One Out of Line

One Out of Line

The Story of a Wisconsin Farm Boy's March Through Life

Joseph C. Hedrick

Timmus Ridge Publishers

Published by:
Timmus Ridge Publishers
1217 Rhea Place
Vista, CA 92084-4346

Design and Layout
MEA Design Group
Escondido, California

ISBN 0-9774369-0-X

Printed in the United States of America

DEDICATION

In memory of my grandfather,
Isadore Hedrick

ACKNOWLEDGMENTS

First and foremost I must acknowledge the major contribution of my wife Betty who so cheerfully processed draft after draft of this book. This required her to work from my handwritten drafts, which meant a great deal of "deciphering" some of my scribbling. In addition to her perennial cheerfulness, I need to acknowledge her curiosity, infinite patience and initiative that sent her to computer web sites when research was needed. I could not have written this book without her help. She somehow survived the hectic hours connected with the production of this book, and earlier had produced more notable works on her own: Diane, Cathryn, Joyce and David.

Thanks also to my brother Ronald who refreshed my memories of life on the farm while we were growing up, and nephew Mike Hedrick who brought me up to date on modern day farming. Also to other members of the family who provided information and photos, or proofread and critiqued along the way.

Another key player did the design work, prepared the printer-ready digitalized disk, and provided liaison with the book's printer. Mary Ellen Alton (MEA Design Group) is a fellow member of my Escondido (California) Kiwanis Club. Our Thursday noon club meetings provided timely opportunities to "swap" material in what I learned is a time-consuming and complex process. How comfortable to work with someone you know and trust in a venture such as this.

CONTENTS

Maps

PROLOGUE

I said to myself, "This is it! You will either be dead or dying within the next couple of hours." One thing I knew for sure; we would fight it out to the bitter end.

It was well below zero as I lay on my stomach in the snow. I was 8000 miles from my Wisconsin farm home. The date was 27 November 1950. The sun was sinking low in the west and darkness could not have been more than an hour off. My location was in the Taebek Mountains of North Korea, 100 miles south of the Yalu River and Chinese border. To add further to the geographic isolation, was that our rifle company's location at the time was in enemy territory, approximately four miles from our friendly front lines.

In addition to this already unpleasant situation was our involvement at the time in what we humans have visited on each other over recorded history—warfare! For the approximately 175 men in Baker company, 1st Battalion, 7th Marines our combat patrol was at the time involved in an intense firefight with a large enemy force that appeared to have us surrounded.

PART 1

Growing Up Years

CHAPTER 1

One Out of Line

The weather was typical for a Wisconsin fall day in early October. The day was cool, yet bright and sunny. The year was 1946 and my primary job on the farm that day was to shock the corn not needed for silage.

Silage was the first priority for the corn crop. Typically the corn was cut when well along in maturity, yet green enough so it fermented when chopped and blown into a silo. A horse drawn corn binder harvested the standing corn, one row at a time, by cutting the stalks off about six inches from the ground. After a predetermined number of stalks were accumulated in a bundle, they were tied automatically with twine, and the bundle was dropped to the ground. These bundles were typically seven to nine feet in length and weighed from twenty-five to thirty-five pounds.

Right after the noon meal, ideally on the same day the corn was cut, the farmer loaded the corn bundles onto his horse drawn wagon. The bundles were then hauled to the silo where a noisy tractor-powered silage cutter/blower chopped the corn into small chunks and blew it into the silo. The silo was basically an airtight cylindrical structure approximately fifteen feet in diameter and thirty feet high. In time the corn fermented and served to provide an appetizing and nutritious meal for cattle in the winter.

Not all corn was destined for the silo. Some of it would be shredded. The corn shredder was another tractor-powered machine. It separated the golden ears of corn from the stalks. In the process it chopped up the stalks which then could be used either to feed cattle or be used for their bedding. Since the shredding process might not happen for weeks, we had to take steps to protect those golden ears in the bundles still on the ground. If the bundles were left on the ground many of the ears of corn would rot away under the assault of rain and snow. Wild animals and birds also had easy access to the corn if left on the ground. To protect the bundles we assembled them in shocks in the field where they had grown.

The shocking process involved using a sawhorse device made of honest to goodness heavy oak two-by-fours. The sawhorse was used to stack upright approximately fifteen to twenty bundles of corn. The sawhorse weighed about seventy-five pounds, and as noted, each bundle weighed twenty-five to thirty-five pounds. Once the proper number of bundles were stacked around the sawhorse a rope and pulley were used to draw the bundles together, like a woman's corset, about two-thirds of the way from the bottom. Then the pulley was clinched and twine was used to secure the assembled bundles; and now we have a shock of corn. Hard work, but healthy hard work. Now when it rained the water cascaded around the shock for the most part. The water that went into the shock ran down a given stalk to the ground.

One of the rules of farming, at least for German farmers, was to keep their farms as neat as possible. That meant those corn shocks had to be lined up straight as an arrow. To ensure this alignment was maintained, the sawhorse was dragged along the same row to the spot selected for the next shock in that row of shocks.

Somewhere along the way I accidentally drifted over a row (about three feet) and set up one shock out of line. I noticed the error when I moved forward to build the next shock—but who wants to tear down one of those monster shocks and then rebuild it? Particularly so since it is now late afternoon and even eighteen-year olds tire. Then too, is one out of line all that bad?

Now if this aberration had been located on any of the 140 other tillable acres of our farms it might have gone unnoticed. For that matter, it could have been on any other row in this particular field and might have gone unnoticed. But as luck would have it, all Dad had to do was turn towards Mother during the meal (he looked at Mother often—they did have ten children after all), and there through the kitchen window behind her, neatly framed by two small barns, was that long row of corn shocks, with one shock out of line. He expressed unhappiness at what to him was this unseemly sight. I did not respond.

Ah, but for me this was the straw that broke the camel's back. All the real or imagined frustrations of working for my dad on the farm, or maybe just working on a farm seems to have come to a head at that moment. I then and there quietly resolved to escape the farm in the only way I knew how—by joining the military—heretofore something of a tentative consideration.

CHAPTER 2

North Half of N.E. Quarter (N½ of N.E. ¼),Section 19: Township 26 North, Range 2 West

On 1 February 1858 the Federal Government deeded eighty acres of land to George Hedrick, my great-grandfather. The legal basis for this transaction were the provisions of the Northwest Ordinance passed by Congress in 1787. The area embraced by the ordinance, the Northwest Territory, eventually became the states of Wisconsin, Illinois, Michigan, Ohio and Indiana. A small parcel of what is now Minnesota, that area east of the Mississippi River was also included in the Northwest Territory.

The family treasures the original deed signed by then President James Buchanan. The custodian of the document and current owner of the farm is Michael Hedrick, the original grantee's great-great-grandson.

The farm was typical of those carved out of the millions of acres in the Northwest Territories. It took the form of a neat squared box measuring approximately three-quarters by one-quarter mile. I am not sure of this, but it seems much of the tillable land in this area was open prairie when the first farmers took over. If most of the land was clear, no doubt there was still the need for considerable tree removal and grubbing of stumps over the early years to increase the tillable acres.

The buildings were located in the northeast corner of the farm. This was generally sloping ground and at the time a wooded area. This was a logical choice since the trees provided a readily available source of building material, firewood, and a large degree of protection from those cold winter winds that blew out of the northwest. Water may also have been a factor. The lower elevation on the site chosen reduced the depth needed to drill for water. No doubt a further consideration was that compared to the rest of the farm, this part was relatively unsuitable for cultivation.

In retrospect, this was perhaps not the best site for the buildings. Future generations decried the slipping and sliding that took place as horses, cattle, and humans tried to navigate under alternating muddy or icy conditions. I remember carrying pails of milk from the barn up-hill to the milk house where a separator isolated the cream from the milk. Under icy conditions this two hundred-foot trek could be tricky. When this was the case it was not unusual to see elongated patches of milky white ice here and there between the barn and milk house. Another problem with the side hill location was associated with power driven equipment used on the farm. Machinery used to thresh grain, fill silo, shred corn and grind feed, accompanied by their tractor or steam engine power source all had to be leveled. This was accomplished by a laborious combination of digging holes and using blocks of wood.

At any rate, many a Hedrick lost his right to heaven when certain language was required to adequately express the proper degree of displeasure at the many prat-falls and related incidents occurring on this side hill. "Temporarily" lost their right to heaven, I should add. This was a Catholic community after all. During fair weather seasons there was confession on Saturday night; during winter one could confess their sins before mass, thus the slate was quickly cleared.

Eventually a township road (now Kendall Avenue) cut through the northeast corner of the farm leaving approximately two acres and the buildings cut off from the rest of the farm. This meant cattle and horses needed to be escorted across the road to the pastureland via a series of gates. This was clumsy and time consuming.

Before I leave what I will from now on refer to as the "home farm" I want to mention the eight acre forested area on the southwest corner of the farm. This was too far from the farm buildings to be pastured by milk cows or horses. As a result it served as summertime pasture for young heifers needed to replenish the herd. Among the variety of trees were many hickory nut trees. Where you have hickory nut trees in Wisconsin you have squirrels. Where you combine squirrels with a young man, a rifle, and a good hunting dog, you have a little bit of heaven on earth for that young man and his dog. A little tough on the squirrels though.

In June of 1924 my grandfather Isadore Hedrick purchased a neighboring farm from Alvina Bucholz. I believe the farm came on the market after the death of her husband. This farm had been originally deeded by the federal government to a John Beebe on 20 February 1857. The signature of President Franklin Pierce graces this deed. The abstract of title for the Bucholz farm reflects thirteen owners over the years, with a man named Kasper Arnold owning it on four different occasions.

The Bucholz farm was where my dad took his bride to live in 1925. This is where six of my nine siblings and I were born, and where all ten of us were raised. Today the same house, now independent of the farmland, is home to a paternal niece (Denise Mulvaney, daughter of Ronald Hedrick) and her family. She is a great-granddaughter of Isadore Hedrick.

Throughout my growing up years this farm was commonly referred to as the "Bucholz farm" or "Bucholz place." For the sake of differentiating one farm from the other I will continue to use the term "Bucholz" farm and "home" farm.

The Bucholz farm originally consisted of 100 acres. Unlike the home farm this farm was blessed with a house and related buildings all on level ground. But the much larger and more modern barn on the home farm dictated that this be the focal point for the dairy effort.

The Bucholz farm in turn was also neatly squared. In the late 1860s four acres were deeded to the Chicago and Northwestern Railroad for their right of way. A part of this four-acre parcel, on the northeast corner of the farm, bordered at a remote point the Fred Goetz farm. This geographic fact permits me to say, with a large degree of accuracy, that I subsequently married the girl next door.

Here again this isolated four acres required a couple of gates, one on each side of the railroad tracks for moving cattle from one side to the other. If this was bad news, the good news was the railroad built and maintained the fences and gates. This small parcel was also used to pasture young heifers.

Equal in joy to me as the squirrel woods on the home farm, was the trout stream running through this four acre bottomland across the tracks on the Bucholz farm. It meandered for about a quarter-mile through our farm with a few holes over six feet deep. These holes changed locations, thunderstorm by thunderstorm, with there being an abundance of catchable and friable fish in the creek. Many locations along the creek permitted one to cool off on a hot day. Later on in life I heard it referred to as "skinny-dipping."

Approximately one-fifth mile separated the barn on the home farm from the house where we lived on the Bucholz farm. The Bucholz farm had two small barns, but as noted, all the milking was done on the home farm while I was growing up. Under certain winter weather conditions this could be the longest one-fifth mile in the world. But those cows had to be milked and winter chores completed, no matter how high the snowdrifts or how cold and blustery the northwest wind might be.

The Bucholz farm had approximately forty acres of woodland stretching all along its northern boundary. The forestland generally dropped off the workable tableland into a valley where the railroad was built and where the creek was located. Sturdy oaks and other hardwoods produced many railroad ties and an inexhaustible supply of firewood, fence posts, and other lumber needs.

Appendix A reflects the land use for the two farms. As can be seen from the building layout in Appendix B, a Wisconsin family farm in that era was like a functional little village in itself.

The farms are located on what is called Summit Ridge. Although well known locally at the time, it's unlikely many maps showed Summit Ridge as a place name. Earlier mention was made of the home farm buildings being on a side hill. Actually, there's a general rolling tilt to all of the land on Summit Ridge. When the fields are flush with crops this unevenness is hidden. But this is Wisconsin's rolling hill country after all.

The name Summit dates back to 1870-73 when the Chicago and Northwestern railroad extended their line from Baraboo through Norwalk to Sparta (see map page 508). The high point on the roadbed between Norwalk and Sparta, i.e. the summit, was located at a point in the valley below the home farm and only a few yards from the northwest corner of the Bucholz farm. Eventually a small community was established at Summit. In its heyday eight to ten houses and a railroad depot/post

Homes in Summit, late 1800s (Monroe County, Wisconsin pictorial history).

office sprung up in this tiny enclave. One of those homes was my paternal grandmother's first home after her arrival from Germany in 1893. A second home housed my maternal great-grandfather, Charles Geoghegan and his family. All the families living in Summit were associated with the railroad in one way or another.

Summit Depot, late 1800s (Monroe County, Wisconsin pictorial history).

Farmers from the ridges bordering this narrow valley traveled "down Summit" to pick up their mail (rural free delivery did not start until 1900). Additionally, the railroad made it possible for local farmers to ship farm produce and wood products, to receive necessities, or to travel. One of the farm products shipped out was barley. This was sent twenty miles west to Bangor to make beer. For many years a total of six regular passenger and four to five freight trains ran daily, plus several special freights. The passenger fare was two cents per mile. For twelve cents passengers could make the round trip to Norwalk. Some of the young ladies from the area commuted to Norwalk High School via the rails. (The boys usually went to work full time on the family farms after finishing elementary school.) As a further example of rail fares at the time, the cost to travel from Norwalk to Madison was two dollars, to Chicago six dollars.

One of the daily passenger trains was the fast "midnight express" running from Chicago to Minneapolis. On many nights I awoke to hear the lonesome wail of its whistle as the train barreled along through our farm. (More on the railroad and its ties to my family follows in chapter three.)

I remember only three homes standing in Summit, two of which were lived in during my growing up years. It might be more accurate to say only one was lived in full time. The old cellar of my maternal grandmother's home is still discoverable if one knows where to search.

The urban center of our life, two and one-half road miles away, was the little village of Norwalk, population around 335 at the time. (More on Norwalk in chapter four.) The economic engine driving the village at the time was the creamery. Farmers brought their milk products to the creamery to be turned into butter and cheese. There was at a minimum weekly shopping trips to Norwalk. Sparta, the seat of government for Monroe County was located twelve miles from our farm and had a population of approximately 5000. We shopped here a great deal less, maybe once every couple of months. The really big city was La Crosse; a Mississippi River town located thirty-five miles from the farm with a population of 30,000. For our family, a shopping trip here occurred once each year, usually before the start of the school year.

The center of our lives outside of the family was St. John's Catholic Church and the one room rural school we attended. The church was two and one-half miles from our home by road, or about a mile if we walked via an old road through Summit. During the time I was growing up this old road was no longer serviceable for vehicles. The one room school was one and one-fifth miles away.

CHAPTER 3

The Chicago and Northwestern Railroad

I grew up when railroading was at its prime—romantically and commercially. People viewed railroading as exciting and romantic as modern generations view air and space travel today. The men who operated these powerful black locomotives were called "Engineers." The public placed them on a pedestal much as we do airline pilots today. I was proud that my maternal granduncle, Tom Geoghegan, was one of those larger-than-life heroes who was an engineer on a passenger train at the time.

Most families who lived on Summit Ridge were largely isolated from the world, with little diversion from the routine of farming. Of the fifty-five families who lived on the ridge only five had railroad tracks adjacent to or running through their farms. Of those five only two, the Goetzs and Muehlenkamps had children of my generation, and both families lived some distance from the tracks. Ah, but we Hedricks were the lucky ones. At least one-half mile of track ran through our farm and our house was less than one-third mile from the tracks. Furthermore, access was all downhill over a combination of well developed cow paths and a rough wagon road. I thoroughly enjoyed watching the trains go by. On those occasions when sound carried just right, and the steam locomotive was laboring under a heavy load, I could hear the huffing and puffing as the train traveled westbound out of Norwalk. On those occasions I had five to ten minutes to reach the scene before the train passed my favorite vantage point on the northwestern tip of the farm.

When I was deemed old enough to go off on my own to view the trains I was warned not to get too close to the locomotive. The theory was that suction from the locomotive's twelve fast-turning drive wheels, each wheel seven-foot in diameter, could pull one in and chew them up. Until I realized this was just a ploy to keep me from getting too close, I took the warning seriously. To be on the safe side, I sat on the ground as close as I dared to the passing train—grasping with all my strength fistfuls of grass with both hands as the ground shook beneath me. Since there was a crossing right at the summit, all this thunder and hissing of steam was accompanied by a long blast of its mournful whistle.*

A good part of the joy in watching the trains go by was just plain getting there. I loved to run and did so often for the pure joy of running. Once there I watched in awe as this 122 foot long black monster approached, belching clouds of grayish black smoke from its funnel, along with sending out clouds of steam from its two, or on some locomotives at the time, four cylinders as it labored to climb over the "summit." Remember this was the highest point on the Norwalk-Sparta run so trains from both directions labored to varying degrees to climb over that high point located right at my favorite vantage point. I exchanged waves with any visible humans; first the locomotive crew, then those passengers who were aware of my presence. If it was a freight train the brakeman could be counted on to wave back from his tail-end position in the caboose. Now

---

*Mention was made in the previous chapter of pasturing young heifers on the four acre isolated bottomland next to the railroad tracks on the Bucholz farm. Imagine the initial reaction of these young animals to the presence of those noisy intruders going past their then new pastoral home. Initially there were many "speed" runs with tails high in the air.

and then a hobo or two waved back from the open door or top of a freight car. Then it was uphill for me going back home after this brief flirtation with the romantic world of railroading.

Whenever possible I tried to be in the vicinity when a train was due. For example, if it were necessary to bring the cows home from pasture in the evening, why not time the chore to coincide with the east bound four-thirty freight train? During blackberry picking season I arranged to pick berries in the patch next to the tracks around two p.m. and wave to the crew and passengers on a Minneapolis bound train. In the late fall and winter months, my dad and I spent many hours harvesting wood in the woodland bordering the tracks. Even in the middle of sawing down a tree, with the then customary two-man crosscut saw, Dad stopped to watch the train go by.

The railroad through our land was built in that era when our nation was having a heated romance with railroading. In May of 1869 a coast to coast link was established when the tracks of the Union Pacific and the Central Pacific were joined at Promontory, Utah. Where the railroad went, prosperity followed. As a result towns and cities fought to be on a railroad line.

As noted earlier, in 1870 the Chicago and Northwestern decided to extend their line from Baraboo to Sparta. A major undertaking on the line was the construction of three tunnels between those two cities (see map page 508). Two were 1680 feet in length and were located near Wilton and Kendall. The granddaddy was three-quarters of a mile (3810 feet) long with its eastern entry one-half mile from our farm. Initially the railroad considered avoiding having to build two of these tunnels. The first was the tunnel between Wilton and Norwalk. More important was the second, the three-quarter mile tunnel between Norwalk and Sparta. Should the railroad have exercised this option, the line would have run through the farming community of Ridgeville. The center of Ridgeville, as defined by a Lutheran church and near by tavern and store, was approximately three cross-country miles from the future railroad station at

Summit. Presumably, the track would have swung northwest before entering Wilton (from the east) and then followed county trunk "M" to reach the high ground on Ridgeville. After crossing the farms in Ridgeville, the line would descend into Coles Valley and on into Sparta. This prospect excited the folks in Ridgeville at the time to the point where a land survey was conducted for city-sized plats. In the final analysis, Ridgeville's elevation of 1450 feet lost out to Summit's 1250 feet. Another factor was the more gradual gradient of two-to-three percent as the tracks climbed the 220 feet from Norwalk (elevation 1030) to Summit over a three mile run. The tunnels were determined to be cost effective and construction began on the long tunnel near our farms in 1870.

The tunnel was bored through solid rock using hand labor, black powder, mules and oxen. It took three years to complete (1870-1873). The cost was 1.5 million dollars, around 20 million in year 2005 dollars. (I will recount later my grandfather Isadore Hedrick's role as a young boy in caring for the oxen and mules used in the tunnel construction project.) Construction began at both ends. At the mid-point an airshaft was drilled from the surface into the tunnel. This developed into an ice cave where ice remained on the wall throughout summer months. Although the airshaft remained dangerously open, locals, to include my dad, accepted the hazards involved in obtaining ice. The shaft was located on my maternal Aunt Helen (Alphonse) Muehlenkamp farm. For the Hedrick family the ice was used for making homemade ice cream.

The ice cave remains an attraction to this day. Its location is only a few hundred yards from what is now Kayak road. Despite the danger, some cannot resist the siren call of the cave. I must admit to a trespass on the Muehlenkamp property to show the cave to my children. In May of 2000 some members of a high school graduating class staged an unofficial and underage drinking party in this area. In time, the police showed up and one person, trying to escape, fell into the cave and was injured. Given our litigious society, a lawsuit evolved.

In the process of drilling the airshaft, an aquifer was tapped with near artesian qualities. A wooden trough was built in the tunnel ceiling to divert this steady flow of water to a drainage channel on the side. As one approached the center of the tunnel, the sound of falling water, with a little imagination, sounded like an approaching train.

The tunnel was wet. In addition to the aquifer tapped by digging the airshaft, springs and freshets hampered the digging. The problem of water wasn't over when construction was completed either. In wintertime, the inside of the tunnel was relatively warm, while freezing cold outside. The freezing and thawing process would have crumbled the rock around the entrance. To keep this from happening, huge double doors were installed on each end to seal in the warmer temperature. Watchmen were hired in winter months to open and close the doors for passing trains. Shanties were placed on each end for the watchman during his twelve hour shift. A variety of signals were in use to warn the watchman of an approaching train. The most sophisticated was an alarm transmitted by a signal wire on the rail that activated a bell in the watchman's shanty when

Watchman's shanty at east end of tunnel.

the train was approximately a quarter-mile away. Additionally, red and white flags were used for daytime signaling and lanterns at night. Obviously red meant stop—white to proceed. The shanty was furnished with a bunk, but in practice the watchman got little sleep what with the need to constantly open and close the doors.

Earlier I mentioned my maternal Uncle Tom Geoghegan being a locomotive engineer. His brother Jack was a tunnel watchman who worked one of those twelve hour shifts. Uncle Jack stayed with us in the winter while he worked the six p.m. to six a.m. shift. Despite our large family, finding an empty bed was no problem. By the time Uncle Jack arrived at our house after his shift (around 7 a.m.) we had many empty beds, and he was back on watch long before family bedtime that evening.

Later, our neighbor Clarence Dittman was one of the watchmen. At the time his shift ran from midnight until noon. Clarence's post was on the far west side of the tunnel. If the snow cover permitted, Clarence cut through his and our land to reach the tracks—still a two-mile walk in wintertime. If the snow cover was heavy, he traveled a longer route, using the road taking him past our house. Many a night I saw only his lantern swinging back and forth as he made his lonesome way to the tunnel shanty. How brave I thought he was. I was convinced the night teemed with wolves, mountain lions, bears and other wild and ferocious animals. My worst fear was concentrated on the black panther, a member of the wild cat family. Not only was Clarence out there at night all alone with all those beasts, but a large part of his trek was through heavily forested areas—where these beasts lived. Then too, how about the "bogeyman, hoboes, witches, etc.?" Weren't they increasingly active at night as well? Finally there was the weather: this is wintertime in Wisconsin after all. On one occasion, Clarence was snowbound for three days in the shanty before being able to walk to a nearby farm. Clarence remembers being ravishingly hungry.

On one occasion, I accompanied Clarence during his winter watch (no doubt against railroad rules). I was eleven at the time. This would be my first time to enter the tunnel. Was I excited at the prospect? You bet I was! Excited and apprehensive. My mother packed plenty of food and drinks for my twelve-hour shift. Clarence stopped by around ten or ten-thirty p.m. and off we went. Somehow the night and the dark forest didn't seem all that frightening in the company of this heroic figure. First we walked the one-fifth mile to the home farm barn, then down the old Summit road for one-half mile to where the little village of Summit once stood. Then we followed the tracks west for one-half mile to the eastern end of the tunnel. After a quick courtesy check with the watchman on duty in the shanty, we ducked through a small door into the dark dank tunnel with only the eerie light of Clarence's hand-carried lantern to light the way. After the three-quarter mile trek through the tunnel, we exited through another small door and there, on the right, was our shanty home for the next twelve hours. Again, a brief friendly greeting to the relieved watchman who then headed west down the tracks by the pale light of his own lantern.

The small shanty was barren except for a coal burning stove, a bunk, and a heavy wooden chair. Its only light was the pale illumination from Clarence's lantern. We took off our heavy outerwear and turned immediately to our food. We were not alone. A couple of mice quickly made their appearance, and apparently they were used to being fed. Clarence enticed them to take pieces of bread from his hand. One can appreciate that this was one of the few diversions for Clarence and his fellow watchmen.

At 12:30 a.m., the first of several trains came through. This was the previously mentioned "midnight," a fast passenger train bound for Minneapolis that would be emerging from the tunnel as it headed west.* The giant doors were swung open, and we stood on the side of the narrow gorge waiting and watching. I wanted to move closer to the cliff and away from the tracks, but there was no room. Soon a light was discernible deep in the tunnel. Then, with a thunderous roar, this one million pound black

---

*The railroad companies used their most powerful and fast locomotives to pull these "prestige" express passenger trains.

monster shot out of the tunnel. I stood close to Clarence as the cars thundered by. The next spectacle was the heavy volume of thick black smoke emerging from the tunnel. Eerie! After the smoke had cleared, the doors were closed and we went back to feed mice, and for me, catch snatches of sleep. The next train was an eastbound freight that approached through the wider gorge from Sparta and disappeared into the tunnel. Impressive, but not as awesome as when westbound trains exited the tunnel. I suppose there were the usual four to six trains traveling one way or the other during our twelve-hour watch. I'm sure I was a tired, but happy boy when I arrived home.

Another interesting engineering feature related to the rail line was the flume. Shortly after the line was open a heavy downpour sent a torrent of water down a valley running north-northwest from the tracks and washed out a section of track. A ten-foot deep, fifteen-foot wide and four to five hundred foot long flume was constructed of wood to catch and divert the water away from the tracks. The lumber quickly rotted and was rebuilt with large flat granite stones and concrete. The twelve inch wide ledge on the top of the flume walls made for relatively easy walking. This was more often than not the route I traveled on my way home after catechism classes held at St. John's Catholic Church in the summer time. Walking on top of the flume also negated the need to cross an old wooden bridge that spanned the flume at the terminal end. In summertime, the area under the bridge was overgrown with brush and weeds—the perfect place for those dreaded "trolls" to hang out.

When the tunnel was completed in 1873, and the line opened for traffic, a depot was established. As noted earlier, since this was the highest point on the fourteen-mile run between Norwalk and Sparta, they named it Summit. The elevation of two to three feet for each one hundred feet of horizontal travel required helper locomotives for most of the freight trains on the three-mile up-hill run from Norwalk to Summit. From the other direction, the climb from Sparta to Summit was gradual and extended over ten miles, so there was no need for helper locomotives. A siding was built at Summit to provide a place to park the helper locomotives in order to keep the main line open. The siding also permitted the parking of freight cars that delivered goods or were loaded with produce to be shipped from the area. As steam power increased the helper locomotives were not needed. I do not recall ever seeing a helper locomotive. The siding remained, largely unused until use of the line was discontinued in 1965.

As mentioned above, I do recall seeing and waving to hobos. These were the depression years and the heyday of the hobo. These men "rode the rails" as they moved from place to place in search of work, or as was most often the case, just for the sake of moving from place to place. The railroad did its best to discourage these free rides, primarily from the standpoint of safety for the individual. One of the dangers was the tunnel. If a person was standing or kneeling on top of a freight car they could be injured or killed by the low tunnel entrance. To alert the individual to this danger, thin wire rods extending downward from wooden beams were installed at each end of the tunnel. These rods, which all but brushed the top of a freight car, served to alert the standing or crouching rider far enough in advance of entering the tunnel so he could either jump off the car or lie down flat. I am not sure how this worked in practice. The idea of lying flat on top of a freight car with smoke enveloping you must have been a frightening experience. Even at twenty miles per hour, a couple

Hobo alert wire (east end of tunnel).

of minutes were needed to travel the three-quarter mile involved. Survivable apparently—if one kept their cool. At times the hobos jumped off the freights at either end of the tunnel and walked over the ridge to reboard the next freight at the other end. Now and then these men stopped at a farmhouse along the way for a handout.

Despite the proximity and mystique of the tunnel, those who lived in the area rarely ventured any closer than the tunnel entrance. The track right of way was understandably a non-trespassing area, and locals were generally law abiding. Then too, both ends of the tunnel were relatively remote from farms and villages. The east entrance near our farm was by far the most inaccessible. The approach from this direction ended in a narrow quarter-mile corridor that was spooky to begin with. With a little investigation, one could determine the times for scheduled trains, then make the half-hour walk through the tunnel between trains. But what if unscheduled freights or work trains came along? Survival, if one did not panic, was assured—but it would have been frightening. But kids will be kids, and we Hedricks lived too close to the tunnel to be totally in awe of it. I recall on one occasion four or five of us from the area walked to the east entrance. We knew we should not have done so, and once there, we were nervous and apprehensive. I don't recall the season, but we assumed the watchman was in residence—and that it would be Henry Dittman, Clarence's brother. We further assumed he would treat us gently, and maybe demonstrate opening and closing the double doors. We debated which of us was to knock on the shanty door, and at last I volunteered. My knock was soft—and fast. "No one there," I said as I returned to my fellow trespassers—and we quickly headed for home.

Our family's involvement with railroading also included my dad who worked for a time as a section hand. When his younger brother (Joe) was old enough, Dad was relieved of his full-time job helping his father on the farm. Dad was single at the time, lived at home, and no doubt continued to help out on the farm during the busy seasons to pay for his meals and board. The railroad association ended when his brother Joe died at age twenty-three from complications following an appendectomy. I recall on several occasions Dad expressing his disappointment about his lost opportunity for a railroading career, and how he might have preferred railroading to farming. I really don't think he meant it though, since obviously, he enjoyed farming.

On one occasion while on the job, Dad and his co-workers decided to take an unauthorized break to play cards. What better place than in the tunnel where they could guard against the unannounced arrival of the section boss. They went to the center, where the water falling from the airshaft muffled whatever sounds they made. Coats were spread over the tracks and play began by lantern light in the otherwise pitch dark tunnel. They knew the tunnel was no place to be when a train went through, but they knew the schedule. Imagine their surprise and fright when a westbound "unscheduled" work train bore down on them. The surprise arrival was in part due to the fact that the train was now on a downhill run towards Sparta. Furthermore, this was the center of the tunnel and water falling from the aquifer all but drowned out the sound of the approaching work train. The players had enough time, and common sense to dive into the water filled ditch on each side of the tracks, and to stay there until the smoke cleared.

(Hey Dad, I don't ever remember goofing off like that while I was working for you on the farm.)

Shortly after the line between Baraboo and Sparta was fully functional, a decision was made to build a spur track to Cashton, a village twelve miles southwest of our farm. The plan was for the tracks to cut through another portion of the Bucholz farm, climb up through a valley leading to our one room Bohn School, and then across the ridge to Cashton. Construction proceeded to the point where a few hundred feet of roadbed was completed. This stretch of elevated landform is still visible on the Bucholz farm. Changing economic conditions cancelled the project. Good news for the farm. If this line had been completed the woodland and pasture portion of the farm would have been chopped up once again with a significant loss of land and yet another set of clumsy gates.

In its heyday from 1873 to 1925, this line carried all the traffic be-tween Chicago/Madison and Minnesota, North and South Dakota, and Northern Iowa. During the period 1873-1910, a maximum of six passenger and numerous scheduled and unscheduled freights traveled the line everyday. From 1911-1925 freight trains decreased but the six passenger trains continued to run. Passenger service dropped to four in 1925 and two in 1948. The last passenger train went through the tunnel in 1948, close to two years after I joined the Marines. In that year President Harry Truman's 1948 campaign train traveled this route on his presidential whistle stop tour. Many of the locals journeyed "down Summit" to wave to the President as he passed by. The last freight went through in 1965. In 1966 the tracks were removed.

The tunnel also played a role in the Cold War. The Monroe County Civil Defense Unit designated it a fallout shelter capable of holding 1900 people.

In summary, the Chicago and Northwestern railroad line that ran through our farm remains a warm and cherished part of my childhood memories. Not only do I remember how much I enjoyed watching and waving to passing trains, but also the involvement of my two maternal granduncles, neighbor Clarence Dittman, paternal grandfather, and my dad.

CHAPTER 4

Norwalk

Norwalk—population 335 when I first took note of the sign outside the west end of town; but oh my, what those 335 could do. I was jealous of the kids in town. No farm chores to do. They had electricity. They walked only a few blocks to school, for the most part on sidewalks—and on level ground. What really annoyed me though was the time they had to play ball, from after school until dark in early fall and late spring, and all day long if they chose to do so in summer.

Like other small towns in rural America, Norwalk residents were for the most part dependent on local farmers for their livelihood. One might exclude a few railroad employees, the postmaster, and to a degree, the clergy.

Despite the preponderance of German immigrants in the area, a man named Selium McGary of Scotch-Irish descent laid claim to the land on which Norwalk now stands. Born in Vermont in 1829, Selium arrived in the area with his wife in 1852. Eventually the honor of naming the town fell to Selium. The name he chose was Norwalk after Norwalk, Ohio.

"Going to town" was a fun event in our lives. This was especially true if one was in the close company of an adult. They could usually find a nickel to buy a kid candy or an ice cream cone.

Many businesses thrived (or at least survived) during the time I was growing up. The co-operative creamery, owned by the farmers, was the main economic engine in Norwalk. Farmers who brought their cream and/or milk to town on occasion stopped to have feed ground, or buy feed at one of the two feed mills. Horses were the engines for farming so a harness shop flourished as well. Farm machinery and repair parts were available at two implement dealerships. Farmers picked up their bi-monthly milk checks and transacted other banking business at one of the two banks. Now and then there was a need for lumber products, or a store built storage shed, brooder house, etc; a lumberyard took care of these needs. The two hardware stores were often frequented, not only for hardware items, but for firearms and ammunition as well. Three grocery stores met the needs of the village and surrounding community. One, called the "Mercantile" was a department store—but on a small scale. It had one floor and a three-sided wrap-around balcony for displaying its wares. The rear of the second story also provided living quarters for the proprietor. In addition to groceries, the store sold clothing and fabric, shoes, kitchen supplies, toys, and other miscellaneous items. The Mer-cantile also acted as an exchange for the farmer's excess egg production. Eggs could be traded for groceries and merchandise, or sold for cash. An added attraction to the store for me was that my paternal Aunt Matilda (Tilla) was one of three clerks in the store. Another store in town sold women's apparel only.

Another business in Norwalk purchased poultry. These were either hens that had outlived their productive usefulness, or the surplus roosters that had arrived with the then unisex batch of baby chicks purchased in the spring. I also remember selling my rabbits here on at least one occa-sion. For selling hogs, surplus cattle, sheep etc. the farmer called upon Norwalk's Kroeger Trucking to haul his animals to stockyards in Chi-cago. This trucking firm also was available to haul machinery, logs, fur-niture, etc. Here again I had a connection. My maternal uncle, Richard

Berendes, was one of the truck drivers. I viewed this trucking firm second only to the railroad in terms of prestige and romance.

Main Street in Norwalk looking south (1938).

The two-block main street also embraced a drug store, along with a furniture store/funeral parlor combined, with the proprietor living upstairs. Two new car dealerships (Ford and Chevrolet) and two or three combination gas stations and repair shops met the area's automotive needs. There was a cobbler shop that in addition to repairing shoes also sold rugged work shoes and boots, and a blacksmith to take care of the horse's feet. On occasion I rode our workhorses to Norwalk to have them shod.

The "de facto" news center in Norwalk was the barbershop on Main Street run by Charley Tigwell and Percy Woodliff. If you wanted to be clued in on the latest happenings, often much embellished, you needed to be present here day by day.

There was also a post office and train depot. A one-horse drayage service moved freight back and forth between businesses and the depot. A restaurant was located on Main Street, and a volunteer fire department and a marshal to enforce the law did their part to meet the public service needs of the village.

My favorite merchant in Norwalk was Jim Betthauser who ran one of the two feed mills. We did most of our business with Jim and he and I hit it off. When his next door business neighbor, who owned the lumberyard died, Jim was the executor of this man's will. In that roll he saw to it that Harold McGary's 30-30 caliber Winchester lever action deer hunting rifle came my way.

Finally, there was the telephone central. Telephone service was organized to serve Norwalk and the surrounding communities in the early 1900s. Most farm subscribers were on a series of "party lines" tied into the switchboard in Norwalk. For those living in town the operator manually connected the caller to the requested party. But those on a party line could communicate with each other without the help of the central station operator. Usually about ten families were on a given party line. Those of us without electricity used batteries to power the phone and ringers. A coded ring on the party line alerted a given family to a call for them. The code (ring) for our home was two shorts and a long. The caller produced this code by turning the hand crank on their phone. You will appreciate given the manual dexterity difference of people, especially as they aged, the coded rings were at times not all that distinct.

Can you see another problem here? Assume ten parties, "A" through "J" are on a given party line. Let's say "C" calls "E" using "E's" coded ring. All other eight parties hear the coded ring and know it's not for them. They then ignore the ring—right? Not necessarily. News was scarce and here might be a bit of news to spice up the day. "C" and "E" would be wise to assume that at least some of their eight fellow party line members were listening in. From time to time, if not all batteries were up to a certain charge, the volume dropped to where "C" or "E" might have to ask listeners to hang up so they could hear each other. It follows that courtesy dictated you listen before ringing on a party line.

So far "A" through "J" can talk to each other without the assistance of an operator on their party line. Now assume "A" wants to talk to a subscriber on another party line, or a subscriber in Norwalk. Now "A" rings the telephone central in Norwalk (one long ring) and an operator manually does the necessary switching to make the connection.* The operator could also ring other switchboards in other communities to provide long distance service throughout the country. But the quality of these long-distance calls was usually marginal at best.

What with all the human activity involved in this manual system wrong numbers were bound to happen. Wrong number in one sense, but since most everyone knew each other these "accidental" hook-ups provided an unexpected opportunity for a chat. There was a separate code neighbors on a party line might use in an emergency. Assume a neighbor's house was on fire: two long rings alerted all households on that party line to the emergency and the need for help.

The central telephone exchange in Norwalk operated on the "folksy" side. If people heard the fire siren the switchboard was deluged by calls. The custom at the time was to ring church bells when someone died. Again, many calls were made to the switchboard operator inquiring as to who passed away. Local merchants on occasion advertised via this central office. The operator gave an extra long ring on all the party lines the merchant wanted to reach, and then announced whatever a given merchant was promoting.

As the number of tractors increased on the farms a fuel delivery firm based in Norwalk delivered fuel to the farms. Another service based in Norwalk was a mobile feed grinding operation. Those who did not want to haul grain to the mills in Norwalk, and who were not equipped with the machinery to grind their own, could arrange for this truck-mounted rig to roll up to their granary and grind away. An elementary and high school served the village, as did four churches. A newspaper, the Norwalk Star Herald published weekly and a dairy on the edge of town provided for home milk delivery in the village. A dentist and a doctor also served Norwalk. The doctor was Judson S. Allen, the quintessential model of the

---

*When my maternal grandfather called our home he first rang the central in Norwalk, then asked for "2-1 on 137" (two shorts and one long ring on party line 137).

old time country doctor. He served the area for forty-six years before re-tiring in 1963. House calls were willingly made and I suspect he delivered all of the Hedrick siblings, seven of us at our home. Patients seldom made appointments; they just dropped in when medical attention was needed. Before the automobile came along he made his calls in a horse and buggy. In the winter he used a team of horses and sleigh. At one point, after cars came along, he replaced the front wheels of his car with skis so he could travel around better in the winter. If needed, he also supplied the neces-sary ambulance service. This was fast ambulance service by the way; Doc Allen knew how to "put the pedal to the metal."

Doctor Allen was a frequent visitor at our house. He had an infec-tious dry sense of humor. I can remember him saying to Mother, "Now Frances, don't worry, Ronnie (then age nine) will be out plowing the back forty in a day or two, etc." When he retired in 1963 a grateful community declared a special day for this good and decent man. He was presented a 1963 Oldsmobile in appreciation for his service to the community.

Then there were the three taverns. As a general rule each had its own "hard core" of loyal customers. One seemed to cater to the older or retired types; most of whom could be found playing cards. Another ap-pealed to the middle aged and more sedate crowd. The younger set and party types made up the hard core of the third tavern's clientele.

You could not be sure where you might find a given individual who you knew was in town; other than you knew he was likely to visit at least one of the taverns. Let's say you know your friend Mike is in town and you have a need to contact him. First you checked tavern "A", and while there had a five-cent draft beer while awaiting the expected arrival of Mike. Mike doesn't show up so on to tavern "B", etc. Mike and you might not meet on this occasion, but what a great time you were likely to have sopping up those five-cent beers in your conscientious attempt to track him down.

Pete Schreier's tavern deserves special mention. In the hall above the tavern was what today would be called a community center. You name it, and if it drew a crowd, the event was held in this hall. Everything from high school basketball games, wedding dances, the spring prom, stage shows, charitable benefits, graduation ceremonies, roller skating, to community meetings were held here. This second story hall with its one narrow stairway was a near perfect example of a firetrap. Added to the fire danger were the heavy vibrations so evident in the bar below as the dancers above danced a foot-stomping polka. Thank heavens for no problems during this period—for what would the community have done without this hall?

One-mile southeast of the village, on Highway Seventy-One, was a nightclub called Hollywood. Built in 1932, this was a place to kick up your heels to a live band on Saturday nights. Hamburgers were served on dance night, and chicken at twenty-five cents a plate on special nights. Hollywood burned to the ground in 1943, before I was old enough to frequent the place.

Norwalk merchants staged at a minimum, an annual Christmas parade and Fourth of July celebration. They were fun, but what I really enjoyed was the Tuesday night free movies. The movies were shown in a couple of outside locations over the years—weather permitting. Movie studios tailored their offerings for rural and small town America. They were action filled, fast paced melodramas and adventure films aimed at we less demanding patrons. That was okay with us; the theme after all was shopping and socializing for the adults, and eating goodies for the kids. The village supplied wooden benches, but it was advisable to bring your own chair. Those who did not, and found the benches filled had to either stand, sit on the curb, or lean against an adjacent building.

These were wise merchants. There was indeed heavy shopping before and after the movie. The women and children far outnumbered the men at the movie itself. Many of the men preferred to spend their time in one of the friendly taverns. My expanded discourse on taverns does not imply heavy drinking was the norm. To the contrary, public drunkenness was rare, as were disturbances due to drinking. Think of the television show "Cheers" and you have the same kind of friendly gathering place in the taverns of Norwalk.

My routine for a Tuesday night at the movies began with my grandfather Hedrick giving me a dime—and what ten cents could buy at the time. I started out at the drug store candy counter to purchase an unbelievable amount of inexpensive candy for five cents. I then went next door to Pete Shrierer's tavern. In a separate room next to the bar Pete was selling freshly popped and lavishly buttered popcorn. The cost, five cents for a two-quart bag. Pete had attractive daughters, one of whom, Helen assisted her dad in dispensing the popcorn. Pete popped and packaged up the popcorn. My thrill was handing Helen the nickel and her handing me a bag of popcorn. How romantic.

The little village of Norwalk nestles in a relatively narrow valley and looks as picturesque as the villages you see on picture postcards from Europe or the New England states. The village has an especially warm and endearing spot in my book of childhood memories.

CHAPTER 5

The People of Summit Ridge

By and large, the population of Summit Ridge and most of the surrounding area was of German extraction. The great majority traced their ancestral roots back to Southern Germany. A few Polish and fewer still Irish blended in. My mother's maternal grandparents were fully Irish and she one-half Irish. That one-quarter Irish blood in me is a full license to celebrate St. Patrick's Day. As can be imagined, Ellis Island in New York City played a major role in my ancestors' trek to America.

If you were to draw a circle two miles in diameter from St. John's Catholic Church on Summit Ridge you encompassed all but a few of the fifty-five family farms in the parish at the time I was growing up. Of those fifty-five farms, only five were located in adjoining valleys. The rest of us then could be categorized as "ridge runners."

In this homogeneous group of fully functioning farm families, fewer than five were not Catholic. That said, in no way was this minority discriminated against. Their children blended easily into Summit Ridge's two one-room schools (Bohn and Goetz schools).* The families in turn

---

*Two other one-room schools, Conger and Oak Grove, were located on the northeast and southwest fringes of Summit Ridge. A few families from Summit Ridge attended these two schools.

interchanged freely on cooperative farm chores and non-religious social events.

Understandably the immigrant settlers tended to stay together based on religion and ethnicity. Summit Ridge was, as noted, for the most part Catholic. Then, at a point two miles northeast of the Catholic Church, a colony of Lutheran farmers populated an area called Ridgeville. Southeast of Norwalk was Spring Valley, where farmers belonging to a branch of the Methodist church lived on their string of farms, and so on throughout other communities.

Despite this religious and ethnic compartmentalizing, everyone got along fine on those occasions when they intermingled. Of course the Catholics, as was their wont at the time, were quietly convinced that non-Catholics could not go to heaven.* At best they went to the netherland of Purgatory, where even un-baptized Catholic babies had to spend eternity. As a result, Catholic babies as a rule made a quick trip from the womb to the baptismal font. Further insurance of future heavenly bliss was provided by naming children after saints—a stern requirement at the time.

Clarence Dittman, who has already been introduced as a neighbor and railroad tunnel watchman, was one of those few who fell into this religious minority on Summit Ridge. Worse still, the Dittmans practiced no religion at all. What might have been viewed as more shocking was that Clarence and his wife Martha lived in a common law marriage. Was this a problem for my saintly and one-hundred-percent Catholic Mother? Absolutely not! I am sure she must have yearned to be able to play a role in converting the Dittmans to the Catholic faith. The promise was that no one would be denied the joys of heaven if they were to play a meaningful role in converting one to the Catholic faith. As far as I know my mother didn't make any overt moves to convert the Dittmans. The Dittmans were welcome in our home and we in theirs. Clarence was a frequent caller since the road to Norwalk took him right past our home.

---

*On the lighter side, the more liberal minded Catholics viewed Protestants as Catholics who merely had the misfortune to flunk Latin.

At the time, before radio and television, farmers passed up no chance to stop and chat with one another.

Our own community within the community of Summit Ridge embraced twelve families. The cement binding us together was the cooperative effort in that great farming event of the year—threshing grain. A good part was hard work, but it was also a major social event with absolutely great meals. Smaller groups split off for less labor-intensive projects, such as shredding corn, sawing firewood, repairing well pumps, etc.

Our other closest neighbor after the Dittmans was the Steinhoff family. Both were approximately one-half mile from our home on the Bucholz farm. These two neighbors were much like extended family, quick to help each other in an emergency or lend a hand when needed.

The Dittman farm was located at the end of the road (now Kennedy Avenue) and on the nose of a spur ridge. The bad news was there was not much tillable land, which in turn dictated a smaller herd of cattle than his neighbors. The good news was that most of the land was forested, which meant excellent hunting. The same fishable creek that ran for one-quarter mile through our farm meandered for three-quarters of a mile through the Dittman bottomland. As was the case with the Bucholz farm, the railroad tracks resulted in this bottomland being separated from the farm proper. The Dittman family consisted of Clarence and his wife Martha, and Clarence's elderly parents. The next chapter will introduce Clarence in a more comprehensive way.

The Steinhoff family operated three farms. They farmed more land than any other family on the ridge. The patriarch of the family was Joe, a widower. His four children, along with a brother and an unmarried sister, all assisted in meaningful ways with the farming operation. Joe's other two siblings, a brother and sister, were unable to contribute physical labor during the time I knew the family due to health problems. With their large pool of seven healthy laborers, the Steinhoffs worked rings around the rest of us. Where we might be able to haul in four to five wagonloads of hay in an afternoon, the Steinhoffs could easily triple that amount.

They were a wonderful family, who I remember as perennially smiling, friendly, and cheerful neighbors. Their home farm was about a mile from another of their farms, which in turn was close to our one-room school. Many a truck trip was required between the farms. There was no doubt but that they would pick us up if we were on the road to or from school. That could mean as many as five Hedricks jammed into the truck cab along with the driver.

Mention was made earlier that only one family lived full-time in the once thriving little village of Summit while I was growing up. This was the Christ family. The family consisted of the widowed mother, Frances, and two unmarried daughters, Gertrude and Laura. The daughters were roughly the age of my parents. Although less than one-half mile from either of our two farms they were truly isolated. The old Summit road no longer could be used for vehicles and they had no horses, nor any means of stabling horses. Their location in the valley denied them any view of another inhabited house or farm building. Until the Summit depot closed they could take the train to and from Norwalk and Sparta. After the depot closed they had to walk—and walk they did; to and from church when weather permitted, and to the home farm for milk and to pick up their mail. For their major needs, i.e. groceries, fire wood, etc., they depended for the most part on the Steinhoffs. (Joe Steinhoff was a nephew of Frances.) These were the depression years and there was a polite concern for so-called hobos working their way up to our farms from the railroad. Yet here was this family of three defenseless women living right next to the tracks. As far as I know, neither they nor we were ever bothered by hobos.

In summation, I don't recall there being any kind of serious neighbor versus neighbor animosity on Summit Ridge while I was growing up. Petty jealousies occurred now and then, or a tiff over school policy on occasion, but nothing to seriously mar the day-by-day spirit of shared experiences. The same could be said for the inter-relationship of neighboring communities surrounding Norwalk.

With our world at the time extending little more than two miles in any one direction, we were in effect, an island. Our literary link to the outside world, at least during my early years, was strictly through newspapers and a couple of farm magazines. Summit Ridge families pretty much all fell into the same economic pot, although a few in one section of the ridge did have electricity. At the time this was a community of small farms in the heyday of small farms in our country, bonded even closer by a shared religion, large extended families, and one-room schools. It might be said, given the rather primitive conditions in which we lived, that we youngsters on Summit Ridge were twentieth century children growing up in a nineteenth century world.

CHAPTER 6

Clarence Dittman

$\mathbf{F}$armers are in many ways quite competitive. Somewhere near the top of the list is getting certain seasonal chores done, not only in step with the season, but ideally a day or so before your neighbors. For example, the big seasonal chore was haying. This process stretched over four to six weeks. How sweet it was to finish ahead of the neighbor(s), and then to flaunt the fact by going fishing. One needed to time this trip so your neighbor(s) in the field saw you driving down the road, cane-fishing poles lashed across the top of your vehicle.

Haying was the big event, but so it went with the spring seeding of grain and corn, then cutting and shocking grain and corn; filling the silo, etc. Another major chore was fall plowing, although here the joy was just getting done since plowing took place in late fall when it could often be quite cold—usually windy cold.

Individual farmers also claim the right to judge their neighbor's farming methods. Woe to he who does not march lock step with the rest of the herd when the season dictated that certain work be done. In a polite sense the non-conformist is made the object of a degree of scorn and derision. Yet in a way, comforting to have a few of these non-conformists

Clarence Dittman (left) and maternal uncle Frank (Bud) Berendes enjoy a story and a beer.

around since it made the rest feel a bit superior.

Most farming communities have a few of its members who go about their farming methods in a relaxed manner. I think our next door neighbor, Clarence Dittman, exemplified this type of farmer. Make no mistake about it, given the choice Clarence preferred to hunt, fish, and trap rather than farm. I feel quite certain that if there had been uninhabited-forested mountains to the immediate west, this is where we would have found Clarence Dittman spending his working life as a mountain man.

Picture this if you can. It's a hot, sultry morning in mid-June of 1938. The farmers are dedicating themselves to mowing hay, raking in rows that which was felled the day before, and in general, gearing up for a busy afternoon. There's hay to be hauled to the barn and it must be done before one of those frequent summer afternoon showers came along. Now a cloud of dust catches the eye, which indicates a vehicle moving on a country road. Who could it be? Since the mailman has gone it can only be another local farmer. Someone must have had a machinery breakdown and is rushing to town for a repair part. Of course; why else would a farmer be wasting these precious hours of sunlight? As the vehicle materializes out of that cloud of dust it's not a machine part we see lashed to the top of the vehicle, but rather those beautiful, long cane-fishing poles. Clarence and his wife Martha are off to try for bass at Lake Tomah—and are symbolically thumbing their nose at the system.

Clarence only postponed the inevitable. Long after everyone else was through haying Clarence was picking away at this major farm chore. The hay crop at this point had hardened (over ripened) but was hauled into Clarence's hayshed even though his livestock were likely to reject it next winter. My dad and other neighboring farmers were not above smiling, and on occasion making quasi-snide remarks as trucks hauled hay back to Clarence's farm during the winter. Either his cattle refused to eat the hay he had harvested, or he ran out. In any event, this seemed to be an annual ritual.

So it seemed to go with Clarence and all his farming chores. He was either late (with most everything pertaining to farming), did things halfway (fencing), or not at all (cutting weeds).

If Clarence was not all that great a farmer he was an excellent mechanic. He liked to tinker. At one point he was working on a perpetual motion device sophisticated enough to impress the local high school science teacher. His skill as a mechanic was often called on to keep our three temperamental one-cylinder Johnson and Johnson engines running. On both farms the engines were a backup to pump water in the event the windmills did not produce enough. The engines also powered washing machines on both farms. This process was particularly critical in our home of twelve. No engine power meant hours of heavy work with a washboard. On the home farm the engine also powered the cream separator, although as a back up (often used) there was a hand crank. Finally, a lonesome Johnson and Johnson engine pumped water for the young stock kept in the small patch of woodland (squirrel woods) in the southwest corner of the home farm.

Clarence's farm was in turn run down, especially the barn and other outbuildings. There was old rusting machinery sitting here and there. The manure pile reached as high as the barn in the wintertime. Here was another cardinal sin since most farmers, even in the dead of a Wisconsin winter, moved this valuable fertilizer to the fields. Although the fertilization aspect was important, so was the appearance of the building area. All this did not seem to bother Clarence at all.

Clarence loved to hunt, fish, and talk to people. If a neighbor were anywhere near the road when Clarence drove by, his car was brought to a stop and a neighborly chat ensued. It's significant to note the other fellow usually politely terminated these chats. Clarence could also be called a storyteller, and on occasion told some pretty tall tales. It is true that on occasion he "slanted" the truth a bit. But no harm was done. He was at his best telling stories to children, although I am not sure they were stories to Clarence. As I recall, most of my siblings and I clustered around Clarence during his visits. He usually involved us in the conversation or otherwise enthralled us with his stories, and many of them were repeats.

Clarence was a heavy cigarette smoker. He rolled his own and the finished product was more flat than round. Clarence rarely took the cigarette out of his mouth while he talked. My sisters still giggle when they recall our mother trying to anticipate when to hand Clarence whatever passed as an ashtray while smoking in our house.

Throughout the summer, as a rule, I was sent by my dad to help Clarence out with various chores. One of the more pleasant chores was cultivating corn. Clarence didn't have a tractor so I rode and guided a horse while Clarence walked behind manhandling the cultivator. Clarence's farm was laid out in such a way that all his fields terminated at the edge of a wooded area, or a line fence, which in turn was wooded. Wooded means trees, and trees mean shade, and shade beckons in the most irresistible way on a hot day. So here we sat. Clarence invariably picked up a small stick to alternately scratch in the dirt, chase and squish a bug, or draw rough diagrams usually depicting techniques related to hunting and fishing. If Clarence and I were contented in this leisurely repose, imagine how happy the horse had to be? Clarence also regaled me with stories of alleged goings on when my parents and their peers were young. This did not quite seem to fit in with what I thought I knew of all those proper people. But for the most part, we talked of hunting and fishing, and life in general.

Clarence's wife, Martha, was in turn a pleasant person. She was also a much more industrious individual who didn't really appreciate Clarence's lack of industry. At times she came upon Clarence and I as we lazed around. On one such occasion this interruption came as too much of a surprise. It set Clarence off on an angry tirade in a raised voice. Then, as soon as Martha departed, he quickly shifted back into conversational voice and continued, "Then Joe, you throw a stick or stone and the squirrel will think you're walking around the tree and will move to where you can then line the squirrel up with your rifle, etc., etc."

There was yet another facet of Clarence's behavior that shocked or amused many. He was a professional at swearing who could muster up a string of profanities permitting him to cuss for minutes without ever using the same word twice, or breaking stride. On one occasion, Clarence and his wife took my younger brother Noel and me fishing. We had arrived at the lake and Clarence was standing next to the car, his head inside, working on something or other. His wife, apparently about to ask a question said, "Clarence." As he made his move to stand erect he hit the back of his head. Clarence was off. He was at his best on this occasion. Sheer poetry! My brother and I will frequently recount the event since it's permanently etched in our memories. We agreed that although swearing may not be proper, you have to stop and admire someone who is an expert in his field.

Clarence could come up with humorous ways of expressing himself. My siblings and I still chuckle when we recall the time Clarence was trying to find the precise word(s) to describe to our mother how something moved quickly and with many gyrations. He stumbled and stammered as he searched for that right word or phrase. In the meantime, we are on pins and needles waiting for him to finish the description. Finally he blurted out, "Frances, it jumped around like a fart in a bottle."

And to think, I came ever so close to shooting Clarence Dittman!

I don't suppose I was any different from other farm boys in our area who progressed through a series of shoulder-fired weapons. It started with an air rifle (BB gun), then on to a single-shot 22-caliber rifle. The next three in order were a 410 and 20 gauge shot gun, and on to a 30-30 caliber Winchester lever-action deer hunting rifle. The air rifle, and later the 22 caliber rifle were my constant companions as I moved about the farms to the point where they could be viewed as appendages to my body. This was especially true in the fall and winter months when there was more time to play. The weapon sat in the corner of both my grandparent's and our own kitchen along with the coats and boots where it could be easily gathered up as I headed outdoors.

I was forever pestering sparrows with the air rifle, but they were after all considered pests on the farm. Doves were also a frequent target, but they ended up as a tasty meal. For obvious reasons I was not allowed to do any random shooting of sparrows or doves during the nesting season. Then there was my imagination. I stalked tigers and lions, and at the critical moment fired off a shot. This was at a time in my life when I was quite sure that wild animals, especially wildcats (panthers) were present in our area. I can recall on occasions foolishly shooting at the moon, raising the rifle several degrees to compensate for the distance the pellet or bullet had to travel. I only recall killing one wild animal with my air rifle for no reason at all. I have often wondered why I can still visualize the precise spot where I stood at the time, where the chipmunk in turn was located in a gully, and that I remember the pellet hitting the animal right under an ear. I recall feeling guilty as this little animal went through its death throes—and I still do.

I was about twelve at the time of the incident involving Clarence, and had graduated to carrying a 22-caliber rifle. One evening I was traveling the one-fifth mile from our home to help with the milking on the home farm. The temperature was cold enough to be wearing gloves—but otherwise it was a bright moonlit and altogether beautiful night. The road made a sharp left turn as one approached the barn with a dirt bank on that side obscuring my view beyond the turn. I was carrying the rifle, and as usual, there was a round in the chamber, but with the safety on. When I was a few yards from the turn, from behind the bank, came this creature snarling and growling, making all the sounds I expected a wild animal to make. Could this be the much feared black panther? Here was the moment of truth. I peeled off my right glove, no doubt put the safety off, and aimed the rifle at the creature—then, without firing, I turned and ran towards home still carrying the rifle. At this point the "wild animal" burst into raucous laughter as Clarence arose from his crawling position on hands and knees. I was too frightened to tell Clarence what had nearly occurred. I certainly did not tell my parents or anyone else either. I would have lost the use of my rifle in an instant. I suspect this is the kind of occurrence one suppresses in their memory. To this day it brings back unpleasant thoughts to think of what easily might have happened. I suppose I could chalk this occurrence up to a dry run. Approximately ten years later I would remove a glove and hunt for the trigger of my rifle on a hill mass near the Chosin Reservoir in North Korea.

Clarence continued living on the farm after his wife died. Around this time he retired from dairy farming and rented out his land. He usually spent his retirement days in the small town of Norwalk, three miles from his farm. A small railroad retirement check and income from renting his farmland to my brothers sustained him. He was a commuter who left the farm at around nine a.m. each day and returned in the evening. Time was spent talking to old friends or sitting silently at the bar in a friendly tavern that became the center of his life. Not only was there social interaction with others, but meals were served in the tavern as well. The community sheltered him, when the conditions under which he lived suggested he should become a ward of the county.

My younger brothers and their families who were living on the farms generally monitored Clarence's coming and going. His not driving by for a day or so was cause for concern. On several occasions one or the other of my brothers checked on him. On one of those occasions my youngest brother Paul found Clarence dead in his home. The date was 18 January 1982.

What follows is a letter I felt compelled to write upon hearing of Clarence's death. The letter was subsequently printed in the local newspaper.

> January 24, 1982
>
> Editor
> The Monroe County Democrat
> Sparta, Wisconsin 54656
>
> Dear Sir:
>
> I was moved to set down the enclosed eulogy on hearing of the death of a long-time Norwalk resident, Clarence Dittman.
>
> I hope it a fitting tribute to the man from a neighbor boy who remembers him so well, and with so much affection and respect.
>
> I would be pleased if you could print the document since its purpose is to pay public respect to a most unforgettable gentleman.
>
> Thank you for your consideration of this matter.
>
> Sincerely yours,
>
> Joseph C. Hedrick

SO CLARENCE DITTMAN IS DEAD…!

The word of his passing reached me in California around 1 p.m. on January 18th. I believe he had been found dead only that morning. It took a few long minutes before I could dampen the rush of memories, and set aside, as best I could, the sadness so as to continue on the job.

I trust there was the standard obituary, and standard church service to commemorate his passing. That is not to demean those processes, but those processes in turn are unlikely to fit the needs of this unique individual. Neither will this of course, but I will have the satisfaction of having tried.

In many ways Clarence didn't fit into the farming community where I grew up, and where Clarence spent his entire life. He wasn't the passionate, industrious farmer that his neighbors seemed to be; and oh my goodness, he didn't go to church on Sunday. Clarence might be said to be profane, but those of us who knew him were aware this was his way of expressing himself. He certainly meant no disrespect.

It's a tribute to the man, and his neighbors, that he was warmly accepted as a full-fledged member of our farming community despite those minor deviations from the rule.

Clarence was a good and kindly man. As I recall, he was one of the first to respond to a neighbor's need, and to do so double-quick if it were an emergency.

Clarence had a special fondness for children. A pity that he and Martha were childless. I suppose as a result we ten Hedrick children, as his closest neighbors, benefited in a special way.

As the oldest boy in the family I became a major beneficiary of the man's kindness—indeed, wisdom. Since we inevitably finished haying, grain cutting, etc. ahead of Clarence I was often sent by my father to give Clarence a hand. I looked forward to those assignments since it seems we were usually at the "end of the row" where the shade trees along the line fence beckoned us to stop a spell. There, a great deal of my practical education took place.

I often hunted and fished with Clarence. He taught me how to coax the squirrels around a tree; how to wait out the circling fox; how to fish for the elusive trout that populated the creek running through our farms; and a host of other skills related to nature's scene. And for raw excitement, imagine an eleven year old accompanying Clarence on a midnight to twelve noon stint as a tunnel watchman. First the eerie two mile hike by faint lantern light across the winter landscape, then the mile hike through the tunnel, and finally the warmth of the small shack at the west end of the tunnel. The highlight though had to be the old "midnight" roaring out of the tunnel while we stood just a few feet away in that narrow canyon.

I think Clarence was especially proud when I joined the Marines. He assumed, and rightly so, that his hunting and rifle training would be put to good use in that organization. I remember too how rather embarrassed I was at Clarence's emotional welcome home when I returned from Korea.

So this good and kindly man is dead. I am pleased, and proud that my two younger brothers looked in on Clarence from time to time over his last years. Clarence was in his eighties after all, and he lived alone in a remote farmhouse at the end of a country road. It was my youngest brother Paul, who drove the half-mile back to Clarence's place, as he had many times in the past to check on his welfare who found Clarence dead.

Clarence was the last of a generation of decent and generous giants who tilled the soil on our end of Summit Ridge. I remember them all with great respect and affection. But I will always have a special feeling for that one man who took time out to teach, to talk, and to listen to a kid.

I am not sure how the world would judge a man like Clarence Dittman. I know this though: it's unlikely that I will ever "reach out and touch" another man's sons the way Clarence reached out and touched my brothers and me.

CHAPTER 7

St. John the Baptist Catholic Church

After the family, the church was in so many ways the center of our lives on Summit Ridge.

St. John the Baptist Catholic Church was close to the geographical center of Summit Ridge. According to local church lore, Saint John was selected as the patron saint of the church because many of the parishioners were named John. This included John Muehlen-kamp who donated the land on which the church was built. Then too, the first pastor was Father John Metzler. The church was built in 1878, with a rectory added in 1900. By

St. John the Baptist Catholic Church

the time I was born, the priest had established his residence in Norwalk and St. Johns became a subordinate mission to Norwalk. The old rectory, a big white square building, became the home of Alex (Pete) and Rosemary Kroeger and their family. Pete paid rent by maintaining the church and cemetery. This included stoking the furnace for winter Masses.

Shortly after building the rectory in 1900, an attempt was made to establish a parochial school. A fine two story brick building was built. The first floor was intended to be classrooms, the second floor living quarters for the teaching nuns. Unfortunately, money problems resulted in the second floor being left unfinished (as it remains today) and no parochial school was built. Over the years this building was put to use as a church hall, for catechism instructions, and related church activities. Most all the young women in the parish had their bridal shower in this building. With the addition of a kitchen, it served, and continues to serve as a center for social gatherings and fundraising events.

Summit Ridge was indeed Catholic. All but three of the fifty-five families on the ridge were members of the parish. We were still governed by the standard 19th Century spiritual book in which Catholics were told:

> You may be a poor man—striving by wearying, ceaseless toil for a poor living; you may have had little schooling; you may lack comforts of this life and feel envious sometimes to see your Protestant friends so much better off in this world's way...but there is something you possess which our poor friends with all their wealth cannot purchase –the true religion of Jesus Christ.

We are told that President Kennedy's maternal grandfather, John "Honey Fitz" Fitzgerald (1863-1950) was sure a Catholic would be struck dead if they were ever to enter a Protestant church. I don't recall ever being told that directly during my early days, but I wonder if it didn't come through as an unspoken rule. At any rate, I do not recall ever setting foot in a Protestant church during my nineteen growing up years on Summit Ridge.

The church at the time rigidly adhered to the proposition that human love must be subordinated to love for the church. In May of 1944,

Kathleen Kennedy, the granddaughter of "Honey Fitz" and sister of a future president, married an English Anglican. The President of Catholic Manhattan College wrote to Rose Kennedy (Kathleen's mother) promising to pray each day that God would give Kathleen the opportunity to repair in full measure "the mistake into which human love had led her."

And Rose Kennedy did not have only daughter Kathleen to worry about. At one point she learned that her son and future President Jack, was dating a Protestant girl. Her reaction was to send him a one-year's subscription to the Catholic Digest magazine.

In the Catholic Church's view, marrying a Protestant was permitted as long as he or she converted to the Catholic faith and brought the children up as Catholics. Violate that rule and you might continue to attend Mass, but could not receive the sacraments. Parents saw themselves as failures if one of their children married a Protestant who did not convert. Marry a divorced person—don't even think of it! As late as 17 April 2003 Pope John Paul II issued an encyclical reinforcing the church teachings that divorced Catholics who remarry cannot receive communion. The encyclical further reminded Catholics who remarry after divorce that they are living in sin.

But let us not be too hard on the Catholic Church as it relates to the matter of divorce. Protestant religions too had their restrictions on divorce at the time. History reminds us that King Edward the VIII was forced to abdicate the throne of England in 1936 when he chose to marry Wallace Warfield Simpson, a divorced woman. This was the only abdication in English history. Not until 1960, during the reign of the current monarch Queen Elizabeth II, was a divorced person allowed in the presence of the Queen—and then only if that person was the blameless party in a divorce.* Today, three of the current Queen's four children are divorced.

---

*A nobleman in that pre-1960 era whose marriage had been annulled was allowed by the Church of England to re-marry—but could not be invited to Royal events. In a sense he was told you might be allowed into the Kingdom of Heaven—but not the Royal Palace.

Celebrations in the Catholic Church formed an organic unit, which consisted of three festivals or seasons. Christmas preceded by Advent, followed by Epiphany; Easter proceeded by Lent; and Pentecost, followed by the rest of the church year. Through this cycle, times of waiting alternated with times of fulfillment; the lean weeks of Lent with the feast of Easter and Pentecost; and times of mourning with seasons of rejoicing.

How well I remember the lean weeks of Lent from the viewpoint of a child. During the forty-day Lenten period, adults and children were expected to give up something they "enjoyed" in order to better appreciate the suffering of Christ. The goal for us children was to fast and abstain from eating any candy during Lent. Somehow or other all the children found a box of some kind, usually a shoebox. What fun to check, day by day, that box with a small, yet to us, impressive growth of candy. What temptation to have at least one piece of candy—what torture to resist that temptation! So over those ten years I participated in this process how many years was I able to carry through without breaking the fast?

ZERO! ZIP! NUNO! NADA!

Another memory of the Lenten period was the daily rosary. Right after the evening meal we knelt, using chairs for a bit of support, to say the rosary. The same happened at my grandparent Hedrick's house (there was no escape) and throughout the Catholic community. On a lighter note, for some reason the rosary often produced a "giggling" outbreak. This was assured if someone were to fart. Even my mother was not immune from the giggling process. But this only delayed the inevitable; going methodically through all five decades of the rosary.

On Friday evenings during Lent we gathered at the church for Stations of the Cross. This was after farm chores were done, usually at 8 p.m. I was a Mass server (altar boy) for thirteen of my growing up years. The best job for an altar boy during this service was to carry the cross. This job didn't require having to kneel or genuflect—just to "stroll" along with the group. Two of us carried lit candles, with no protective device to catch and hold the hot wax. We (the three altar boys and priest) moved down the center of the church as we made our way past each of the fourteen stations hung as pictures on the walls. We stopped at each station where the priest first said a short prayer. Then we genuflected and the priest said another much longer prayer. Finally we knelt for the Our Father, Hail Mary, and Glory Be to the Father. Then the choir sang a short refrain as we moved to the next station. So it went for all fourteen stations.

Somewhere around the second or third station the hot wax overflowed the well at the base of the burning wick. If you held the candles perfectly straight the wax cooled as it ran down the candle and did not reach your hand. But with getting up and down while genuflecting, it was nearly impossible to keep the candle straight. How we hated that first splash of hot wax hitting our hands. It didn't burn, but it got your attention. A little bit of happiness was having enough wax covering your exposed hands to where additional hot wax merely piled up.

Despite our remoteness from the centers of fashion, Easter Sunday was "dress up day," especially for the ladies and girls. The emphasis was on new hats (bonnets) and gloves. The little girls were particularly pleased with their new attire. At that time a hat or scarf of some kind had to be worn by women and girls while in church. This gave the ladies considerable leverage when working their husbands for a new hat. If a brightly colored, maybe even gaudy hat was acceptable, a sleeveless dress for the ladies was definitely not.

The next major church event was Christmas, specifically Christmas Mass. Ideally the Mass was said at midnight, but the senior parish in Norwalk commanded the one priest for this prime time slot. In order to preserve the image of midnight Mass ours was at 5 a.m. on Christmas day—while still dark. I remember the near darkened church lit only by six candles on the altar (six candles for "high" Mass, two for "low" Mass). One of the better woman singers sang *Silent Night* to open the service. Pure magic! In my days this spinner of magic was my maternal Aunt Agnes.

On Christmas and Easter Father Mechler expanded the Mass server force from the usual four to ten. These six additional servers (i.e. recruits) occupied the space between the altar—where the regular servers knelt—and the communion rail. For us "veterans" this could be entertaining at times. In those days there was frequent genuflecting during the Mass. These recruits were used to genuflecting to a kneeler six inches off the floor. No such kneelers for them on the altar. As a result the recruit's genuflections ranged from what resembled deep curtsies to bone-jarring thumps as they tried to compensate for the lack of accustomed kneelers.

Reverend Edward Mechler

Yet another somewhat comical aspect of this expanded group of Mass servers was how we moved on and off the altar. We had only a typical thirty-inch wide door leading from the sacristy to the altar. This meant we had to alternate going up and down the two steps to and from the altar. I don't recall our ever having problems getting on the altar with some degree of orderliness, but not necessarily so coming off after Mass. First of all, the Masses were longer on Christmas and Easter. As a result we were all anxious to leave the altar. This was particularly true of the recruits who had to remain close to stationary throughout the Mass. We also knew that on these significant occasions of Christmas and Easter Father Mechler gave each of us a sack of candy. At any rate, the exodus was invariably sloppy at best. One after another the recruits bounced off the door jams as they hurried to leave the altar. On one occasion, as the group stood around Father Mechler, looking sheepish, he asked us what our fathers were likely to do if the cows were to move through the barn door in the manner in which we had just done so?

The candy from Father Mechler came only on Easter and Christmas. We four regulars were irked that we received the same amount as the recruits. Further, these recruits were mere ornaments, stage dressing if you will for these two major church events.

Hey there Father Mechler—we are your four regulars who are on the job fifty-two Sundays a year plus holy days, weddings, funerals, and Saturdays when you had catechism instructions, etc. We're the guys who had to learn all that Latin, to include the lengthy Confiteor and toss it back to you on cue. We poured the wine and water twice during Mass and handed you a small towel on each occasion to dry your hands. Who rang the chimes at Consecration and Holy Communion, and who carried the paten to ensure no communion host dropped while you were giving out Holy Communion? Remember too Father, one of us took up a collection of pennies from the first three rows of boys and girls so you could buy new vestments. Finally Father Mechler, did you forget who supported you during Benediction? As a matter of routine you added to the length of the service with Benediction right after the Mass proper. The four of us, your regulars, were the ones who fired up the extra ten to twelve candles and brought the large monstrance to the altar from the sacristy, along with that elegant robe you wore during Benediction. Speaking of "firing up," we also ensured that the small piece of charcoal was red hot when you placed it in the censer. Ah yes, I remember the sweet fragrance that came from the censer when you sprinkled incense on that red-hot charcoal. We also noted that you held the censer in your right hand at the height of your breast and grasped the chain near the censer cover. The left hand, holding the top of the chain was placed on your breast. All the while, your right elbow was tucked in close to your side. Then you raised the censer to the height of your eyes, gave it an outward motion all the while ensuring that the censer ascended towards the object to be honored, and then immediately brought back to the starting point. This constituted a single swing. For a double swing the outward motion was repeated, the second movement being more pronounced than the first. We may have been simple farm boys Father Mechler, but we took note of all this. We also divined (no pun intended) that the dignity or importance of the person or object being honored determined the number of swings.

So, did we four regular Mass servers form a union, or otherwise ever let Father Mechler know of our gripes relative to the candy issue? Are you kidding? No way! That giant, this man of God who to most, if not all parishioners was to varying degrees Jesus Christ incarnate. No, we had to be satisfied to reflect on Matthew, chapter nineteen verses thirty: **"Many who are first shall come last, and the last shall come first."**

Another significant church related event in our lives was called "Sister School." Early in the summer, right after public school was over and before the labor-intensive job of haying began, two nuns arrived to conduct two weeks of religious school for school age children. School ran from Monday through Saturday. We Hedricks, probably five maximum at any one time, walked the one-mile to the school by way of the old Summit road. The road, no longer usable for automobiles, was tree lined and shaded along most of its entire length. Wild flowers abounded along the route. My sisters arrived home with flowers for Mother daily. The day began with Mass followed by catechism instruction until three p.m. Instruction was held in the building once intended to be a parochial school. With the need to divide forty to fifty children in teachable groups even the unfinished upstairs was used. One of the jobs for the nuns was to prepare that year's crop of first communicants. On the last day of Sister School, a Saturday, these youngsters made their first confession. To add to the children's apprehension was that the confessional was a foreboding place to begin with. Its location was in a dark windowless corner in the back of the church. The children were well schooled on what to do and say once they entered this closet sized enclosure. "Bless me Father, for I have sinned, this is my first confession. I...." It must have been entertaining for the priest to hear the sins of these six-year olds.

The following Sunday was the big day. The girls, conscious of how beautiful they looked in their spotless white dresses, veils, stockings and shoes were happy to be so dressed and the center of attention. Unknown to these little girls at the time, the next event whereat they were likely to have a similar "dressed up" experience would be their weddings. The boys in turn wore white shirts and trousers—and did not appear to be all that comfortable or happy to be so attired.

For the rest of the fair weather year, Father Mechler conducted catechism on Saturday morning—preceded by Mass. Mother made sure we knew our catechism lesson since Father Mechler held parents strictly accountable. I recall on one occasion being anxious to leave the house to observe pig butchering. Neighbors had already arrived and the process was soon to begin. "Not until you learn the seven sacraments," said Mother. I probably memorized and rattled off "Baptism, Confirmation, Penance, Holy Eucharist, Holy Matrimony, Holy Orders and Extreme Unction" in record time so I could be turned loose.

Our mother would have won warm praise from the church hierarchy for the manner on which she did her part to indoctrinate the teachings of the Catholic Church in her children.

Is it any wonder that I remember how pleased my Mother was when, at around age seven, I told her how lucky I felt being a Catholic and an American?

In the winter months Father Mechler occasionally conducted a "dreaded" unannounced catechism quiz in place of the Sunday sermon. Embarrassing enough to display your ignorance when only he and the rest of the class were listening for the right answer, but now your parents, relatives; indeed the entire parish was there to closely monitor the process. I don't recall that he ever quizzed us Mass servers, but that didn't mean we were not apprehensive of his doing so.

On a biennial basis the Bishop visited to confirm the next crop of youngsters about to enter their teen years. In the process we became "Soldiers of Christ." The process involved his quizzing us on the catechism and being physically slapped on the cheek. In practice the slap was but a light tap, but in anticipating the event we thought differently. Here again the quiz took place in front of the entire parish. Now not only were the children and parents in a position to be embarrassed, but also Father Mechler. An abscessed tooth seemed to be a preferable trade-off to avoid going through this ritual. My class was saved from the expected questioning by my older sister Elaine. She engaged the bishop in a long, drawn out discussion on the question he asked her. I was too frightened at the time to do much but review in my mind the possible question he might ask me. Apparently though, the bishop was enjoying this exchange with my sister and the discourse went off in several related directions. The bishop wrapped up the questioning by suggesting Elaine should be teaching catechism. Can you imagine how happy this must have made my parents—and Father Mechler?

The reader by now knows that I was a regular Mass server at St. John the Baptist Catholic Church for thirteen years. We were told that the right place at the right time for Lana Turner (of Hollywood fame) was when she was spotted by a talent scout while working in Schwab's drug store in Hollywood. We were also told the snug sweater she was wearing at the time helped as well. For me, my location at the aisle end of the pew the day Father Mechler picked two new Mass servers did the trick. Don Ziegler and Bob Rapp were graduating off the altar and I, along with my maternal cousin Jim Muehlenkamp, were to join Leander Ebert and Delmar Donskey as regulars on the altar. I was age six and cousin Jim Muehlenkamp was approximately six months younger. He and I carried out our Mass serving duties until I joined the Marine Corps.

There was a rather rigid regimen relative to where you sat during Mass. All the adults had assigned seats with their names printed on the pews to ensure no mix-up. All the boys of school age were assigned to the first three rows of pews on one side of the church, with the youngest being in the front pew. The same for the girls on the opposite side. This placement served two purposes. First, it placed the children where they could easily view the altar. Secondly, the knowledge that parents, relatives, and other adults could easily monitor their deportment kept even the most recalcitrant among them in line. Eventually the young ladies graduated out of those seats and joined their parents. This was not for long since marriage or jobs soon took the ladies out of this safe harbor.

The boys graduated to the **bullpen!**

A balcony-like loft is located over the entry way and confessional area of the church. On one side was the organ and choir. On the other side was the bullpen. This earthy identification does not imply that less than fervent Catholic young men occupied its spaces. But let's be realistic: the bullpen was out-of-sight, and some of the occupants in all likelihood partied heavily the preceding Saturday night. What then could be better than to have done your duty by attending Mass and yet being able to pick up a few "Zs" in the process?

In the meantime the boys and girls had to put in their time in those front pews. For most, the then ritualistic Mass with all its Latin could be sheer boredom. As noted, with parents and a host of relatives and neighbors behind you, there was little to do but to be on your best behavior and sit as still as you could for one hour or more.

Contrast that with serving Mass. We were "stage center" with only the priest out starring us as human components of the Mass. Our uniform was a black vestment (robe) called a cassock and a white top called a surplice that indeed made us look like little priests. As noted earlier, we were able to bound about the altar. Any period of prolonged kneeling or sitting was punctuated by frequent moving here or there as we performed a variety of tasks. We did have to stay alert. When the priest said "Dominus vobiscum" (the Lord be with you) we had to be ready with "Et cum spiritu tuo" (and with your spirit). And how about "Ite, Missa est" (go, you are dismissed) at the end of Mass? Our response was "Deo gratias" (thanks be to God). We tried not to put too much vocal emphasis on this last response, but we knew we spoke for most of the congregation.

The confiteor! We enjoyed saying the confiteor. The Latin seemed to roll off the tongue. I remember it still:

> Confiteor Deo omnipotènti, beátæMariæ semper Virgini, beáto Michaéli Archángelo, beáto Joánni Baptistæ, sanctis Apóstolis Petro et Paulo, ómnibus Sanctis, et tibi, Pater: quia peccávi nimis cogitatióne, verbo, et ópere (now strike breast

three times as you say) mea culpa, mea culpa, mea máxima culpa. Ideo precor beátm Maríam semper Vírginem, beátum Michaélem Archángelum, beátum Joánnem Baptístam, sanctos Apóstolos Petrum et Paulum, omnes Sanctos, et te, Pater, oárre Pro Me ad Dóminum Deum nostrum.*

Somewhere along the way I was assigned two jobs that further broke the routine. While my fellow servers knelt at the altar during offertory, I retreated to the sacristy, picked up a small collection basket, and made the rounds collecting pennies from the six rows of boys and girls. This collection was used to purchase new vestments for the priest. When I finished the task I rejoined the others whose knees had to be feeling some discomfort. Better yet was my assigned job during Holy Communion. There was a near military-type precision demanded of those who approached the altar rail. As far as I know this was Father Mechler's way of adding more reverence to the sacrament. The first ten communicants lined up in front of the communion rail. When those ten judged they were all lined up there was a group genuflection. Then in unison they walked up the two steps and knelt at the communion railing. In the meantime the next ten had assembled in a line behind those receiving communion at the railing. Those at the railing remained kneeling until the last had received communion. Then as the priest started back down the line they all stood—backed down those two steps, and in unison with the ten formed behind them, genuflected and returned to their seats. And so it went. Can you imagine how confusing and embarrassing this had to be for visitors to the church?

Once again I left my three partners kneeling at the altar while the one hundred plus parishioners received communion. As a rule, all those over

---

*I confess to Almighty God, to Blessed Mary, ever Virgin, to Blessed Michael the Archangel, to Blessed John the Baptist, to the Holy Apostles Peter and Paul, and to all the Saints, and to you Father, that I have sinned exceedingly in thought, word and deed, (strike breast three times as you say) through my fault, through my fault, through my most grievous fault. Therefore I beseech Blessed Mary, ever Virgin, Blessed Michael the Archangel, Blessed John the Baptist, the Holy Apostles Peter and Paul, and all the Saints, and you, Father, to pray to the Lord our God for me.

St. John's Altar and communion rail (1930s photo)

age six received communion. It might raise some eyebrows if an otherwise eligible person did not trek up to the communion rail. My job was to be at Father Mechler's left side so I could place the paten* under the chin of the person receiving communion. A host (communion wafer) is viewed as the "body and blood" of Christ and having it fall to the floor could only be viewed as traumatic. This did not happen during my time, and I am quite certain I would remember if it had.

At that time in the church, all those receiving communion had the host placed on their tongue. I noted over the years the different sizes, colors and textures of many tongues. I noticed too that some of the folks opened their mouths wide and stuck their tongue out as far as they possibly could. Others did so only to where the tongues just cleared the lips. Still others merely opened their mouths, which required Father Mechler to put a little spin on the host to ensure delivery. I wonder how many tongues I observed over the years, or put another way, how many times

---

*An approximate seven inch in diameter plate-like device with a handle.

the folks on Summit Ridge stuck their tongues out at me. I remember another soft and warm incident that occurred while in the communion process. Somehow I had mustered the necessary two or three dollars and purchased costume jewelry as a Christmas present for a young lady I was dating at the time. I remember how pleased I was to note her wearing that jewelry when she received communion at that year's Christmas Mass. I should not have been so smug. After all, this young lady was an attractive blond and no doubt received similar, but more expensive jewelry from others whom she dated. Being a kindly and thoughtful person, she wore what I had given her knowing no doubt that I was likely to be a close observer while she knelt at the communion rail.

Another ritual was confession. As noted above, the confessional was located in a dark windowless corner in the back of the church. The priest sat in a darker still closet sized enclosure. On either side were smaller enclosures one entered through a curtain, then knelt on a kneeler. When the priest opened a small sliding door you saw only a shadow of his head and shoulders—but you were now "on stage." While waiting for your turn in the confessional we were told to pray to God for forgiveness while the priest heard the confession of the person on the other side. Doing so with fervor and total concentration reduced the possibility of eavesdropping.

Catholics of that era were encouraged to go to confession as often as they could since Penance (confession) was one of the seven sacraments. This meant additional "sanctifying grace" could be earned just by going through the process—sins or no sins to be forgiven. Those of us who really needed to go to confession appreciated the "cover" provided by the saintly older women standing in line with us. Who after all could say for sure who really needed to go to confession and who simply wanted to earn (i.e. bank) additional sanctifying grace. Another fairly effective cover was to position yourself behind an adult male. In the course of a given days farming, they probably had occasions to verbally express themselves with words and phrases not entirely proper. Another choice, playing the odds again, was to time your arrival in line so you were behind one of the young single men or woman. This is not to cast aspersions on any of the foregoing groups, but you gambled that their transgressions were likely to eclipse yours. The theory was that Father Mechler would then see you as a "lesser" sinner.

Father Mechler had established a predictable pattern to the confession routine. Penitents came and went with something of the same time differential. One worried that you might be counseled at some length while in the confessional. All your friends, family, and neighbors might wonder why it took you so long to clear the confessional.

Not only did Father Mechler have a predictable pattern relative to time for each confession, but this also extended to the penance assigned for your sins. The usual was an Our Father, Hail Mary, and Glory be to the Father—and you might be surprised what in the way of sins that penance served to excuse. The usual routine was for penitents to return to a pew, kneel, and say their penance. Now how long does it take to say an Our Father, etc.? Spend too much time on your knees and folks might again wonder "how come?" Break out a rosary and tongues were likely to wag. One way out was to say only the routine Our Father, etc., leave, and then finish out your penance sometime later—but this was discouraged. You were expected to say your penance in the Lord's house.

But there was a way for the heavy sinners to avoid these possible embarrassments. For example, those who leafed too slowly through the women's undergarment section of the Montgomery Wards and/or Sears Roebuck catalogues. Since we received both catalogues this was double exposure for me. For those who wanted to escape the scrutiny of their fellow parishioners, the answer was to go to confession elsewhere. Since an element of suspicion arose if you didn't go to communion on Sunday, nearly the entire parish showed up for Saturday evening confession in fair weather months. In winter time confessions were heard before Mass. In an emergency, saying a "sincere" act of contrition, if "really" sincere, might absolve your sins. I often used this prayer when I found myself in the fields a long way from the farm buildings with a thunderstorm likely to catch me in the open. In summary, on a given Sunday morning more than likely the church was filled with parishioners, all in the state of sanctifying grace – a stern prerequisite for receiving Holy Communion.

No coffee or donuts were served after Mass at St. Johns, but there was much socializing—except in the wintertime. Parishioners were expected to attend their own parish's Mass, and no one missed Mass without a compelling excuse. Therefore, you could count on seeing your fellow parishioners on Sundays. Nearly the whole congregation gathered in small groups to chat. Along with the purely small talk, business was conducted, primarily among the men.

There was one family living on a farm about a city block from the church. They usually walked to Mass. The mother and five daughters seemed as alike as peas in a pod—all neatly dressed and wearing the same soft smiles. Since our church embraced two school districts (both one-room schools), as a rule I saw this family only on Sundays. I was impressed by the family and their seeming wholesomeness and demeanor. Little did I know then that I would return on military leave in 1953 to marry the oldest daughter.

If folks on Summit Ridge were good Catholics, they expected something in return for their loyalty, devotion, and prayers. Openly asked for during group prayers were bountiful crops and healing of the sick and injured. In our home a candle was often lit when a particularly severe thunderstorm with accompanying heavy winds rolled though the area. This to remind the Lord that we were "good Catholics," and in a sense, to lay off the heavy stuff.

I suspect most Catholic mothers in my day hoped and prayed they would have the opportunity one-day to say, "My son is a priest!" Mother pushed the idea often—but softly. Usually this was done in conjunction with mentioning that somehow the family would find the money to pay for the necessary schooling.

At one point when I was about twelve, my maternal Aunt Agnes was talking to a few of us Hedrick children after Mass. She mentioned that my brother Noel, four years younger than I, was likely to become a priest. She had noted how his lips constantly moved in prayer during Mass. I objected vociferously to this. After all, I reminded my Aunt Agnes, I was an altar boy and if anyone were to become a priest it was likely to be me!

So life went on. He who objected vociferously to our Aunt Agnes' prediction became a career Marine; he whose lips constantly moved in prayer became a Catholic priest.

No discussion of St. John the Baptist Catholic Church could be considered complete without mention of the adjacent cemetery. Here lie the mortal remains of several generations of parishioners. My wife and I find it "sweet sadness" to visit the cemetery on our annual visits to Wisconsin. In addition to our departed parents, grandparents, aunts, uncles, and a host of other relatives, are others we knew who are buried here. Here lies Lloyd Ziegler, who at age twenty-one was killed on Iwo Jima during World War II. He was my wife's first cousin, and my inspiration for joining the Marine Corps. The grave of our neighbor Frances (Mamie) Christ is the one grave in the cemetery I helped dig. As noted earlier, Frances, a widow and her two unmarried daughters lived in one of the three homes still standing in my days in what was once the thriving eighthouse community of Summit. Frances' husband Pete had been a railroad section foreman maintaining the tracks through Summit. And here is the grave of Pete Semann, another of the giants who tilled the soil on Summit ridge while I was growing up. Young men at that time not only had the duty to farm, but on summer Sunday afternoons they were expected to play baseball for the Summit Ridge team. I remember one game in particular in which Pete played. Uniforms were a rarity so Pete played second base in his overalls, as did most of his teammates. A blazing liner was hit toward second base, seemingly destined to go over the head of Pete. I'm sure Pete was as surprised as anyone when he leaped high to grab that line drive. The catch was the basis for a time out as the crowd and his teammates cheered.

As I pause at Pete's grave, I am also reminded of the sentimental account of his funeral. Pete was musically inclined with his instrument of choice being the violin. Pete also enjoyed the "sung" songs. At the time of Pete's death, the parish priest was an accomplished singer. During Pete's final illness, Father Scheckel often visited Pete in the hospital. During each visit Pete asked him to sing a song entitled *Be Not Afraid*. Since this was a hospital, Father Scheckel obviously could not do so. At Pete's funeral, the priest mentioned this frequent request, then looking toward Pete's casket he said, "Okay Pete, here is *Be Not Afraid* just for you." There wasn't a dry eye in the church. Fittingly, musical notes are inscribed on Pete's gravestone. And so we amble, row after row past the approximate 300 gravestones in the cemetery with many conjuring up memories similar to those of Pete Semann.

The reader will appreciate that the other Mass servers and I developed a close relationship with Father Mechler. He was the only priest at our parish during my growing up years. He arrived at St. Johns on 23 March 1927. I was born on 14 October 1927. Coletta Ebert was the first baby born on Summit Ridge to be baptized by Father Mechler. I was the second, and the first boy he baptized. I went directly from the altar to the Marine Corps in January of 1947. Father Mechler was transferred to a parish in Cook's Valley in April of 1947.

A Catholic upbringing was woven tightly into the fabric of my life during those early years. My moral compass was set and the launching pad readied for whatever life had in store. The subject of becoming a priest has been mentioned from time to time. I recall considering this role as I approached the end of my first enlistment in the Marines. In the meantime, the military chaplains could count on me to be a daily attendee at Mass or rosary service whenever possible.

CHAPTER **8**

Family History

On the Hedrick side we know little of the family history beyond my great-grandparents, and not all that much about them. My paternal great-grandfather was George Hedrick (1820-1906). His wife, my great-grandmother was Christina Rosenberg (1827-1903). Assuming Christina was fully Jewish, as her surname suggests, would result in my generation being eight-percent Jewish. I suspect we wouldn't have passed Adolph

Great-grandparents George and Christine (Rosenberg) Hedrick

Hitler's racial purity test.

Both George and Christina were born in Bavaria, Germany. We believe they came to this country sometime around 1856. They were living in the community of Bristol (Dane County), Wisconsin where my grandfather Isadore* (1857-1951) was born. Bristol was a farming community just east of Madison. In 1858, George moved his family by oxen team to the area later called Summit Ridge where he homesteaded what is still today the Hedrick family farm. The trip took them through heavy growth of forest, grass, and weeds on the side of whatever passed as a road on that 120-mile trip. One imagines the family traveled in a self-contained wagon, carrying their food and sleeping in or under the wagon. One suspects too that it must have taken at least a week to make the trip. From time to time they saw piles of rocks higher than the surrounding grass and brush. These had been placed there by earlier travelers as a guide for those who were to follow.

Great-grandfather George was a wagon maker by trade. He walked the seven miles by road (five if he traveled cross-country) to a wagon shop at Ridgeville. Since his son Isadore was two years old in 1858, I assume the farm was not actively worked until Isadore was old enough to participate. Then again, Great-grandfather George may have farmed, and as time permitted worked as a wagon maker.

Part of my grandfather's earliest recollection of life on their new farm was of seeing a band of fifteen to twenty Indians crossing the farm a few hundred yards from the house. Memories of the massacres that occurred during the Black Hawk War with the Sauk and Fox Indians still lingered in the minds of settlers. My grandfather acknowledged being frightened stiff. He also mentioned the frequency of seeing bears, which was something else to strike fear in the heart of a child.

My grandfather found a great employment opportunity when the railroad tunnel was constructed in 1870. Fourteen year-old Isadore was

---

*Named after Saint Isadore, the patron saint of farmers.

hired to care for the approximately fifty mules and oxen used on the east end of the tunnel. A tent was erected in a flat area down the hill from his farm home, approximately one-half mile away. At around six p.m. he took over control of the mules and oxen when the drivers finished up their days work. He unharnessed, watered and fed them, and cleaned up the temporary stable. Before dawn he arrived at the stable to feed, water, cleanup, and harness the animals. I often wondered how much he was paid.

My paternal grandmother was Barbara Semann (1877-1965). Her parents were Adolph and Barbara (Sell) Semann. I often asked my grandmother about her early life in Germany. She was the only close relative I knew who remembered life in what was so often referred to as the "old country." Her responses were general, leading me to believe they were routine. Why should they not be? She was born in a small town called Elfershausen (Bavaria), Germany. The little church in Elfershausen still stands today. It's called "Maria Himmelfahrt," which means Assumption of the Blessed Virgin.

She was fifteen in 1893, when along with her mother and five siblings they left their village home in southern Germany to journey to America. Her father had preceded them by approximately a year. She was much more animated in telling about her journey to America. The train trip across a large part of Europe, the ocean crossing, then the train trip to her new home in Wisconsin. At age fifteen, an exciting and largely enjoyable event. Understandably, life on the ocean liner was the most exciting and impressive for her. Her family settled in one of the eight houses in Summit. That old home can still be identified by the cave cellar dug in the side of the hill.

A tragedy occurred five months after the family was reunited. Her father was killed while in the process of cutting firewood near their home. I still wonder what her father did for a livelihood, and what were his plans? I suspect the railroad was involved. I wonder too how the family survived without a breadwinner. The answer to the last question no doubt is neighbors and relatives.

Probably no one now living had a better opportunity to learn a great deal more about my grandmother's early years than I did. I spent considerable time growing up in her house, and ever so happily ate many a meal at her table. She was a great cook! I also had numerous opportunities to visit with my grandmother's five siblings. They were all likeable and easy people to talk to; all that was missing were my questions.

Isadore Hedrick and Barbara Semann were married on 5 March 1897. My father George (1898-1981) was the second of seven children born to this union.

Grandparents Isadore and Barbara (Semann) Hedrick

On my Mother's side (Berendes) much more is known of preceding generations.

On the paternal side of her family my generation can trace our roots back nine generations to grandparents Phillipi Herman Steinhoff (1660-1718) and Anna Elisabeth Cames (1662-1732). They lived in Udorf (Westphalia), Germany. My great-grandmother was Ida Franzisca Steinhoff (1847-1924). She was also born in Udorf, Germany and came to this country in 1852 with her parents and two siblings. Her husband and my great-grandfather was Frank Berendes (1835-1898). He came from Prussia, Germany.

I am quite sure I would have liked great-grandfather Frank. First of all, he came to this country from Germany as a stow-away. Then too, he came from Prussia, that generally barren area of Northeast Germany made up of largely disconnected stretches of sandy wasteland, marshes, and somber pine-forested hills. Prussia was more than the name of a country; it represented a military way of life. Prussia was the home of the true German warrior class, the so-called "Junkers." He arrived in time to fight in this country's great Civil War. After the war, in 1865, he purchased a farm on Summit Ridge from the railroad. In order to encourage railroads to expand, the Federal government awarded vast tracts of land, usually on either side of the railroad right of way. The railroad then could dispose of this land as they wished. This farm was but two miles from the small community of Summit where his future daughter-in-law and my grandmother Mary Geoghegan (1880-1918) grew up.

On the maternal side of my mother's family we have the Irish. My great-great-grandparents were Thomas Geoghegan (1773-1861) and Elizabeth Buckley. They lived in County Cork, Ireland. My great-grandfather was Charles Geoghegan (1846-1917). He immigrated to this country and initially lived in Brooklyn, New York. There he met another Irish immigrant, Anna Healy (1852-1930) originally from County Claire, Ireland who was working as a priest's housekeeper. They were married at St. John's Catholic Church in Brooklyn, New York on 9 August 1877.

After moving to Wisconsin Charles and Anna lived in LaValle, Wisconsin before moving to Summit. They initially lived at the western side of the tunnel in Farmer's Valley. This was where my maternal grandmother Mary was born. Later they built a house in the newly developed settlement of Summit one-half mile east of the tunnel. Charles labored as a section hand on the railroad all his working life.

My maternal grandparents were John Berendes (1877-1948) and

Maternal grandparents John and Mary (Geoghegan) Berendes

Mary Geoghegan (1880-1918). They were wed on 25 November 1902. My mother Frances (1905-1971) was the second of nine children born to this union.

A tragedy also visited this side of the family. My grandmother Mary died in 1918 in the great flu epidemic that swept the world after World War I. She left behind nine children, ages one to fifteen. My mother was the oldest daughter. She was fourteen years old. A widowed paternal grandmother (Frances Berendes) moved in to fill the role of mother and housekeeper. When my mother was nineteen her grandmother died and my mother took over as housekeeper and surrogate mother until she married at age twenty.

CHAPTER **9**

Extended Family

My dad worked two farms. My paternal grandfather who owned the farms was able to assist to only a limited extent. While still a young man with a large family to raise he had been injured in a farm accident. He had been struck in a leg by the tusk of a boar (male pig). He ignored the wound and blood poisoning set in. His life was saved by Doctor Jones from Rockland, a community approximately twenty miles from the home farm. He spent the winter recuperating while brother-in-law Julius Semann moved in to help run the farm.

My grandfather, Isadore Hedrick, was seventy years old when I was born. I remember him walking with an obvious limp; otherwise he was a healthy man. I also recall him helping with milking, doing barn yard chores in the wintertime, and mowing hay. I am not sure when he stopped hoeing corn. I do know he was still hoeing corn while in his early nineties. He must have enjoyed breaking the routine of his retirement by working in this way for a couple of hours each day. Hoeing corn involved cutting out the weeds that were using up some of the soil nutrients, and in general loosening the soil around the corn stalks. This permitted the roots to breath better and the loose soil was better able to catch and hold rain water. Naturally, the corn hoed grew taller than the corn not so tenderly cared for. The neighbors accused my grandfather, good naturedly, of only hoeing in about ten feet from the roadside fence line before hoeing back on another row, etc. As a result, all the rows of corn in that field looked great as one traveled along the road.

Four adults were living in my grandparent's home at the time. In addition to my grandparents there was Aunt Tilla who, as noted earlier, worked at a store in Norwalk called the Mercantile. She was making about forty dollars a month. All of Summit Ridge was in awe when in 1936 she bought a brand new Chevrolet sedan. The price was just under $500. The other person was Aunt Lena. She had been somewhat crippled by polio, but was nonetheless a hard and productive worker. This applied not only to helping her mother in the house, but also with assisting in the morning and evening milking and some of the fieldwork. She was my mother's age, yet more a buddy than an aunt to me.

I suspect that my grandmother or Aunt Lena was looking out the kitchen window one morning or evening and noted my older sister Elaine and I going to or from school. It must have been cold weather time and what they saw was a potential wood carrier in that young grandson/nephew. A deal was then struck with my parents. I stopped off on my way home from school to carry in the next day's supply of wood to their house. In return, I ate supper at my grandmother's table. After supper, Aunt Lena and I joined Dad to do the evening milking.

Remember the home farm was on a side hill to begin with. The trek from the woodpiles to the house was up a relatively steep incline making it a "huff and puff" job in any season. Now add to the chore the effects of snow, ice, rain, etc. and you can see where a kid could earn his supper.

Lucky me! First of all, I did not have to compete with whatever number of siblings gathered at the table for food at home, especially for dessert. My grandmother baked many a pie that she cut into six slices. Usually only five of us were at the table; and guess who received the extra piece of pie? A little different situation if the dessert was cake. Then only five pieces were served, one for each person at the table.

Another benefit of eating the evening meal at my grandparent's house was being saved the round trip of walking to and from our home since I would have had to return to the home farm for evening milking. Then too, consider how busy my mother had to be with a house full of children compared to a healthy grandmother who could pretty much dedicate herself to kitchen chores—and she had a well deserved reputation as an excellent cook. In my mind's eye I still see her bending over the stove or scurrying back and forth from the pantry to the kitchen stove. Finally, imagine how delightful for me to be the only kid at a table with four doting adults. I don't suppose it hurt at all that I was my grandparents/aunts first grandson/nephew, and was named after their son and younger brother who died at age twenty-three.

In the meantime I had to earn my supper. First there was the need to carry seven to ten armfuls of wood to fill the kitchen range woodbin. The slope of the ground precluded the use of a sled, small wagon, or wheelbarrow. The wood was outside; and many times it had to be dug out of the snow. I had to be sure to knock off as much snow as possible before gathering up an armful. The kitchen woodbin was filled from the outside. A drop-down door in the kitchen provided access to the wood. This was located four feet from the kitchen range. Usually wood was moved directly from the woodbin to the stove as needed. If there was a need for a hot fire in a hurry, perhaps to heat the oven to bake bread, a certain number of pieces of wood were laid next to the stove for a few hours to better ensure the sticks ignited quickly and burned hot.

Next there was the need to carry the heavier pieces of firewood (chunks) to stoke the Round Oak space heater. Another seven to ten armfuls were stacked on one end of an open porch. I didn't have to be too particular here relative to leaving some snow and ice on these chunks since the Round Oak firebox could all but ignore these trivial impediments.

Stoking the Round Oak heaters seemed to have been acknowledged as the man's job. At our home Dad did so in the early morning and at bedtime. Since he was usually home for noon and evening meals he could also stoke the fires at these times as well. That still meant Mother had to stoke the stove as needed during the day. My grandfather was the full time stoker in his home. To do so he had to venture out on the open porch, which could be extremely cold and blustery in the wintertime. Usually a couple of trips were necessary to fully stoke the stove.

As time went on and I matured, I took on additional chores. One was carrying water to the house from the well about 100 feet away. Another was splitting wood. I took over this job from my grandfather. The blocks as they came from the harvesting operation could be twelve to fifteen inches or more in diameter. They then needed to be split into at least quarters for chunk wood for the Round Oak space heater, and into ten or twelve relatively small sticks for the kitchen range.

I ate most of my evening meals, and many noon meals while growing up at my grandmother's table. In the early years, when Dad was basically a hired hand, he ate the noon meal here as well if the farm work at the time was of a certain nature. Sometimes a hired man took his meals at my grandmother's table. One such person was Leonard Steinhoff, a man who for many years worked in temporary jobs, moving from farm to farm as needed. He was a dependable and an especially conscientious worker. As a result, he was much in demand. Being a hard worker, he also developed a keen appetite and enjoyed my grandmother's desserts as much as I did. Now I had a problem! Remember my grandmother cut her pies in six pieces. Normally only five of us were at the table making it a given that the extra slice of pie came my way. Now here was Leonard at the table to make six. But there was still hope. On occasion my grandfather passed on dessert. If Leonard were at the table the odds were he would do so. (My grandfather referred to Leonard as "the governor.") Both Leonard and I shifted our eyes from that last piece of pie or cake to my grandfather, and then back to the dessert. Grandfather took his sweet time, knowing we both were agonizing over his decision. Perhaps one out of five times he ate the dessert. One out of five Leonard won the nod. The other three times it came my way. After one of these shutouts Leonard remarked to my dad, "Damn kid, he doesn't do anything and yet he gets the best food."

To carry this association of Leonard and myself further is to see why I may not have been his favorite kid. One time he volunteered to re-install the tongue on a toy wagon. He took out the old cotter pin, then looking at me, gruffly said, "Where is your tongue?" What else could a kid fully one-quarter Irish do but stick out his tongue? I recall Leonard exhibiting no sense of humor at the time. But Leonard knew how to get even with me. Although hired men may have taken their meals at my grandmother's table, they slept at our house. I was their bedmate. As noted, Leonard had a keen appetite. He also loved candy. He also had money to buy candy. He also ate candy while in bed. He never offered me a piece of candy.*

Leonard Steinhoff was in many ways considered a member of the family. My wife remembers, and appreciates that he was the first non-relative to visit her in the hospital in conjunction with the birth of our son. (I was in Vietnam at the time.)

After I had taken care of stocking the day's quota of firewood, I joined my grandfather on one of the two window-side chairs in the kitchen. Grandmother was busy making supper and pleasant cooking aromas filled the kitchen. There was a small magazine rack between the chairs. In addition to current magazines, Grandfather kept a map of the United States and another of the world here. Grandfather was quite a reader. He subscribed to three farm-related magazines, two local newspapers, and a national newspaper, the Milwaukee Journal. He read the Journal closely each day. Here he was, all primed with the day's news and with no one to share it with. Then I came along. Initially we just talked about the news, insofar as a grown man could talk to a seven or eight year old kid about national and world events. Before long he was pointing out map locations

---

*Leonard went on to serve his country in World War II as a member of the Army's occupation force in Germany. While stationed there he met the woman he would marry and bring back to America.

to me. That led to his encouraging me to read certain articles. Then we discussed the article, referring as necessary to the U.S. and world map he kept handy in the magazine rack. Initially our discussions concerned the many New Deal recovery programs then underway in the administration of President Franklin Roosevelt. (A handsome framed picture of the President hung in the kitchen.) How my grandfather did it I cannot say, but through him I became conversant with what was called the "alphabet soup" of federal programs enacted to pull us out of the depression. For example, the CCC (Civilian Conservation Corps), the WPA (Works Product Administration), NRA (National Recovery Act), etc., etc. (This knowledge of New Deal programs got me in a bit of trouble later in school.) Soon world events took center stage. These are the mid to late 1930s with Germany's dictator Hitler and Italy's dictator Mussolini much in the news. So was the abdication in 1936 of the King of England (Edward VIII) to marry an American divorcee, Wallace Warfield Simpson. The Spanish Civil War also started in 1936 and my grandfather was "on top" of that development as well. By the time Hitler marched into the Rhineland (March 1936), Austria (March 1938), and Czechoslovakia (March 1939) I was holding my own in the discussions. It must have been interesting for my grandfather to watch me mature as related to discussing world and national events with him. The news came particularly hot and heavy when in September 1939 Germany invaded Poland. At this point I was close to twelve years of age. Like most Americans, we were alerted to the Japanese attack on Pearl Harbor by radio. This was a Sunday afternoon and I was at home. But not for long. As soon as I heard the news I ran to my grandparent's home. My grandfather and I had much to discuss. Over those tumultuous war years, he and I followed unfolding events and the maps relating to these events like hawks.

The image of waves of Japanese planes striking the fleet on 7 December 1941 was deeply imbued in our minds. One morning in early spring of 1942 I was operating the tractor while preparing the ground for spring planting. A loud noise, above that of a noisy tractor, alerted me to six aircraft approaching out of the sun. They were flying low, perhaps no more than 100 feet off the ground. At first I was thrilled, the next moment the thought hit me that these could be enemy planes. I stopped the tractor with the intent to jump off and cower under the machine. Before I could do so six Army Brewster F2A-3 Buffalo fighter/bombers roared right over me in a tight formation.

The normal routine for us, after reading the paper, was to talk in the kitchen while waiting for supper. In the winter time the pace of farm work lessened and we took a long break after the evening meal before going to the barn for chores. Grandfather and I then moved to the living room where the Round Oak heater was doing its duty warming the room. Grandfather sat in his rocking chair and I would lie down in a warm two-foot wide space between the heater and the wall. The "sweet spot!" This was made all the more comfortable due to the wooden wall paneling ra-diating added warmth back to my reclining body. The only light came through the door from the kitchen where a kerosene lamp hung. Under these absolutely perfect conditions we talked, and talked, and talked over world events of the day. And what world events to discuss! Hitler invades Norway, Denmark, France and the Low Countries. Much discussed too was the U-boat (submarine) warfare conducted by the Germans. Then there was North Africa, Russia, Pearl Harbor, Guadacanal, D-Day in Eu-rope, etc., etc. We did not confine our discussing to what had occurred, but also to what was likely to occur, or what should occur. In that latter role my grandfather and I were assuming the roles of generals plotting "grand strategy."

We spoke so many times of Hitler, Stalin, Mussolini, Roosevelt and Churchill that I felt I knew these men. The first two were tyrants of the first order; the third comes down in history as something of a buffoon; the last two were men of great stature. I am a great admirer of Winston Churchill and am somewhat in awe of having lived in his time. Then there was the death of President Roosevelt on 4 April 1945. Both my grandfather and I were relatively quiet that evening. At no time do I recall my grandfather ever talking down to me, nor do I ever recall being the "smart aleck" teenager in our discussions. How I hated the clock when it dictated I leave this warm nest and great discussion to head to the barn for evening chores.

As radio became a reliable medium, we listened to the six p.m. news to augment what for the most part we had already read and discussed. As much as Grandfather enjoyed hearing the news presented verbally by an announcer, he viewed with a certain amount of disdain anyone who did not work with his or her hands for a living.

One of the spin-offs of reading newspapers at a relatively early age was running across words I didn't understand. After reading of "rape" in a certain context on a couple of occasions I found a private moment to ask Grandfather what it meant. He ever so delicately told me.

I was in time also my grandfather's chauffeur. We took the old Ford model "A" truck to go shopping in Norwalk or Sparta. I also recall on several occasions loading the truck with chicken crates and going off to buy chickens. Our pick-up point for one of those trips was less than four miles from the farm. As we drove home and reached a point about a mile from home I noted his looking from left to right, then he said, "Ah Joe, we are back in God's country."

Did I bond with my paternal grandfather? You bet I did! He ranks up there as one of the most influential persons in my life. The interests in history and geography he awakened and nurtured have remained with me to this day. Another term not in use at the time, but so applicable here is "quality time." My grandfather and I sure had our share of that precious commodity.

In concentrating on my grandfather it may appear that I am slighting my grandmother. She operated on the quiet side in many respects. I don't recall her ever entering the discussions going on with my grandfather and I. For that matter, neither of my aunts participated either. Then again, what chance did they have when competing with a couple of "experts" who had just read the daily paper? My grandmother though could hold her own in conversations more to her liking, i.e. family, cooking, her garden, price of eggs, etc. There was many a conversation in German between my grandparents. I did not ask what they were discussing. I assumed the conversation was not for my ears. I remember when Grandmother's favorite song was *You Are My Sunshine*. When two or more of her grandchildren were available she often asked them to sing this song. She then closed her eyes, clasped her hands in her lap, and smiled softly while listening. *You Are My Sunshine* is a song frequently sung by my Kiwanis Club. I have not yet failed to choke up a bit as a flood of memories hits me when the song is sung.

The two other members of the household previously mentioned were also influential in my formative years. Aunt Lena was another adult in the household I interacted closely with. She was in many ways an understanding big sister. I don't recall, despite our near daily association, her ever displaying anger or frustration. And what a worker! Finally there was Aunt Tilla, she who awed Summit Ridge by buying a new car while most were driving ancient clunkers. Amusingly, my dad often commented disparagingly on her spending four dollars to have her hair done. Aunt Tilla expanded our entertainment horizons by frequently taking us older children to movies in Sparta. This was something my parents simply could not afford to do. She also remembered to bring me a gift when she returned from her annual vacations. I remember one gift being what was called a Little Big Book. Called "little" because it measured only four inches wide by six inches in length, but "big" because it measured three inches thick

There was another wonderful grandparent in my life on my maternal side. As noted earlier, John Berendes had been widowed when his oldest child was fifteen. He was left to raise nine children and he didn't remarry. When his sons were old enough to help in a meaningful way on the farm he became what was called a road patrolman. This involved maintaining the crown on approximately eight miles of rural gravel road with a horse drawn road grader. This was necessary to ensure water ran off the roadway and into an adjoining ditch. I suspect since this was during the depression he took on this job to help pay off a farm loan. He was a warm and kindly man who could be counted on to have a candy bar handy for his visiting grandchildren. We lived approximately three miles apart and visit exchanges were frequent. We also had the opportunity to check in with grandfather Berendes (Grampa John as we called him) at Sunday mass. His youngest child, a daughter Agnes, was his housekeeper. Four of his sons also lived on the farm at the time. The Kroeger trucking firm in Norwalk employed Richard. The youngest son Frank (Bud) ran the farm. Anthony (Manny) and Charles (Chuck) worked at various jobs, for the most part in a role titled "hired man." They both inherited their fair share of Irish blood as was evidenced by their "good ol' boy" conduct. Put another way, among the otherwise rather dour Germans they were "fun" types. Uncle Chuck in particular was a happy-go-lucky sort, popular with young and old. One found it difficult not to succumb to his infectious smile and laugh. Manny and Chuck were also much into baseball—and were proficient at the game. As a result, we played a great deal of baseball when visiting Grampa Johns, with emphasis on the fundamentals, i.e. base stealing, sliding into base, pick-offs, run-downs, bunting, etc.

Uncles Richard, Manny and Chuck Berendes all served in the Army during World War II.

In addition to our grandparents, thirteen paternal and maternal aunts and uncles, and many cousins lived close enough to maintain close contact and help out in an emergency. One of them, my paternal Aunt Josephine, played out one of those family roles when I was age seven. I had developed abdominal pains and Dad took me to see Doctor Allen in Norwalk. The doctor diagnosed the problem as appendicitis and hustled me the thirteen miles to Sparta's hospital. When Dad returned home to render his report my mother was concerned. There I was, at this tender age, all alone in the hospital. She called Aunt Josephine, who lived in Sparta, who in turn hustled right over to assure me the family had not abandoned me.

Members of the extended family had a tremendous influence on us children. All were excellent role models and they had little or no competition from outside sources. The combination of extended family, parental influence, and the teachings of the church served to set our internal gyroscopes for life's journey.

CHAPTER 10

Parents

My dad and mother grew up on Summit Ridge on farms approximately three miles apart. Both attended Summit Ridge's St. John the Baptist
Catholic Church, but different one room rural schools. Their initial attempt at dating was frustrated by her father. He applied the common rule
prevalent at the time that young women didn't date until they were eigh-

teen. She was seven-
teen at the time of
their initial attempt
at courtship.

And date they did
when she reached age
eighteen. Over their
three-year courtship,
Dad visited by horse
and sleigh in the
winter, or he walked
the three miles. As a
rule they remained

George and Frances (Berendes) Hedrick

at her home on those winter visits. In the summertime he either walked or borrowed his father's model "T" Ford. Now the couple could range away from her home, her father, and eight siblings, seven of whom were younger than she.

At this point I will mention again the responsible role my mother played in her early years. As noted, her mother died in the great flu epidemic following World War I in 1918. My mother was fourteen at the time, the second oldest of nine children, and the oldest daughter. A widowed paternal grandmother (Frances Berendes) took over the household, but she died five years later when my mother was nineteen. From then on until she married at age twenty she was the "woman of the house." Not only did her father lose a daughter when she married, but also a housekeeper, cook, and surrogate mother for seven younger brothers and sisters.

One imagines an initial much reduced workload when she moved from all the many chores she left behind to those associated with only her husband and herself. Ah, but that would change!

My dad operated a bit on the serious side, as was the typical mode of those who are German. He was a hard working man and frugal, as is also typical of Germans.

At the time of his marriage Dad was basically a hired man for his father. He enjoyed the benefits of a rent-free place to live and the produce from the farm, which included meat and milk. Also included was an unlimited supply of firewood. This was Wisconsin after all and a Wisconsin winter demanded a large amount of firewood. But he did not enjoy any regular financial remuneration. If Mother's egg money didn't fully support the need for clothing and staples, Dad would have to go, hat in hand so to speak, to ask his father for money. This unhappy situation evolved eventually into Dad getting one-half of the milk checks, then later into one-half ownership of the farms, farm equipment, and livestock. When my grandfather died, Dad bought out his five sisters to become sole owner of the farms.

For at least twenty-five years after his marriage Dad rose before dawn and trudged the one-fifth mile down to the home farm to do the morning milking. That one-fifth mile between the two farms was not exactly a level "walk in the park." From the Bucholz farm to the home farm the ground sloped down at a five to six degree grade. Fine for going down, a bit more of a chore coming up. If going downhill was easy, the bad news was that in the winter the cold northwest wind was in your face. The good news was you could accelerate a bit going up hill back to the Bucholz farm with the wind on your back. After morning milking he trudged back to the Bucholz farm for breakfast. After breakfast, back to the home farm in the winter to do chores, i.e. barn cleaning, feeding the animals, etc. In the late spring, summer, and early fall he was involved with tilling the soil, harvesting the crops, and fall plowing. The home farm was the launching pad for all fieldwork. At noon he was back at the Bucholz farm for dinner. (Dinner was at noon on the farm.) After dinner, back to the home farm for afternoon chores in the winter, or to become fully involved yet again with the field chores in other seasons. At some point on winter days he needed to find time to care for about ten heifers kept in one of the two barns on the Bucholz farm. Not too labor intensive, he cleaned out the barn and fed them hay twice each day. Since they were not milk producers or carrying calves they did not rate silage or ground feed. They did need water, so in freezing cold weather he had to fire up a water heater immersed in an outdoor water tank. Around six p.m. he was back for supper at the Bucholz farm. After supper he trudged back once again to the home farm for evening chores. At around eight p.m. he arrived back at the Bucholz farm to end his workday.

This routine went on seven days a week, but there was no fieldwork on Sunday. Still, there remained those six round trips each day in conjunction with milking, feeding the cattle, and cleaning the barn. Naturally when I was old enough I was woven into this routine. Is it any wonder farmers viewed their sons in many ways as horses?

Still clear in my mind today was an event occurring during one of those Wisconsin blizzards. The storm came up while I was at school. My older sister Elaine must have missed school that day due to illness. I was in the first grade at the time. I recall being frightened wondering how I could make it home alone, not realizing the teacher would not let us leave school during blizzard conditions. How happy, I mean downright happy I was to see Dad waiting for me in the entryway. We had quite a trip home that afternoon. Luckily the trip was eastward with the full fury of the wind on our backs. The first leg, made in near darkness, was fighting our way through snowdrifts straight down the road for one-fifth mile. We then cut to the left at Dick Steinhoff's farm to work our way down a small valley that led to the community of Summit. This was the same valley through which the spur railroad track to Cashton was once intended to run. The snow depth was still heavy but the trees protected us somewhat from the fury of the storm. From Summit we worked our way up the old Summit road, still shielded by heavy tree growth that ended at the barn on the home farm. From there we walked the one-fifth mile up the road to our home on the Bucholz farm, again with the howling wind on our back.

Another fond memory took place while Dad and I were in the process of cleaning oats prior to spring planting. The process, a dirty one, involved my turning a blower with a hand crank while he poured oats in the hopper. In the process, the chaff and dust was blown away and large plump kernels of grain emerged ready for planting. At one point we took a break and he put me on a scale. "Seventy five pounds," he said with mock surprise, "you are half-a-man." Wow! Half-a-man. I remember being thrilled. What a landmark! What a step up the ladder! I was no longer a boy; I was half-a-man!

Dad also introduced me to flying. The occasion was one of those barnstorming air shows that traveled the country at the time. This one took place on the Semann farm, right next to our rural school. A piper cub and a biplane (two wings) were the attractions. For two dollars you could go aloft in the piper cub. Dad and I took a ride. Our flight time permitted a comprehensive over flight of our farms, and we both marveled at the sight of them from 1000 feet. The ride ended with a dive over the crowd and an abrupt pull-up that forced us down in our seats. Dad cared for this not at all—but I was hooked. My interest in flying eventually led to flying lessons and soloing; and coming ever so close to becoming a military pilot. As for the air show, it pretty much ended when the biplane hit the top branches of a tree right next to the house (and the crowd). Some torn fabric on the plane and scattered branches here and there were the only damage from this rather foolhardy stunt.

After evening and noon meals Dad usually sat back and relaxed for a few minutes. We kids on the other hand took advantage of this break to play work-up softball in good weather. On a few occasions Dad joined us, and what fun to have him do so. With me pitching, Dorothy at first base and Dad at shortstop we had a pretty tight infield. What a shame Dad had so little time for this sport; I think we could have developed him into a quality player. I remembered all this when the time came for me to play with my own children in outdoor games. I am quite certain my children will give me high marks for doing so. Then again, I didn't have Dad's evening and weekend work routine to hinder me.

Dad's experience with finances were such that he tolerated absolutely nothing that could be considered a foolish expenditure, or any other action that could mark one as a spendthrift. He was frugal to a fault. On one occasion, in his presence, I passed up a nickel (yes, five cents) in change from the proprietor of a small store on Summit Ridge. I was royally chewed out! On another occasion I bought my little dog Corky a can of dog food at Christmas. Wow! That did not sell at all either. Who ever heard of a farm dog eating store bought food? Another example of his thriftiness was the manner in which he monitored my use of the family car. He was generous in allowing me to use the car, but not in putting what he considered excess mileage on the car. The typical entertainment at the time was a movie. The nearest theater was in Sparta, approximately twenty-four miles round trip from our home. I knew that on at least one occasion he checked the odometer. As a result I was forever after wary of his doing so. I knew he did not expect me to deviate from a presumed route. What then did I have to do when I wanted to go the additional miles to catch a movie in Tomah? At that time one could easily disconnect the speedometer cable. This is what I did on several occasions after ensuring that at least twenty-four miles were added to the odometer. The inevitable happened; the small drive shaft that extended a quarter of an inch from the speedometer cable became entangled in some wires in the dash and broke. Dad was far from happy. The good news was that I don't think he ever had it fixed. Once again this experience was in my mind as my own four children used the family car. I did not want them to provide open taxi service, but I never checked the mileage. Odometers by this time were tamper proof so they did not have the option of being able to disconnect the device.

During the first part of my freshman year in high school I rode to Norwalk in a car driven by a fellow student, John Berendes. He also provided transportation for three other students. I believe we paid John a dollar a week for the service. Later a different arrangement was made. About this time we began delivering milk to the creamery seven days a week. Why not combine my need to attend school with the necessary daily delivery of milk? I was too young to legally drive so we turned to Bob Kruk, two years older and also in high school who was working for his uncle, our neighbor Ed Kruk. The plan was for me to load up the milk and drive the half-mile to the Kruk farm. Here Bob took over and together we first delivered the milk to the creamery, then went on to school. After school Bob drove the truck to his uncle's farm and I then drove the rest of the way home. That's the way it generally worked. On one occasion I begged Bob to let me drive all the way to the creamery and he agreed. While in Norwalk a vehicle stopped suddenly in front of me and I could not. No damage to the other car, and minor damage to our truck. A few bent radiator pipes as I recall. I confessed to Dad before he noticed the damages. Understandably, he was not happy.

I said Dad was frugal. Life's experience taught him this lesson. This was not generally fully appreciated by me. On one occasion we were on what I suppose was our annual shopping trip to La Crosse. No doubt this was just before the start of the school year. At lunchtime, much to my surprise and chagrin, Dad proposed to take the bologna sandwiches we brought along into a tavern to be eaten. I was too embarrassed to go along and was left sitting in the car.

Although difficult for me to pry cash out of my dad, he was generous when it came to giving me carte blanche access to the farm's animal feed supply for my rabbits, beef calf, and pig raising projects that I engaged in over the years. He was not too happy about how much feed was involved, especially for the pigs—but he hung in there with me. More on these enterprises in a later chapter.

Working in the woods was a joy to Dad—I thoroughly detested the routine. I knew we needed firewood, fence posts and wood for lumber projects, but I thought this was an ideal job for a hired man. Work in the woods occurred in the wintertime when the farmer had only routine chores related to the dairy herd to perform. All too often it was uncomfortably cold to begin with, and what with the snow your work gloves were wet in no time. But then again what better time to work in the woods? The unending work of raising and harvesting crops did not demand his undivided attention at this point in the cycle. There were no leaves to add to the weight of trees and branches, or otherwise interfere with the process. The underbrush had disappeared and the insects that might have plagued us were long gone. Finally, if it were cold and uncomfortable now, imagine how hot and sticky it might have been at other times of the year. Yet there remained the plain hard work of it all. Invariably the work was done on a slippery side hill. We used a two-man crosscut saw, and with my enthusiastic dad at the other end there was no way I could slack off. The trimming of branches was a bit easier since I was on my own doing this. And it could be dangerous. Trees could snap when they fell and shoot backwards instead of the intended direction of fall.

Once on the ground the tree had to be sawed again and again to reduce them to manageable lengths. At some point horses were brought in to snake the logs to a pile, producing again a danger from logs whip lashing one way or the other. We did stop to watch the trains go by. I appreciated this break in labor, and always enjoyed observing this spectacle. I was happy when three p.m. came around. At this point I was sprung to do the late afternoon barn chores. What a pleasant change to clean out the barn, carry in straw for bedding, climb up the silo chute to throw down the needed cattle feed for that day, and finally to let the cows back in the barn and make sure all the cattle were locked in their stanchions. In the meantime Dad made sure he was left with enough "one-man" chores in the woods. Usually this was the labor-intensive job of further splitting logs, using a sledgehammer and steel wedges, all the while moving them about with a cant-hook. The cant-hook was a device used to roll logs around both for lateral movement or to reach another point on a log to permit further splitting.

On one occasion I was present when Dad asked his father for money to replace our aging Ford model "A". In the only rather heated argument I heard them have, Dad won the right to harvest enough railroad ties to buy a car. Many a tree fell on the farms to assemble the logs that eventually ended in cut-to-order saleable ties. I am glad I was too young to be involved in this project. Dad's goal was 1000 ties. The railroad inspector accepted 885 and paid ninety cents for each. Dad had to deliver them to the railroad siding in Summit and load them on a freight car. The result was a used 1939 Oldsmobile. Something of a problem car as I recall—a lemon in today's vocabulary. My problem with the car, as noted above, was that the speedometer cable entangled itself in the dash wiring when disconnected.

Mention was made of the danger in working in the woods. As noted earlier, my paternal grandmother's father was killed while cutting firewood for his family. My dad came close to being killed or seriously injured when a portion of a felled tree whipped around while being towed by a tractor. More poignant was the death of neighbor Dick Rapp in 2001. He was killed while using a front loader to move tree limbs. What made this particularly sad was that Dick at the time was a seven-year veteran of living with a heart transplant. He was sixty-eight at the time of his death.

Radio finally came along, and I suspect Dad had what could be termed a "love-hate" relationship with this medium when it arrived at our house. I should say radio arrived to us in fits and jerks. The major problem was power. We did not have electricity and apparently no dry cell batteries were available for radios in those early days, or else we could not afford them. We were left with a wet cell car battery that had to be transferred from the car to the house if we wanted radio entertainment. The vacuum tubes in early radios used a great deal of power, and car batteries, even when fully charged were not all that efficient at the time. As a result, listening time was short and then the now power depleted battery had to go back to the car for re-charging. Fortunately the radio conked out before the battery was completely discharged. Although not enough battery power remained to use the car's starter, there was enough to provide the necessary spark when hand cranking the engine.

Assuming there was an evening program we wanted to catch, the routine in those early days went something like this. After evening chores were done Dad disconnected the car battery and with alligator clips attached it to the radio. We all gathered around to listen—as long as the battery held up. All too often the cut-off occurred right in the middle of a broadcast.

Dad liked listening to the "blow by blow" broadcast of boxing events. One of the big boxing events at the time was the second fight between Germany's Max Schmeling and Joe Louis, the so-called "Brown Bomber." In 1936 Max knocked out Joe Louis and Adolph Hitler was happy. Further proof of the "master race" theory for Hitler. Joe Louis went on to earn the world's boxing championship. Hitler is now unhappy with this situation and insisted that his Max Schmeling have another crack at Joe Louis. First of all, Joe Louis is a Negro, another group Hitler was not a fan of, and he wanted the world's heavyweight crown to come to Germany. Now occurred not only a major sporting event, but one with major political overtones as well.

The re-match was in May of 1938; local time around eight p.m. Dad made sure evening chores were done on time. The wet cell battery was transferred from the car and connected to the radio. Joe Louis knocked out Max Schmeling in two minutes and four seconds. Dad heard the first one and one-half minutes of the fight before the battery died.*

Later we graduated to a wet-cell battery independent of the car. To keep it charged a wind machine was installed on the house. The problem was that in addition to vibrating the entire house the machine shrieked, moaned, rattled and whined as it turned at different speeds depending on the wind. Unfortunately too the device was not all that efficient. We had to wait until 1945 for electricity to finally provide a stable power source.

I recall on only one occasion Dad physically disciplining me over my growing up years. It occurred after Sunday mass when I was five or six, and still occupying a seat in one of the front rows in church. Apparently he observed my misbehaving and on the way out of church I was cuffed. I suspect the reason I remember it so well was that it occurred as a public cuffing.

On balance, my relationship with my dad was typical for a young man growing up on a farm where one interacted so closely with one's parent on a daily basis. I don't ever recall that we argued vociferously; he pointed out mistakes I made, and scolded, as was his job; I no doubt sulked, the typical response of a teenager.

In the meantime, my mother was not having morning coffee with the neighbor women nor playing a round of bridge in the afternoon. She was kept busy cooking, sewing, laundering, and trying to keep the house clean for her ten children and husband. Add to that her near total responsibility for the family garden in the summertime, and year round

---

*I had a little better luck, but by a critical small margin, with a wet cell powered ground to aircraft radio while on a combat patrol in Korea in 1950.

involvement with the chicken and egg operation. In the winter she added the chore of nursing sick children to her many duties. All of this was under relative primitive conditions—yet with a perennially cheerful and pleasant demeanor.

If farm fathers looked upon their sons as "horses," the mothers likely viewed their daughters in much the same way. As the daughters matured they helped out in a meaningful way with all the household chores. More than likely one of the most important chore was that of baby-sitting younger siblings.

I mentioned remembering only on one occasion my dad physically disciplining me. I remember several "warm" spankings from my mother, plus numerous "heavy" scoldings at other times. What did I do to incur my mother's wrath? Imagine this: she had nursed one hundred baby chicks through those first critical couple of weeks in their lives. Now the combination of warmer weather and maturing chicks permits them to run around out of doors. At this point in their lives the only object these chicks have seen move, other than each other, was a human. As a result, a human is viewed as a surrogate mother. Thus they are relatively tame and still cuddly cute. With that many tame baby chicks close at hand they are easy to catch, even for clumsy children. My little sister Dorothy and I were playing outside. I was four or five and Dorothy three or four. I found a one or two quart fruit jar and cover. Then, with Dorothy helping, I stuffed baby chicks into the jar until it was full. Then the cover was screwed on and the jar proudly presented to my mother. After all, I had observed the canning process so I thought we were contributing to the family's food supply. I do not remember being spanked, but I must have been. Nor do I recall my one year older sister Elaine being involved in this incident, but she remembers a "warm" spanking for failing to adequately supervise her younger siblings.

Sometime later Dorothy and I were involved in another massacre of chickens. We had been keen observers as our mother chopped the heads off chickens. This usually took place on Saturday afternoons in late summer on into early fall with the roosters then being the centerpiece for the following Sunday's noon meal. (Of all the meals in my lifetime nothing stands out like those Sunday noon meals of fried chicken, mashed potatoes, gravy, hot biscuits, and homemade noodle soup.) We children were tasked with catching the roosters. At this point chickens were not all that tolerant of humans and retreated if you approached them closer than about six feet. The solution; a seven or eight foot stiff wire with a hook at one end just the right size to snag the rooster's leg. We then delivered the rooster to Mother. She tucked the rooster's wings next to its legs and held it in her left hand. In her right hand was the ax. She then laid the bird with only its head extending over a block of wood. Down came the ax and off went the head. She then tossed the bird far enough away so its death thrashing did not bloody her or us bystanders as the rooster "danced around" for a few seconds after they were released, all the while spewing out blood. Mischievously we referred to this as the "Saturday afternoon massacre."

There was a small depression by one of the barns that filled with rainwater. It wasn't a big deal, six or seven inches deep and about fifteen by twenty foot in size. What fun, I thought, to chop the heads off the chickens and toss them into the pond where I expected them to "walk on water," at least for a while. No baby chicks this time, Dorothy and I had graduated to the big time. No baby chickens from my mother's point of view either, these were laying hens. I moved a block of wood to one end of the pond, found the long handled ax, and started to work. Dorothy or I caught the chickens with that long rigid wire with a hook at one end to grasp and hold the chicken's leg. After one whack I tossed the chickens into the pond. I was not strong enough to wield the ax with authority so most of the chickens, other than temporarily being knocked for a loop, survived. I seem to recall massaging the necks of six to eight chickens before we either ran out of immediately available chickens, or we simply lost interest. I don't recall any repercussions. Finding a few dead chickens with mutilated necks wouldn't have been all that unusual. Dogs or wild animals would have been suspected. Perhaps had I been a little older at the time, or the ax a little sharper, Colonel Sanders of Kentucky Fried Chicken fame might have found a serious competitor by the time he started his chain of restaurants.

I remember too on one occasion while in my teens, Mother finding what was considered obscene material belonging to me. Can you imagine what passed as obscene material sixty plus years ago? Probably one notch above the panty and brassiere displays in the Sears' and Ward's catalogues of that era. She was angry, really angry and spared no words in verbally berating me. Thank heavens I was too old to spank. I'm quite sure Father Mechler, or even the Pope would have been less harsh with me.

I also provoked my mother to take stern action in conjunction with my misuse of an air rifle, or BB gun as we called them. My age was ten, the other actor my brother Noel who was six at the time. We had just arrived home from Sunday Mass and apparently Noel and I were already at odds with each other when we climbed out of the car. In a flash I grabbed my air rifle from the porch and Noel took off running towards the barns. I fired, but purposely aimed wide. Mother caught all this as she was exiting the car. I don't recall how long before I saw my air rifle again—but a deserved punishment, and rather lenient under the circumstances.

In general, my relationship with my mother was smooth as silk. I can recall only one occasion of hurting her feelings. It seems on this occasion, which occurred when I was well into my teens, I griped about the food. I believe it was a breakfast meal. As I was on my way to the home farm Dad caught up with me. He looked me in the eye and said softly, "You made your mother cry," and then he continued on. His words hit me like a ton of bricks, and I still recoil with sadness at the remembrance. The situation called for an apology, but that did not occur.

Mother possessed and manifested in large measure the knack the Irish have of getting a kick out of small incidents. Our mode of transportation best remembered was the Ford Model "A". This two-door sedan was often "packed" with Hedricks, especially on Sunday trips to Mass or when visiting relatives. One evening we were returning home around nine or ten p.m. When we arrived home, Dad got out of the car to open the gate (kept closed to keep the sheep in). Seven children were in the car. I was eight or nine at the time. No doubt Mother, the baby (Ronald) and next youngest (Helen) were in the front seat. The other five of us were sitting or standing in that cramped back seat. There was a great deal of crying and whining. Finally I blurted out, "Shut up—a half-dozen of you." Mother did some quick mental calculations, then let out a hearty chuckle. I thought that a pretty good trade-off for what might have been a deserved scolding.

Of the many chores Mother had to perform, there was one I thought particularly onerous. That was washing clothes for her family of twelve in the wintertime. The washing machine was in what was at one time the milk house on the Bucholz farm. A not at all dependable Johnson and Johnson one-cylinder engine powered the washer through a series of belts and pulleys. (As noted earlier, Clarence Dittman was a key person in keeping those temperamental engines running.) First of all, it was a good idea to ensure that the hand-cranked engine was in working order before proceeding with the washing chore. If the engine was not operable it meant laborious and time-consuming work with a washboard. Assuming the engine was working, warm water had to be dipped from the kitchen-stove reservoir and carried the approximately 100 feet to the milk house. Once a given load of wash was done it went to the clothesline. Now the job was attaching the clothespins in freezing weather. At the end of the day the clothes, stiff as boards were carried into the house and stacked here and there until they thawed out and dried.

At some point the determination was made that we needed a new washing machine. The one selected had its own attached gas engine and cost eighty-five dollars. There was no such amount of money available. The answer was to plant and harvest cucumbers on a small plot of tillable land on approximately one-quarter acre in the northwest corner of the Bucholz farm. (This was my old favorite spot for viewing passing trains.)

Those of my siblings old enough at the time will remember the hours we spent in the hot sun that year picking cucumbers to earn enough to buy the washing machine. For some reason we really hated that chore above all others on the farm. Each week's pickings were hauled the twelve miles to Ontario where they were graded and sold. We did it—Mother bought her washing machine although the major chore of washing remained. I think those of us who labored in that patch of ground still shudder a bit when we view the field today.

When Mother had spare time, usually in the evening, she spent the time darning socks, mending clothes, and sewing. Dresses, pajamas, aprons, etc. flowed from her foot powered Singer sewing machine. The fabrics for many of these garments were those gaily-printed flour sacks of the time. Mother was also the barber in our house.

Although her enthusiasm was kept in check, no one in the family welcomed the Spring/Summer and Fall/Winter issues of the Sears Roebuck and Montgomery Wards catalogues more eagerly than did Mother. Not only was it a "wish book" for her, as it was to the rest of the family, but she did a great deal of practical ordering from these catalogue giants. Upon receipt of the order a near Christmas atmosphere prevailed as each item was lovingly unpacked. Other family members stood in line for their chance to thumb through the catalogues. I was fortunate to have access to my grandparent's catalogues. I dwelled on those pages reflecting carpentry tools and hunting/fishing supplies. The catalogue firms also distributed a Christmas catalog with a clear emphasis on toys. Now here was a real "wish book!"

Mother was lucky in one respect since she was not required to help out with the farm work. My dad, Aunt Lena, and to a limited extent my grandfather did all the farm work. As my grandfather phased out I was phasing in. But still, what a monumental job mothers of that era had to perform in the process of raising a family. President Roosevelt's wife Eleanor may have paid women like my mother the ultimate complement. Eleanor was a "dynamo" of energy who in addition to being the "eyes and ears" for her polio stricken husband, wrote a daily newspaper column entitled *My Day*. This is what appeared in the article she wrote on 24 February 1944.

> I sometimes wonder how the people who are so impressed by my energy can fail to realize that any woman with a family who does all of her own work is doing in the course of a day twice as much as I ever think of doing. Just getting the meals and cleaning the house and doing the laundry, not to speak of taking care of several children, who in winter are bound to have the ailments that come the way of all children, will fill up more time and demand a more active life than I live at any time. In the few concentrated periods when I go on trips I may be nearly as active as the normal housewife, and then only because I follow the schedules which other people map out for me.

I remember only one occasion when there was a strained relationship between my parents. Apparently Mother had danced, in Dad's opinion, too enthusiastically with a fellow parishioner. I suspect Mother was rather pleased; did I not note a look on her face that could lead one to this observation? At any rate, this all blew over in a couple of days and mealtime chatter was soon back to normal.

When there wasn't a need to hurry to the fields my parents engaged in pleasant conversations after meals while sitting at the table. Dad fired up his corncob pipe, sat back and discussed the news, problems, plans, neighbors, family, and a host of other topics with my mother.* As I recall, each had equal time for their contribution making for a pleasant flow of conversation. The rest of my siblings disappeared, but I found it interesting to listen in. Then too, my peers in the families were sisters one year older and one year younger than me—and what boy wants to play into that crowd (unless its an outdoor game like softball)? From their standpoint, my age and predictable conduct was such that I would have been "frozen out" of playing their games or otherwise engaging in their activities anyway.

---

*Grandfather's copy of that day's Milwaukee Journal made its way to our house each evening and was fodder for discussion the next day.

Their candid discussions were informative, and as noted, quite interesting. One of the topics, extending over several weeks, was the kidnapping and death of Charles (the Lone Eagle) and Anne Lindbergh's baby in 1932, and the follow-on trial of Bruno Hauptman in 1935 for the crime. I recall in the discussions during the trial one or the other of my parents asking the other, "But then, how do you explain the ladder?"* Another event provoking a long discussion was the crash of the German airship Hindenburg at Lakehurst, New Jersey in May of 1937. The death toll was ninety-two and the cause of the fire and crash remains a mystery to this day. Was it lightening? There was a storm in the area. Was it sabotage? Adolph Hitler had been in power since 1933 and many in the world would have liked to see Hitler discredited.

On a sadder note was the obvious deep gloom and sorrow that overwhelmed my parents when a neighbor farmer, friend, and fellow parishioner was killed in a highway project accident on 28 April 1934. Gene Ziegler was thirty-eight and left behind a pregnant wife and five children. I believe he was participating in a government project permitting farmers to work off farm loans in what were then depression years. A wave of sorrow hit Summit Ridge again in March of 1945 when Mary (Mayme) Ziegler, Gene's widow, was informed of the death of her twenty-one year old Marine son on Iwo Jima.

Another tragedy that led to much discussion was a plane crash on Summit Ridge mid-afternoon on 29 April 1932. A small plane, carrying a honeymoon couple and the pilot crashed while trying to make a forced landing due to motor trouble in a late spring snowstorm. The field, with many wood stumps in it, was located next to the road (now Kayak Road), about 100 yards north of George Schaller's barn, and approximately one-quarter mile north of our one-room rural school. The plane was on a flight from La Grange, Illinois to La Crosse, Wisconsin. The young lady was killed instantly, the two men seriously injured. There were not that

---

*Bruno Hauptman was convicted and executed.

many aircraft flying the skies in 1932, and I suspect it was rare that one flew over Summit Ridge. I remember, as one not yet five years old, visiting the site on the day of the crash. This was my first view of an airplane, although it could not be identified as such in its crumpled state. I was particularly in awe of the fact that a person had died in the crash.

For the most part, entertainment consisted of visiting relatives and card parties in the wintertime. There was a time when, on one or two summer evenings each year, my parents attended plays put on by a traveling troupe called the Robinson Players. These productions were performed in a tent in Sparta. I don't ever recall my parents going on vacation, or going to a restaurant to eat while I was at home. There was of course the summertime Tuesday night free movie in Norwalk, but movies at a theater were rare.

Life for my parents had to be like a trip back in time. No cash to speak of, no electricity, and no running water. Living conditions for them at the time were in many ways similar to Colonial America times.

Despite the economic issues and relatively spartan living conditions, I feel my generation that grew up on Summit Ridge could be considered in so many ways as having been born with a "silver spoon in our mouth." As inferred in the previous chapter, our parents, along with the extended family, made us feel so secure we thought we were rich. Ours were "Old World," loving yet strict parents who, along with extended family, were the role models who gave us our bearings. Peer pressure, to do this or that, which might have conflicted with our parent's rules, was not present to mar the relationship between children and parents. The entertainment industry, to the extent we were exposed to it, was at the time "wholesome."

CHAPTER 11

Siblings

I was born around ten a.m. on 14 October 1927. I joined my sister Elaine in the George and Frances Hedrick family. Dorothy, Noel, Joan, Helen, Ronald, Paul, Carolyn and Mary followed over the next sixteen

Author age two

years. Elaine and I shared the honor of being the two oldest grandchildren on both sides of the family.

I was named after a paternal uncle who died at age twenty-three from complications following an appendectomy operation. There was the lingering and dark suspicion that my parents were tempting fate by naming me after a deceased uncle who died so young. This apparently came up again and again as I passed through childhood illnesses of the time. This was particularly true when, at age two, I was seriously ill with pneumonia. What really raised a black cloud was my own appendectomy operation at age seven in the same hospital where my namesake died. As if to tempt fate once again, I turned twenty-three on a ship heading for a combat amphibious landing in North Korea; the same age as my Uncle Joe when he died.

Elaine and Dorothy, approximately one year older and one year younger respectively, were my obvious playmates. Noel, four years my junior was too young to be a remembered playmate. The rest of the family, from Joan five years younger on down through the youngest, Mary, were generally viewed as my little brothers and sisters to be loved and enjoyed—but not as playmates in the true sense of the word. But when it came to a work-up softball game, there were times when we could field seven Hedrick children who could all catch and hit a ball.

Although too young to be a playmate, my sister Joan was the right age for what I recall as a warm "big brother—little sister" relationship. She was also at the right age to catch a ride home from school on my old rickety bike. Not at all a comfortable seat for her; she sat on the frame between me and the handle bars, grasping the handles tightly, feet out and away from the front wheel—and happy as a lark. Later Joan did yeoman service for me by ensuring the twenty-two pigs I was raising were provided with fresh drinking water four to six times per day (depending on the temperature).

I'm sure the two oldest girls closest to my age were typical little girls with typical interests relative to play. I in turn am sure I did my duty as a little boy in tormenting them. I suspect the two oldest girls had no problem at all when my paternal grandparents welcomed me into their home in return for carrying in the wood supply. As a result, we were separated from each other during what would otherwise have resulted in a large degree of interaction during the prime time at home after school, and for a part of Saturday and Sunday. It did not take long for boys to be woven into the farm routine; thus once again in my case a large degree of isolation from other members of the family occurred.

Like Mother, my sisters were not required to assist in farm work in any meaningful way. The isolation of the milking barn from our home was a factor, as was the assistance rendered by my Aunt Lena and grandfather. In time my brother Noel and I took part in the farming role while our sisters helped our mother in the home. This was not the situation for all families on Summit Ridge. Case in point was my wife's family. The first five children in the family were girls. As a result, from the day her parents started their life together, her mother and then the girls were deeply involved in farm labor. A boy finally arrived, but at this point my future wife was seventeen.

Earlier I mentioned the difficulty we had with reliable radio service. Somewhere along the way wet cell battery power became more dependable. As a result radio listening became a regular feature in our home. One program was broadcast from WLS in Chicago while we were in the process of getting dressed and ready for school. "Uncle Joe Kelly" filled the air with kid type chit-chat. At some point each school day he broke out his "magic telescope" to count how many children were dressed and ready for school. The competition was between boys and girls and each day he announced the winner. We went for it hook, line, and sinker. Later on we children became fans of The Lone Ranger, The Vampires, The Shadow, etc. as presented on radio. For the adults there was Jack Benny, Amos and Andy, Fred and Gracie Allen, Fibber McGee and Molly, and Edgar Bergen and Charlie McCarthy.

My oldest sister Elaine embraced radio with a passion. Through her efforts she had the rest of the family mimicking the various programs of interest. One popular show at the time featured singers Lulu Belle and Scotty—a husband and wife team. There was also Patsy Montana and the Arkansas Woodchopper—all radio entertainment icons of their day. Elaine organized impromptu skits around these characters—she was "always" Lulu Belle. Since I was both unavailable, not to mention unwelcome, brother Noel was selected to play all the male leads. Those of my siblings who were old enough to participate in Elaine's efforts appreciate the entertainment her organizational ability and leadership provided.

This was especially true in the winter months when weather and road conditions restricted travel. My mother too enjoyed observing and listening to this happy group of aspiring entertainers.

Elaine's really big production was the then popular Lucky Strike (cigarettes) *Saturday Night Hit Parade*, where the top ten songs on the charts for that week were played. She had those siblings who were old enough to know what was going on sit in a circle while she, referring to notes, reminded them of which songs were climbing week by week, and which were falling, etc. I enjoyed listening to the songs, but certainly didn't want to be part of Elaine's brigade of amateur performers. Then again—I wasn't invited.

We all need to thank Elaine for entertaining our mother. Mother was by nature a cheerful person and quick to smile and laugh. As Elaine matured, her (Elaine) antics, conversational ability and sense of humor kept my mother chuckling. There came that time, early in her high school years when Elaine worked for her room and board in Sparta (twelve miles from home). She continued to work in Sparta for a time after high school graduation as well. A highlight for my parents, especially Mother, was to have Elaine come home on weekends to regale the family with stories, laced with humor, of her experiences. Frequently Mother asked me to go to Sparta to bring Elaine home for the weekend. Since I liked to drive I was eager to make the trip.

Thanks to sister Elaine, for many years I was "Bub" to my immediate and most of the extended family. The name "Bub" derived from her early effort to say "brother." I must have been about ten when I told my mother I wanted to be called Joe. She put the word out, and I was amazed and pleased at how quickly Bub was dropped. Along the way I was accorded the honor of naming one of my siblings. There was a likable young man named Jerry Bolden who worked as a hired man in the area. I thought the name "Jerry" was absolutely tops. When a baby brother, eleven years my junior arrived on the scene, my parents acceded to my wishes and accepted Jerome as his name, with Paul as his second name. I don't recall anyone ever referring to him as Jerry or Jerome—it was always Paul. My sister Elaine had a great deal more success with my being called "Bub."

Elaine was also involved, innocently as it turned out, in my running away from home. I was in the second grade at the time and on the way home from school I used a profane word(s). Elaine immediately said, "I'm going to tell Mother." The thought of her doing so struck the fear of God in me. I was keenly aware Mother did not tolerate profanity from her children. Of course Mother never had to maneuver on the home farm's side hill either. I suspect I may have been on probation for other offense(s) as well. At any rate, home was not for me at that point in time. As Elaine entered the house I took off for Summit via the familiar route used to reach my favorite train viewing location. At the time three homes were standing in Summit with the Christ family living in one of the homes. I took refuge in a woodshed at one of the houses and wondered what in the world to do next. This was late fall and whatever I was wearing home from school was not enough to ward off the evening chill. Darkness came early, and there I was with witches, goblins, and bogeymen—not to mention wild animals all around me. I kept looking out the woodshed at the soft lamplight radiating from the Christ home and was tempted to throw myself on their mercy. I also knew I would be turned in and was not quite ready for that. Finally I left the woodshed and started working my way up to the home farm. For a while I settled in across the gully from the barn. Lantern light came from the open door and windows so I knew milking was in progress. Around seven p.m. I went into the barn where my grandfather was milking alone. "Joe," he said, "everyone is looking for you."

I don't remember there being any punishment. Then again, there usually isn't in cases like this. Elaine apparently didn't snitch on me. She knew as well as I our mother's likely reaction and chose not to rat on her little brother. I suspect it wasn't the physical punishment I feared as much as realizing how disappointed my mother would be in me, knowing I had taken the name of the Lord in vain.

I will recount later another involvement with foul language that arose to embarrass (and educate) me. This was in March or April of 1951 while in Korea.

I have made the point on several occasions that dollars were hard to come by during the depression years I grew up in. Imagine the shock and surprise to the family (and community) when sister Elaine, then in her early teens, came into approximately $700. Our great-maternal uncle, John Geoghegan, a life-long bachelor, had named her as the beneficiary of a life insurance policy. Uncle Jack was the relative who stayed with us in the wintertime in conjunction with his job as a tunnel door watchman. The money was wisely banked for her further education after high school.

Sister Dorothy, one year younger than me, is remembered as the girl who eagerly embraced the home economics classes when she went to high school. She introduced us to a separate salad dish before the main courses along with other related nutritional food and table manner issues. I don't recall any of us being critical or of making fun of her for bringing these strange nutritional items or behavior modifications to the dinner table. I only recall being impressed. Something Dorothy could not change, had she wanted to, was to have the entire family involved in a single conversation topic. With up to twelve of us at the table several different discussions were bound to be going on at the same time.

We came close to losing Dorothy to scarlet fever when she was seven. This disease was especially hard on young children. Scarlet fever was characterized by a sudden high fever, often rising to 105 degrees in the first hour, accompanied by a deeply red congested throat, swollen tonsils, a puffy face and a scarlet rash spreading over the entire body. Dorothy had to be totally isolated from her siblings. The rest of us siblings went to live with our Hedrick grandparents for six weeks. Dorothy and our maternal Aunt Agnes (then age eighteen) who came to care for her were isolated from all human contact for those six weeks. This was not a new experience for Aunt Agnes. The year before she had performed a similar chore for a nephew with the same affliction. Another seven-year old in the community, Mary Ann Ziegler, daughter of Mary (Mayme) Ziegler, died from this illness the same year Dorothy was afflicted.

This was a lonely time for Dorothy and Aunt Agnes. Their lonesome ordeal was made somewhat more bearable by the "daily" visit of a neighbor. Clarence Dittman could be counted on to stop by on his way home from his twelve-hour shift as a tunnel watchman. These visits were by necessity conducted through a window.

It seems someone was often ill in our family. Sickness, especially in the wintertime was prevalent and worrisome. I can remember gathering around a crib in a near darkened room on one occasion while Mother led us in reciting the rosary for a seriously ill infant.

Despite the many dangers lurking on the farm, injury accidents were rare in our family. Brother Noel fell off a small building and broke his collarbone, but this could have happened anywhere. The only true farm related injury happened to brother Ronnie when he was five and I thirteen. This was spring planting time and I was operating the tractor digging up ground for planting. My dad, with a three-horse hook-up, was seeding oats. Ronnie was sitting on a narrow platform on the back of the seeder, on which Dad was standing while driving the horses. A series of interlocking gears served to measure out the kernels of oats at a prescribed rate. These gears were fully exposed, and at one point, an inquisitive little boy placed his fingers where he could catch kernels of oats. **Ouch!** A couple of fingers were drawn up into the gears. I heard Dad yelling above the sound of the tractor and ran to the scene. At this point Ronnie's fingers were extracted but he was in severe pain. I carried him the half-mile home while Dad trotted the horses back to the barn. As we approached the house on the home farm our Aunt Lena saw us and ran out with an understandably concerned look on her face and the anxious question, "What happened?" I don't recall Ronnie crying, just barely audibly moaning.*

---

*Ronnie was left with a couple of slightly deformed fingers as a result of this injury.

A common practice at the time was for children in the summer months to stay with grandparents and aunts and uncles. These visits lasted for one to two weeks. This started when children were seven or eight years of age. Although a degree of homesickness was initially felt, it did not take long to acclimate to yet another loving family among our rather large extended family. Imagine you are my next youngest sister Dorothy. At age eight you are one of seven children. Now off you go the two miles to visit your maternal Aunt Helen Muehlenkamp and her family of four boys. Three of the boys were about her age so she has playmates. From being one of seven at home she is now for awhile, the center of attention. In the meantime, the Muehlenkamp boys are getting used to having a girl in their midst. Finally, a pleasant diversion for the Muehlenkamp parents as well to entertain this little visitor. For Dorothy, this was an opportunity to adjust to a new environment, despite a degree of homesickness at first. Bottom line is she learns that here is yet another family who loves her.

For me these vacations were usually spent at my maternal grandfather John Berendes' farm where four uncles and an aunt provided plenty of excitement. Another place was the Muehlenkamp family where two of the boys were close to my age.

The time between returning to the house after evening chores and bedtime was short for me. Our large dining room table was a hubbub of activity, especially when school was in session. Some were doing their homework, others playing games. The girls took turns combing Dad's hair while he contentedly read the paper. Both he and the "combers" seemed to enjoy the process.

It is hard to imagine not growing up in a large family—especially on a farm in that era. The children had playmates and the healthy experience of sharing. For the parents, in addition to normal parental enjoyment of watching their families grow, there was the promise of future household and farm help. Speaking of sharing, yes, we all shared the same galvanized laundry washtub of water for our Saturday night bath. The ritual generally started with the youngest and worked up to include Dad. This was a typical routine for farm families at the time. Yet, a modern industrial nation saw the need to ban "all bathing" for the "entire population" except on Saturday and Sunday. The date this rule was imposed was 5 January 1940. The country was Germany—and the reason for the law was to conserve soap during World War II.

The family (1948 photo). Front row left to right: Carolyn, Ronald, Mother Frances, Father George (holding Mary), Paul. Back row left to right: Helen, Elaine, Author, Noel, Dorothy, Joan.

CHAPTER 12

My Dog Corky

When I was about eight, my folks returned from a shopping trip to Sparta with an offer I couldn't refuse. They had learned of the availability of a litter of pups and suggested that if I could earn the $2.50 asking price I could buy one of them. To raise the money I was granted full access to our two Dutchy apple trees. These apples, although not considered desirable for eating, were excellent for cooking and baking.

No doubt I had been begging for a dog of my own. We routinely had what was termed a "cow" dog. This was usually a collie that took naturally to herding cattle. A properly trained cow dog, when verbally directed, raced off to where the cows were grazing or had gathered, and through barking and "polite nips" at the heel, moved the herd towards the barn. These dogs were kept on the home farm and I certainly couldn't consider them my dog.

The going price for a bushel of Dutchy apples was $1.25. Try as I might, I could not quite fill those two baskets to the point of overflowing, and this was what the buyers expected. As a result, I had to settle for $1.00 per bushel. If that was bad news, the good news was that my parents either came up with the fifty cents needed, or the sellers cut the price for the pup. Knowing how tight money supply was in our home at the time I'll bet Dad worked for the fifty-cent reduction. After all, the owner of the pups ran a small store and he probably saw it as good business to keep a customer happy.

This little black and white pup, commonly referred to as a rat terrier, came to our house from Sparta late one afternoon. The next morning my job was to "watch cows." The usual practice of farmers was to fence off their fields on either side of country roads. This was necessary and required since cattle were often driven along the road to go to and from summer pasture. It was a common sight to see the farmer's herd strolling along a public road morning and evening while looking hungrily at the growing fields of corn, oats, alfalfa, etc. Approximately two-thirds of the width of a road's right

Sister Carolyn and author holding Corky.

of way was open for grass growth. The grass growth in turn benefited from the lime dust generated by traffic on those gravel roads. Farmers hated to see any milk producing grass go to waste, so periodically they allowed the herd to graze along these roadways. Since these were public roads with no gates at either end someone had to be stationed at each end of the road to ensure the cows did not go beyond established limits. One of the ideal grazing areas was the nearly three-quarter mile stretch from the barn on the corner of the home farm to where our land ended and Clarence Dittman's began. Since the road ended at the Dittmans this was also a quiet stretch of road. On this particular day I had the Dittman end. There was a rough wooden ramp leading from the road into our field right on the dividing line between Dittman's and our land. A perfect place for the pup and I to sit in the warm sun and become acquainted. For the better part of three hours Corky was stroked, tickled, cuddled, rubbed and talked to. The word bonding wasn't part of the vocabulary for this type of association at the time, but it surely must have occurred since Corky was indeed my dog from then on.

I am amazed, thinking back, that Corky was allowed to become a housedog. He must have automatically trained himself since I cannot imagine my mother having time to train him, or my siblings having done so. Even then this little dog with his short hair had a tough time in the winter. Can you imagine how he "hustled" to return to the warm house after being turned out to make his bathroom call on a cold winter day or night?

From a functional point of view, Corky paid his way as a hunting dog and by killing rats. He was after all a rat terrier. Not only was he an excellent rat killer, he was enthusiastic in the process. When time permitted, I flushed out rats and Corky killed them with one crunch of his jaw. There were three places on the farm where I could find rats to satisfy Corky's killer instinct. One was in the pigpen; another was the corncrib, and the third, the granary. There was no shortage of rats on the farm.

Like most any dog Corky liked to chase cats. He was lucky since cats abounded on the farms. Most of the cats could be found in the barn on the home farm. They generally lazed around wherever they wanted to. Before opening the barn door I held Corky back until I was sure the cats had little time for reaction—then turned him loose. The cats sought safety in several locations. Their favorite was the stone and concrete base supporting the barn proper. This was seven or eight feet from the floor and provided about a foot of space all around the perimeter of the barn. If I were feeling extra frisky (or mean) I placed Corky on this wall for another show of "scatter the cats."

Corky was also a social dog; at least when weather permitted. Unlike any other dog any of us ever heard of, Corky visited two of the neighbors on a regular basis, usually when I was in school. We have no idea how this started, but given the hospitality at each home he visited, it's not surprising the visits continued. His first call was usually the friendly Clarence Dittman house, one-half mile from home, where he was welcomed to come into the house after he yipped to announce his presence. No doubt he enjoyed a certain amount of affectionate pats, and perhaps a snack. At some point he asked to leave and then traveled, usually cross-country, to the also friendly Joe Steinhoff home. Here he enjoyed not only the company of two other housedogs but also the attention of three to four doting Steinhoff women. Later in the day he made his way home. On a given day he might decide to reverse the procedure relative to which home he visited first, or he might choose to spend all day at the Steinhoff home.

What Corky really liked to do was hunt squirrels. Not only was he very good, but again, he was enthusiastic. Squirrel hunting season in Wisconsin extended from sometime in early October to mid-November. At this point the young squirrels had been raised and the breeding season had not started. Thinning out the squirrel population was considered desirable. Corky and I then could be seen as doing our civic duty in that regard.

Given a choice, squirrels prefer to travel on the ground as they forage for nuts, corn, etc. Naturally they climb the nearest tree when they sense danger. Unfortunately for them, they left a scent Corky zeroed in on and tracked to whichever tree the squirrel climbed. At times you saw the squirrel jumping from tree to tree heading for its home or a better hiding place. Usually though, the squirrel hunkered down immediately in what it considered a safe spot in the tree Corky identified it as being in. As one approached, the squirrel usually heard them and moved around the tree to stay out of sight. In the meantime Corky is barking up a storm, and in his excitement trying to climb the tree. At the same time I'm trying to spot the squirrel by attempting to move quietly around the tree. Sometimes I was successful by finding a stone or large stick I could throw to the opposite side of the tree from where I was standing. More often than not the noise caused the squirrel to move back to my side, and right into my gun sight (as Clarence Dittman suggested they would). From the squirrel's standpoint, the bushy tail nature provided them to stabilize their body as they moved through trees could be fatal during hunting season. The hunter could spot the tail ninety-percent of the time. There was still the need to have the squirrel show their body, but more often than not the tail gave them away.

Sometimes I could not spot the squirrel in the tree. Either the squirrel had traveled unseen to another tree, to its nest, or other safe haven. In the meantime Corky only knew he had treed a squirrel, and after a while stopped barking and gave me an eyeball to eyeball look that said in effect, "Hey boss, I did my job, what's holding you up from doing yours?" On those occasions I walked away and called Corky to follow me. He was quick to obey, and I don't think there was ever any hard feelings given the speed with which he searched for the next scent. Usually though I quickly spotted and then shot the squirrel, and Corky was right there to give it the coup de grace. Then he lost all interest. Dead rats and squirrels did not interest him. Without a word or move by me he went off searching for the next scent.

Squirrels were usually active at dawn and late afternoons. In the interest of safety, they preferred to do their feeding close to groves of trees to which they could quickly retreat when danger lurked. Both humans and squirrels prized hickory nuts for their tasty and crisp meat. As a result farmers many times left a hickory nut tree to flourish in a cultivated field and worked the land around it. At times squirrels were careless, and two or more could be found in these trees with close to a zero chance of escaping the hunter.

My take was usually four to six squirrels each day. I believe five was the limit. Given the farm chores to be done I could only squeeze in a couple hours of hunting on a given day. I found it a joy to wave a batch of squirrels to Dad as he did the fall plowing with the old Fordson tractor. A cheerful wave and a smile back from him—we all liked squirrel meat.

As a rule I found Corky waiting for me when I arrived home from school. When I was done with chores we could go hunting. Occasionally he overstayed his visit at the Steinhoff farm (like those farmers who over-stayed their trip to town on milk check day). My mother or Aunt Lena telephoned the Steinhoffs, and if Corky was there he was booted out and told he was needed to go hunting. I wasn't at all happy to be kept waiting, but Corky sure looked cute coming flat out to return home for what he had to know was a hunt.

I could hunt without a dog of course. With luck, but most of all with patience, I stood for awhile and watched for movement on the ground or in the trees. If no luck, I moved on to a second area and began the routine again. I liked hunting with Corky much better.

Somewhere along the way Father Mechler heard about Corky's hunting prowess. One Sunday after mass he asked me if he could team up with the two of us? Serving Mass for this man of God was one thing, but to be a fellow huntsman with a man I was in awe of was mind-boggling for me. However, on at least two, maybe more occasions we teamed up. We usually started at St. John's Catholic Church and hunted the woods that dropped off to the railroad tracks in the old community of Summit. Our plan was to take turns shooting the squirrels. Father Mechler's eyesight was not the best at this time and when he was unable to spot the squirrel he asked me to fire away. Either way, we split the bag of squirrels fifty-fifty.

Much to his displeasure, Corky was not allowed to accompany me when hunting rabbits. Corky was pretty safe at the base of a tree while I shot the squirrel out of the treetops with a rifle. Rabbits though are usu-ally hunted with a shotgun while they are on the run. This could be dan-gerous for a dog that might be right on the rabbit's tail. Corky was also my steady fishing companion. He often meandered off while I fished out a given hole, but from time to time checked back in with me.

On one occasion I located the spot where Mother had hidden a choc-olate cake. I ate what I thought was prudent, given the threat of being discovered, and then gave a large sized chunk to Corky. Then we were off to round up the cows for evening milking. We traveled at least an eighth of a mile with Corky carrying the piece of cake locked in his mouth. How could he resist not gobbling it down? Much to my surprise he then ran off to one side and hurriedly buried it. I often wonder if he ever retrieved, or tried to retrieve the cake. No doubt the ants had a great feast

When my two oldest sisters entered high school one or the other, or both, convinced my mother dogs did not belong in the house. I suppose this particularly applied to farm dogs with their access to so much in the way of offensive material. I suspect the basis for this was my sister's high school home economics class. Corky was indeed banished to the barn, despite what I thought was the convincing argument I made to my mother that Corky should stay in the house and my sisters should go to the barn. I'll bet if I had promised her I would study for the priesthood, my argument might have been successful. I remember taking him to the barn, for at least a while. No doubt this banishment occurred during other than cold winter days since this barn, with only its few heifers to provide body heat wasn't warm. Surely it would have been too cold for a little short-haired terrier. Besides, my mother and dad had developed a liking for Corky as well, and in a short time he was back in the house.

I left Corky behind when I joined the Marine Corps. Before I returned on leave fifteen months later he had been killed in an accident. Corky had followed my dad to the garage, and in his old age, was not able to move out of the way as the car was backed out.

The terms bonding and quality time were mentioned earlier in conjunction with my paternal grandfather. The same was true of Corky. Unless you have enjoyed the experience it might be difficult to imagine the close communion of a boy and his dog, especially when "on the hunt."

CHAPTER **13**

Bohn School

Bohn School was named after George Bohn, a school board member at the time the school was established. Records indicate it was established in 1864. The school was located on the southeast corner of what is now Kendall Avenue and Kayak Road on land donated by the Semann family. The agreement with the Semann family allowed for the use of the land as long as the school functioned. When the school closed in 1962 the land reverted back to the Semanns. Today the site has been woven back into the Semann farmland with there being no hint this corner once embraced a school.

We lived a little over a mile from the school that all ten of us Hedrick children attended. At one

Bohn School

point, five of us were making this trek at the same time. The first leg was
the road from our house to the barn located at the corner of the home
farm. Here we took a shortcut past the barn, then cut between the granary and chicken coop, on down past the milk house and corn crib, and
then back onto what is now Kendall Avenue for the rest of the journey.
There was a distinct pecking order in our walking arrangement. My older
sister Elaine walked in the right-hand path. I say path because the dirt
and gravel roads at the time ended up as two wheel paths. As the second
oldest, I headed the procession in the left-hand path. The other three
followed in an order I don't remember, but I'll bet Joan, the youngest,
was third in line in one or the other columns. Think of it now; the right
hand position is the place of honor. For example, our country's flag is
always flown or positioned on the right of other flags. A senior official or
military officer is positioned on the right. We certainly weren't aware of
this rule of protocol—yet we seemed to have naturally assumed it, based
on our ages.

At any one time there were twenty to thirty students in the school
spread out over all eight grades. School hours were the same for all
grades. The routine was for the teacher to call one grade up front at a
time, although at times she combined two grades. The rest of the children worked quietly at their desks while waiting their turn to be called
front and center and take their place on the rough benches. For those not
up front, and all caught up with their assigned deskwork, a small library
containing light reading material was available. Those of us not in front
with teacher often found it difficult to disassociate ourselves from what
she might be teaching. The reader will recall my mentioning how familiar I became with the "alphabet soup" of programs associated with President Roosevelt's depression era programs. All this learned with my grandfather's encouragement and participation. This knowledge came close to
getting me in trouble one day at school. One or two of the upper grades
were up front reciting. I was at my desk doing assigned schoolwork. I
heard the teacher ask, "Who can tell me what the initials WPA stands

for?" Silence! She posed the question again—and still no answer. Finally I could stand it no longer. I practically shouted, **"Works Products Administration!"** Dead silence in the school as I cringed in embarrassment. Teacher did not approve at all of this spontaneous outburst.

In addition to the school, three other buildings were located on the grounds. Two of these were separate outdoor toilets for boys and girls, each with wrap around facades to ensure privacy. The fourth building was a woodshed.

In the winter, a furnace located in the partially finished basement heated the school. The furnace did a fair job, although it could be cool around the outside walls, especially if a cold wind was blowing. The school was east-west oriented with the southern side naturally the warmest. Only two trees of any size stood on the school grounds so there was little natural protection from the elements. The seating arrangement resulted in the first and second graders occupying the desks on the relatively colder northern side of the school—the seventh and eighth graders, those on the relatively warmer southern side. The usual routine in winter was for one of the local farmers who lived close to the school to fire up the furnace on a Sunday night and set the dampers to assure a slow burn. Upon arrival on Monday morning teacher tossed blocks of wood onto the bed of coals and opened the damper to heat the school. Before leaving at the end of the school day, she filled the furnace, turned the damper down, and next morning usually found a bed of coals to fuel the wood.

Most of us arrived at school quite cold and began the day by standing over and around the one large floor register to thaw out. Naturally there was pushing and jostling as we crowded toward the warm center of the floor register. On occasion, the fire went out overnight and teacher found a stone-cold furnace when she arrived the next morning. One teacher, Miss Silha (now Mrs. Maurice Poss) who taught three years from 1935-1938 remembers one such occasion. The outside temperature was forty degrees below zero, and it was sixteen degrees below zero inside the school.

Although the teacher was central in keeping the school warm, one or more of the older boys also played a role. Before the end of the school day, wood was carried into the basement by those assigned, to meet the next day's fuel requirements. Miss Silha does not remember any snow shoveling during her three years, nor do I during my eight years in the school. Possibly one of the neighbor men did the chore—or we waded through the snow to reach those two outside toilets and woodshed.

Another need was for water. Two of the older boys made a trip before school each morning to one of the neighboring farms with a shotgun can* to "fetch" the water needs for the day. One trip in the morning sufficed in the wintertime. On warm days in early fall or late spring, a second trip at noon might be necessary. Usually the source for water was the George Schaller farm, about one-fifth mile from the school. If there was a heavy snowfall or under blizzard conditions George Schaller delivered the water when he brought his children to school by horse drawn sleigh. The water was kept in an unheated entryway of the school. On really cold days we had to break through a thin layer of ice with the dipper for a drink of water. I recall the trip was long enough, and the water heavy enough so that we usually stopped and rested now and then on the way back to school with a full can of water. On one of those trips my partner and I, during one of those rest periods, hid in the ditch alongside the road as first or second grader Norman Schaller ambled down the road towards school. As he passed my partner and I tossed rocks at Norman to frighten him. His mother Celia observed this and let us know of her feelings. We were terrorized! First of all, might Celia paddle us? What if in addition to paddling us she also reported the event to teacher? Our parents? Father Mechler? After all, she couldn't tell from her vantagepoint that we were

---

*A shotgun can resembled the shells used in shotguns in that its proportion of diameter to length approximated that of the shell. The can was the standard container for a variety of liquid carrying needs, with its major use being to carry milk. Its elongated shape permitted two cans to be carried easily by one person. This shape also permitted two kids to team up in carrying the can with its three gallons of water from the Schaller well to the school.

tossing rocks in a playful manner. To Celia it may have looked like we were stoning her little boy with malice aforethought. I suspect as a result of this event I bonded closely with George and Celia Schaller. They were close to the top of the list of people I (later my wife and I) visited at their home on my trips back to Wisconsin. I'm sure on each of those occasions we brought up the rock-tossing harassment visited on her young son, and laughed about it. No doubt there's a degree of truth in the saying that "humor is nothing more than chaos remembered in tranquillity."

We carried our lunches. I think all of us had metal lunch buckets. Nothing fancy in the way of food; probably a fried egg or peanut butter and jelly sandwich. Perhaps an apple too. There was usually swapping during lunch. In the late 1930s George and Celia Schaller established a small grocery store and gas station at the junction of what is now Highway Seventy-One and Kayak Avenue. If little sister Dorothy and I might have beaten Colonel Sanders in the fried (or canned) chicken industry, could not the Schallers have cornered the Seven-Eleven convenience store business? With George farming and mother Celia running the store, there wasn't time for packing homemade lunches for the children. As a result they showed up with "store bought" goodies in their lunch pails. How jealous the rest of us were. After a while, the Schaller children grew tired of this fare and were open to swapping. One could exchange a peanut butter and jelly sandwich for a package of cream puffs or other delicious dessert like items. Our mothers must have wondered why their children begged for extra peanut butter and jelly sandwiches.

When I was in the sixth or seventh grade, the state of Wisconsin established a program resulting in our having hot lunches. Dad was on the school board at the time and I remember his involvement in setting this program up. The state provided funds to purchase a double burner kerosene stove to heat water in a large kettle. We brought jars of food from home, likely restricted to one or two-cup size to be placed in this kettle of hot water a half-hour before lunchtime. My favorite was macaroni and tomatoes. I'm sure teacher had help from older students—but yet another chore for her.

Speaking of additional chores: in the winter time teacher also ensured that the younger children's coats were all buttoned up, had their gloves, scarves, and boots on, and were in general all bundled up before heading home from school. Older siblings, in their haste to leave, could not necessarily be counted on to ensure that their younger brothers and sisters were ready for the hike home in cold weather.

Two major social events occurred during the school year involving the entire community. The first was the Christmas program. Teacher decided what plays to stage, what songs to sing, and what speeches to be made and selected the actors and actresses. No doubt she prepared many of the costumes too. Rehearsal periods were set aside at near the end of the school day—and what a treat alone to break from the schoolhouse routine for "show time." A few days before the evening performance the older boys dragged the low sawhorses and planks from a dark corner of the cellar and set up the stage. A wire was stretched across the room to hold the curtain. Now a couple of dress rehearsals and we were ready for opening night. All the people who lived in the school district could be counted on to show up, whether they had children in school or not. An oil-fired lamp casting a soft white glow did its best to light up the room. We children all sat up front on wooden benches. Our guests sat in the school seats and in extra chairs brought in for the occasion. Warm applause greeted our amateur efforts. In conjunction with this event, we students drew names for exchanging gifts. Later Santa Claus arrived to pass out the gifts and bags of goodies to the students. No doubt the teacher paid for these bags of goodies.

Valentine's day was also a special event—but this involved only teacher and students. The central idea here was to receive a large batch of valentines from your fellow students. Better yet, collect more than anyone else did. This counting primarily involved the girls. I think teacher passed out candy too—or else Valentine's day might not be remembered by me as a fun occasion.

A second major event was a picnic at the end of the school year. Again the entire community participated via a potluck routine. We perennially "hungry" types really enjoyed this event, and what an array of food graced the tables.

Not unlike most students, we at Bohn School were especially lively at recess and during the noon lunch break. During pleasant weather, the younger children could be found playing on the swing set. For the older ones, the activity was usually softball. At any one time ten to fifteen boys and girls could catch and hit a ball with a fair degree of athletic ability. Games of work-up were lively events, at times made all the livelier by the absence of an umpire.

In the late fall, when too cold to play softball, and before snow permitted sledding, we played a game called Prisoner's Base. Two trees served as respective safe havens. We divided up into two teams and proceeded to taunt each other by moving away from our respective safe havens. Opponent "X" tried to tag you and unless you returned quickly to home base you ended up as a prisoner and was held in jail near your opponent's safe haven. But if someone from the home team left home base after "X", they could tag "X" and now "X" is a prisoner. If legally tagged you went to jail where your team members tried to rescue you. If your team member made it to "X's" jail without being tagged, both you and your rescuer had safe passage back to your home base. Each team was busy, both trying to rescue their own prisoners and protect the prisoner (s) from the opposite side from getting rescued. At the end of recess the team with the most prisoners won. Once again there was no umpire so imagine the disputes as to who was or wasn't vulnerable to being tagged and sent to prison, and who "legally" was rescued.

In the winter there was sledding. The schoolyard sloped down hill from the road on which the schoolhouse fronted. (As noted, all the land sloped one way or the other on Summit Ridge.) A sled run ended after a short distance at a three wire barbed fence leading to the Semann farmland. What to do? First we pulled the bottom strand of barbed wire down and placed a board on top of it to hold it down. Next we piled snow over this set-up to permit sleds to ride over the board and wire. Then we pulled the middle wire up and tied it to the top wire. Now we had the necessary vertical clearance to ride our sleds through. In this way, we tripled the length of the sled run. This worked fine if only one or maybe two piled horizontally on the sled. But accidents still occurred when the top person on the sled collided with the middle wire.

Hey teacher! You also have to be a nurse!

Right after a snowfall and before the schoolyard was tracked up, we played a game called Fox and Geese. We needed most of the schoolyard to set up this game. First we made a circle about 100 feet in diameter. Then a second circle was made inside this circle with a diameter of about 90 feet. Next we constructed four lanes at the 0, 90, 180, and 270-degree points. Now the fox, starting from the center attempts to catch one of the geese who then becomes the next fox. All participants were required to stay in the lanes previously laid out. After a while, the corner cutters, or an over eager fox, or frightened geese destroyed this once neat symmetrical game arena.

One of the exciting events in winter was watching the snow plows come through. Snowplows at the time were neither powerful nor fast—but they were noisy. As a result roads remained blocked for long periods of time. On those rare occasions when the plow came along while we were in session, teacher interrupted the school routine so we could watch from the windows.

I had four teachers during my eight years at Bohn School. The one I remember best, and still stay in close touch with is Miss (Anabel) Silha (now Mrs. Maurice Poss). No trip to Wisconsin is complete without having breakfast with Mrs. Poss. She was eighteen when we met at Bohn School in September of 1935. I was in the second grade. Teacher preparation at the time consisted of one year training at what was called a "normal" school following high school. Her usual job routine was to be at the school from 7:30 a.m. to 5:00 p.m. Another couple of hours was set aside

Mrs. (Silha) Poss and author (2004 photo)

in the evening to correct papers and/or plan the next day's school activities. Her starting salary was seventy-five dollars per month for nine months.* She paid sixteen dollars per month for room and board at a neighboring farm, the home of Dick and Dorothy Steinhoff. She still remembers the wonderful meals Dorothy served. There was no extra charge if she stayed the weekend. In the winter, she often found it necessary to exercise this option. There was no paycheck during the summer months so she returned home to help her folks with the tobacco crop.

At the time I was in grade school, we had a wonderful County Superintendent of Schools, Miss Ollie Swanson. She was Monroe County's academic boss for rural schools and all rural schoolteachers kept a wary eye peeled for her surprise visits. Miss Silha remembers one January day when the main road from Miss Swanson's office in Sparta was known to be blocked a mile from the school. Miss Silha was quite certain she'd have no visit from the boss under these conditions. Miss Swanson's car was indeed blocked, but she trudged the mile to the school. Miss Silha was quite sure she panicked, but all went well.

Speaking of visitors and a boss, our mothers visited the school periodically. I am sure this occurred at least once a year for my mother. Rather a strange feeling knowing she was in the back of the room, no doubt monitoring your every move.

If we Hedricks journeyed to school as a group, I usually traveled home

---

*My starting pay twelve years later as a full time Marine was also seventy-five dollars per month.

independently, especially in the early fall and spring. There was all that gravel on the road, just the right size to throw, and those tempting fence posts and trees to throw them at. Unfortunately for one of the Steinhoff farms, I was right handed and their land was on my left as I walked home. Then too, the ground sloped towards their land so the fence posts were at the perfect height for targets. This made for quite a game of pretend baseball. If the post or tree was hit I called it a strike. Miss the post or tree, and I called it a ball. Per the rules, three strikes and the imaginary batter was out; four balls and he walked. Then to the next batter, etc.

Mention was made of how the entire community was involved in the school. Before the start of the school year, the ladies volunteered to give the building a thorough cleaning. This was repeated at the end of the school year. The men volunteered to do whatever heavy chores were involved. I remember helping Dad install a swing set when he served on the school board.

Consolidation of schools led to the demise of one-room rural schools. Bohn School closed after the 1962 school year. The building was purchased by a neighbor and former student, Leander Ebert, who used it as a machine shed. As noted, the land that the Semann family had allowed the school to use reverted back to them and is now part of a larger farm field. The other major rural school on Summit Ridge was Goetz School. This school was built with bricks so it could not be moved. It too later served as a machine shed. Today it's not much more than a heap of bricks. Unlike the Bohn School site, which has been returned to cropland, that "pile of bricks" marks the exact location of the old Goetz School.

To wrap up the Bohn School experience is to acknowledge June of 1941 as my graduation from the eighth grade. How proud my parents, relatives and neighbors were to learn I was the class valedictorian. For that matter, I was the number one achiever in my grade for all eight years. In candor it should be pointed out that I was also the only member in my grade all eight years.

CHAPTER **14**

Economy of the Time

From 1922 to 1929 the nation witnessed a dynamic surge of production, bringing nearly seven years of unparalleled prosperity to the American people—with the notable exception of those living on farms.*

The farmer's peculiar plight at this time was an outgrowth of World War I, which ended in November of 1918. During the war, farmers were encouraged to increase production, with government assurances that foreign nations would continue making large purchases long after the war ended due to the disruption of farm production in much of war-ravaged Europe.

With the encouragement of bankers, many farmers unwisely borrowed heavily to purchase additional acreage and expensive equipment to work the land. When the war ended, the previous consuming nations found themselves broke and deeply in debt. As a result demand fell and at the same time the nation's farmers were harvesting bumper crops. The law of supply and demand resulted in the price for the farmer's products being pushed so low that in many cases it did not pay to har-

---

*A study made by the Brooking's Institute at the time reported the average income for the nation's seventeen million farm families averaged less than $1000 a year.

vest the crops—or raise and sell meat-producing animals.

Not only were the farmers in trouble, but so were those banks who had loaned money to the farmers. A rash of bank failures in the mid-1920s was an indication the economy was heading into choppy waters. The combination of a dismal world economy, along with many in our own country buying stocks on ridiculously low margins were key factors in bringing us to the brink. When "Black Tuesday" arrived on 29 October 1929, the New York Stock Exchange plunged to its most devastating one-day loss in its history. At that point the rest of America caught up with the farmer. **Welcome all to the "great depression!"**

During the 1920s, many farmers throughout the country struggled to save their family farms from foreclosure. In the meantime, the depression resulted in increasing numbers of unemployed. By 1932, one in every five workers—over twelve million, were unemployed. Thus the demand for the farmer's products fell to an all time low since the laid-off workers did not have money to purchase his products. The farmer in turn comes out of an economic depression a year or more after the rest of the country. It takes that long for the newly re-employed industrial and service workers to enter the market place in sufficient numbers to create increased demands for the farmer's goods.

No matter what your political persuasion, then or now, there was little doubt but that the farm relief legislation enacted during the first one hundred days of the Roosevelt administration in 1933 saved many farmers from losing their homesteads.

One of my earliest recollections was of my parents talking about families facing particularly hard times; with the major calamity being the loss of their farm. No doubt other families discussing the same topic had determined our family might be one of those needing help. During one of these after the meal "table talk" sessions, I recall Mother mentioning that she was aware of a move to provide food and clothing for our family. Presumably she let the benefactors know, no doubt with profound thanks, that no aid was needed.

If times were not all that great economically speaking, prices for goods were in turn low. For example, a postage stamp was two cents, milk ten cents a quart, gas twenty-one cents a gallon, and bread nine cents for a twenty ounce loaf. A new six room, two car garage home in Detroit, Michigan could be purchased for $2800; and $5000 sufficed to purchase a new Spanish style seven room stucco home in Beverly Hill, California.

My growing up years coincided time wise with those great depression years. It wasn't until the start of World War II, in September of 1939 that our nation slowly came out of the depression. The basis, sadly enough, was major armament purchases from overseas nations embroiled in the early stages of World War II.

As family wealth went on Summit Ridge, we Hedricks may have been near the bottom rung of the ladder. My parents had the largest family on the ridge, ten children to the nearest competitor having seven. If we were poor, we children were certainly fooled. I don't ever recall being really hungry, or of not having sufficient warm clothing to wear in the wintertime.

CHAPTER **15**

Sources of Farm Income

T he major source of farm income came from the dairy herd. Most farmers at the time had between fifteen and thirty milk cows. I suspect ninety-five percent of the total labor effort on the farm was devoted to feeding, milking, and otherwise providing for the cattle.

Initially, in my experience cash income came from selling the cream that was separated from the raw milk. A device logically called the separator did the job via the principle of centrifugal force. A one-cylinder Johnson and Johnson engine powered the separator. As mentioned previously, this same engine was used to run a washing machine and pump water if the windmill-driven water pump was not able to keep up with demands. If the engine wasn't working, or there wasn't a large quantity of milk, we could power the separator by a hand crank. The whole milk, fresh from the cow, was poured into a large bowl at the top. As the milk passed through the whirling discs, the heavier cream was diverted out one spout and the lighter skim milk out the other. The skim milk went to the pigs and cats.

The cream went into a can where it accumulated for a couple of days before we took it to the creamery. This creamery was a cooperative owned by the local farmers around Norwalk. In the summer, these cans of cream were submerged in a small tank of cold water. The water was pumped daily from a subterranean well by either the windmill or engine. This kept the cream from spoiling. In the winter, the cream was stored in the milk house where a small stove kept the temperature above freezing.

At various times along the way, the farm wife dipped into the can for whatever cream she needed for food preparation. This could be for salad dressing, whipping cream, and on rare occasions, home made ice cream. The milk we drank came straight from the cow to the table. We also sold milk to the Christ family who lived in one of the houses in Summit, and to the Frank Roy family who lived in a house on one of the Steinhoff farms. They paid five-cents for two quarts of whole milk.

The cream was weighed and tested for butterfat content in conjunction with delivery to the creamery. This was rather important since the Jersey and Guernsey cattle produced less milk, but with a correspondingly high butterfat content. Holsteins and Brown Swiss on the other hand were heavy milk producers but with a relatively low butterfat content. As a result, one hundred pounds of Guernsey cream commanded a better price than the same amount of Holstein cream. The Hedrick's were in the minority with their herd of Guernseys, as were the few families who had Brown Swiss. Since Summit Ridge had no Jersey herds, that left the big black and white Holstein as the major breed. Today (year 2005), Holstein herds are near universal on the ridge.

After the cream had been weighed and tested, the creamery produced butter, cheese, etc. I can still see those one pound packages of butter we picked up directly from the creamery. A record was kept and the cost was subtracted from the bi-monthly milk check (not cream check). Since the butter was not paid for in cash, there was a tendency to view the product as free. As a result it may have been overused. One of the families used so much butter some jokingly remarked they used butter for wagon axle grease.

We hauled our own cream to Norwalk, but most farmers relied on a hauler. As was noted earlier, the Kroeger brothers provided this service, along with hauling cattle to market and meeting the other hauling needs of the community. Their truck picked up the cream, farm by farm, along with orders for butter and cheese. When the hauler returned a few days later, he brought with him the butter and cheese ordered a few days before. How we independent haulers, with our couple cans of cream, hated to end up behind a Kroeger truck at the creamery with it's eighty plus cans of cream. Before a powered conveyer system was installed, each can had to be hand lifted to the loading dock, then poured into a collecting tank and weighed. Each farmer had an assigned number stenciled on his milk cans. This facilitated recording of the pounds of cream he was later paid for. The Kroegers with their large number of cans had to be especially careful to unload the cans in numerical order. The conveyor system speeded up the process, but one still felt a pang of frustration if one of the Kroeger trucks was in line, or worse yet, turned in just ahead of you.

Somewhere along the way the system went to whole milk instead of cream. The volume of milk now required daily delivery to the creamery. In the summertime, the evening production went into a cooling tank. The same for the morning production in warm weather since we ate breakfast before delivering the milk. Occasionally in the winter, the roads were impassable. At these times, the milk accumulated or was delivered by sleigh if horses could move through the drifts. There was a much reduced volume of milk in the wintertime and chances of spoilage was unlikely so the farmer could live with this interruption if it were but for a day or two.

Twice each month was payday. This meant a visit to one of the two banks in Norwalk to pick-up and cash their milk check. Except in the busiest of times, like haying, threshing, etc. this was a great excuse to spend at least an hour in town. This also provided a great opportunity to discuss the events of the day, and what better place to do so than in one of the three taverns in Norwalk. If you think "Cheers," the bar in the television series was a friendly place, it could be viewed as downright "uppity" compared to the bars in small town rural Wisconsin.

Some farmers, despite their best intentions when they started out from home, spent more than the few hours they had allocated for the trip to town. On those days, many a milk cow's head turned during the evening milking when the otherwise businesslike farmer all of a sudden burst into song. At times, due to inclement weather, there was no way one could do farm work. If that day happened to fall on a milk check day—well, the taverns might do a little better business than usual. I can remember on a couple of occasions when Dad, who was not a singer, did some serious "humming" in conjunction with the evening milking. My Aunt Lena and I exchanged amused glances at those times.

Then there were the chickens! Chickens were usually the province of the farmer's wife. Most all the farms had a flock of at least 100 laying hens, and I suspect all of the activities associated with this project were a jealously guarded prerogative of the farmer's wife. The eggs were gathered daily and those not required for family food needs were packed in egg crates. Usually on a Saturday night, certainly on a Saturday night in the summertime, the eggs went to market. For the two-mile trip to Norwalk the crate(s) of eggs competed with us children for the limited space in the back seat of the car. I suspect if seat belts were in use at the time, the crate(s) of eggs might have been belted up rather than the humans. There at the general store, the mercantile as we called it, the eggs were counted and graded.* In time, those eggs found their way to major cities in the Midwest. In the meantime, the store now owes the farmer's wife "X" dollars, which she could collect in cash, or as usually happened, use to purchase food and clothing. In most cases the wife had to come up with additional funds, but not in all cases. My Grandmother Hedrick amassed over the years, what to all of us was the small fortune of over $100 in egg money at one point in 1944. But my grandmother was not feeding ten

---

*A hen could be expected to lay 200 eggs a year. A flock of 100 hens then could produce 1666 dozen eggs. Assuming the family consumed 366 dozen, 1300 dozen could be sold. The average price for eggs in the 1930s and early 1940s was thirty cents per dozen. Thus around $400 might be added to the gross farm income from the chicken flock.

children or buying clothing for them. Although egg money might produce spendable income for a few, like my grandmother, for most it merely reduced to some extent the cash needed for purchases of food and clothing. Today (2005), one would have to hunt far and wide on Summit Ridge to find a single chicken kept for the purpose of egg production.

Most farmers raised a few pigs, perhaps ten to twenty. The main purpose was for a portion of the family's meat supply. This required four to six pigs for the two Hedrick families. Since a sow gave birth to from eight to twelve piglets, surplus pigs were raised and sold for cash. Pigs thrived on skim milk, which was a by-product from separating the cream (for sale) from the raw milk. It would have been a shame to waste all that skim milk. Besides, pigs fed skim milk produced the most tasty meat products. The process on our farm was to carry the necessary amount of ground feed (a mixture of corn, oats, barley, or wheat) to the milk house. As soon as the skim milk came from the separator we mixed it with the feed to make what we indelicately called "slop." This mix of ground feed and warm skim milk was then carried to the pig stable and dumped into troughs. Since the skim milk was warm this was "warm slop." Talk about happy pigs or "eating high off the hog!"

The trip from the milk house down (and the operative word here is down) to the pig stable was not without peril. This was a treacherous trek, downhill all the way, with a particular steep decent around a 180-degree turn at a concrete barrier just before entering the stable. Imagine that trip on ice in the wintertime.

Pigs today are a rarity on Summit Ridge. To some extent, this was the result of going from selling cream to whole milk—so no more skim milk. The major reason though is that it doesn't pay to raise only a few pigs as was done in the past. A few are still raised to accompany beef cattle and clean up the whole corn the cattle do not digest. The old pig stable still stands on the home farm but is used now to shelter calves and young heifers in the winter.

Other means of raising cash was to keep a flock of twenty to fifty sheep, and a few did this. Income came primarily from wool, but they could also be sold for meat. The shearing process was a wide-eyed wonder for us kids. I was amazed at how accepting the sheep were to the process of losing their coats of wool. They did not appear to struggle while being sheared. They were set on their haunches and within a minute were turned loose stark naked. I could be mistaken, but it seemed to me they looked and acted like they were embarrassed. Since this occurred in the spring, the sheep had to appreciate losing their warm woolen coat as summer approached. A temporary problem for the lambs was their not being able to recognize Mom without her woolen coat. Not to worry, Mom was quick to seek her babies out and let them know all was still okay between them. We kept a flock that was free to roam all around our house and other farm buildings. No need for a lawn mower, but a need to be continually opening and closing gates as vehicles/wagons and pedestrians came and went. Oh, and watch where you step too. Rabbits, goats, ducks and geese also made their way into the inventory of farm animals for the purpose of meeting food needs, or for extra income.

The many acres of forestland on most farms provided all the firewood, fence posts, and lumber needed, plus additional income from selling ties to the railroad. Finally, selling surplus apples might bring in a few dollars. The Steinhoffs had approximately an acre of apple trees and there were about twenty apple trees in a small orchard on the home farm. At our home, approximately ten apple trees and one cherry tree were scattered around the built-up area. But no more. Orchards have gone the way of the chickens and pigs. I suspect one would have to search carefully to find an apple tree on Summit Ridge today.

Somewhat independent of farms themselves was the income enjoyed by many of the single young men and women as "hired men" and "hired girls." With the large families at the time, there was usually enough of these two groups to go around. Leonard Steinhoff and two of my paternal uncles, as mentioned earlier, were more or less permanent in that role. Here and there one might find a truly permanent hired man who lived with and was treated as a member of the family. For others, only a temporary job if their own families could spare them, and another family had a temporary need for them. In some cases, a young man advanced from being a hired man to renting a farm, and from there to farm ownership. Childbirth resulted in many a young woman finding temporary employment as the new mother recuperated, for the most part in bed, for approximately two weeks. Temporary employment might also be available for young women during spring housecleaning and produce canning time. During school vacation, young ladies often worked all summer for another family, usually a relative who did not have a working age daughter(s). I remember my sisters Elaine and Dorothy as young women being so employed. Today's young farm women, who at one time could find employment as hired girls, are out there competing with their city cousins for jobs at McDonalds, Baskin and Robbins, etc.

For the young men there was the need for temporary help at harvest times and for harvesting wood. Another source of temporary employment was to go "out west" and work harvesting grain. One heard "Bill went out west" and immediately the mind conjured up the romantic image of the old west and Bill was viewed as a hero on horseback. In practice, "out west" equated to approximately 300 miles to the open prairie farmland of western Minnesota or the eastern Dakotas. Much as was the case with school age young women; the young men could also find summer employment on relative's or a neighbor's farm. My brother Noel, four years younger than I, was available to be so employed. He found work each summer at one place or another once old enough to earn his pay.

Our home was not unusual in having a constant parade of hired help passing through. I felt the hired men to a degree were subjected to more work than they had bargained for. He might be hired strictly for the purpose of working in the woods, and yet after his full day of being so employed was expected to help out with the morning and evening chores as well.

Today, as with the case of young women, young men prefer jobs in neighboring towns and cities. Still, a few are employed on a permanent basis as farm workers.

Then there were the two entrepreneurs on the ridge, Bernard (Bud) Rapp and George Schaller. Both had location, location, location going for them. Bud Rapp at the "T" intersection of what is now Kayak Road and Kermit Avenue; George Schaller at the key intersection of what is now Kayak Road and Highway Seventy-One.

Bud Rapp was the first of the two to branch out to a degree from farming. First of all, it should be mentioned that Bud also had one of the larger dairy operations on the ridge with a fine set of buildings. In addition, he operated a sawmill where others could bring their logs to be cut for railroad ties and other lumber needs. But the heart of his entrepreneurial operation, the "jewel," was a tavern he established in his milk house after prohibition had been lifted. Bud maintained his own icehouse to preserve and cool the products he sold. The tavern was open only during fair weather months and then generally only on Saturday nights and Sundays. Saturday nights were probably best, but Sundays were quite busy as well. First of all, probably half of the Catholic families on Summit Ridge went through that "T" intersection on their way to and from church services. Since Bud's farm was only one-fourth mile from the church, the rest of the families had only a short jog to reach his farm. If the farmer had a little cash in his pocket this might be an opportunity to buy the kids a candy bar and soft drink to share, and maybe something a little stronger for him and his wife.

Sundays in the summer were especially good days for business. Summertime was baseball time and Sunday afternoon was game day. Bud had pastureland adjacent to his buildings that passed as level ground for a baseball diamond and home games were played here. Drinks, candy, etc. were available from the tavern. Before the umpire called "play ball" the cows were chased to one end of the pasture. From here they gazed back contemptuously at the humans who had invaded their domain. But they left reminders behind to ensure the players did not forget whose territory was being trespassed on. As a result, some of the slides into second and third base would have put the immortal Ty Cobb to shame—assisted by what we euphemistically called "cow pies."

In the 1930s the tavern was often the "launching pad" for baseball games played in neighboring communities. One of Kroeger's trucks from Norwalk, outfitted with a cattle rack, arrived at the tavern to haul the team and spectators to that Sunday afternoon's game.

Another way Bud used to bring in the crowd was to sponsor dances, especially wedding dances. These were held in his machine shed. My earliest recollection of observing such an event was in 1934 when I was six years old. The occasion was Margaret Kapellar and John Rapp's wedding dance. I watched in absolute awe as grown-ups grasped each other and whirled around the floor. This was the first time for me to observe normally reserved adults jumping up and down to intoxicating polka music.

George and Cecilia Schaller's enterprise was introduced earlier in the Bohn school chapter. They initially started out building an automotive garage along with gas pumps and a small grocery store. The year was probably 1938. It could have been a winner as a garage since vehicles at that time needed frequent repair. The building had been erected, about 2000 square feet in size when a state inspector showed up. I am not sure if George had scheduled the inspection, or if the inspector just happened to come by. (There was a suspicion the state might have been "tipped" off to this projected new business.) The inspector pointed out to George what he needed to do to comply with state safety laws. Whatever the requirements were it killed the project. I recall George puffing on his pipe and looking downcast. His dream of bettering his economic position in life was shattered. After the inspector left some of those present, who were helping construct the building, suggested George ignore the inspector. After all, one commented, "You will probably never see him again." George though complied with the law and settled for running a small grocery store and gas station. The Schallers also built a small (200-300 square foot) one room building next to the store. I believe that this was intended as living quarters for the person hired to run the business day-by-day. I'm not sure it was ever used for that purpose, but I do recall occasional teen-age Saturday night dances in the building.

The store was a favorite hangout of mine. I was at times a volunteer gas station attendant. A hand pump was used to fill a clear glass tank. A customer would drive up and ask for "X" gallons. I then pumped the "X" gallons into the clear glass tank marked off to show the volume of fuel ordered. Then gravity took over and the customer had his gas. Most of all though I just "hung out" with the "good-ol'-boys" of Summit Ridge whenever I had free time. I was also at times a paying customer. At this point in my life I was a great fan of store bought sliced bread. Schaller's store was one and one-half miles from our home. After evening chores, when I had a dime to spare, I often walked to their store to buy a loaf of bread and then walked back home. As a rule the rest of the family was in bed when I arrived home. I broke out the butter and ate slice after slice of this delicious bread.

In summary, the dairy herds drove the economic engine for the great majority of farmers on Summit Ridge—but don't discount the contribution made by that flock of chickens.

If the average farmer on Summit Ridge had to fight for their dollars—how about their children who had a desire for a little spending money? Specifically, how about Joe Hedrick?

Although the job didn't pan out, I was employed early in life on my grandfather Berendes' farm. The job was to pick the stones off this particular field. I had a two or three gallon bucket and I was to pick and dump three buckets full of stones on a pile as I worked the field. For each pile I would be paid five-cents. Right next to the field was a large pile of stones that had accumulated via pickings over the years. I was caught early on filling my bucket from this pile and carrying them a short distance to make three-bucket piles in the field I was assigned to clear.

I also made a little change catching gophers. The county paid ten-cents for each gopher tail produced. I was too young to set a trap so I drowned them out. Since water had to be carried in pails the process was done in those fields near the house. I enlisted my younger brothers and sisters to help me carry water. All likely avenues of escape (holes) were blocked and water was then poured into the remaining hole. My dog Corky waited eagerly by the hole while I or one of my siblings poured water in the hole. He was a sure-fire bet to catch and kill the first gopher that emerged. I stood by with a club to kill at least one of the remaining gophers likely to emerge. The gophers came out fast and quickly found their bearings to enable "broken field running" making it extremely difficult to club them. In summary—some success, but I didn't get rich, nor did my dog or siblings ever end up being accidentally clubbed.

My first remembered income or allowance was the dime Grandfather Isadore Hedrick gave me in conjunction with the summer time Tuesday night free movies in Norwalk. I'm not sure for how long this went on, but the time came when Dad became half-owner of the farm operation and responsible for labor. Surely I must have received an allowance, but I honestly cannot remember Dad ever paying me a penny as an allowance. I suspect when I went out for an evening, or to this or that event he gave me money. As noted above, and will be mentioned again below, he was more than generous in allowing me to use the raw feed available to support my various income producing projects I engaged in along the way.

I recall the badgering I had to do to obtain the money to fix up my uncle Joe's old bicycle I discovered one day in a dark recess of the home farm garage. About this time a maternal cousin, Jim Muehlenkamp, purchased a brand new bicycle—beautiful balloon tires and all. How neatly it absorbed the bumps in the gravel or dirt field roads. The difference between my hand-me-down bike and Jim's was like the difference between a Communist East German Yugo and a Cadillac. His bicycle cost nineteen dollars. I set about calculating that if Dad paid me an allowance of "X" per week (or month) I could purchase a like bicycle in "Y" amount of time. I rehearsed carefully the precise wording I intended to use in my proposal, and picked what I thought was just the right time. Dad never had to make an easier decision in his life: in mid-presentation the answer was an emphatic, disdainful, and convincing "NO!"

In the meantime, my kid brother Noel, four years younger, is making five dollars a month working for an uncle. (Noel would learn about Dad's allowance policies when he had to stay home and fill in for me after I joined the Marines.) It wasn't a matter of fairness with Dad; he simply didn't have the cash at that point in time. As a result, I was forever grubbing for money. At one point a neighbor agreed to pay me twenty-five cents for each skinned and gutted rabbit I delivered. He didn't realize how many rabbits a cash hungry kid could deliver at one time. I think I presented seven in the first batch. We finally settled on two per week. Another means of raising cash was skinning the young calves that died for one reason or another shortly after birth. The Steinhoff family also permitted me to skin their dead calves. The hide sold by the pound; about a dollar for a Guernsey calf; one dollar and twenty-five cents for a Holstein. Much like a vulture, I cheered the death of calves on our farm and the Steinhoff farm.

Although not a money making venture, I once contracted with a mail order firm to sell packets of flower and vegetable seed. If I sold the required amount I was to receive a guitar. The picture showed an adult with a full-sized instrument. Our friendly neighbors humored me by buying the product and in time I did receive a guitar, but one much smaller than the one advertised.

Then there was collecting and selling scrap iron during World War II. I remember in particular the windfall from the Bohn farm (my maternal Aunt Anna). During World War II there was a shortage of many articles since the nation's near total production effort was devoted to war material. As a result, my old hand-me-down bicycle commanded a few dollars when I sold it. I also recall working for a few Saturdays in conjunction with installing electric power lines. This involved cutting trees to clear pathways for the power lines. Now I didn't mind working in the woods since the job paid twenty-five cents per hour. This was in 1944 when our end of Summit Ridge was in the process of finally being provided with electricity.

Although an innocent party, I was also involved in a rather bizarre method of picking up a few dollars.

This money-making event took place at weddings. Right after the wedding Mass, and before anyone left the church, Father Mechler allowed the two Mass servers involved to leave the altar. We picked up one of his "cinctures"* he conveniently left out for us in the sacristy. Via a side door off the sacristy we quickly made our way to the front door of the church to be in position for what might be termed legal "bush-whacking." One of us stood on each side of the exit with the cincture (rope) stretched across the opening. People leaving the church were expected to make a donation. (Since the cincture was part of the priest's vestments the good Catholics of Summit Ridge would not think of pushing by.) Nickels, dimes and quarters accumulated in whatever we used for a collection pot. The Groom and the Best Man were both likely to contribute a dollar each. Strangers at the ceremony probably followed the example of the crowd. No doubt they assumed the collection was for the wedding couple. After the last person had left the church the two of us hastened back to the sacristy to count our loot—with Father Mechler an amused observer. I no longer recall what amount we collected—perhaps three to five dollars, and it was all ours. This polite form of legal bush-whacking at weddings has since been discontinued.

All the above was honest labor, with the possible exception of what occurred at weddings, and I am proud of my efforts in those projects. Another moneymaking venture was a bit on the questionable side. In

---

*The cincture was a linen cord twelve to fifteen feet in length that served as a belt. The priest used the cincture to "cinch up" the alb. The alb was a loose fitting white linen robe reaching to the ankles and covering the entire body. While applying the cincture the priest said this "vesting" prayer: "Gird me, O Lord, with the cincture of purity and quench in my heart the fire of concupiscence, that the virtue of continence and chastity may abide in me."

late summer, Monroe County held its annual fair in Tomah. Folks brought their cattle, pigs, poultry, jellies, jams, etc. to be judged for cash prizes. One assumes folks brought their best products to be judged. In the case of livestock competition, it was by breed, presumably pure-breds with no taint of strange blood in them. I thought I saw a means to make some money showing sheep. We had approximately twenty in our flock; the Steinhoff's, about fifty. Both flocks were a mixture of Hampshires, Shropshires, Leicesters, Suffolks, etc. As a rule I could usually find individual sheep resembling a given breed in our flock, or the Steinhoff's flock. First step was to select sheep resembling a given breed from the two flocks. Annie Steinhoff, not being in any way in-volved in this conspiracy, helped me sort out probable candidates from their flock. Now I have ten to twelve animals, some of which could qualify by appearance to look like they could be Shropshires, Hamp-shires, etc. Somewhere I found a "rickety" two-wheeled trailer, and on the day before the fair, set off on the seventeen-mile trip to Tomah. Probably around mile twelve a tire flattened on the trailer. I remember standing on the side of the road, most unhappy and wondering what to do. What I did was roll on into the fairgrounds on a flat tire—thor-oughly embarrassed. A neighbor, Leander Ebert was most helpful and did his best to show me the ropes. I think he felt sorry for me, although probably embarrassed to be associated with my animals and me.

The next step was to check the competition in neighboring pens. If I counted only two Shropshire ewes, and I have one that looks like a Shropshire; well, third place is worth a few dollars. Hey, what's this, only one Leicester ewe; I have two that with a little imagination could pass the appearance test—and by default here is the prize money for second and third place. So it went as I orchestrated the placement of my sheep in various breed-judging categories. At the time for showing the animals, I swallowed my pride and took my entry into the judging ring. Leander Ebert, good guy that he was, helped out if I had more than one animal to show in a given category. I suspect the judge was disgusted; I seem to recall he eventually told me so. Still, he either had to award at least three ribbons (likely) or else he didn't have the heart to say in effect, "Your sheep are not in the right class!" Spectators who knew their sheep were grinning, which added to my embarrassment. I don't recall how much money I netted—but I cringe a bit to this day when I reflect back on that episode in my life.

But there would be more honest pay-offs along the way. There was an organization for young men at the time called "Future Farmers of America (FFA)." A companion organization existed for young girls. Are you not surprised, that given the times the organization was called "Future Homemakers of America (FHA)?" We in the FFA were expected to have income producing projects. Our parents were expected to cooperate in this venture. My first project was a small plot of popcorn. This should have been a moneymaker. I don't think shelled popcorn was available in retail stores at the time—but it could have been. Still, I should have been able to undersell the competition. As it turned out, I merely supported the family's popcorn needs. The next project involved rabbits. My mother's chick brooder coop was empty in late fall so I moved in a couple of does and a buck. **Sha-zam**, baby rabbits—many baby rabbits! It wasn't long before Dad took note of how much farm feed they were eating. At one point he slyly suggested the rabbits were eating more hay than the cattle. When spring arrived Mother needed the brooder house for that year's flock of baby chicks so most of the rabbits went to market. I suspect I made a few dollars here.

In high school I naturally was enrolled in an agriculture class. Once again, we were required to have a farm related project. On occasion the agriculture teacher visited the farm to check on the project. I recall raising a beef calf one year, sheep another, but I really hit the big time with pigs.*

I couldn't have had a more cooperative parent in this venture than

---

*I have up to this point, and will continue to use the term "pigs" even though a pig is considered a "hog" when it reaches its market weight of 180 to 200 pounds.

was my dad. First of all, he let me use about an acre of alfalfa land for the venture. Pigs prosper when allowed to graze and they are remarkably clean when given the space to establish a remote area for their "toilet." In a way, he also gave me permission to drag two pig huts from the home farm and place them in this field. What he said was the huts were in too poor a state of repair to be moved. I took this statement as a qualified yes. I did a little repair work on these small huts, mounted them on skids, and one day when he was off shopping, I used the tractor to move them to the field. When he arrived home and saw what had occurred he uttered not a word of objection—obviously he was surprised—maybe even impressed.

In this particularly successful year of pig farming I started off with two sows. One was a spotted Poland China, the other a Chester White. Tony Goetz, a farmer living two miles away allowed me to breed the sows to his Poland China boar. This was a walking road trip with me carrying a long stick to deter the boar from turning into yards or fields along the way, and to have it turn where I wanted it to do so. All I had to do was place the stick to the right or left of its eye and this deterred a turn, or if held there, caused the boar to turn. One aspect I could not influence was the speed, despite my pointing out over and over that I had two "ladies" waiting for him for a three-week "romantic stand." The boar poked along at his own speed (slow), grunting each step of the way. I did not enjoy that round trip in such close proximity to the same sex pig that seriously injured my grandfather. This was afterall a 600 to 700 pound animal.

If sister Dorothy practiced what she learned in her high school home economics class, I did the same when it came to my agriculture classes—and specifically as related to raising pigs. Any animal profits from exercise. For pregnant females it's even more important. It's winter and I have two sows scheduled to farrow in April or early May. Deep snow covering the ground pretty much restricted the sows to a small outside area next to the pig stable. What to do? First I dug a narrow path about fifty feet in one direction, then made a sharp "U" turn and dug another path back. Back and forth and back and forth ending up with a couple hundred yards of reasonably cleared paths. Then on a daily basis I took a bundle of corn, such as was shocked in the first chapter, and placed it at the distant end of this labyrinth of paths. Show the sows once that a bundle of corn is at the end of the path and they will waddle out there daily. If no bundle of corn was available I tossed a few ears of corn out for feed. Bundles were best since the sow now has to fight and tussle with the stalks to reach the ears of corn buried in the bundle; the result added exercise.

Shortly before the end of the 114-day gestation period, the two sows were moved from the stable on the home farm to that field of alfalfa. I knew the first to farrow (give birth) would choose one of the two huts, the second sow had no choice but to take the other. I wondered which hut the first to farrow would choose. One hut was a simple "A" frame, the other a bit larger with four sides and a sloping roof. A threat to newborn pigs was that their mother would crush them as she moves about while giving birth, and in those critical first hours right after birth and before the piglets gather their strength (and survival instincts) to move out of the way as mom gets up and down. The one hut had a railing approximately eight inches off the floor and eight inches from the side. The newborn now had a space into which they were either pushed or scrambled as mom ponderously moved about. The sides of the "A" frame hut sloped to provide much the same protection due to the manner of its construction.

The day arrived in late April or early May when the Spotted Poland China sow began gathering clumps of grass to build her nest. Which hut did she pick? Neither. Her spot was under a tree alongside a fence. If she were to farrow here there were no rails to protect her young. I felt I had no choice but to be a mid-wife.

I did not sleep for most of that night. An altogether mild evening and I had to wonder if the sow calculated in this factor when choosing to give birth outdoors. It can still get cold in Wisconsin in late April and early

May after all, and that mild weather could change in a hurry. At about three a.m., the baby pigs began to arrive. I had placed jugs of warm water wrapped in towels in a couple of bushel baskets. In the literal sense, the piglets received a warm welcome. As the baby pigs arrived, each weighing a little over two pounds, I dried them off with a towel and placed them in the warm basket. The sow seemed oblivious to my presence, getting up and down or rolling from one side to the other during the birthing process. From time to time I placed the early arrivals at a nipple to nurse—but they went back in the basket fast when their 500 to 600 pound mom moved around.

Naturally I wondered how many little ones there might be? As noted earlier, a sow normally produces from eight to twelve young. I was aware that each one of these little pigs that survived was likely to be worth about forty dollars in six months. This was like Las Vegas as mom kept pumping out those little pigs one after another. In the meantime I'm pumping out the standard Catholic triad of prayers (Our Father, Hail Mary, and Glory be to the Father) pleading for more, more, more piglets. When the birthing process was over, twelve healthy piglets had made their appearance—all in less than an hour. Now the really fun part of lifting them all out of the baskets and placing them so they could grasp a nipple for their first full meal. At this point, I left for a half-hour and when I returned, all was okay; so I decided to go to bed. When I checked at six a.m. mom had moved her entire family into a hut, and being female, she naturally picked the larger of the two huts.

My folks were much amused at all this, and yet they had to admit there had been no losses in the litter—and a teenage boy could be doing something worse on an April or May night. The Chester White sow gave no warning she was about to farrow. One morning there was her living litter of ten she had delivered in the "A" frame hut. One did not survive. Not bad, twenty-two healthy baby pigs—wow, I am in "hog heaven." Sometimes it really pays to be Catholic!

Another recommendation in the process of raising pigs for market was to give them room to roam. The alfalfa field provided this feature, along with nutrients from the alfalfa. Another was to allow them to eat all they wanted. Pigs, unlike humans, will not "pig out."* I built a self-feeder as one of my high school projects. This was a box-like device permitting feed to automatically drop down into a trough as needed. The feeder was divided into two bins, the larger containing ground feed, which varied as the pigs developed towards their ideal market weight of 200 pounds. Early on it might be heavily weighted with oats, then gradually increasing the corn and/or barley content. Finally, a smaller section of the self-feeder contained "tankage." This is a feed made from the bones, tendons, and other parts of animals. Tankage contained the remaining minerals and nutrients needed to promote rapid growth. The pigs left on their own, knew how to balance their intake of feed and tankage needed as they matured. Then there was the need for water. Since I was out in the fields most of the day, my little sister Joan carried fresh water to the pigs three or four times during the day. In the process, she made sure they never ran out of water, and that the old water was dumped out. These were pampered pigs.

Something else learned in high school was how to castrate male pigs. This assured more rapid growth, which meant a larger paycheck, and in less time. I suspect those little male pigs saw me as "Mack the Knife." I showed no mercy, we are talking dollars and cents here after all.

In the meantime Dad was keeping a wary eye on this operation. The granary bins and corncrib were already suffering somewhat. At the eight-week level he suggested/encouraged me to sell the entire lot. At this point in their lives the pigs are weaned from their mother's milk and are marketable as "shoats." Farmers who did not want to go through the fuss and bother of the farrowing process bought shoats to fatten out. I backed

---

*Pigs get a bad rap! As noted, if given some room to roam they are clean animals, in fact cleaner than most other farm animals. They rank ninth in intelligence in the animal kingdom; ahead of cattle, horses, and sheep. Perhaps the supreme insult is the term "eat like a pig."

away from this suggestion, and good guy that he was, Dad said no more.

I do recall nearly scraping the granary and corn crib bare. The ear corn went from the crib to the granary where I shelled* and sacked it. Grain was in turn sacked. Both the granary and corn crib were located on the home farm. This "midnight requisition," as it might be termed, was done after evening chores and after Dad had returned to our house on the Bucholz farm. The next day I took the sacks of grain and corn to Norwalk to have it ground in conjunction with hauling milk to the creamery. At this point in the fattening process the twenty-two pigs were eating up a storm. As a result, I was a regular and frequent customer at my friend Jim Betthauser's feed mill. "Frequent" because I could only shell so much corn in the time I had on a given evening. Since the cows and horses were on pasture and the chickens found plenty of insects to eat, the rest of the farm animals did not compete for the grain in storage. After threshing in August, the granaries were filled again, and it was in August, September and October that the pigs were really devouring feed.

I am not sure how the grain supplies held up during the winter of 1947—I was out of there in January of that year. I don't think Dad ever again opened the granary and corncrib to his other three sons. He gave them a heifer calf with no charge for its maintenance. When the heifer produced a calf, the calf was theirs as well. More important for my brothers, there was then the steady daily income from the milk of his animal(s).

Early October of 1946 arrived and the pigs were at their market weight of 200 pounds, two weeks ahead of schedule. One day a Kroeger truck showed up and off to market they went. At twenty-cents per pound on the hoof I was looking for around $880. The price of twenty-cents per pound was set by a World War II Price and Wage Control Act to prevent inflation of food prices. At this point the war had been over for

---

*In the process of shelling corn the corncobs, now stripped of their kernels, were still of some value. They could also be used for kindling to start a fire, or to feed a fire. Indelicately as it may be, I must mention that the cobs could be used as a substitute for toilet paper. This need might arise when the old Sears Roebuck and/or Montgomery Wards catalogues were used up.

fourteen months, but price controls were still considered necessary on foodstuff since there remained the need to feed a still hungry and war ravished world. While the pigs were on their way to market these controls were lifted, and in the open market the price surged to around forty-two cents per pound. I am not sure who was happier when Dad brought the check for approximately $1800 home—he or I. I wonder too if he had ever handled a check that large. The $1800 was enough money to easily buy a new car at the time. In year 2005 dollars, $1800 would equate to $18,000—still enough to have purchased a new 2005 car.

I was in the Marines a few months later leaving the money largely untouched for nearly two years. I did buy brother Noel and sister Joan bicycles, balloon tires and all. Noel tells me I made $100 available to him during Christmas 1947 to buy gifts for the family. I also recall having Aunt Lena tap the money to buy and mail me a portable radio while I was stationed at Camp Pendleton in 1947. I have no idea at this point in time as to why I did not purchase it myself from the Post Exchange on base or a retail store in Oceanside. Not surprisingly for the times, the radio was the size of a small suitcase. Finally, I provided a no interest loan to my parents so they could install running water and indoor plumbing in the house.

In summary, over the long term I could hardly complain about the economic benefits that came my way while working on the farm for my dad.

CHAPTER 16

Homes on Summit Ridge

There was little variation in the homes on Summit Ridge. Most were of wood construction, with at least two being built of brick or stone. The one made of stone, a stately structure, was where my maternal Aunt Helen Muehlenkamp lived. The stones used came from the mid-tunnel shaft that was dug in conjunction with building the railroad tunnel. This shaft was located on the Muehlenkamp farm. All wood frame

Hedrick home (1930s)

homes were painted white—except ours. I remember being ashamed that our home's exterior was the only one showing no evidence at all of ever having been painted.

The homes in that era (late 1920s to early 1940s) and appliances therein differed little from those of the mid-1850s on. Kitchens were relatively large since most of the meals were served here. I suspect all homes had carbon copies of the wood fired kitchen ranges. In addition to the top cooking surface, and commodious oven just below, two warming ovens were located above and slightly in back of the cooking surface. To round out the stove's features there was a large reservoir for heating water located on the side of the range. The baking oven had a temperature gauge, but for the other food preparation chores, a judgment call was required as to when the cooking surface was at the right temperature for this or that cooking need. With time and instructions from mothers and grandmothers, farm girls became experts at the food preparation trade with these ranges.

In addition, these ranges heated the kitchen in the wintertime (it also heated the kitchens in the summertime). Another function was to heat the flatirons used to iron clothes. One or more flatirons were placed on the cooking surface to heat up. The "spit test" determined when the flatiron was judged ready. If not hot enough—no results; if too hot—look for scorch marks on the item being ironed. At least two flatirons were used; one heating up while the other was in use. The top of the stove was also used for toasting bread—but we had to watch carefully or the bread quickly turned black. The cook did not usually toast bread; this was something we kids did at times to round out a meal.

The wood for the range was split into small pieces since the stove's burn box was relatively small. The cook could control stove temperature by the number of sticks fed into the stove. On the home farm, as noted earlier, the wood was stored in a bin accessible from both the outside porch and kitchen. In our house, the wood was kept in an enclosed but unheated porch.

All the home's potable water needs were pumped by hand from an outdoor cistern. On both our farms, these cisterns were approximately 100 feet from the house. We considered it one of the unpleasant chores to "fetch a pail of water." At least this was a level trip on the Bucholz farm. The side hill on the home farm made it more of a chore—especially in the wintertime. In the wintertime too we often had to contend with a frozen pump. This required carrying hot water from the house to melt the ice so we could start the flow. We were constantly reminded of two safety-related issues in the wintertime. One was to be ever so careful around wood burning stoves. The other was don't place a moist hand, or God forbid, your tongue on a cold pump handle. We generally observed the stove rule, but I'll bet most of us lost some tongue flesh to a water pump handle as we "experimented." I suppose this is a part of the "wet paint" syndrome. Our home also had a rain water cistern and pump next to the house. Water from the roof was diverted into this cistern and could be used for other than drinking and cooking needs. I do not recall ever pumping a pail of water from this cistern.

The kitchen also had a wash basin and an adjacent pail for water. The same dipper used to drink from was used to ladle water to the wash basin and for cooking needs. Throw away water and other kitchen refuse went into what we indelicately called the "slop pail." The pail was carried outside and emptied periodically. As noted, my grandparent's kitchen also had a social area where my grandfather and I read the papers and discussed events. The only picture I recall hanging in either kitchen was a neatly framed one of President Franklin Roosevelt in my grandparent's kitchen. There was a silver dollar sized patch on their kitchen door leading to the porch. This marked the spot where one of their two sons accidentally fired a shotgun blast through the door. During hours of darkness a standard kerosene lamp hanging from a fixture on the wall lighted the kitchen with pale yellow illumination. To think that people today pay a premium to dine under this type of soft lighting. The kitchen was the normal entrance and exit to and from the outside. Thus there was a need for a clothes rack in the kitchen to hang all those heavy winter coats and caps, plus a place for boots, gloves, etc.

The living/dining room was where the family gathered when too cold to use the porch or outside areas. In Wisconsin, that covered most of October through mid-May at a minimum. Today it would be called the family room. Here the family played various games, read, studied, conversed, etc. Unlike the kitchen with its kerosene lamp, an oil fired Aladdin lamp provided white light for this room.

I suspect each house had an attic for storage. If ever a home could have used attic storage space, ours was the one. Yet the attic was next to worthless for doing anything but drying out ears of popcorn. To access the attic, one had to straddle the width of the stairs leading to the second story along a three-inch wide board on each side to reach a small platform landing. At best, a tricky process since there was nothing but open space straight down as you moved, spread eagle wise, along those narrow strips of board. Once at that small platform landing you could kneel to open the relatively small lift out door to gain access to the attic.

Our home had four bedrooms with two on the second floor. One large upstairs bedroom accommodated all my sisters. One bedroom, off the dining room/living room was often the family's sick room. With ten children and the uncontrolled childhood diseases at the time, this was a busy room in our house, especially in the wintertime. Bedrooms were for sleeping or to recover from an illness. I don't ever recall "hanging out" in my bedroom, or napping there.

Many of the homes had parlors. Ours did not, but my grandmother Hedricks did, and she governed it like many a woman of her time. The parlor was a showroom to be viewed from the threshold, and to be occupied only during deathwatches, courtship, and piano lessons (Christmas, well, maybe). Parlors as a rule were the only room where you might find a carpet. As a result, most of us grew up with linoleum or wood floors. Many a married man, supposedly head of the household, did not have the opportunity to enter the parlor until he died. Grandmother Hedrick's parlor was definitely off-limits. I am not sure under what circumstances she might have opened the parlor up. It was not opened for Christmas while I was an observer, but then her big dining/living room met her empty nest needs in those years. Luckily no funerals occurred while I was growing up. Although two of her daughters married while I was on the scene, I don't recall her parlor playing a roll in either the courtship or marriages. I'll bet it did not! Since both weddings took place in pleasant weather the porch and/or outside lawn areas were most likely used. Then again, I did not hang around the wedding scenes any longer than I had to. I was best man at my Aunt Tilla's wedding, but I broke away as soon as I could to go squirrel hunting. For all I know they may have partied long and hard in the parlor. Despite all the time I spent in my grandmother's house, and the warmth of our relationship, I seem to recall only a brief glimpse into her parlor at one point when the door was left slightly ajar. But what did I care about a parlor; my grandmother's kitchen was what I was most interested in.

Mention was made of the kitchen stove having to heat the kitchen during cold weather. For the other living area downstairs, we relied on the previously mentioned reliable Round Oak heater. We used two of this type heater in our house. Only one heater was needed in my grand-parents' house since the parlor was not used. These stoves as a rule sat about two feet from an inside wall. The stove had absolutely no guards to prevent accidentally touching the hot surface and suffering painful burns. At times the stove glowed cherry red. Despite the presence of children ranging from toddlers to rambunctious teen-agers I do not re-call any serious burns suffered by anyone in our large family. The two-foot wide area between the stove and the wall was in wintertime the "sweet spot." The floor was usually "toasty" warm, plus the wall-radi-ated heat so the entire body was warmed while lying on the floor. This was a great place to nap.

These stoves were quite efficient and yet if you moved to the perim-eter of a room, particularly an outer wall, you could be uncomfortable.

The homes at that time were not insulated. Our house was wide open to the northwest from whence came the cold winter winds. How helpful a grove of trees would have been, like the grove shielding the buildings on the home farm. To reduce to some extent the cold air from getting into the house, we first wrapped a three or four foot wide strip of tarpaper around most of the house. After tacking the tarpaper in place we stacked horse manure mixed with straw up to the top of the paper. Horse manure provided insulation against the cold and was odor free.

As a result of the cold weather, we also had to share our house with a certain number of rats and mice. The mice could be little thieves since they invaded the pantry through small cracks here and there. As a result, we were forever trapping them. The rats were more an annoyance as they clambered up the inside space between the plastered walls and the outer boards of the house. Both the mice and rats liked the ears of popcorn they found in the attic.

Look to heavy blankets to keep warm if you slept in an upstairs bedroom. My routine was to undress quickly in my upstairs bedroom and shiver my way to warmth under a ton of blankets. One of the old stand-by blankets in our home was a horse blanket. The blanket was so heavy I had to wonder if they took the horse out. Since my bedroom was on the northwest side of the house, the coldest room in the house, I used the horse blanket. When called in the morning I picked up my clothes and rushed downstairs to join Dad at the Round Oak stove that was just starting to heat up. We stood there in our long johns, close to the stove, turning slowly until all parts of our body were relatively warm. Then we slowly dressed for morning barn chores. The rest of the family awakened later to a relatively well heated house.

The stove required frequent stoking, particularly during cold spells. Unlike the kitchen range's need for finely split wood, the Round Oak accepted a large volume of chunks or blocks of wood. To ensure a decent nights sleep, Dad stoked the stove to its limit at bedtime (eight to nine p.m.), then set the damper to reduce the oxygen supply so the wood did not burn too fast. A red-hot coal bed was absolutely necessary in the morning to ensure the wood tossed in quickly ignited. As was noted earlier, there was plenty of woodland to produce all the wood we needed; all that was required was the labor to harvest it.

With wood burning stoves there was always the danger of fire, particularly chimney fires. Depending on the type of wood burned, a certain amount of combustible material attached itself to the chimney flues. Now if the heat escaping up the chimney grew too hot, a fire could erupt in the chimney, or material stored next to the chimney could ignite. How to prevent this from occurring? Be careful setting the stove damper, by burning hard wood, and by keeping combustibles away from where the chimney went through the up stairs rooms and attic. Safety could be enhanced too by cleaning the chimney flues at least once each year

We had no indoor bathrooms during my days on the farm. The kitchen wash basin was where we all washed our hands and face, brushed teeth, and where the men shaved. This small area met most of the functional needs now met by the modern bathroom. The kitchen was logically the place for our large family to cycle through a galvanized metal wash tub for the weekly bath, usually on a Saturday evening. The absence of running water meant there was no indoor toilet. For the very young or ill this meant a chamber pot, for the rest, an outdoor privy met our needs—and that could be sheer torture on a cold Wisconsin day.

Then there was the home's underground indispensable cellar—the farm's refrigerator and winter supermarket. Since we had no electricity for refrigeration, we depended on the cellar to store our perishables between meals. A relatively cool fifty degrees was maintained in the heat of summer. This was enough to store butter, milk and other perishables between meals. In the winter, the temperature hovered around sixty degrees even on the coldest days. Rarely could either a winter or summer meal be prepared without a couple of trips "down cellar" for foodstuff. In the summer added trips were required to first retrieve perishables (especially butter) for the meal, then return them after the meal.

The major role for the cellar was to store food for the winter season needs. During the mid and late summer growing season our garden produced not only enough food to satisfy the daily needs for a family of twelve, but enough to preserve (can) all that was needed for the winter months. Bushels of tomatoes found their way into sealed jars with another product being tomato catsup. Peas, beans, carrots, asparagus, rutabaga, onions, cabbage, horseradish, lettuce, radishes, squash, cucumbers—you name it and we grew and preserved it. Raspberries and blackberries grew abundantly in the woodland area and the home canned variety was one of my favorite winter desserts. Field corn, at a certain point in its development was edible, and added zest to our meals. Peaches and apricots were purchased by the bushel for canning. Apples: I think we had at least thirty apple trees of at least six different varieties on our two farms, plus a few more growing separately in the wood and pasture land. In addition to canning, a large number of apples were stored whole in barrels and bins in the cellar. I remember many a winter evening when Dad took a lamp from the kitchen or lit a lantern for a trip to the cellar where he selected a couple of apples to eat. Potatoes may have been particularly prized since we were of immigrant stock and all remembered the stories of the great potato famines that on occasion swept across Europe—as occurred in Ireland in 1845-47 when about 750,000 died. We also had a cherry tree, but it was a sporadic producer. A few farms had arbors of grapes, and how I envied them. Beef, pork, and chicken also made their way into cellar shelves via the canning process. Despite this cornucopia of foodstuffs finding their way into the cellar, the idea of canned baby chicks that sister Dorothy and I tried to introduce never did catch on.

The fall of the year was particularly rewarding as relates to the final collection of food for the fast approaching winter months ahead. We went with horses and the box wagon to the fields for loads of potatoes, cabbages, and a smaller supply of pumpkins. The potatoes and pumpkins ended up in large bins in the cellar. Much of the cabbage ended up as sauerkraut in large twenty-five gallon earthen crock jars. Potatoes were loose in a bin and amounted to many bushels. Add to all that the barrels of apples and row upon row of canned preserves and you had a virtual supermarket in the cellar.

You can perhaps imagine what a joy to walk down the steps into the cellar in the late fall. First of all there was the delightful aroma of the mix of fresh apples, cabbage, potatoes, pumpkins, onions, etc. Then there was the color. On shelves sat row after row of canned fruits and vegetables radiating green, red, brown, yellow and a number of variations of colors in between. No doubt more important, particularly to our parents, was the comfortable feeling of security and pride in knowing the family would be well fed in the months ahead. I still feel content when we return from a week's worth of grocery shopping knowing we have food in the house. Imagine the feeling when you look at your cellar shelves and see enough food to last throughout the late fall, the long winter, and early spring seasons; and realize that you grew, harvested, and preserved all you see.

Although separate from the house proper, three other buildings were closely related and need mentioning. The first was the milk house. On the home farm this was truly a milk house where the cream was separated from the milk. As mentioned earlier, this was also where we mixed ground feed with skim milk that was then carried to the pig stable. On one wall tools, especially carpentry tools were hung. This was also the clothes laundering room, and where my grandfather dressed out the pigs and beef into various cuts of meat in conjunction with the butchering process. It seemed to me he thoroughly enjoyed this task, perhaps in part because at his age this was one job he could do, and he knew he did it extremely well. There was a small stove that heated the milk house, which meant it could also be a friendly "social" place in the wintertime. Dad, Aunt Lena and I finished evening chores with our respective "tidying up" duties in the milk house. Dad and I still had the one-fifth mile to hike home and on cold winter nights that warm building was hard to leave. As a result, the three of us chatted a while before going our separate way. Many a winter afternoon I cracked and ate the rich meat from hickory and butternuts in this friendly little oasis. At our home, the milk house was used primarily for the clothes washing process, and to a limited extent, for tools. Associated with the milk house, indeed, as an adjunct thereto, was the well. In my day we were able to tap water located in layers of limestone at approximately the 200-foot level. Over the well was a windmill that ideally kept the cistern and water tanks filled at no charge for power. As a back up there was that oft-mentioned one-cylinder Johnson and Johnson engine.

Another building was the outside toilet—and it had many names other than toilet. Examples were privy, the john, the can, and outhouse. Other terms could not be used in polite society. The term "house of easement" as used by English aristocrats at one time never did catch on with the folks on Summit Ridge. Although many of these outside toilets were of solid construction, I don't think we had any made of brick. Watch out on Halloween! For sure some of the outhouses would be tipped over as part of the hi-jinks surrounding that event.

The last building was the woodshed where firewood could be protected from the weather. We had a large woodshed conveniently located next to the house, and on level ground at our home. There was no wood shed on the home farm. That's how I earned my keep—digging wood out of the snow and lugging it up a steep incline to the house. Should the reader wonder, I was never taken to the woodshed for disciplinary purposes.

Despite a few shortcomings, our old house served us well. Electricity came our way in 1945 and running water and indoor plumbing in 1947. Over the years the house has been expanded and modernized, to include an addition to the second story. Despite this addition, the house still generally reflects the same structural external appearance—except the exterior is now painted a dazzling white. A two-car garage is now attached to the house. As noted earlier, a paternal niece, Denise (Hedrick) Mulvaney and her husband Pat are raising their three boys in the old house. The house on the home farm was destroyed by fire, and a ranch type home was built to house Mike and Amy Hedrick and their two girls and two boys.

Hedrick home (2004)

CHAPTER **17**

Rhythm of the Seasons

Introduction

Ask most people who live in the northern climes what they especially like about their area and the answer will probably be of enjoying four distinct seasons. All who live in these areas are keenly aware of the changing seasons, but nowhere is the impact of the changes more profound than on the farm.

Those of us who were lucky enough to grow up on a farm were blessed with the opportunity to see the food we ate develop from seed placed in the warm spring earth. And what an introduction to the world of the "birds and the bees" as we closely observed the procreation of farm livestock. We then watched and waited with eager anticipation for the bounty to follow. First there was fresh produce from the garden in early summer. Soon thereafter, the roosters that had arrived with what at the time of arrival was a unisex batch of baby chicks found their way to the dinner table. Summer was the time too for family picnics, more ice cream than usual, and Koolaid.* I wonder how many gallons of that

---

*I learned later that we on Summit Ridge were not referring to this drink by its right name. Early in my military experience I learned its correct name was "panther piss."

drink we consumed over the summer months? We thrilled as well to the summer time harvesting of hay and grain that was destined to provide feed for the livestock over the long winter months. In the fall, the final spaces in the cellar were filled with potatoes, apples, squash, cabbage, etc. And how about observing the chemical action in those big earthen jars where our home grown cabbage was turned into sauerkraut? This was also the time to harvest the corn crop, then plow the many acres for next year's crops. All along the way we observed the fleshing out of livestock being raised to replenish or add to the inventory—with some to be sacrificed for the family's meat supply and cash income. This was the time too to bring the young heifers home from the remote pastures and introduce them to their winter quarters. These heifers did not see much of humans, nor humans of them over the summer and early fall months. They were on their own during this time with only the need for pasture and water. As a result they had a tendency to operate on the "wild" side. Finally the winter slow-down which permitted us to "sit a spell" after meals and otherwise relax somewhat. Unfortunately, for me this also meant a certain amount of time working in the woods, a job I thoroughly detested.

Spring

In the early spring, as we walked the mile and one-quarter home from school, there came that day when we heard an unusual sound; here a gurgle, there a low roar. The thick carpet of winter snow was melting with water moving towards the valleys. Since most of the ground sloped markedly on Summit Ridge there was an added degree of velocity to the runoff. Then too, the ground was still frozen solid in the early stages of thawing so all melted snow was free to travel. Day by day the volume and roar of the water increased, particularly so behind the barn on the home farm. Here a deep gully lined with rocks provided a spillway for melting snow from surrounding fields. At one point, the water cascaded over a particularly steep section with what to us kids was a Niagara Falls like roar. A little frightening, and yet a joyful sound—proof positive that spring was on the way.

Along with the arrival of spring came the animal-birthing season. Most important was calving. The timing was important since a cow logically produces her maximum amount of milk in the months immediately following the birth of her calf. She will then be in top form as a milk producer when turned out on grass pasture. Arriving in the barn on those early spring mornings we were often greeted by newborn calves. Unfortunately there wasn't room in the barn for birthing pens. The cow's natural motherly instinct to nuzzle and lick dry her calf was more often than not frustrated by her being secured in a stanchion. Still, on occasion the newborn found the strength to move between mom and a neighboring cow to reach the manger where mom could do her natural duty. These same energetic youngsters probably stopped for their first meal outside the womb along the way. More often than not the calves were in the gutter. We lifted and guided them to their mother's teat for presumably their first post-birth meal. We looked forward to seeing these little guys when we came to the barn in the morning. On occasion I witnessed the birthing process during the day. Initially this was an astonishing sight to my then young eyes.

No doubt a joy for the farmer to see the calf as well, but was it male or female? If male it nursed for a few weeks and then was sold for around ten dollars as veal. In this case all the farmer really had of worth was a "freshened" cow. What the farmer really wanted, in addition to the freshened cow, was a female calf. Here was a future milk producer who could replace older animals in the herd. The older animals in turn commanded a fair price. In some cases they were still young enough to be productive milk producers. Buyers constantly roamed the countryside to buy up this type animal for shipment overseas.* Dad was especially effective at haggling with the buyers over price. For those animals

---

*While we humans were confined for the most part to the geographic limits of Summit Ridge, some of our cows were traveling the world.

no longer valued as milk producers, we received a fair dollar amount by selling them for slaughter.

What joy, what reckless abandon, what exuberance the cows exhibited on that magical day when they were turned loose on green grass. Even the oldest of the animals all but leapt in the air with joy. This "freedom to roam" came after being confined to a barn from mid-October to mid-May. True, on most days, weather permitting in the wintertime they were turned out into a small barnyard for an hour or two. Otherwise they were held in place by a stanchion in the barn. Then too, the menu during this time may not have been all that great; cured hay, fermented corn silage and ground feed. No way could that compare with eating lush green grass while roaming at leisure through the pastureland. Initially, even the fresh green grass was passed up as they gloried in the "open range" by romping like children.

Although the horses and sheep on our farm were also kept indoors during the winter months, the cows were the only animals that demonstrated this degree of exuberance that made them look foolish to me. For that matter, I don't remember the young stock (future milk animals), who had been out on pasture the previous year, acting with the same enthusiasm. It had to be a remembered joy of the "old times" triggered when that barnyard gate opened for the first time on a warm spring day in May.

Cows are comfortable animals to be around. They are not nearly as friendly as a dog or cat, or as approachable in the open as are horses—but still domesticated. As with most animals that move in groups, one of their members is a permanent leader. My two youngest brothers, Ronald and Paul put this behavior to a test one day. They forced the leader aside and held her back while the cows were moving as a group down the road from pasture to barn. Another cow moved into the lead and maintained this leadership position. When they permitted the isolated leader to rejoin the herd she moved slowly but surely through the herd to resume her leadership position. No bumping, no shoving, but convincingly done.

Now and then a cow gave birth to her calf while on summer pasture. Usually she found a secluded spot on the forty acres of woodland pasture. I first had to locate her, then carry the still wobbly-legged calf back to the barn. The cow exhibited no concern when I picked up her calf and cradled it in my arms—but she followed close enough behind to keep nuzzling her newborn. You really had to appreciate motherhood at a time like this. Despite this apparent universal lack of concern relative to humans handling her newborn calf there has been at least one exception. A news item out of Norway, Iowa dated 5 May 2002 has as its headline, *Cow Fatally Mauls Man*. Apparently Bruce Schulte, age fifty, was trying to rescue a newborn calf stuck in the mud. One assumes the calf vocally indicated discomfort, which prompted the mother to react as she did. A veterinarian, quoted in the story, stated that a cow can be protective but it's unusual to turn on a farmer. I am glad there was no known occurrence like this lurking in the back of my mind as I carried calves home from the woods. What if the calf were to suffer some discomfort from being lifted or cradled, and communicated that discomfort to its attentive mother? I think I'd be leery of repeating that process today based on what happened in Norway, Iowa. This was a "mad cow" case if ever there was one.

When chickens were given their first opportunity to venture outdoors, after four to five months of winter confinement, they seemed not quite sure what to do. A few ventured out—then more—and finally the entire flock became excited. Why not, what with insects to devour along with blades of grass. The chickens now pretty much found all the feed they needed on their own. Egg production went way up—and those humans with discriminating taste buds swore that eggs and foodstuff made from eggs tasted better due to richer and better textured yokes. The same discriminating taste buds also swore to the added tastiness of fried chicken.

The hens returned to the safety of the chicken coop at night—and we ensured the doors were closed after dark to protect the flock. Most of the chickens continued laying their eggs in boxes provided for that purpose in the coop. Others could not be counted on to be that disciplined. The farm provided any number of places for them to hide their eggs.. We stumbled on these nests from time to time and now the question; are the eggs spoiled or not? The test was to put them in a pail of water. If they floated they might be okay, but were not sold and were opened delicately by the cook. The egg sinking was proof positive that the egg was rotten. I usually threw these eggs against the barn, a tree, or other objects. The sulfur smell was horrible!

On occasion a practical use was found for a rotten egg. As dogs went through their mischievous and "constantly hungry" puppy stage they might develop a taste for eggs. Since the chicken coop was open during the day, the eggs were there for the taking. The pups didn't realize that you don't mess with the farm's egg production without incurring the wrath of the farmer's wife. I can still see Dad holding the pup's mouth open while he popped in a rotten egg. The rotten egg treatment did not work on this occasion. The pup was caught a few hours later devouring eggs in the chicken coop. No doubt the answer in this case was to keep the dog tied up for a time.

Along with the newborn calves we welcomed baby lambs on our farm. How entertaining these lambs could be, much more so than the calves. The sheep were not monitored as closely as the cows, plus the approximate twenty ewes were kept in a common pen. As a result, the lambs might be a couple days old before we noticed them. Twin lambs were common, so over the birthing season approximately thirty lambs might be added to the inventory. The lambs were "frisky" from the start and forever energetically bounding about. They seemed to enjoy jumping straight up into the air or chasing each other around. Another activity was jumping up and standing on mom's back. Only their mom allowed this latter activity.

Those little lambs were indeed cute, but there was a distinct downside to their birthing for me. The ewe carried her lamb(s) for approximately five months. We did not maintain a male (buck) so it was necessary to borrow the animal from another farmer. That farmer for several years was Ernie Brandau, who lived about seven miles from our farm—all seven of those miles across an open wind-swept ridge. Sometime in late November or early December Dad and I would set off, after evening chores, in the old model "A" truck to pick up the buck. The buck was placed in a pen sitting loose in the truck bed. I was assigned the duty of riding in back to ensure the pen didn't tip or unduly move about as we rounded corners or as the animal moved. It was invariably a cold, indeed a miserably cold trip. Our top speed was approximately twenty miles per hour. We slowed to five to ten miles per hour on the five ninety-degree turns on the route to ensure the pen did not tip over, and just a bit over that speed on other curves. A few weeks later we repeated the process when the buck was returned to the Brandau farm.

About this time we also welcomed approximately 100 baby chicks into the farm family. Most of these chicks arrived by mail, 100 to a box. Four compartments separated them into twenty-five each. There they could keep each other warm during transit and yet not crowd each other to the point where some might suffocate. The farmer watched closely for the mailman when he knew the "chicks were in the mail." Some farmers used incubators to hatch chicks using fertilized eggs produced on the farm. Since there was no electricity, kerosene heaters were used in the process. These heaters were temperamental so it took conscientious watchfulness over the three-week incubation period to keep the eggs at the right temperature. My Hedrick grandparents had this type egg hatchery. I remember only one time that they used it while I was an observer. The incubator was kept in the house near a stove. I seem to recall too that the number of chicks hatched was disappointing.

The chicks may have kept each other warm by being tightly packed in a box but they could not eat or drink under those conditions. Newborn chicks have a reserve of body fat permitting them to live without food or water for whatever number of days were involved in the shipping process. When turned loose they scurried off in all directions, each on his own.

With no more mutual body warmth they needed a warm shelter kept at around eighty degrees. We called this shelter the "brooder coop."

The process of nursing baby chicks far enough along in life to where they no longer needed artificial heat was a worrisome undertaking. The chicks succumbed quickly if the temperature dropped below a certain point. In part this was due to suffocation as they crowded together. Cold spells in the springtime after all were not unusual. Here again a temperamental kerosene heater was employed. This meant frequent checking of the brooder coop day and night until the combination of warmer weather and developing feathers permitted a degree of relaxation.

Watching a hundred baby chicks scurrying about in the brooder house was most entertaining. At one point or another during the first few days, when the chicks were at their cutest, all the family had an opportunity to see the show. There was all this scurrying about, accompanied by soft chirping as they went about their business of eating, drinking, and socializing. We all thoroughly enjoyed watching the show.

The sex of chickens was important too. We were looking for future egg layers. Not until the combs came out could the males be identified. No problem. At this point the farm's entire crop of chickens were living largely off the land, and thanks to the "Saturday afternoon massacres," most farmers wives ensured that few if any males (roosters) made it to the chicken coop to eat winter feed.

Then we had to contend with the "lone rangers." When the chickens were turned out in the spring we could count on at least one or two hens in which the nesting instinct was strong. These had mated along the way and were now laying fertilized eggs. These hens usually found an out of the way place to lay their eggs, then proceeded to hatch them. At some point the hen showed up with ten or more baby chicks in tow, seemingly proud as punch. They were made most welcome.

As noted earlier, chickens, and the income from eggs was usually within the province of the farmer's wife. In our home, Mother certainly was the ever so conscientious "mother hen" in this process.

Eagerly welcomed also were the baby pigs. Cute as could be in their early days as well. Their life span was destined to be short, except for those few kept as brood sows. By early winter of that same year they were either on their way to market or had been butchered by the farmer. In the meantime they lived, let's say, "high off the hog." As noted, in my day we initially skimmed the cream off the milk and sent the cream to market. The skim milk was surplus and was fed to the pigs who loved it. Timing is everything. Cows produce at their maximum in the late spring and early summer, so all that skim milk is conveniently available at the critical time needed for the hogs to maximize their growth rate. Meat from pigs fed on skim milk was considered much tastier than from those fed only ground feed. Unlike cattle and chickens, the farmer was looking and hoping for male pigs. Most were slaughtered after six months and the castrated males grew the fastest and thus produced more meat when butchered, or brought more dollars when shipped to market.

To round out the birthing process, we could also count on new kittens showing up, and from time to time, a litter of pups. On rarer occasions a colt joined the newborn on the farm. Some farmers kept geese, ducks and goats and they too did their part in producing young in the springtime. Apart from the domestic animals and fowls, even the casual observer could not but notice and enjoy the proliferation of new life amongst the animals and birds in the wild.

Perhaps more mundane than the birthing process, but equally welcome was the "greening" of the countryside, to include those most welcome spring flowers. There was also the need to plant seed in the ground. The greening happened naturally, but seeding was a carefully choreographed process. The farmer couldn't look at the calendar and say, "Ah, it's April tenth, time to plant the oats." He observed the weather pattern carefully as well as the condition of the ground. Perhaps too it might be wise to keep an eye on what the neighbors were doing.

First though there was the need to pick stones. How we hated this chore. As many family members as possible went to the fields with a team of horses and the "box wagon."* Even today (2005), these fist-sized rocks continue to find their way to the surface as a result of the year's frost upheaval. In winter, the frost level on Summit Ridge goes down to about six feet. The upward pressure exerted during the spring thaw serves to move the rocks up through the soil. The next job, if it had not been done in the fall, was to spread lime on the tillable land being rotated from raising hay to corn. A spreader was attached to the back of the box wagon. The lime, spread at the rate of three ton to the acre neutralized the pH in the soil.

As noted earlier, the individual farms at the time were relatively small, eighty to one hundred acres. Some of this land was wooded, or otherwise devoted to summer pasture. That left "X" number of tillable acres for planting. Now came the necessary arithmetic calculations. An acre of tillable land will produce a certain volume of crops, which equates to animal feed. Take this a step further and you can see where the number of farm animals that could be supported was dependent on the crops that could be reasonably expected from the acres involved. Thus a farm of ninety tillable acres could support a few more animals than one of sixty acres, etc. The farmer with twenty-four milk cows made more money than he could with twenty, etc. It also follows that he had to work harder.

Now back to the spring plantings. First of all the ground had to be prepared. As a rule, the fields on which the current year's corn and grain crop was to be planted had been plowed the previous fall. Next, the soil had to be loosened so that the newly planted seed had a soft bed in which it could easily germinate and take root. This was a time-consuming and boring chore going over those tillable acres with a ten-foot wide spring harrow. I remember it being horse drawn, but by the time I became involved as a laborer we used a tractor. The oats, wheat and barley seed was usually that which the farmer had set aside in his granary from the

---

*A device called a "reach" permitted the same set of wheels (metal wheels in my day) and sled runners to accept cargo carriers of different lengths and configuration. The reach was a "full" dimensional two by four made of sturdy oak with the length adjusted with a series of holes and a pin.

previous year's harvest. A necessary first step was to sift the grain kernels through a hand-cranked device whose large fan served to blow off the chaff, the weed seeds, and any light grain kernels so that only fat and healthy kernels were left to be planted in the ground. From time to time Dad added some sort of foul smelling chemical in powder form that thoroughly irritated the lungs. (Today that chemical is expressly forbidden to be used in the manner we used it then.) Not a pleasant chore, and usually done after evening chores—by lantern light if necessary. Initially we used our own corn for seed, but early in my experience we purchased hybrid seed corn. Finally there was hay (legume) seed. In some years clover seed was hulled (same process as threshing) in the fall of the year. The usual routine though was to purchase legume seed.

Now the planting; a great deal more interesting given that seeds were actually going into the soil, yet equally time consuming. Initially, for grain and hay seed planting, we used a horse drawn box seeder. This seeder, and later its replacement the grain drill, was about ten feet wide. The grain was placed in the larger of two boxes and gears dropped a measured number of seeds as the seeder or drill moved along in the field. If the farmer's plan called for this field to be harvested for hay the next year, he placed hayseed in the smaller box to be similarly dropped to the ground. The grain was the "nurse crop" for the hayseed since the grain sprouted quicker, grew faster, and kept out the weeds. With the box seeder there was the need to cover the seed since it had been dropped on top of the ground. Some seeders had small chains attached that covered the seed and smoothed the ground as they were dragged along behind the seeder. On our farm we used a device called a "drag." This served to protect the seed from birds and gave the seed a better chance to germinate. The drag was about fifteen feet wide and relatively light for a team of horses to pull. It consisted basically of four or five pieces of wood, probably two by fours set about a foot apart at right angles to the direction of movement. Four to five inch metal spikes protruded through the wood. These rows of spikes were arranged, row by row, so that their protrusion covered all the seed with soil. At one time we used a Ford model "A" truck (converted from a two door sedan) to pull the drag. This was considerably faster than using horses, more fun, and no need for a Wisconsin driver's license.

Eventually a "drill" replaced the box seeder. Now the seeds were literally drilled into the ground. Now no need for the follow-on dragging action, but we still did so to make doubly sure the seeds were covered with soil. At some point a tractor replaced the truck in pulling the drag. This permitted us to extend the width of the drag to approximately twenty feet. After the sowing of grain and legumes came corn planting—usually in the middle or end of May. In our inventory of farm equipment was a hand-operated corn planter. A rather ingenious hinged device that measured out a couple seeds at a time in conjunction with insertion in the first couple inches of soil. I did not use it—nor did I observe it being used. It might have had some applicability for planting sweet corn in a small garden. My recollection is of the old horse drawn two-row planter. The corn was placed in two cylindrical cans, one for each row. Each held approximately three gallons of seed corn. Measuring gears ensured that only two to three seed kernels went into a given hill and that each hill was a pre-determined distance apart.

Of all the crops that Dad closely monitored, he seemed to show the most interest, if not reverence for the corn crop. I recall our visiting a newly planted cornfield after chores one evening. He knelt in the field and carefully pushed away the top half-inch of soil. There it was, a curled up yellowish green blade that told him the seed had germinated. I still recall this episode as a near religious event. If garden space was at a premium, we might plant pumpkin seeds in the same row as the corn. This was done by hand since only a few plantings produced an abundance of pumpkins. These plantings were usually placed in an obscure corner of a field, or in a short row of corn as was sometimes dictated by the lay of the land.

Concurrent with planting field crops was that of the farm garden. Like the nurturing of the baby chicks, this was usually the sole province of the farmer's wife, to include close to totally her labor. She asked only that the ground be plowed and harrowed; and that she have first call on the farm's best fertilizer (chicken manure). Here then, in the richest soil on the farm, using a taut string to ensure straight rows went the seeds or plants that in time led to lettuce, tomatoes, carrots, squash, cabbage, radishes, and cucumbers. Also beans, peas, strawberries, onions, and maybe watermelon. Also, asparagus and rhubarb sometimes grew in the garden, but these did not need to be planted year by year. Again, as in the case of crops to support the farm animals, the size of the garden was based on the number of mouths to feed. Not only did the produce result in tasty and nourishing meals early in the summer through early fall, but also via the canning process, a cornucopia of produce was preserved for late fall and the winter ahead.

The amount of potatoes required for the family dictated the need for much more ground than could be supported by the garden. The potato crop was usually planted in long rows next to the corn. Another crop normally rating its own separate field was popcorn. As a rule this was a small plot here or there that could not otherwise be efficiently farmed with machinery. Other edible crops prospered naturally on their own. Apples, cherries, blackberries, raspberries, hickory nuts, butter nuts etc., were all available with little effort or expense required by the farmer. With the exception of apples and cherries, the remainder grew wild in the wood and pastureland of the farm.

Another major chore in the spring was repairing fence that had deteriorated over the years, or had been damaged by the past winter's heavy snow or frost upheaval action. This was the number one project on those days in early spring when too wet to work in the field. By this time the frost had left the ground and the soil was moist for a couple of feet from the absorbed snowmelt and spring rains. Off we went with the truck or horses and box wagon, loaded down with farm produced wooden fence posts along with barbed wire, hammer, staples, fence stretcher, post mall, and posthole digger. The term posthole digger was a misnomer since all it did was open a hole in the ground with its beveled end. That was enough of an opening since the six-foot wooden post had been sharpened so its tapered end fit tightly in the hole. This resulted in the pole standing straight while the farmer hit it as often as necessary with an eight pound post mall to drive the post to a sufficient depth into the ground to where it locked in as solid as a rock. Then came the easier part of stretching the barbed wire and securing it to the posts with staples. When necessary to work in woodland or on steep hills, we could not reach the fence line with the truck or horse-drawn wagon. That meant carrying all the tools of the trade to the site. Either way the results were often pretty enough to where we stood back for a bit when finished and admired our completed work.

The first priority was the "line fence" separating one farm from an-other. In our case, our two farms bordered the land of six neighboring farms. The saying that "good fences make good neighbors" was especially important to farmers. No one wanted a neighbor's livestock to wander onto his property to eat or otherwise trample crops. A given farmer's re-sponsibility for his share of the line fence was determined in this fash-ion. At some point in time, maybe a hundred years ago or more, the two landowners met, face to face, at the exact mid-point of their common line fence. Each then faced right and his responsibility for installing and maintaining the fence was that portion from where he was now facing to the end of their common adjacent land. This was not necessarily as fair as it sounds. For example, we Hedricks had a comparatively open and level section as compared to the Dittmans. Their one-half quickly dropped off to rather steep woodland. On the other hand, there wasn't all that much to tempt livestock in woodland or on steep hills so only one or two strands of barbed wire was adequate. Many times trees could be substituted for the fence posts. On the other hand, tempting fields of hay, oats and corn required at minimum three strands of taut wire on fence posts, ideally standing straight as soldiers. Farmers also had their own internal fenc-ing needs wherever they fenced livestock off from their own croplands. Want some trouble Mr. Farmer? Fail to maintain the fence around your wife's garden with the result that livestock find an opening and eat and/or trample the garden crops.

In conjunction with spring planting, Father Mechler resurrected the prayers he had suspended after all the crops were gathered the previous fall. This was the so familiar—one size fits all—Catholic triad of prayers, the Our Father (Lord's prayer), Hail Mary, and Glory Be to the Father— introduced by the phrase "For favorable weather and good crops." This prayer was said after the Mass and Benediction, and was added to the other prayers that were offered for special intentions as he knelt at the foot of the altar. At times it could be raining on the farmer's new mown hay as the prayers were being spoken, leaving the farmer to wonder if his prayers were being heard. Worse yet, assume the farmer cut hay Saturday with plans to haul it in Monday. Normally the hay was hauled in the day following it being cut but no farmer was going to work on the Lord's day. You can bet your life the farmer kept a wary eye on his neighbor parishioners to make sure they didn't cheat. Sunday as it turned out was a beautiful day for making hay. Sunday night it rains. Damn!

Although Father Mechler's prayer was rather specific—for favorable weather and good crops—the farm family was likely to ask for more than that. Much like the legislation processes in Congress a certain amount of amendments were attached—in this case, silently attached. For example:

> Please Lord, don't let that brooder coop heater fail to keep the baby chicks warm, and watch that unisex mix of chicks. Please let the great majority of the chicks be pullets (female). And could you keep an eye on my sows so they don't crush their offspring as they lower their ponderous bodies to rest and/ or nurse. And Lord, in addition to hale and healthy calves, it certainly would be appreciated if the great majority of those calves were female. After all, future milk producers are much more valuable than the males. The males might bring ten to fifteen dollars as veal after I go to the expense of nurturing them for a month with their mother's milk. I'd really rather harvest the milk for sale to the creamery. Further Lord; don't interpret that favorable weather and good crops too narrowly.

It's possible that a grasshopper or armyworm infestation could come along and wipe out the good crops the favorable weather produced. And Lord, do watch that hail; you know what hail can do to tender leaves and the process of photosynthesis. And don't forget Lord, we are farmers, and our ability to support your church in large part depends on at least a favorable bow in the direction of my foregoing requests.

I had my own special intention. "Please Lord, don't let me end up a long way from the farm buildings during a thunder and lightning storm." These storms began in the early spring and made all too many afternoon visits through early fall while we were engaged in fieldwork. I don't know if others were braver than I was, but for me those storms were frightening.

Also part of the spring scene was our rural school's end of the academic year picnic, and the church's Lent and follow-on Easter Sunday ceremony. As noted earlier, we Mass servers could look forward to a sack of candy on Easter Sunday from Father Mechler.

With that we all settled back in eager anticipation of a bountiful year and were reasonably sure all our prayers for these special intentions would be answered. In the meantime, the cows are giving more milk which means larger milk checks; and the chickens are laying more eggs that will result in less cash needed for groceries and clothing.

Summer

Summer and the living is easy. These were the words to a popular song, but summer was hard work for the farmer. Yet, if the work was hard, this was usually a labor of love for him, not necessarily so for his children.

First of all there was haying. The start of haying served as a clear line of demarcation between spring and summer. Haying involved several weeks in June and nearly all the month of July. How we hated to miss the Fourth of July celebration in Norwalk. But if there was hay to be made, we were in the fields. Now and then, due to weather conditions we might not be able to harvest hay on the Fourth of July. On those occasions we were able to attend the celebration in Norwalk, therefore we knew what fun we were missing. On our farms we usually harvested around one hundred wagon loads of hay at the usual rate of four to five loads per day. This was a mix of tender clover and alfalfa hay for the cows, and coarser timothy hay for the horses. The more nutritious alfalfa and clover went to the milk producers who were probably also carrying calves. The horses had a much-decreased workload in the wintertime and could subsist satisfactorily on timothy hay. Timothy had the further advantage of producing more hay per acre than other legumes and grew well on poorer soil. In fact, timothy hay was viewed by many as a first cousin to the weed family. The haying process was often interrupted by rain. During these rain delays a variety of miscellaneous chores were waiting to be accomplished. When possible we squeezed in cultivating corn, repairing fences, cutting weeds, or doing other farm related chores.

From the farmer's viewpoint, as relates to haying, the routine ideally flowed in this sequence. Hay was cut (mowed) over the morning hours under a bright sun. The drying process, ideally enhanced by a soft breeze, continued throughout the rest of the day and on through the next morning. Late that same morning he raked the hay cut the day before into rows (windrows). He might also break a stem here and there to confirm that the moisture content was just right. That afternoon four or five loads of hay were hauled to the barn, leaving a neat clean field where the hay had lain in windrows that morning. As noted, the hay to be hauled in the following day had been cut that morning, and would be drying under a bright sun and soft breeze.

Why shouldn't the haying process proceed in this fashion? After all, had he not prayed for "favorable weather and good crops" the previous Sunday? Alas, from time to time it rained on the hay before it could be hauled to the barn. This served to lower the nutritional value to some extent, but only marginally if ideal drying weather followed the rain, and this particular cutting was not rained on again. Since the rained on hay was now bunched up in windrows the drying process was slowed. This was especially true of broad-leafed clover hay. Many times we walked down those long windrows manually turning the hay with a fork so it dried faster. If the hay was rained on repeatedly, or did not dry over a couple of days, it turned brown and lost much of its nutritional value. If hay were put in the barn too wet there was a risk of burning down the barn. The wet hay enkindled itself through the process of spontaneous combustion. At a minimum, the hay was likely to mold.

As noted, the haying process began with cutting the hay. I took over this chore from my grandfather at some point. First there was a need to prepare the horses. Ideally they were first brushed (curried) but I usually skipped that part. Then the need to harness the animal. Harnessing a horse is similar to programming a VCR, i.e., complicated. I jest, but there was a step-by-step procedure. First a collar was placed over the neck and latched. At some point the bit and bridle were put in place. Then approximately forty pounds of harness was draped over the horse and buckled here, there, and everywhere. Then I led the horses outside individually and attached those connecting straps that made them a team. Next drive them to the mower where one horse steps over the tongue so they straddled it. Next move up front and attach the neck yoke to each horse, then lift the tongue of the mower and place it in the ring on the neck yoke. Now to the back and hook each horse to its own singletree. The singletree in turn is on a whipple tree (or evener). Finally I was ready to pick up the reins and drive to the field.

I still remember the names of our horses over the years. They were Ruby, Blossom, Topsy, and Topsy's colts King and Lou. Topsy was Dad's favorite, and as a result she was selected to foal the colts. When Topsy died, and the rendering works came to haul her away, Dad turned away and said to me, "I can't look." I worked primarily with Topsy's colts King and Lou. My overall experience with horses left me with a quasi-negative feeling for the animals. I admired them for the necessary work engines they were, and how they hung-in there when on the job. I had to be constantly aware they could kick, and be on guard while working behind them as was necessary when hooking them up for fieldwork or cleaning the barn. One could also be stepped on as you moved around them during the harnessing process, and on occasion they might bite. At the end of the day we led the horses through a series of gates to their nighttime pasture across the road from the farm buildings. These were understandably happy horses at this point. In sheer exuberance they kicked their rear legs high in the air before trotting off to graze. For me that meant moving out of the way fast. Today, where most might admire a beautiful horse, I visualize a can of Alpo dog food.

The mowing process was a slow, boring, and yet a comparatively easy job. The five-foot sickle cut an effective four-foot swath* as one went round and round a given field. On occasion a stone or bunched up hay stopped the cutting action and I had to dismount from the mower to remove the stoppage. There was a lever to disengage the cutting blade from the drive wheel so if the horses started moving I could avoid injury. Rarely did I use it. After cutting for an hour the sweet smell of drying hay was in the air, and what a pleasing smell—especially when mowing clover. The fun part came when I was down to the last few swaths in a given field. At this point the rabbits and other wild life were driven from what had been their sheltered home. Tough on the displaced wildlife, but the hay field had to be cut so I enjoyed the diversion.

As an adjunct to the mowing process was the need to periodically re-sharpen the cutting edges of the approximate twenty individual triangular shaped cutting knives. The combination of slicing through tons of green hay plus repeatedly hitting stones called for re-sharpening; usually three times each week. If a stone broke off a knife it had to be replaced before the mower went back to the field the next day. This involved pounding out two soft metal rivets, replacing the knife, and then pounding the new rivets down to where they held the knife securely. Then there was

---

*Today the tractor driven mower cuts a nine foot swath and at a much faster speed than did the horses.

the process of sharpening all twenty knives. This was usually done after chores in the evening since we didn't want to waste those precious hay making hours on something that could be done during the last light of a summer day. My job was to turn the grind stone. This solid stone was about the size of what is now an emergency tire for many cars. The absence of ball bearings or gears resulted in the need for the application of pure muscle power to keep the wheel moving. Dad guided the individual knives along their running surface in what seemed to take forever.

As the morning wore on, the horses now thirsty, hungry, and tired wanted to head for home. When we arrived at the end of a field closest to the barn, or the road leading to the barn, they tried their best to turn in that direction. It took some effort on the reins to keep them on the job. Although tired, they moved at a brisk pace when we finally did head for home at noon. First there was a long cool drink of water for them, followed by a generous helping of oats and a better grade of hay than they were fed in the winter when their workload was much reduced. For that matter, they were not fed oats in the wintertime at all. The horses remained in harness during their noon break. They would be back at work that afternoon.

My first job in the haying process, long before cutting hay, was driving a team of horses while loading hay in the fields. The horses pulled a hay wagon with a rack approximately twelve feet wide by twenty feet long. A hay loader was attached to the back of the wagon. The hay, cut the day before, had been raked in rows that morning, assuming no rainfall delayed the natural drying of the hay. Driving the team was a piece of cake as one traveled along a given row of hay, one horse on each side of the row and the hay loader following faithfully behind the wagon. Its metal tines picked up the hay and moved it up an incline ramp to be dumped in the back of the wagon. But at the end of a row there was usually a ninety-degree turn. Since the loader was some thirty feet behind the horses, keeping the row between the horses resulted in the loader missing a large chunk of hay on corners. The answer for a seven or eight year old kid was to apply some trigonometric functions and make a judgment call as to how far to drive the horses off the row (straight ahead) and then turn gradually back to the row of hay. If done right, the hay loader tracked the row of hay leaving nothing on the ground. I had better be proficient at this since Dad was known to be intolerant of missed hay on these corners. The hay left behind detracted from the otherwise clean field. This was no more acceptable than a shock of corn being **out of line**. Usually we took time in our next trip to the field to swing by and collect that clump of hay with a pitchfork.

So there we were, proceeding down the field with the hay loader pumping hay to the back of the wagon. Dad positioned himself at the back with a fork to distribute the hay. Initially he built up a six-foot high base in the back half of the wagon. Then came the front part. I stood on one corner of this still clear front of the wagon bed while Dad tossed hay in the other corner. My understanding of the rules was that I was to be alerted when it came time for me to move to that corner just covered with hay. But usually a forkful of hay, loaded with dusty chaff washed over my sweating body. When I turned to give him my ice cold, little boy angry stare, he either failed to see me, or had a mischievous grin on his face. So it went, for Dad spreading hay over that 360 square foot of surface area and me trying to judge when forkfuls might come my way, all the while making sure that hay loader tracked the windrows.

In an earlier footnote, mention was made of a "reach." As noted, this sturdy length of a full two by four-inch oak timber served to connect the same set of wheels or sled runners. Now and then it broke if subjected to twisting action. This could happen as you crossed an otherwise navigable ditch, especially if the ditch ran at an angle to your direction of travel. This twisting force on the reach was exaggerated if on a slope—and this is Summit Ridge after all. This could be avoided if the person driving the horses or tractor was alert, and made sure that first the front, and then the back wheels hit the ditch or depression at the same time. (It was okay to miss a clump of hay under these circumstances.) Imagine how unhappy

Dad was when that reach snapped? Now guess who was blamed?

One afternoon we were routinely loading hay from a field of clover. Scattered fluffy white "cottonball" clouds floated in the sky. Otherwise, it was a sunny and pleasantly warm day. A soft cooling breeze added to the idyllic conditions prevailing at the time. Farmers called this kind of day "perfect haying weather." The pleasant aroma of clover filled the air. Different colored fields of corn, grain, and hay combined to produce a kaleidoscope of colors as the sun ducked in and out of the clouds. An altogether pristine day with the air quality as pure as it could be. Today's most rabid environmentalist would have been ecstatic if there to take it all in. The field was next to the woods with tall trees obscuring the skyline to the southwest. Suddenly low black clouds accompanied by rolling peals of thunder boiled over the woods. Usually Dad kept a wary eye on the horizon for these fast moving surprise afternoon storms. Once spotted, the hay loader was quickly unhitched and we headed for the barn at a trot with whatever hay was then on the wagon. On this occasion the trees blocked his view of the horizon. I couldn't believe Dad would do such a foolhardy thing, but here he was, really angry, and while shaking his fist at the approaching storm he yelled, **"Favorable weather and good crops!"** I thought we were goners. To begin with, as noted earlier, I am scared stiff of lightning and there he was shaking his fist at the gods. As far as I know only Henry VIII had dared to cross swords with the Catholic Church in his quest for a divorce from Katherine of Aragon in 1533, but his quarrel was with the Pope, a fellow human. But here Dad is quarreling with the Deity itself. We survived, but that partial load of hay, along with Dad and I were thoroughly soaked.

When loaded, the wagon full of hay resembled an enlarged jellybean. Now I could lie down on the sweet smelling hay, fifteen feet off the ground, and enjoy the five to fifteen minute ride to the barn, perhaps to even fall asleep. An empty wagon, running as it did on steel wheels, seemed to magnify every bump on the road or in a field. But with a mattress of soft and sweet smelling hay twelve feet thick it felt like I was being rocked in a cradle. The spell was broken when I heard the horse's hoofs hit the wooden barn floor as they pulled the load of hay into the barn. Next we unhitched the horses and led them, one by one out through the narrow opening between the fully loaded wagon and adjacent haymow. Then the horses were hooked up again as a team to do their large part in the process of unloading the wagon.

In the meantime Aunt Lena had pulled the carrier and unloading fork along the steel carrier rail located at the top of the barn. The carrier stopped at the mid-point on the rail that positioned it directly over the wagon. The fork was then pulled down. Next she stuck the fork into the hay in a location where approximately one-fifth of the load at a time was lifted into the storage area, or mow as it was called. For many years the fork used resembled a large staple, with two prongs about four-foot long and with a two-foot space between. A small three or four inch hook on the bottom of each prong was pulled up after embedding the fork in the hay. Dad was up in the mow ready to distribute the hay evenly around the entire area. A haymow on each side of the driveway encompassed four-fifths of the upper barn area. Hay had to be distributed over this wide area by manual labor. Distribution was necessary for two reasons. First, it better ensured that whatever moisture was in the hay safely dissipated. (As noted, a fire could result from a process called spontaneous combustion if the hay was too moist.) The second reason was the hay could then be relatively easily removed in layers from the haymow later in the winter.

When Aunt Lena was ready I was told to move the horses. "Giddy up" was the command to the horses. The whipple tree dragged along the ground for a few feet then literally shot up in the air as the loose rope reached its limit and the large fork full of hay started up to the track rail approximately thirty feet above. When it reached the rail it locked into a device called a carrier that then moved the hay horizontally along the track. Once the hay reached the point where Dad wanted it dropped he yelled "now" and Aunt Lena released the fork full of hay by pulling a trip rope attached to the fork itself that served to disengage the small hooks on the bottom of each prong of the fork blade. At times Dad used a long stick to sway the fork full of hay as it hung at some point on the horizontal track. On command Aunt Lena tripped it at the right moment. It took approximately five such cycles to unload a wagonload of hay.

Aunt Lena was careful not to stand under that forkful of hay, weighing a ton or more, as it moved up to the carrier. A mechanical malfunction, although this was rare, could result in the forkful of hay dropping back to the wagon. Most often this happened when she accidentally tripped the load before it reached the haymow. She was after all moving about on unstable hay and on occasion she accidentally stepped on the trip rope as the load ascended. When this occurred, the load was tripped before reaching the haymow. Less of a problem occurred when the carrier had not locked in at the midpoint on the overhead rail. As soon as the load started up, the carrier took off on its own. As noted, no big problem. Stop the horses; pull the carrier back and ensure it locks in, then "Giddy up" again to the horses.

Physically distributing the hay around in the mow was hard work, and the stifling heat made it worse. As a rule it took about a half-hour to unload, and we processed four or five loads of hay on a given day. The fork sticker had to be careful on the last three cycles to ensure that the fork did not accidentally pick up the hayrack. Not at all a good idea to send the hay rack up to the hay mow. At my end, the moment the forkful of hay started moving horizontally along the track, the rope and whipple tree dropped, again like a rock, and the horses turned around on their own and started back for the next cycle. Exceptions to this routine occurred when the fork full of hay did not travel far enough along the horizontal rail. After the shouted directions from the haymow were relayed to me the horses had to be turned back around. They objected to this break in the routine. Now we had to be careful not to pull the rail mounted carrier with its forkful of hay too far or it lodged against the end of the rail. If this were to happen, and we were lucky, the only damage was a broken rope.

There was yet another opportunity to break the rope on which the entire unloading process depended. After the horses returned to the start position for the next load, thirty to forty feet of rope lay on the ground. When Aunt Lena pulled the carrier and fork back along the rail for the next forkful of hay the rope was drawn back through a pulley. This pulley was firmly anchored at one side of the large entrance doors, and a few feet from where I stood before driving the horses forward. At this point the rope made close to a ninety-degree turn as it passed through the pulley. The carrier and fork alone represented a goodly amount of weight. Now add to that the extra effort needed to pull the rope along through the pulley, and at best the assembly could only be moved in fits and jerks. The fits and jerks were not only due to the weight involved, but the horses at times stepped on the rope in the process of turning around back at the starting point. After the horses had turned around, I dropped the reins and immediately began pulling the rope in—but until then Aunt Lena had to "huff and puff" as she struggled to set up the next cycle. We needed a dedicated "rope puller." This person started pulling the rope in through the pulley as soon as the forkful of hay was tripped and the horses started back. If done smartly, Aunt Lena's effort was reduced by fifty percent, plus the horses did not step on the rope. Eventually younger brother Noel grew into being the official rope puller.

Now back to the possibility of a broken rope. When the rope was pulled back through the pulley, it had to be laid out neatly so the rope didn't bunch up in front of the pulley when the horses started pulling it forward. If snarled, and the horses were not stopped in time, the rope could break. That happened from time to time—and once again, an understandable unhappy farmer up there in the hay mow—and a "scared stiff" kid down below.

In time I graduated from driving horses to loading hay in the field. Since we were using a tractor at this point I had no opportunity to toss forkfuls of hay on my little brothers or sisters. I also graduated in the unloading process from driving the horses to sticking fork, then to distributing the hay in the mow. Hay balers came along a few years after I left the farm. Today hay balers "kick" bales of hay into a following wagon and an elevator moves the bales up to the hay mow.

On those days when too wet to cut or haul in hay I was often allowed to go fishing. Finding earthworms for bait was no problem. As a rule all I had to do was pick up a board or stone and I could pick and choose. Naturally I selected the long and fat worms. The creek on our farm was approximately one-half mile away through the woods and across the railroad tracks. My dog Corky was my constant companion. I started off around nine or ten a.m. and fished the best holes on the Tony Goetz and Clarence Dittman farm along with our own farm stream. This took about four hours. The fish ranged in size from four to eight inches, although now and then I might catch one larger. These were strictly pan fish. One of the highlights of going fishing was treating myself to long, cool drinks from our farm's spring. The water ran under the railroad tracks and where it emerged there was a soft blanket of moss like grass. It would have been easy to fall asleep on this soft mattress, but sleeping wasn't on the agenda what with the joy of fishing. None-the-less, I took the time while lying there on my stomach to drink my fill—then stopped for a spell—then tanked up again and again on this delicious spring water. Corky, who drank downstream from me needed only a few laps before he was off.

Throughout the growing season, as time permitted we cultivated corn. This was not necessarily a must-do chore, but the process eliminated weeds competing for soil nutrients and broke up the soil to permit the ground to better catch and hold water. This produced the same results as when Grandfather Hedrick went out with his hoe. Usually the corn was cultivated at least once during the growing season, ideally twice. As noted, corn cultivation occurred when too wet to cut or haul in hay. At the same time the cornfields had to be dry enough for a horse-drawn or tractor cultivator. With horses we cultivated one row at a time. With the horse-drawn cultivator, I sat in a metal seat close to the ground and riveted my eyes on the shovel blades cutting into the soil. Foot pedals, much like pilots use to control aircraft, permitted the blades to be moved approximately six inches from right to left to avoid digging up hills of corn that deviated from a straight line. These uneven rows occurred when in the process of planting, the horses failed to walk in a perfectly straight line. Rain, etc. could also cause a given hill of corn to be shifted out of line. With a team of horses who knew how to straddle a row of corn, and fixed concentration on the part of the human, you could move the digging blades close to the corn and heap dirt around the stalks to further stifle weed growth. A lever controlled the depth of the blade penetrating the soil. With the tractor-mounted cultivator we could cultivate two rows at a time. But be careful; you had to be absolutely sure you followed the exact two same rows previously planted by the two-row planter. Once oriented to this tactic, a steady eye on a given row of corn ensured that a left or right jog on one row corresponded with the hills of corn in the other row. The digging blades were further apart since no foot pedals were available for making minor deviations. Additionally, there was no team of intelligent horses straddling a row of corn so the tractor operator had to avert his eyes from the rows of corn from time to time. But you could move at a much faster speed with the cutting blades and as a result, throw more dirt around the stalks to stifle weed growth. My problem with the tractor cultivator was not in starting off on the wrong two rows of corn, although that happened, but with wondering off altogether in drowsiness. On those occasions I stopped and did some hurried remedial re-planting by hand.

While all this cultivating and weeding was going on in the cornfields, be assured that weeds had even less of a chance of survival in my mother's and grandmother's gardens. Time was found to ensure that not only were there no weeds, but that soil was kept loose all around the plants on a continuing basis, weeds or no weeds.

Another onerous chore ranking right up there with picking cucumbers was cutting or pulling out "bull" and "Canadian" thistles before they blossomed and spread their seed. These were two of the more prolific weeds that sprung up, usually in patches, in both cultivated fields and pastureland. The Canadian thistle was so insidious as to require the appointment of a "weed commissioner" to ensure farmers kept this weed from spreading. In my day our neighbor Ed Kruk filled this position.

In the meantime we watched and thrilled to the growth of all that had been planted in the fields and garden, along with the growth and development of all the farm animals born in the spring. About this time too we enjoyed fresh produce from the garden to include those ever-delicious strawberries mixed with rich cream. Blackberries and raspberries that grew wild found their way to our table, along with some of the early eating and cooking apples.

But the farmer continued to worry about the weather. Would prayers for "favorable weather and good crops" be answered? Wind was of particular concern, as was the absence of sufficient rainfall at critical times in crop and garden development. Another concern was the infrequent, yet feared infestations of locust (grasshoppers). These insects migrated in swarms. No one knows why. They could destroy or damage growing fields of alfalfa, clover, corn and oats. I recall only one such occurrence. The grasshoppers seemed to move in a cloud from north to south across an east-west road bordering the home farm. Army worms were another threat. Again, I recall only one occasion and these too moved from north to south in a large mass. I am not sure as to the damage either of these pests did. I suppose they may have merely filled their stomach's needs as they passed through without devastating the crops.

Summer was baseball time. The Chicago Cubs were the big league team we avidly cheered for. On occasion a lucky few went to a game at Wrigley Field in Chicago 250 miles away. We who could not conceive of traveling so far to such a significant event saw them as heroes. We all knew of and followed the various star players of that era. How about Chicago Cub's catcher Charles L. (Gabby) Hartnet hitting that home run as evening shadows fell on Wrigley Field in 1945? As a result the Cubs were in that year's World Series. Unfortunately the Detroit Tigers beat them, and this was the last time (to date) that the Cubs won the National league title. Worse still, the last time the Cubs won the World Series was in 1908. And how about Lou Gehrig, known as the "Iron Man?" Called the iron man because of the 2130 consecutive games he played in over fourteen seasons with the New York Yankees. His lifetime batting average was 340 in thirteen seasons with the Yankees. I recall clearly a day in 1941: we were playing softball during the noon hour while attending summer catechism classes (Sister School). Father Mechler drove up, called us off the field and told us Lou Gehrig had died.*

Then there was our own Summit Ridge team that played on Sunday afternoons, weather permitting. If not all, at least most of the folks from Summit Ridge showed up for games, whether at home (Bud Rapp or Ollie Muehlenkamp farms) or away. Some, but not all of the players had uniforms, most a bit ragged. Those who did "strutted" a bit. From time to time the team was short a man or two. When this occurred, one of the Summit Ridge spectators who came to enjoy the game found himself on the playing field (talk about being drafted). Having come to enjoy the game he was wearing something less than his "go to church" finery, but still dress-up clothes, usually a white shirt and new or close to new Oshkosh-b-gosh overalls. We also mustered some talented young ball players at Sister School. We now had assembled in one place the Catholic students from all of Summit Ridge's rural schools. Two standouts that come to mind were Lawrence Donskey at first base and Lloyd Ziegler playing third base. Since our playing field was rather restricted, being the then still vacant portion of the cemetery, we had to play softball instead of baseball. The cemetery kept encroaching on our playing field. What was an open third base the year before was now covered by the Swartzlow's gravestone. I can still see Lloyd Ziegler fielding grounders or line drives in front of or by reaching over that marker. Father Mechler often umpired the games. Not on one occasion did anyone dispute his calls. Perhaps not openly, but sister Joan is still ticked-off about being called out by

---

*At age thirty-eight of amyotrophic lateral sclerosis, now commonly referred to as Lou Gehrig disease.

Father Mechler when she tried to stretch a single into a double.

I was not considered talented enough to win a regular spot on the Summit Ridge team. Perhaps the best that could be said was that I was a better fielder than a hitter. I do remember on at least one occasion reaching first base (I was probably walked). Frank Kruk was the opposing team's catcher. I remember the "good ol' boys" discussing Frank's prowess as a catcher and they agreed he did not have a strong throwing arm. With that bit of "insider information" I took off on the first pitch and found the second baseman holding the ball as I approached. On another occasion Dad scheduled me to drive part of the family to visit relatives on a Sunday afternoon outing. I no doubt mustered every ounce of mid-teenage nastiness and stubbornness to escape doing so. In the process I lost my right to drive to the game site in Melvina. I hitchhiked to the town and noted only nine of us were there from Summit Ridge. At last, I thought, I have another chance to start. But that did not occur. The manager of the Summit Ridge team picked his friend from another community to round out the team. Disappointing and embarrassing!*

Right after haying, sometime in late July or early August, the process of harvesting the grain crop began. This was another labor intensive and time consuming venture as the horse drawn grain binder cut its five-foot swath through the fields. In the process, bundles of oats, barley, rye, or wheat tied with twine were dropped to the ground. Next came the chore of shocking these bundles. This was done to minimize damage to the grain from rain before threshing. First we took two bundles and leaned them against each other so they both stood upright. We next placed two more on either side. If you used two caps, two more bundles could be placed on either side of the first two already set in place. Next came the

---

*Others too were embarrassed in not being picked to play. One was our current president (2005) George W. Bush. He was a pitcher on the Yale freshman baseball team. On this occasion Yale was behind by ten runs. The Yale manager strode out to the pitcher's mound and signaled the umpire that he was making a pitching change. The manager then looked for a moment towards the bullpen where George "W" Bush was warming up. Then he signaled for the second baseman to take the mound.

rain guard. A bundle (maybe two) was flared out and placed over the top of those standing for rain protection. As noted, these were called "caps." No job on the farm could compare with this for "sustained" drudgery. You needed to wear a long sleeved shirt to protect your arms from the sharp ends of the cut stalks. On hot days this was most uncomfortable. This was an all day job, day after day. One worked up a tremendous thirst in the process and younger siblings were kept busy carrying drinking water to those of us involved in this labor.

As with shocks of corn, we built grain shocks in a straight line. Not only did this look better, but in the process of threshing, straight rows of shocks facilitated the loading of bundles since horses now could follow along side a given row without use of the reins.

At times a windstorm hit just when the grain stalks were top heavy with fully developed kernels of grain. As a result, fields or portions of fields were so flattened that the grain could not be harvested. Usually though the grain was left lying at an angle where it could still be harvested, but only by cutting in one direction. Now instead of driving all around the field, cutting as you went, it was necessary to "come back empty" after reaching one end of the field. In the process the cutting time was nearly doubled and shocking was more difficult since the bundles were ragged.

As soon as the grain was cut and shocked we launched into threshing. This occurred in mid to late August and sometimes extended into early September. Grant Wood painted a well-known picture in 1934 called *Dinner for Threshers.* Except for the timing I could be in that picture. On many occasions I sat around tables such as the one depicted in this picture as we moved from farm to farm during the three or four years I participated in the threshing process. It's one thing to grow old, yet another to be able to look back and say that I was once a part of a ritual that was both romantic and historic. Much like being able to say, as was noted earlier, "That I lived during Winston Churchill's time."

Threshing was a combination of hard work and social involvement. Indeed, it was something like a holiday event despite the hard work.

Dinner for Threshers *by Grant Wood – 1934 (Art©Estate of Grant Wood/Licensed by VAGA, New York, N.Y.)*

The highlight was the meals, and the piece-de-resistance was the meat dishes served at the noon and evening meals at whatever farm we were threshing at. The wives were on the spot; this was probably the most stressful task they were called on to perform all year as related to cooking. Much to the delight of the men, the women tried to outdo each other relative to the meals served. Farmers returning from a day of threshing had better be prepared to be de-briefed on what was served at the noon and evening meals that day. This was especially true if the wife still had to feed the threshers. I suspect in most cases the men ravenously ate their meals and went off without a word to the cook(s). But there was an exception. On one occasion we were threshing at the Clarence Berendes' farm. His wife, Laverne, served us a new dish (to us) called "heavenly rice." I am told this was a combination of cooked rice laced with pineapple and marshmallows. A pretty fancy dish for a bunch of farmers of that era. The men actually interrupted their eating to let Laverne know how delicious the dish was. It really was delicious, I couldn't believe anything could taste so great.

Our threshing group involved twelve farmers. One year we started the process from one end of the string of farms, the next year from the other end. A farmer was expected to contribute one man for each farm he owned. Until I was old enough to join the workforce Dad hired a man since we had two farms. As a rule, four to six wagons and teams of horses were involved in hauling grain from the field to the threshing machine located in the farmer's barnyard area. The farmer having his grain threshed usually furnished one team and his closest neighbors the others. Others worked in the fields breaking down the shocks and pitching the bundles up to the driver on the wagon. If we were short of men, the wagon driver pitched his own load from the ground. Others worked carrying the grain in large elongated sacks to the granary, and for some of the grain, up a stairs in the granary to bins on the second floor. As the bins filled there was the need to move grain to the back of the bins. One or two others built the straw stack, an extremely dirty job as threshed straw along with dust and chaff was blown with some force out the blower.

The first task in building a straw stack was to make a judgment call— and a major judgment this was. What size stack do I build? Make it too large and you will not have enough straw to build the necessary dome that will ward off moisture from rain and snow. This could result in rotted straw. Make it too small and the excess straw will have to be blown aside where it will likely rot before it can be used. There was also the need to continually stomp the straw down, particularly in the center so the dome wouldn't cave in and allow moisture to enter. This kept the one or two men constantly moving straw with their forks while stomping, stomping, and stomping.

There was one man who tended the blower. This tubular mechanism, ten to twelve inches in diameter could be telescoped out approximately twenty feet and swung approximately 100 degrees from side to side by hand operated gears. Ropes in turn permitted turning the head of the blower to different angles. Via hand signals, experience, and common sense the blower operator and straw stack builders went about their business.

Then there was the engineer (one of the farmers) easily identified by an oil can that seemed to be an appendage to his arm. The engineer kept the machinery running and made repairs as necessary. Finally there was the man who filled the sacks as the grain came from the hopper. The hopper filled with grain separated from the stalks by the threshing action. At the one-half or one bushel level the hopper was set to trip and the grain dropped down a cylindrical chute to the sacker. At the finish of threshing for a given farmer a count was tallied and the farmer paid so much per bushel for what was threshed on his farm. Thus the more grain you harvested the more you paid. Eminently fair to the smaller farmer.

Initially in my threshing experience the Steinhoffs furnished the threshing machine and steam engine power. This machine could only be fed from one side so only one wagon at a time could unload. With approximately eighteen men in the crew the capability was there to process the grain at a faster rate. The farmers formed a cooperative and purchased a larger threshing machine that could handle a wagon unloading from each side of the machine. This served to speed up the threshing cycle considerably. A large tractor also had to be purchased by the cooperative to power this new and larger threshing machine. The money collected year by year by the cooperative, farmer by farmer, was used to meet the expense of running the machinery, especially to replace worn belts, etc.

As noted, the threshing machine itself was initially powered by a steam engine. How it huffed and puffed as it did its chore. The engine was approximately fifty feet from the threshing machine with power delivered by a belt. It's amazing that on those occasions when this belt broke no injuries occurred. The belt slapped together whenever the threshing machine was overfed, or if ragged or wet bundles had to be digested. The sound at those times was like a thunderclap. At the same time the steam engine (later a tractor) coughed and snorted in anger. In fact the whole environment around the machinery was dangerous, what with exposed gears, pulleys and belts by the score.

For children the first and most important job was to **stay out of the way.** Danger was everywhere around the machinery with its unprotected pulleys, gears, and belts. The ten plus year olds helped in the relatively safe granary. As noted, grain piled up in front of the bins where the grain carriers by necessity had to dump it. There was a need then to shovel it to the back of the bin. Hot, dirty work and a necessary chore, yet fun. For me this was my initiation to the threshing process as it related to necessary work. Young ladies, not yet old enough to work in the kitchen, might be assigned the job of delivering water to those pitching bundles in the field. The usual routine was for one of the teamsters to bring jugs of water as they traveled back and forth from the farm's built up area to its fields. At times both boys and girls might ride along with the teamsters to pick up a load of bundles. The thrill was being allowed to hold the reins as the horses moved along the shocks of grain.

As a rule the farmer whose grain was being threshed assigned jobs to those not driving teams. The bigger, younger, and stronger men were assigned the job of carrying sacks of grain to the granaries. All our threshing was done on the home (side hill) farm. Here the five or six grain carriers had a 100-foot trek up-hill to the granary. At this point the grain carriers still needed to climb seven or eight steps more to reach the first floor of the granary. If that wasn't enough, bins on the second floor required about fifteen additional steps up a stairs. As a rule we threshed a mix of oats, barley, rye and wheat. A sack of oats, in a good year, weighed around seventy pounds. Those of barley eighty and wheat ninety pounds. Carrying those sacks of grain was without a doubt the hardest job in the process of threshing.

My job as a rule was pitching bundles to the driver on the wagon. There was a routine. First, pluck off the top cap (there for rain protection), then the second cap, then the remaining eight bundles in a given shock of grain. Bundles were not randomly tossed into the wagon. Ideally a bundle landed a couple of feet from the driver with the grain-laden end away from him. As a matter of pride we pitchers tried to place these bundles right in front of where the driver stood waiting for them. He then could arrange his load so when he unloaded the bundles into the threshing machine he rhythmically spun each one in mid-air to ensure the grain laden ends went in first, as was desired. Of all the jobs in the threshing process, pitching bundles in the field was the only one isolated from the otherwise dirty, noisy, and in many ways dangerous work around the machines.

The worst job I ever had one year was at Ed Kruks. My assigned job was to drive his team of horses, an unruly team to begin with. On this particular day not enough men were available to pitch bundles. This meant I had to jump off the wagon and pitch my own load. A well-trained disciplined team of horses responded to voice command to move forward and stop. Ed's team moved forward on command, but they did not stop. That required leading one of them by its bridle. When a pitcher was at last available I still had to use the reins to control the horses, but at least I was now on the wagon. The horses were also skittish when approaching the noisy threshing machinery. One of the men working around the machines had to lead this team, again via the bridle. Accidentally hitting the threshing machine itself with that wide and fully loaded wagon could have ended the threshing for that day, if not for a few days.

We routinely started threshing right after morning chores. The process took close to three weeks since rain forced delays. Some of the smaller farms could be threshed in half a day. We (Hedricks) needed the better part of two days with our two farms. Although we might finish at a given farm at noon, it took close to the rest of the day to break down the operation, then move the machinery (ponderously slowly) to the next farm, then set-up again. Since the machinery had to be level it took time to accomplish this, especially for farmers with side-hill barnyards. The usual routine was to move from one farm to another after the end of a threshing day. The three hours of daylight remaining permitted the move and set-up so that the threshing operation could start early the next morning.

The happiest creatures on the farm after the machinery and men moved on were the chickens. What fun they had digging in the chaff for whole kernels of grain that for one reason or another did not end up in the granary bins. If the chickens were happy, so were the threshers when they celebrated the end of threshing season with a keg(s) of beer. Like threshing itself this event moved from farm to farm each year. This was an evening event enjoyed not only because the big job of threshing was done, but also for the camaraderie and singing. The after threshing beer party was a routine event, but other beer parties were held as well throughout the summer and early fall. Birthdays and anniversaries were obvious examples of what could spawn a beer party. Invariably there was singing as the beer took its effect. In practice, these beer parties were de facto auditions for the church choir.

The last crop processed in late summer, although it could extend into early fall, was making second crop hay. This crop grew up on those fields that had been harvested the previous June or July. This crop was only a percentage of what came from the field earlier. It made up for its lack of volume by having increased nutritional value. Having to put this valuable hay on top of the old hay in the mow, and then having to feed it first was frustrating for the farmer. In an ideal world this more nutritious second crop of hay could be left untouched until the cows freshened in early spring. A certain amount could be piled in the driveway of the haymow area and left untouched until most needed, but this made for clumsy unloading from the hay wagon. In some years, if weather conditions were right, a third crop might be harvested. This was even more nutritional than second crop, but again the volume was reduced from that which was harvested for second crop.

An important actor, as yet not mentioned, also plays a key role on the farm—especially in late summer. This is the bull. All winter long he languished in a back corner of the barn with his harem of twenty ladies so close, and yet so far away. I don't believe he left the barn at all during the winter months. As soon as there was enough grass growth in the spring he was tethered outside along a fence next to the home farm buildings. His twenty-foot chain, which terminated in a ring through his nostrils, permitted him to graze in splendid isolation. As a rule there was enough grass to permit him to be left in one place for a couple of days before moving him along the fence line to a new spot. There was no problem with running out of pasture since by the time we moved him along the entire fence line the grass on the spot first vacated had grown back and was ready for him to visit again. One chore had to be done daily, and that was to lead him to the water tank each evening. I didn't like this job at all. First of all, this is a bull with the size and temperament befitting the species. Then there was the chain we led him with that terminated in his nose. One had no choice at times but to pull on the chain rather hard to force him to come along if he had contrary ideas. That must have hurt, and who is hurting him but a ninety pound kid—and he weighed well over a ton!

We lost at least two bulls to lightning while I was on the farm. The twenty-foot metal chain tethered to a wire fence was the culprit. In both instances lightning struck a tree, then jumped to the wire fence which conducted it to the tethering chain, and as a result—**no bull!**

During late June through early August we bred cows for next spring's crop of calves. The indication that a given female was in heat was if she stood still while another animal mounted her. My assigned duty at times was to watch the herd for approximately fifteen minutes to see which if any of the females were ready to be bred. Now the bull was led, again with that long chain, to the barnyard where his lady was waiting. The twenty-foot chain permitted me to stand well to the side of the couple. I wonder now if when I was first involved in this process I knew what was going on. I do know that what I observed of farm animals breeding in my early years led me to believe human procreation was similar. For example, if there were seven children in a family it followed that the human couple had seven sexual experiences. Today the farm maintained bull for the milk-producing herd has pretty much gone the way of chickens, pigs, sheep, and fruit trees. On nephew Mike Hedrick's farm, once a young animal has been identified as a future member of the herd by virtue of milk production and butterfat content, a consultant, i.e. breeding expert is called in. The question is how can we best ensure her offspring will be the type that will be even more productive? The expert evaluates the animal on some ten to twenty physical characteristics. For example, size of udder, size of ankle, legs, shoulders, chest girth, etc. Each of these body characteristics is assigned a point count. Now, via a computer this animal is matched with a stable of over 200 bulls for the best possible match. Periodically a delivery of specific sperm vials is made to the farm and kept in a barn cooler. When cow "X" needs to be bred, Mike goes to his records and sees that "X" needs to be matched with sperm "Y". Then via artificial insemination the cow is impregnated.

Has this scientific breeding paid off? You bet it has. In my day a productive cow produced about 12,000 pounds of milk each year. Today (2005) the average is 23,000 pounds per cow for nephew Mike Hedrick's herd.* Again in my day, our herd of 20 to 24 milk cows, during their best producing months, could come up with about 800 pounds per day. Mike's herd of approximately 60 cows produces around 4,000 pounds per day.**

Although kept fairly busy in the summertime I still found time to play. On many summer nights there was enough daylight after evening chores to muster my siblings for a work-up softball game. As noted earlier, I could fish on those days when we were unable to work in the fields after a rainstorm. Another pastime was pitting the Chicago Cubs against the St. Louis Cardinals in an imaginary game of baseball. The milk house on the Bucholz farm was the diamond. I tossed a ball up on the roof and as it rolled back down I was ready to swing the bat. If the result were a pop-up and I caught it—the batter was out. If the ball went over the building, and if hit high enough to where I could hustle around in time to catch it—the batter was out. A ball over the building and not caught was

---

*Assuming the average cow is a milk producer for nine years, at the rate of 23,000 pounds each year she would produce 207,000 pounds during her productive years. A California cow, known only as number 289, holds the record. She produced 465,224 pounds of milk during her productive years (presumably nine years).

**The feed provided milking animals plays its part in this increased production as well. Milking animals are served buffet style (all you can eat). The allocation is seventy-three pounds for each milk-producing cow each day. This breaks down to thirty-five pounds of hayledge, twenty pounds of cracked shell corn, twelve pounds of corn silage and six pounds of a protein supplement. It matters not whether it's spring, summer, winter or fall, the spread is there. Automatic unloaders in four silos provide the correct mix and a conveyer takes the feed to a feeding trough. As implied, a dry cow (not producing milk) for that two months period before she freshens does not eat at the buffet table.

a hit. Balls bouncing off the shed or that I completely missed were strikes. It could take me hours to play a nine-inning game.

Fall

Spring came in with the initial soft sounds of melting snow and resultant running water. Summer was rather clearly marked on the day we cut the first blade of hay. The transition from summer to fall was more subtle. Threshing and making second crop hay generally marked the end of summer, and yet, Mother Nature seemed to have trouble making up her mind as to the line of demarcation between summer and fall. I suppose an analogy might be "do I wear the summer white or the fall beige dress to the church social?" Make no mistake about it though; fall was a delightful time of the year on the farm. Not only was the weather more temperate, but squirrel hunting season was right around the corner. Of course school started as well. Although I labored long and hard during the summer I don't recall being at all eager to assume the more sedentary role in school. Fall also saw us rounding up the last of the livestock's winter-feed needs, not to mention that needed for the humans. These gatherings for humans ended up mainly in the cellar. The gardens were producing at their maximum, which resulted in a busy follow-on canning process. Sweet corn was also available in early fall. This could be specifically grown sweet corn, or as was most often the case, field corn harvested just before the kernels started to harden.

If haying and threshing were the most important harvesting operations in summertime, that of harvesting the corn crop in the fall was right up there in importance. This was the last of the farm crops harvested to feed livestock. Like haying, the individual farmer was pretty much on his own. The exception was if he were to shred some of his corn crop. Unlike hay, corn did not have to be dry before putting it in the silo. Actually it needed to be on the green side since moisture hastened the necessary fermentation process in the silo. As a rule we ran a water hose to the silo filler with the water running into the cutting/

blowing blades right along with the stalks of corn.

As noted in chapter one, the first priority of the corn crop, both the stalks and attached ears was for silage to be fed to the milking herd in the winter. Before hybrid seed corn was universally used (which had to be purchased), there was a need to set aside a certain amount of kernel corn for next year's spring planting. Usually the farmer raised pigs for both food and cash, and pigs fatten up best on corn. Thus a farmer might determine that he needed "X" bushels of ear corn for his pigs out of the current years planting. Still, he did not want to lose that nutritional ear corn from the silage fed to the milk cows throughout the winter. After all, milk and its derivative cream was central to farm income.

Like many other cases related to farming, judgments had to be made along the way as how to meet his dairy herd's dietary needs in the wintertime, along with the need for kernel corn for other purposes. Wheat and barley were a fair substitute for corn and could be used to fatten hogs. If the grain crop was bountiful that year he might squeeze by with only the need for seed corn. Another factor was what kind of corn crop did he expect to grow this year? Will the stalks be six or eight feet tall? The larger the stalk the more silage it produced and the one or two ears of corn on each stalk were larger as well. Thus in a mediocre year he might need all twenty acres of corn to fill his silo(s). In a better than average corn crop year fifteen of those twenty acres might do the job, leaving five acres from which to harvest ears of corn. In one of those mediocre years he cheated on the cattle a bit.

Prior to the cutting and bundling operation, at a stage when the ripened ear was easily removed from the stalk, we walked down a row of corn and with a downward thrust "snapped-out" every ear, or every other ear on a given stalk depending on perceived needs. The ears were dropped next to the standing stalk so that subsequent mechanical cutting and bundling of the standing corn did not injure those ears lying on the ground. The husks were left on the ears to protect them from the elements and foraging animals. Now the bundles of stalks, with no ears or reduced ears of corn went into the silo. After the corn had been cut and removed from the field for silage the farmer returned with his box wagon to manually pick up the corn, ear by ear. The box was modified by placing a two to three foot high backboard along one side. This permitted us to toss ears of corn from as far as three or more rows away without overthrowing the wagon. Naturally the more workers you could put on the job the sooner the job was completed. The youngest picked up corn from the row nearest the wagon, and on out four or five rows depending on the number of workers available. The horses didn't stop in the process so the pickers had to keep up. We then hauled what we collected to the corncrib where we manually ripped the husks* off the corn and tossed the ears into the crib. We used a bracket like device over one hand with a steel shank on one end to assist in this process. Since this was slow going the wagon of corn was left by the corncrib and as time permitted we processed the corn. This was usually during whatever daylight remained after evening chores. Not one of my favorite jobs on the farm.

Another scenario might evolve like this in a better than average corn crop year. We first filled the silos with the full-fruited corn from the fifteen acres. No need now for the labor-intensive chore of snapping out corn, then picking it up from the field, followed by husking before tossing the ears into the corncrib. Now the remaining five acres produced all that was needed for other than silage, and the ears of corn were separated from the stalks and stripped of their husks by a corn shredder. Corn shredding was much like threshing, but with a smaller crew. The bundles of corn were hauled in from the fields, then fed into the shredder and golden ears of corn tumbled into the wagon from one spout, and the shredded stalks out another spout to be stacked much like the straw pile built during grain threshing. There was more nutritional value in shredded corn stalks than straw, but not much more. Usually we let the young stock rummage

---

*The husks, after being thoroughly dried often found their way as stuffing in home-made mattresses. One of these graced my bed for a time. There was zero support, and as a result I sank out of sight. Further, it sounded like World War II whenever I moved.

through the stack in the wintertime for any nutritional value it had for them. Like straw it could also be used for bedding. The ears of corn could be shoveled into the corncrib rather than being husked ear-by-ear and then tossed into the corncrib by hand.

Some years the corn shocks were left in the field. In the dead of winter, after the manure was spread I swung by the cornfield. Usually I had to pry a shock loose since bundles had frozen to the ground. The bundles were delivered to the pig stable for the pigs to find and eat the ears of corn buried within each bundle.

At times the corn left over after filling the silo was of insufficient quantity to justify the cost of having it shredded. At those times we went to the field of still standing corn and snapped out the ears, husked them on the spot, then tossed the ears of corn into the box wagon that the horses pulled along as we worked one or two rows. The barren stalks were later plowed under. Unfortunately, not all of a given long stalk was buried. A portion of the stalks ended up sticking out of the plowed ground at odd angles. The process was effective, but it didn't look orderly. Remember most farmers on Summit Ridge wanted their fields to look neat. A more vexing problem occurred the next spring in the process of harrowing the soil for spring planting. At times these stalks bunched-up to jam the harrow. I can attest to the fact that farmer's sons did not enjoy having to stop the tractor and pull apart that tangled mass of old corn stalks.

Of all the tasks associated with harvesting the corn crop, filling silo was the most important and most labor intensive. Like the process of haying, individual farmers usually did this without a neighbor's help. In fact, an individual farmer might be able to do this with no additional help whatsoever. First he positioned the tractor driven silage filler next to the silo. On the Hedrick home farm that meant a bit of digging and/or use of blocks of wood to make sure the machine was reasonably level. Now attach the approximate eight-inch diameter pipes to the filler to whatever height it had to be to reach the top of the silo, probably thirty-feet at a minimum. He started with a "C" shaped pipe that served to direct the upward thrust of the silage 180 degrees to a downward flow into the silo. Then he attached an approximate five-foot section of pipes to this "C" section pipe and raised it off the ground with a rope and pulley. Section after section was attached in this fashion until the "C" shaped pipe protruded into a small door at the top of the silo. Finally, the bottom section was attached to the silage filler. Next he entered the silo and positioned the first of several silage chute doors in place. These were approximately two by three feet and slipped into slots. As the silo filled he added additional doors by hoisting them up with a rope and pulley. In the winter, as silage was used, these doors were removed one by one and lowered back down to a storage area. He might also position the tractor at this time, making sure it too was reasonably level. It all looked neat and businesslike. The silage filler was nestled up to the foot of the silo with its long blower pipe seeming to be an appendage to the silo. The tractor setting off to one side added to the appearance of an altogether orderly arrangement.

The corn was cut with a horse-drawn corn binder. This was usually a morning chore as it was for cutting hay. He cut only what he could process that day (only fresh, green stalks of corn to the silo). At some point the belt from the tractor to the silage filler was attached and made suitably taut. That afternoon he was back in the field for wagonloads of bundles. The bed of this wagon was as wide as the box wagon but twice as long. Bundles were stacked on the rack at right angles to its length. When he arrived at the silage filler the tractor was started and the pulley engaged to power the silage filler. As noted above, since moisture hastened the fermentation that eventually took place in the airtight silo, a flow of water via a hose was often introduced into the cutter/blower fan area. He then began feeding corn bundles into the cutting blades and fans that literally "hurled" the cut corn up the pipe and into the silo. The eighteen-inch cutting blades could be adjusted to slice the corn stalks near paper thin, which was desired. After a couple of days the blades had to be sharpened and adjusted.

The bundles entered the cutting area through two horizontal rollers that moved up and down depending on the size of a given bundle. As he pulled a bundle off the wagon and placed it in the chain driven feeding chute he constantly had to ensure that the bundle did not catch on the lip of a safety guard in front of the rollers. He knew to what level a wagonload of corn filled the silo. Then as necessary he installed silage doors to accommodate the next load of corn. Ideally he also spread the silage around since it fell on one increasingly heaped pile, then stomped it down so the settling pressure was equal throughout the entire area in the silo. All the aforementioned steps he could do on his own, and many often did this by their lonesome.

Dad had it easier since he had both my grandfather and Aunt Lena to help him. First, again via a rope and pulley, he attached a series of pipes, eight to ten inches in diameter and about four- foot long from that point where the silage made a fast "U" turn at the top of the silo. These initially extended down inside the silo to within a few feet of the floor. Now Aunt Lena came from the house or garden when she observed Dad coming home with a load of corn. She entered the silo and with ease swung the pipes to ensure the silage was distributed evenly around the entire area of the silo. In the process she also kept stomping the silage down. She also installed the doors as the silo filled. When I was too small to otherwise help I found it fun to go up in the silo with Aunt Lena. First of all, she let me direct the pipe (which was made of relatively light metal) to ensure the silage was distributed evenly over the entire area. That made me feel quite important. Then too, there was the noise, especially as corncobs and kernels of corn rattled down the pipes, and finally it really smelled pleasant!

My grandfather assisted by standing next to where the bundles entered the cutting area to feed the bundles into the rollers. Now Dad could keep the feeding chute filled while Grandfather ensured the new bundle end was compressed so it entered the cutting blades with next to zero interruptions time wise. This served to speed up the action considerably. As soon as I was deemed old enough to physically, and from a safety standpoint handle the job, I fed the bundles of corn into the rollers. As I matured I naturally graduated to hauling bundles home from the field and unloading them in the feeding chute. Aunt Lena remained on duty in the silo, but Dad and I rotated from the relatively heavy work of unloading the bundles to the soft job of ensuring the bundles entered the cutting area in an unbroken stream.

If I enjoyed the noise the silage made as it came through those light metal pipes inside the silo that definitely was not the case standing within a foot of the cutting and blowing action of the blades. This series of blades and fans whirled at a high speed within a cylindrical shield measuring about five-foot in diameter. The noise alone of that device turning was deafening. Now add to that the cutting and hurling action as bundles were fed in. There was no chance for verbal communication between the one unloading the bundles into the chute and the other standing four feet away ensuring the bundles went efficiently through those rollers. We had to physically gain the attention of the other person and then shout in each other's ear if the need to communicate arose. Once the silo was filled to the brim we backed off for a time to allow the silage to settle. Later we added to the supply of silage in this silo by cutting another load or two of corn to ensure the silo was filled to the brim. Later in my experience on the farm a second silo was built.

On rare occasions in the fall we "hulled" clover to glean the seeds for next year's hay crop planting.* The huller, much like a threshing machine separated the clover kernels from the stems. I suspect this was a one-day operation and only minimal help from neighbors was needed for such a small undertaking.

About this time the different types of deciduous trees were treating us to many bright hues as their leaves turned color. I don't suppose our display compared favorably with what could be viewed in the New England

---

*Today farmers on Summit Ridge depend exclusively on alfalfa for their hay needs. Alfalfa grows faster and produces from three to five years on the same field. A clover field may produce for only two years.

states, but it's hard to imagine anyone from our area signing up for a bus tour to see the fall colors in that area.

One of the last field chores before winter set in and the ground froze was to plow for next year's corn and grain crops. This was the time of year the farmer set-up his next year's crop rotation plan. From one-third to one-half of that summer's hay fields were plowed for next year's corn crop, and the corn ground plowed for next year's grain crop. Planting corn and grain on this same ground two years in a row was to be avoided. This was based on both soil erosion control and soil enrichment. Hay crops (legumes) enriched the soil with nitrogen, plus their root system served to hold topsoil in place. Hay fields could be maintained in this role for two or three years before being plowed for corn. Spreading lime to neutralize the pH of the soil being rotated from hay to corn was mentioned as one of the rituals of spring. Ideally though the lime was spread in the hay fields before fall plowing.

Plowing was a slow process; even with a tractor pulling a gangplow with two twelve-inch blades.* As a youngster I observed Dad and other farmers working large fields with a single bottom horse-drawn plow. A single bottom plow turned about a fourteen-inch wide strip of soil. Imagine the time needed to plow a given field? I had my opportunity to wrestle with this device when it came to plowing for gardens and other small areas where a tractor could not maneuver.

To add to the boredom of plowing was the approaching winter with the accompanying cold winds. I could hardly recognize Dad as he sat all bundled up between those two large back wheels of our old Fordson tractor. Actually I recognized the tractor and assumed Dad was operating it. This tractor was especially hard to start in cold weather. On cold mornings, before starting morning chores, Dad gathered a bed of coals from the milk house stove and placed it under the oil pan of the tractor. The tractor was kept in a shed with the back (east side) open so there was some weather protection. When he came to start the tractor an hour or

*Today on the Hedrick farms a five-gang plow turns over nine feet of ground in one swipe.

two later he was usually successful. I never operated that tractor. When I was twelve or thirteen years of age we bought a new John Deere tractor, and this was to become my baby. I was happy knowing this tractor would reduce considerably my time with the horses. Within days of taking delivery I was excused from school at noon to drive the new tractor while making second crop hay. What a thrill to operate a moving vehicle for the first time. Also appreciated was being six feet in front of the wagon and no longer in danger of Dad tossing fork fulls of hay on top of me.

That old John Deere tractor was subsequently sold, but in 1998 nephew Mike Hedrick tracked it down and had it completely refurbished and painted up like new. I was visiting Wisconsin at the time and under some pretext Mike took me to the shop where the tractor was ready for pick-up. He awarded me the high honor of driving the tractor home. Talk about a sentimental journey! Mike uses the tractor for light work around the farm since it's economical to operate.*

Deer hunting, one of the great holiday periods of the year highlighted late November. The older boys and men looked forward to this event with as much anticipation and yearning as children did for Christmas. Bagging a deer was not only a chance to demonstrate one's hunting prowess, but if successful, for a few days at least your family and friends enthroned you on a pedestal. Then too, the successful hunter brought a new kind and substantial amount of meat to the table. I no longer recall when I started deer hunting. I suspect this was the year I turned sixteen. So popular was this five to seven day ritual that schools turned a blind eye to absences. Father Mechler celebrated an extra early morning Sunday Mass during deer hunting season so the hunters could be in the woods by dawn.

Some hunters were "lone wolves" and positioned themselves at what they knew or suspected was a deer crossing to wait for a deer (buck) to move through. With so many hunters moving around through a limited

---

*That old tractor, along with six others is currently in the inventory of farm machinery on the Hedrick farms.

amount of woods the deer were now constantly moving during daylight. Most hunters preferred to hunt in-groups since it provided for varied assignments and social involvement as well. In a given group most positioned themselves at likely deer crossings; the rest tramped through a section of woods, making as much noise as they could so as to drive the deer towards those waiting at what was judged to be those likely deer crossings.

My first year I hunted with two others, Al and Ruth Mack. We were hunting a small section of woods where one person could effectively drive the deer. This woods was less than a mile from the Mack home in Farmers Valley. On this one occasion Al and I took up position and Ruth drove. Along came this large ten point buck (ten prongs on its horns) and I fired one round with my Winchester thirty-thirty caliber rifle. The deer staggered but did not go down. Al saw it move into a small grove of trees and came upon it lying down. Before he reached the deer a second hunter (not in our party) came right up to the deer, fired a shot at point blank range and put his tag on the antlers. My shot had gone in behind the front legs and would have been fatal but for the coup de grace by the other hunter. Al, who saw all this had some choice words for the hunter, but legally the deer was his since his tag was now on the deer. That evening Dad went to Norwalk to visit this man, who was one of the town's leading citizens. I'm not sure what ensued, but Dad did come home with the deer's head; I suppose with the idea of mounting it. I was told this man was embarrassed and apologetic. I think everyone realized that few of us were hunting for sport, we were meat hunters. In the meantime I was one unhappy young man.

The next day Ruth Mack and I were hunting alone. Ruth again was driving and I was at the same spot as the day before. Here comes another large buck and this time my two shots did the trick. Ruth and I dragged the deer to a farm path and I went to a neighbor to call Dad. Like that $1800 check for the pigs, I don't know who was happier, Dad or I. If the good news was that I bagged a deer, the bad news was I had to return to school the next day. I remember Ed Blewett, the manual training (shop) teacher and also a deer hunter intercepted me in the hall to confirm that I really did bag a deer. He had many questions on the locale of the kill and how it all took place. I was much pleased by this encounter since Mr. Blewett was one of my favorite teachers.

Over the three or four years I participated in this annual ritual I hunted with either the Macks or a group associated with my paternal uncles (Berendes). The Berendes group numbered from five to ten and they combined deer hunting with a certain amount of hi-jinks. During that period I brought at least three deer to the family table. The deer I brought home in 1944 was nearly lost to me. This was one of the war years and ammunition; particularly rifle ammunition was in short supply. As a result I was hunting with a pump action twelve-gauge shotgun. The deer-killing element was a piece of soft metal called a slug that was propelled by the powder charge. I was standing halfway up the Erdman hill when a buck crossed the road about 100 feet from my location. I had three shells. I missed with the first two but dropped the buck with the third. He may have dropped but he was still obviously alive. The slug had gone in his neck and he lay on the road with his head canted at a near ninety-degree angle. I had no more shells and there was no way I was going to use my knife or try to hold him down. I yelled for a fellow hunter, but before one arrived the deer lumbered away with his head at that crazy angle. Our crew tracked him down and an uncle finished him off. I was awarded the deer. Deer hunting continues in the same popular fashion in my area of Wisconsin today. The local paper is plastered with people and their kills, usually the successful hunter posing with their deer in the back of a pick-up truck.

There was another ritual in the late fall involving that year's flock of chickens. We all enjoyed this ritual. Those once cute little chicks were now ready to be moved to the chicken coop for the winter. They had spent the first seven to eight weeks of their lives in the small brooder house. Soon thereafter they began roosting in trees or any other object that permitted them to avoid enemies by sleeping (roosting) up off the ground. By this time most of the roosters (males) had either been butchered for Sunday dinners or sent off to market. The pullets, now six months old were ready to start paying their way by laying eggs. (By the way ladies, your quota is 200 eggs per year.) After chores, ideally on a moonlit night we made the rounds of trees and other heights to "snatch" the pullets from their perches. One did not herd chickens as you could most other animals on the farm. The human snatcher handed the chickens to the human carriers who grasped them by one leg. Depending on the size of the carriers, they each hauled two to eight pullets, head down, to their winter quarters. Mother was there to attach a colored band to the leg of each chicken. A given color identified that chicken as being a product of a particular year. Rarely was a laying hen kept for more than two years. The leg bands, a different color for each year, identified those more than two years old. In fact, since egg production decreases after the hens are a year old, many of the old timers in all likelihood had gone to market before the new pullets were added to the egg laying flock. They were the victims of a culling process that measured the distance between their pelvic bones. Less than a two-finger width, and lady, you are off to the stew pot.

My dislike for the process of harvesting wood has already been mentioned in an earlier chapter. This dislike went beyond felling the trees and then cutting them down to a size that a couple of men or a team of horses could handle. Whether using men or horses, the cut timber, most often lying on a steep hillside, had to be carried or snaked by a team of horses to a fairly level assembly point in the woods. This assembly point needed to be located where a stake sled or wagon could reach it. Here the timber was further reduced through hand sawing and splitting to the equivalent of a two-man load. This might be called phase one. Phase two involved hauling the heavy and/or ungainly pieces of timber to a central location. This could be days, weeks, or months after phase one, as time permitted. Here the timber was eventually cut into blocks for firewood, with a certain amount set aside for fence posts. Sometimes this assembly point was in the woods. If so, the timber could be assembled quickly. But if this was the case, the blocks of wood still needed to be hauled home. Ideally we took the time to haul the uncut timber as close as possible to the wood-shed at home, or on the one quasi-level spot near the house on the home farm. No matter where assembled, the process of loading the timber on a stake wagon or sled was a chore. Ideally a two man job; the heavy and reasonably straight pieces were loaded first. Now the limbs, many still heavy enough to require the labor of two men were piled on top. The limbs were anything but straight and rested ever so tentatively on the timber already loaded. The next limb, also ungainly caused the first limb to whip-saw this way or that. This unexpected shifting of the limbs caused many painful whacks to the head and body. So much for phase two.

Phase three involved cutting the long length of raw timber into blocks of wood, each fourteen to sixteen inches in length. A saw rig was attached to the front of the tractor with a short belt turning a large circular saw. Usually it took a crew of four to efficiently execute the process, but five was better. When we sawed our wood my usual job was to stand to one side of the saw where I caught the blocks and tossed them on a pile. Dad stood next to the saw to do his part to manhandle the raw timber when delivered to him from the pile. Next he made a judgment call on the length of the block, and guided it through the saw. Two men, "A" and "B" carried the raw timber to Dad at the saw; Dad then took over "A's" end, and along with "B" processed the wood through the saw. In the meantime "A" joins "C" to move the next piece of timber to the saw. It really took five men to tango.

From time to time the tractor was moved closer to the pile of still uncut timber. This saved "A", "B" and "C" from having to carry the raw timber so far as the unprocessed pile receded. The move also gave more room for the cut blocks of wood to pile up. So it went hour after hour. Since we had no labor union there were no rest breaks, except for when the tractor was moved. No safety protection either as this thirty-inch in diameter saw whirled around inches from Dad's and my hands. The heavy gloves we wore in view of the cold weather and nature of the work provided a degree of safety. There was one major benefit to all this hard and dangerous work. Since we had a work crew of neighbors we were served a big meal, much like a threshing meal.

In time these blocks of wood were split into chunk wood for the room heaters and smaller pieces for the kitchen range. This though was a one-man job. On the home farm the wood ended up on a jumbled pile near the house where it eventually had to be dug out of the snow. On the Bucholz farm, as noted earlier, there was a large woodshed right next to the house to protect the wood from the elements. As a rule, blocks of wood were stacked neatly in the shed. Even if they were just tossed in, retrieval in the wintertime was a relatively easy chore.

There was yet another sawing job one man could do alone, but two made it easier. That was sharpening fence posts. As Dad eyed a standing white oak tree about to be felled he visualized six-foot straight lengths of the trunk as ideal for fence posts. These six-foot sections were split, via sledge pounded wedges (like Abraham Lincoln used) into whatever bulk sized six-foot length he wanted. These sections were piled around the home farm yard area to await sharpening. Again the front mounted saw was attached to the tractor and Dad angled the posts through the saw so one end was tapered, running approximately eighteen inches to a sharpened point. He could do this alone, but as cut pieces piled up he had to stop the sharpening process and throw them aside. My job was to catch the pieces as he angled the rail through the saw and toss them aside. These scraps of wood later found their way to the various stoves. As we started the process I looked at the pile of raw posts and realized each one required four to six cuts to meet Dad's standard of a sharply pointed fence post. I wondered if we would ever finish this tedious chore.

Now here we were at the end of fall. The granaries and barns are groaning and bulging under the weight and volume of all we had worked to store therein. The cellars in turn were filled with the produce needed to support the human population on the farm. Generally there was a feeling of smug self-satisfaction on all our parts, children and adults alike as to what had been accomplished since we started harrowing the ground back in April.

And by the way Father Mechler, we can now discontinue the prayers said at the foot of the altar after Mass for favorable weather and good crops!

Winter

In the introduction to "Rhythm of the Seasons" I suggested that most people who live in northern climes enjoy the four seasons. You will find many though who do not enjoy winter at all.

The routine changed in the winter. Now farm work evolved around caring for the confined livestock. All in all this was a pleasant change from the labor-intensive spring, summer, and fall seasons. The only noteworthy irritant for me, as has been recounted, was on those occasions when we worked in the woods. Harvesting firewood took on an added significance for us since we needed to supply wood for the home farm as well as our own.

Winters in Wisconsin can be a trial, especially for adults. Like in the heat of summer, adult conversation in the wintertime invariably related to weather conditions. How cold could it get in Wisconsin and how was it measured? Perhaps this analogy will help. In the Naval Observatory in Washington, D. C. an atomic clock measures time to the millionth of a second. Yet in my time a more precise method existed for measuring winter temperature in Wisconsin. One could read a thermometer, but depending on the location of the gauge the readings could vary. Now imagine a farmer entering the local barbershop, where, in conjunction with removing his coat(s) and stomping the snow off his boots, he exclaimed, "Jesus Christ it's cold!" Now, there you have a precise measurement.

The daily winter routine for the farmer began as in any other season with the morning milking. There was no need to start the milking process as early as in the other seasons so we allowed ourselves a half-hour

Winter scene late 1930s (Hedrick Home)

more of sleep. For Dad and I it still meant that one-fifth mile hike to the home farm barn in whatever weather winter had to offer. How delightful to duck into that relatively warm barn, heated by twenty plus cattle, four horses, several calves, and numerous cats. City folks in our modern perfumed society may find this hard to believe, but the odor in the barn was not at all unpleasant. The sweet sour smell of fermented corn silage, not unlike the smell one detects in a modern delicatessen greeted us. The first chore was to feed the cattle silage and ground feed. Next on to the milking. After milking we spread hay in front of the cattle and horses. Then breakfast time for us—a leisurely breakfast at this time of year. Next back to the home farm where the barn was given its first cleaning of the day. The animals remained in their stanchions, stalls or pens as the barn was cleaned. Now what to do with the manure? If it were a particularly vicious day weather wise the manure was dumped in the barnyard to be hauled to the field another day. Most of the time the manure was loaded on a sleigh and hauled directly to the fields where I spread it with a "hand operated" manure fork. But first the horses had to be harnessed. This was a tiresome routine no matter when done. Then we made the trip to the field with me standing on the planks amongst that day's load of manure. The rule was to start at the far end of a given field and work back towards the buildings. But on a blustery cold winter day I had no trouble cheating by finding a convenient area nearer the buildings. I suspect it took close to a half-hour to spread the manure, forkful by forkful, over the ground.* On occasion I rounded out the morning by hauling a load of chunk wood home from the woods or bundles of corn from shocks still standing in the field. Happiness was putting the horses back in the barn, removing their harnesses, and then heading for the warmth of the house.

There was this to be said for my cold weather experiences on the farm. The similar winter conditions experienced a few years later in North Korea did not surprise or terrorize me as it did men from warmer climes, or those who had not ever worked under severe winter conditions.

Unless harvesting wood was on the schedule we could laze around after the noon meal. There was time now for other enjoyable/leisurely pursuits. Conversation time could be extended and time devoted to reading newspapers and magazines in more detail. On occasion I spent a couple of hours rabbit hunting. Often too I spent time cracking and eating hickory nuts and butternuts in the heated milk house on the home farm.

Around 3 p.m. it was time to turn our attention to barn chores. Initially there was the relatively light job of caring for the few heifers and sheep housed in a small barn on the Bucholz farm. The major effort would be devoted to the milk cows on the home farm.

If weather permitted the cows were let out of the barn, both for exercise and to permit a more thorough cleaning of the barn. The relatively small amount of manure was dumped on the ground since it froze to the

---

*Today an automatic barn cleaner empties the manure into a manure spreader that costs as much as a small car. A large tractor remains hooked to the spreader all winter long. This tractor has a heated cab, a radio, and is air conditioned for summer use. Manure is hauled to the field daily whatever the weather or depth of the snowdrifts.

sled boards if left there overnight. After cleaning the barn and carrying in forkfuls of straw needed for bedding, I climbed up through a narrow chute into the silo and threw down enough corn silage for that evening and next morning. Not a tough job, and the aroma of fermented silage was pleasant. Next the silage was delivered to each cow's manger. A metal bushel basket was used with one basket usually holding enough for two cows. Remembered was the long trek with that relatively heavy basket from the silo area to the mangers furthest away. At some point a sack of ground feed was carried from the granary to a bin in the barn. Another one of those fun projects on our side hill, particularly so if it were an icy day. Next a scoop (two to three quarts) of ground feed for each cow, and the cow now has what is the equivalent of a pizza supreme for a human. At this point the barn was as clean as could be, smelling only of corn silage and ground feed. There was a blanket of straw nine to twelve inches thick for the cow's bedding. When finished, and before letting the cows back in, I took time to stand back and admire the scene. The barn door was then opened and the eager to enter animals went to their own stall where they allowed themselves to be locked into stanchions.

To round out the afternoon chores, hay was pitched out of the haymow. Later that evening and the following morning the hay would be tossed down a chute to the barn floor for distribution to the cattle and horses. The cows received the nutritionally rich clover and alfalfa hay; the horses the coarse timothy hay in view of their relatively light work load in the wintertime.

It's now close to suppertime, and other than evening milking, the end of the workday.

Winter milking, especially in the evening, was more relaxed than at other times of the year and not as time consuming. Since the cows were no longer on pasture, their milk production was relatively low (as was the milk check). Cows within a few months of calving were not milked so their bodies could direct all its energy to the calf they were carrying. Time for some "hi jinx." If Dad was no where near to observe, and our respective milking locations permitted, Aunt Lena and I might direct a stream of milk from the cow's teat at one another. I invariably started this, but the "little girl" in all adult women eventually manifested itself and she shot a stream back at me. Then there were the cats. They learned that if they sat in the right place, and stayed alert, a stream of warm milk was likely to come their way. Their mouths opened wide and they minded not at all if that stream of milk splattered all over their face.

Another pleasant winter chore was cleaning out the chicken coop. I suspect this took place two or three times during the winter. Being careful not to let any of the chickens escape from the building, I first moved all the manure to the exit door. Once ensured that the chickens were all well away from the door I quickly tossed the manure out on a pile. The result was a clean but barren chicken coop, and 100 relatively unhappy laying hens. Chickens love to dig and scratch. Where once they had straw, even though dirty straw, now all they had was a bare floor. Next came the fun part for both the chickens and me. Forkfuls of fresh clean straw was carried in and spread on the floor. Now the chickens reacted as did the cows when turned out in the spring. Not only was the straw fresh and clean, but in the threshing operation not all the kernels of grain came off the stalks so there was feasting as well. I found it enjoyable to stand there and watch and listen to the persistent happy clucking of the chickens. Perhaps I stayed there longer than I should have, given all the other chores that still needed to be done.

Yet another chore punctuating the winter scene was grinding feed for the cattle and pigs. Once again Dad placed red-hot coals under the oil pan of the old Fordson tractor so it could do its duty of powering the feed grinder. The grinder was positioned near the granary door and bolted down. Then the tractor was moved into position and the belt attached to power the grinder. Oats, barley, wheat or cob corn was either ground separately or combined together and fed into the grinder. My job was to shovel the ground feed into a bin as it dropped to the floor. A noisy and dirty job, yet not all that unpleasant. Before I was old enough to take on the harder job of feeding grain into the grinder we graduated to having Sylvester Weibel bring his self-contained truck-mounted feed grinder out to the farm from Norwalk. His operation reduced our labor involvement, but was still a noisy and dirty job. On occasion too we sacked up grain and corn and took it to Norwalk to be ground, and at times mixed with other nutrients at one of the two feed mills.*

Remembered as well as Christmas and the Bohn School Christmas program as fun events was wintertime butchering. Logically this was done in the wintertime when the freezing cold temperature reduced significantly the chance of meat spoiling before it could be processed. One or two other farmers came to help, usually Joe Steinhoff and Clarence Dittman. Butchering took place on the home farm. We butchered one beef and four to six pigs to meet (no pun intended) the needs of our family and my grandparents.

Watching the process as a kid was raw excitement. Later as a laborer I still looked forward to this event. The beef was led up to the haymow area where the same rope and pulley arrangement that served to loft hay to the mow from a wagon was readied to string up the beef. First one of the men swung a heavy sledgehammer hitting the animal in the middle of its forehead right above the eyes to stun it. The animal dropped like a rock and immediately its throat was slashed to drain out the blood. Now the animal was hoisted to be skinned, gutted, and quartered. Internal organs that were usable were harvested as well. Later that evening we carried the then frozen carcass into the milk house where my grandfather established his temporary butcher shop to cut up the meat.

The routine was different for butchering pigs. Instead of a hammer blow to the forehead we used a twenty-two-caliber rifle. A pig's brain is about the size of a half-dollar and is located midway between, and an inch above the eyes. This was the spot to hit to stun and drop the pig so it didn't feel the knife cutting its throat. This part of the process took place

---

*The mobile feed grinder and the two feed mills that once thrived in Norwalk are no longer in business. As far as is known no one has blamed their demise on Wal-Mart.

in the pig stable area. We then dragged the pig to a barrel of scalding hot water. This barrel was tilted at about a twenty-degree angle against a two-foot high sturdy table. Now the pig, dead for only a couple of minutes, was rapidly slid in and out of this scalding hot water. Damage to the meat occurred if it were left in the water too long. After five or six dips the hair could be easily removed. Next all the men applied their scrapers to the pig's hide and in a few minutes the pig was completely hairless. Then the pig was hung up and gutted and the usable internal organs harvested. The whole pig was now hung outside where it froze solid before being carried into the milkhouse that evening after chores. The crew then turns its attention to pig number two, etc.

No one ever wrote a romantic love song about how striking was this scene of five or six gleaming white pig carcasses reflecting the light from a bright moon. After evening chores we shouldered a whole pig carcass and carried it to the milkhouse. The weight of the carcass at this point was about 125 pounds. Grandfather Hedrick applied his surgical skills the next day to reducing those carcasses to manageable cuts of pork.

Those of you who have not had the opportunity to enjoy the over-powering delicious aroma from freshly made pig sausage do not know what you have missed. Even for us this was only for one or two days since the sausage meat then had to be immediately preserved. It tasted every bit as good as it smelled. After the first day or two the meat had to be stuffed in casings (pig guts, thoroughly cleaned) and then preserved by smoking.

In addition to satisfying hearty winter appetites a large portion of the meat was preserved for future needs. The kitchen became an extra busy place as the meat was processed. We made our own sausage with a small hand cranked device. There was also the canning process and some of the meat was deep-fried. In this process the sides of the butchered pig were cut into strips. After frying, the meat was placed in a crock-pot or jar and completely covered with grease. The hardened grease (lard) preserved the meat. Another means of preservation was to keep pork meat in salt brine until needed. Sausage and certain cuts of meat, particularly hams and bacon could be preserved by smoking it. The smoking process required a small building, perhaps as small as thirty square feet and as air tight as possible. It also required an abundant supply of small hickory wood branches. The meat was hung on hooks while hickory smoke was allowed to penetrate every pore of the meat. This could take a month or more depending on the size of the meat to be cured. The general rule of thumb was seven days of curing for each one-inch thickness of the meat. The meat was also heavily salted at some point in the process. Once cured the meat could be stored in the cellar until needed. Our neighbors, the Steinhoffs, buried their smoked hams in the granary oat bin to prevent flies from getting to the hams. On our farms my paternal grandmother performed the chore of smoking the meat. The process was time consuming and required constant attention. I remember on one occasion the smoking process did not go right and maggots infested the meat. She was sad and dejected knowing she had let the families down due to the loss of all that meat. My grandmother also made delicacies called pickled pigs feet and headcheese.* Neither of these were favorites of mine. Other spin-off delicacies of the pig butchering process were pig's brains and blood sausage (called "black pudding" in Great Britain and Ireland). Blood sausage is made by boiling down the blood with diced pork fat (or other filler) along with onion and bread crumbs until thick enough to congeal when cooled. Once again, I found it easy to pass on these delicacies. Another chore falling into my grandmother's sphere was the rendering of lard. She did this in a large (forty-gallon) cast iron kettle set over an outdoor fire. The same kettle was used to make soap. This latter process required a large amount of lye; an obnoxious ingredient if ever there was one.

In the meantime school age children and mothers were going

---

*HOG HEAD CHEESE: 1 large hog head, 1½ tablespoon salt, dash of red pepper, dash of black pepper, 1 onion, 1 cup vinegar. Clean hog head by removing eyes, ears, and brains. Saw into 4 pieces. Put in large pot and boil until tender. Remove meat from broth. Pick out bones and cook onion until done in broth. Dip out onion and run meat and onion through food chopper. Mix in peppers, vinegar and salt, put in cheesecloth (today the leg of a panty-hose works real well), hang, let drip overnight. Slice and enjoy.

through their winter routine as well. Children bundled up and walked to and from school. Mothers had the additional chore of guarding their children's health and caring for sick children. Then there was the pleasant chore of feeding the chickens; and gathering the eggs. I think my mother rather enjoyed breaking loose from that house full of children to spend time with her chickens.

I go back far enough in time to remember visiting relatives by sleigh. On many occasions this was at night when there was moonlight to light the way. This was the same sled used to haul manure, but a box replaced the planks used to haul manure. This was the same box used to haul ear corn, cabbage, pumpkins, etc. home from the field in the fall, gather stones in the spring, or spread lime in the fall or spring. We huddled under blankets, including the heavy horse blanket from my bed. Once at the host home the horses were put in their barn and the visiting began. On occasion we also made trips by sled to shop in Norwalk, but these trips took place during daylight hours. The horses were covered with blankets while they waited for the shoppers.

The sleigh was used for trips to Norwalk when either the road was impassable for automobiles, the usual case, or the automobile could not be started in cold weather. We were like most families on Summit Ridge who started with a Ford model "T", then graduated to a late 1920 vintage used Ford model "A".* In 1935-36 the more stylish and streamlined Chevrolets and Fords were seen in the church parking lot, but our family languished in that old Ford Model "A". In the mid-1940s Dad bought a used 1939 Oldsmobile. This was still the family car when I left home in 1947. One of our vehicles was a model "A" that had been converted to a truck by cutting off the back half of a sedan body and adding a wooden box. An altogether reliable vehicle, but often hard to start in cold weather.

---

*The old machine shed on the Bucholz farm stored what today would be a treasure of old horse-drawn personal conveyances. Tucked up in the rafters was a "one horse open sleigh". On the floor was a buggy, configured to be pulled by one horse. I suspect when the machine shed was torn down these relics of the past were tossed.

We kept it in a machine shed, but that didn't keep out the cold. On cold winter mornings Dad and I were faced with the job of starting the truck. No way could the battery turn over that stiff engine: Dad had to crank it. My job was to manipulate two levers on the steering column. This was a "pressure laden" assignment. Whenever starting a model "A", whether using the starter or the engine hand crank, these two levers had to be adjusted. The lever on the right controlled engine speed. Set too low, or not moved to increase engine speed as soon as the engine started resulted in the engine stopping (The person cranking the engine was not too happy if you allowed that to happen.) If set for the engine to run too fast, the engine could be damaged since in several degrees below zero weather it took time for engine oil to warm up to where it could circulate around the cylinders. Then there was the spark adjustment lever on the left that advanced or retarded the spark. It needed to be in the retarded position when starting the car. If not fully retarded the engine could "kick-back" (backfire). If this occurred while using the car's starter, the engine kickback could break the starter drive since the starter itself was still engaged. If the kickback occurred while cranking the car, a sprained or broken arm was not unusual. After I don't know how many attempts at starting—it varied day by day—Dad often removed the crank and banged it across the left front fender. You should have seen that fender! A typical verbal expression used in conjunction with the fender smack was **"Jesus H Christ!"** We never did learn what the "H" stood for.

Wintertime meant outdoor winter games, with an emphasis on sledding and skiing. Much as I envied my maternal cousin Jim Muehlenkamp's brand new balloon tired bike, I yearned for one of those sleighs where the handles were far enough back permitting you to actually twist the steel sled runners to change direction. As compensation Dad built us a rather fancy bob sled with two pairs of runners. Via a rope the front pair could be turned ninety degrees to the right or left. He built several of these for his nieces and nephews as well.

For adults, winter recreation meant card parties, usually on Sunday evenings. The location changed week by week. Now the hosting farm wife was not on her own as she was during threshing. Each family brought sandwiches, dessert, etc. And I do mean families. A given home was jam packed with people of all ages. No doubt the home's entire inventory of kerosene lamps was used to light up the rooms. Most of the women enjoyed chatting with each other more than playing cards, and they also kept an eye on the little children. The rest of us played, or stood around a table and observed the action. Usually we stood behind a favorite friend or relative. If you did, it was a good idea to be very quiet and to maintain a "stone" face. We all knew better than to exclaim, "Look at all those Kings and Queens," and to be sure not to brighten up or smile broadly if the person you were standing behind was holding what you knew were important cards in the game being played. My choice was either Clarence Dittman or my maternal Uncle Chuck. We all knew that at the end of the evening's card playing there was bound to be plenty of food for all.

On milk check day the farmer could now afford to spend a little more time in town. Card playing was popular and "buck euchre" was the game. Five-cents a bump and ten-cents per game was at risk for the players. In those cash-strapped times tension filled the air on occasion as the pot increased in value. Independent of milk check day, there remained the need to take the eggs to market and to shop. With the children home from school this trip was ideally made on a Saturday. This was usually done during daylight hours in winter since Saturdays were not now dedicated to fieldwork.

On occasion I found myself in Sparta, twelve miles from the farm, on a winter Saturday afternoon. Our family routinely made monthly shopping trips to this city of 5000. While there I might be released from parental control and allowed to attend an early afternoon movie. I suspect the cost to attend was a nickel or a dime. As noted earlier relative to free shows in Norwalk, movie studios turned out action filled, fast paced melodramas and adventure films aimed at we less demanding patrons. Imagine then what was offered in an early Saturday afternoon movie for a bunch of farm kids. The movie I best remember was a typical grade "B" Western starring Wild Bill Elliot. In one scene Wild Bill and a few others were cantering along. A shot rings out loud and clear enough to startle me. Wild Bill reigns in his horse; then says to his companions, "That sounded like a shot!" We farm yokels hooted and howled. For heavens sakes Bill, what else could it be but a shot? For a moment I felt quite superior and sophisticated as this silly scene played itself out.

Another remembered joy of wintertime was hot buttered popcorn. This was a treat not available to us once our home grown supply ran out. Earlier mention was made of my attempt to make money raising and selling popcorn. I don't recall that we ever purchased "store bought" kernel popcorn. Their customers were probably vendors like Pete Schreier who sold popcorn in conjunction with the Tuesday night free movie in Norwalk during the summer. Another likely customer was the street vendor in Sparta whose product was available throughout the day and evenings during fair weather at the corner of East Main and Water Streets. Our popcorn went into the attic, right next to the chimney where it dried to the point where it could be easily shelled. Mother timed the feast so the popcorn was ready when we returned to the house after evening chores. This absolutely delicious aroma nearly overwhelmed us. A heavy-duty cast iron frying pan was used and when hot the kernels popped to their full tender potential. Hot melted butter was "lavishly" applied. Since we had many eager customers in our house, a heaping dishpan of popped corn was prepared. On other winter evenings, as noted earlier, apples from the cellar were often on the evening snack menu.

Another winter ritual we kids enjoyed was the evening visits to the Steinhoffs and Dittmans. Aunt Lena was our escort. Although we played games, the hot buttered popcorn is what I remember as the highlight of the evening. I also remember how cold it could be walking home.

Winter meant Christmas with one of the highlights being the Bohn School Christmas program and a bag of candy from Father Mechler. No matter how tight the money supply might be we could count on one store bought gift. One year my hoped for, prayed for, and asked for gift was an air rifle (BB gun). About a month before Christmas one of my shoes wore out. The sole had separated from the rest of the shoe. I knew the shoe was beyond repair. "There goes my air rifle," I thought. I assumed my dollar portion of the family's Christmas funds would have to go for a pair of new shoes. Since this was wintertime I could hide the shoe in boots for all outside activities. When indoors I tried dragging my foot so the sole wouldn't flop, but I knew this would soon be noticed. It might not look quite right for an otherwise healthy kid to be limping around. I avoided detection for a while using a large rubber band cut from an old automobile inner tube. The inevitable happened; Dad spotted this large band around the damaged shoe. The result, a new pair of shoes, and on Christmas morning there was a new air rifle as well.

There was one unplanned and unpleasant chore that all too often came along in the wintertime. That was pulling pump. Why did the need to pull pump occur most often in the wintertime? Wells on Summit Ridge were sunk to an average depth of approximately 200 feet. At the bottom of the well shaft, enclosed in a pipe was a cylinder with a piston. Since we had no electricity, pumping water was dependent on either the one-stroke Johnson and Johnson engine or the windmill. The engine was much preferred since it delivered even power for the up and down motion of the piston at the bottom of the well. In winter these engines were hard to start. As a result we relied on the windmill and the plentiful supply of wind. As the wind rose and fell in velocity the jerking unevenness was transmitted to the piston. In time the piston broke.

A couple of neighbors showed up to pull pump. Ropes and pulleys were positioned on the windmill. A large metal clamp with a vice grip was positioned to hold the pipe as necessary removal and re-attachment of pipes took place. The one and one half-inch galvanized pipe sections were each thirteen-foot long. As they were pulled up they were unscrewed and set aside. The well on the home farm was sunk to a depth of 180 feet, the one on the Bucholz farm 190 feet.* This meant fourteen sections of pipe had to be pulled before we gained access to the damaged piston inside the cylinder. Once the repairs were made there remained the laborious task of reassembling the pipes, section by section, and then lowering them back down the well shaft. As noted, this task was usually required to be performed in wintertime. In addition to the cold, work gloves quickly became wet in the process adding to the misery of the job. In summary, a clearly obnoxious job!

Much has changed to make Wisconsin winters much more palatable. Fast, powerful, and efficient snowplows all but ensure the roads will be open for travel each day. If necessary, sand or salt is spread on icy roads to make them safe for travel. Fuel oil or liquid propane (LP) fired heaters and insulation combine to keep all corners of the home pleasantly warm. But it can still get cold and nasty. More and more of my generation are escaping to the sunbelt during the worst of winter's weather. My wife and I have a total of twelve siblings in Wisconsin and Minnesota. Weather reports are exchanged by e-mail on a regular basis, and from time to time they bemoan their weather plight. We ensure that they hear all about our San Diego (California) area weather in these exchanges.

This may be simple nostalgia—but I still rather envy their experiencing a Wisconsin winter.

---

*The well on the Bucholz farm was recently sunk to a depth of 480 feet; the one on the home farm to a depth of 375 feet.

CHAPTER 18

High School

$\mathbf{A}$ fitting description of my high school years was that they were endured more than enjoyed. Up until two years before I finished grade school, farm boys as rule did not attend high school. Farmers saw their sons as future farmers and those with high school age sons were likely to say, "You don't learn about farming from books." Dad subscribed to this line of thinking but Mother felt differently. Her view prevailed. As a result, I was off to Norwalk High School in September of 1941. The freshman class numbered approximately twenty students. In December of 1941 our country entered World War II. I graduated in June of 1945 and Japan surrendered in August of 1945. Mine was a World War II high school class for all the years of the war.

If my high school experience was to be more endured than enjoyed, I apparently enjoyed my freshman year in Norwalk entirely too much. I am sure this was a shared decision, but Dad informed me that I would be attending Sparta High School beginning with my sophomore year. It wasn't that I misbehaved at Norwalk, but obviously I must not have earned high marks as a scholar.

Transferring from Norwalk High School with its approximately

80 students and four teachers to Sparta's 600 plus student body and 25 teachers was traumatic. From associations in grade school, the church, and frequent visits to the town I knew most of the students at Norwalk. Now at this "big city" school I knew only three other students. One was a neighbor, Mary Rapp. Another my older sister Elaine who, beginning as a freshman, had attended Sparta High School all along. The third was my younger sister Dorothy who was starting her freshman year. Adding to my discomfort were all those "sophisticated big city girls" at Sparta High School who scared the dickens out of me. To make matters worse, another farm kid in the agriculture class humiliated me. Probably at the first, or one of the first class meetings this fellow pointed out to the rest of the class that I was from the "ridge" and could be identified by the red clay on my shoes. All this from a "sand farmer" from out Cataract way. This then taunter eventually became my brother-in-law.*

School busses did not exist. While attending school in Norwalk the logistics were relatively simple. The school was two miles from the farm. As noted in an earlier chapter, fellow student Johnny Berendes provided taxi service. Riding with Johnny was exciting. If he were around today Johnny would be a natural candidate for NASCAR track driving. He was a skillful driver and he drove fast! Each school day our route took us past the Steinhoff farm. Their house and garden were on one side of the road, while the chicken coop was on the other side. The chickens crossed the road to feast on insects and worms in the garden—then returned to their coop. A curve in the road hid an approaching car from the chicken's view. Johnny loved to surprise and scatter them. Each year before St. John's annual chicken dinner fund-raiser the question was asked, "Where could they obtain the chickens needed for the main dish?" Joe Steinhoff, with his keen sense of humor, suggested they send Johnny Berendes over the ridge in his car. A truck could then follow to pick up the chickens.

Later my transportation to school was combined with the daily milk

---

*Dave Sullivan, who married my sister Joan.

delivery to the Norwalk creamery. The minor fender bender I had as an unauthorized (by Dad) and unlicensed driver was recounted in an earlier chapter. Transportation was more complicated when I transferred to Sparta twelve miles away. Before I became a taxi operator for five other students I needed to complete most of my sophomore year. I was almost fifteen years old in September 1942, too young for a driver's license. Several "jury rig" arrangements were made for me to attend school during my sophomore year. One arrangement in particular stands out—and it was **ugly**.

Fort McCoy was a booming Army post near Sparta and many locals were employed there. Arrangements were made with a party in Norwalk to pick me up at Schaller's store, one and one-half miles from our home. Pick-up time was around 6:45 a.m. They dropped me off in Sparta at the junction of Tyler and Main streets. From there I walked three blocks to the school. Luckily the janitors had the school opened so I had a warm place to wait for nearly two hours before school started. After school was out I hung around the school until time to head for the same street junction and my five p.m. pick-up time. After dropping me off at Schaller's store, I walked home in darkness. To make matters worse, this was wintertime and on many of those trips it could be windy cold. I was awakened by an alarm clock each school day. The house was at best cool. No one else was awake. Breakfast was cold cereal. The walk to Schaller's store was made in darkness. At the store I did my best to find a windbreak while waiting for my ride. Five adults were already crowded in this boxy 1920 vintage unheated car. We exchanged not a word of greeting as I took my place in the crowded middle of the front seat. My legs straddled the floor-mounted stick shift. The rest chatted amicably. I can still recall the musty smell of the bodies and car. A half-hour later I was dropped off in Sparta, again without a word being spoken. Likewise for the trip home in the evening, except now there was little conversation between the tired workers.

If the bad news was that this may not have been my parent's finest hour in making arrangements for getting me to and from school, the good news was that this arrangement didn't last long. I assume we paid by the week and I recall on only two occasions paying the driver. I spent the rest of the winter months staying with my paternal Aunt Josephine Nichols and her two young sons in Sparta. Her husband was working for the Army in Chicago as an instructor in an electronics school. I was able to help out with chores—I was an expert at digging firewood out of snow after all. In addition to handling my aunt's wood carrying and snow shoveling needs I also made some money by doing similar chores for her neighbors. I enjoyed not having to do morning and evening chores at home, and how about walking to school on sidewalks—and on level ground? Then too, now and then I could find a quarter to attend a movie.

If I enjoyed not having to do farm chores while living in Sparta, Dad did not particularly enjoy doing the farm work without my help. In early spring of 1943 he bought a used 1920 vintage Chevrolet sedan, a boxy but generally reliable car. At fifteen and one-half I was now old enough to drive and spent the rest of my high school years driving myself, my two sisters, (who could now live at home) and other neighboring students to school. Joe Mosnicka was a passenger for a time; he met us at Schaller's store. Mary and Betty Rapp met the car pool at Bohn school. Betty Rapp became valedictorian of her high school class, due in part I am sure to the efficiency and comfort of the taxi service afforded her. Sisters Betty and Nancy Henderson and June Mlsna, all from Farmer's Valley were also passengers at one time. There was a time when all five of my passengers were young ladies. Perhaps I should have, but I didn't really enjoy the one-hour round trip each day with five loquacious high school girls. The car had no radio, but doesn't it figure that we didn't need one?

By the start of my junior year in 1943 we had upgraded the car to another box-like, but more reliable 1928 model "A" Ford. It sat outside under a pine tree at our home year round—and this model "A" could be counted on to start with no problem. In the winter there was often the need to shovel snow before moving the car. There was no car heater so it was just as well that six of us were crowded in that relatively small car to and from school.

This was wartime with gasoline and tires strictly rationed. Since I was driving to school we were liberally supplied with "A" stamps. So liberal in fact that a number of my classmates were able to use their family cars on prom night via the "A" stamps I could easily spare. A patriotic rule at the time, generally practiced by all, was to drive no faster than thirty-five miles-per-hour. Cars at that time were most gas efficient at this speed. Violators were reminded of their exceeding the limit by other drivers giving them the "V" for victory in Morse code with their horns; beep-beep-beep-beeeeeeep. Tires were especially hard to come by. You had to appear before the rationing board and argue your case. As far as I know we never needed a tire, but I suspect the rationing board would have been sympathetic to ensuring that a de facto school bus remain safe and road worthy.

It's perhaps not surprising that just getting to and from school was the most remembered part of my high school experience. But then there was the academic side of school. I enjoyed and prospered in the agriculture class. Via this class I introduced checking the milk of each of our cows for butter fat content. As noted earlier, the creamery in Norwalk tested the collective milk daily to determine its butter fat percentage with the results dictating the dollar value for the milk. An individual cow could be a dud and bring down the fat percentage and we would never know it. To find that dud a sample of each cow's milk was collected on a monthly basis and tested in the school's agriculture lab. Cows showing a trend for low butterfat content were sent to market as soon as a replacement was available. Another class I enjoyed was manual training and its tough, no-nonsense teacher Ed Blewett. This class dovetailed nicely with my interest and involvement with carpentry projects while growing up on the farm.

I have avoided discussing other academic subjects as long as I could since my record here is less than noteworthy. I didn't have to study much to get by. No one pushed me. Our high school did not have counselors at the time. No doubt the teachers and administrators subjectively saw their farm boy students as future farmers as well. They satisfied themselves in knowing that as a result of the high school tutelage they provided, we would likely have more educational polish than our parents did. I do recall Mother encouraging me to participate in an extemporaneous speaking class, but I wasn't self-assured enough for that kind of involvement. I also remember getting an "F" in English literature. I was shocked and embarrassed, although not surprised. I don't recall any parental scolding—but I suspect there was something said that I don't remember. Possibly my relatively decent grades in history, government, and geography resulted in my getting a "bye" on this one time occurrence of receiving an "F". In general though I just "muddled" along in high school.

I thought the girls were "stuck up." They weren't, but that was the typical view of all too many farm boys who came to school with an inferiority complex. The "big city boys," who were also as a rule the sports heroes of the school, were friendly and went out of their way to be kind and helpful.

I don't recall being self-conscious relative to the clothes I wore. I do remember on one occasion three or four of us boys chatting about clothes during the noon hour. One asked the other how many pairs of trousers he had. "About ten," he replied. I was awe struck; here I was with two pair of rather threadbare trousers and this guy has about ten. I was not at all bitter, nor did I feel sorry for myself; I think I was rather amused at what I saw as this glaring disparity of an item that didn't interest me to any great extent to begin with.

A keen disappointment in high school was not having an opportunity to earn a letter in sports and wear one of those red sweaters with gold rings around the right sleeve. One ring for each year you won a letter in a given sport. I would have enjoyed trying out for basketball and baseball. I had installed half of an old dutch barn door in the driveway area of the home farm hayloft (where it still hangs as of 2005), attached a hoop, and spent much of my spare time shooting baskets. I found it a pleasant diversion on those daily trips to the haymow to throw down the next day's quota of hay. During noontime scrimmages at school I had the reputation of being a pretty fair shot, particularly from the corners. In make-up games my teammates fed me the ball for these corner shots. What we all really loved to play was baseball. As noted earlier, I was not a heavy hitter but could pay my way as a fairly proficient outfielder. But participation was impossible due to the need to drive the school taxi. I was but one of many, who for one reason or another could not participate in after school activities, to include my five passengers.

High school ended for me with no prom night to remember and no class ring. My parents gave me money to buy a class ring, but left it up to me as to how to spend it. I choose to buy carpentry tools.

I don't know who the person was that came up with the motto for me in the senior yearbook. At best it was a left-handed complement. The motto was "Never Over Studious, Serious, or Sad." I'd like to say to this person that what was said then might have had more than a kernel of truth to it. But I went on to earn a bachelor's degree, two master's degrees, a doctorate in law, and attended a Home Depot class on how to install a ceiling fan—SO THERE!

Approximately ninety-five graduates were in Sparta High School's class of 1945. No valedictorian status for me this time, I was "nosed out" of that enviable position by fifty-nine of my fellow graduates.

CHAPTER **19**

Joining Up

On 7 May 1945, a month before I graduated from high school, Germany surrendered to the Allies. In the meantime the war raged on with Japan. My parents and I fully expected I would be called to the colors when I turned eighteen the following October. My thought processes were already debating which military service to join, or should I wait to be drafted? There seemed to be no reason to make other plans.

On 14 August 1945 Japan accepted the Allied surrender terms. World War II in its entirety was finally over. I am quite sure but for the atomic bombs dropped on Japan I would have been involved in the planned 1946 invasion of Honshu, the main Island of Japan on which was located Tokyo. (The island of Kyushu, south of Honshu, was to be invaded in October of 1945).* With the end of the war there was no immediate need to

---

*In February of 1945 Prime Minister Churchill and President Roosevelt met on the island of Malta in the Mediterranean Sea. At this point Germany was considered a defeated nation and the atomic bomb was still an unproven theory. The two leaders and their military staffs agreed that 1947 was the likely year for victory over Japan. From Malta those two leaders flew to Yalta for a meeting with Premier Stalin. Here Stalin stated that Russia was prepared to enter the war against Japan six weeks after Germany surrendered. Our Chief of Naval Operations at the time was Admiral Ernest King, a man not given to excited outbursts or wild projections. When Stalin's statement had been translated he blurted out, "We just saved two million lives."

plot and plan relative to the military. In October 1945 I registered for the draft. There was still uncertainty so I settled back to wait and see—and work for my dad. I suspect about this time Dad and I reached an agreement that led to my raising two litters of pigs in lieu of wages.

Much as I debated with myself which military service to join (had the war not ended), now the debate was what did I want to do with the rest of my life. Little by little the decision to join the military solidified in my mind. From time to time during my last year at home Dad often deemed it necessary, when an issue arose between us, to inform me that next year I might have to work for another farmer. My stock answer was, "Next year I will be in the Army." My mother, unlike Dad, suspected I was serious about enlisting. Dad I suppose saw it as a bluff—much as I viewed his statement from time to time of having me work for another farmer. I wasn't sure why he kept bringing this up. Perhaps he wanted to avoid another "raid" on the granary and corncrib in conjunction with another crop of pigs. No doubt but that I took advantage of working within the family environment by goofing off from time to time. This was something I couldn't imagine doing if working for someone else. At any rate, the threat in one form or another kept popping up along the way.

I mentioned to my Grandfather Hedrick that I was considering joining the military. With a mischievous smile he said, "Well Joe, with your big feet you won't fall over if you get shot." Mother questioned three of her brothers who had served in the military relative to the likelihood of my passing the physical. One told her that with my having pneumonia as a child the likely condition of my lungs precluded the military from accepting me. Another brother said my flat feet would keep me out. What flat feet? Probably no healthier pair of feet ever marched in the Marine Corps. Up to hearing about these predictions I intended to join the Army. Once my uncle's opinions were made known to me I thought, "I'll show you; I'll join the toughest service we on Summit Ridge were familiar with—the United States Marine Corps!"

No doubt the mystique of the Marines seeped its way into our minds as we absorbed the battles of World War II. That mystique was enhanced by the death of one of the men from Summit Ridge. This was Lloyd Ziegler who was killed in action on Iwo Jima in 1945. He was twenty-one years old at the time, and his was the only death among the young men who served in the military from Summit Ridge during World War II. The aura of that, plus the fact that his death occurred in one of the bloodiest battles the Marines ever fought made Lloyd a hero figure to us all, and especially to this now aspiring Marine. Iwo Jima ranks today, sixty years later as the toughest battle the Marines ever engaged in. I am understandably proud that my own involvement in the Chosin Reservoir campaign in Korea (November/December of 1950) is considered one of three of the toughest battles in Marine Corps history. Lloyd served in a rifle company. I am proud to say I spent a good part of the Chosin Reservoir campaign with our battalion's rifle companies.

January of 1947 seemed like the right time to make my move. The farm routine had settled down to the slower pace of winter—and yet the threat of working in the woods hung in the air. The festive seasons of Thanksgiving and Christmas were now history for the year. By enlisting now I ensured getting out ahead of the full fury of a Wisconsin winter. I would go to Boot Camp in either San Diego, California or Parris Island, South Carolina, both with markedly more moderate winter weather.

My major concern at the time of enlistment was the Marine Corps recruiting poster that proclaimed in bold and colorful letters: "Only 100,000 can serve." As a result I wasn't sure what might happen, and thinking the worst, I assumed it would be difficult to enlist in the Marine Corps. As a result my departure from home was on the quiet side. I do not remember saying goodbye to anyone in the family, although I may have patted my dog Corky on the head.

On my first attempt to enlist, neighbor Leander Ebert picked my Aunt Lena and me up after chores one evening and took me to my Aunt Josephines in Sparta. On the way we passed a girl friend's home where I left a box of chocolates in her rural route mailbox. This was the same young lady on whom I had invested approximately three dollars for jewelry that I subsequently spotted when she came to the communion rail. Here already were indications of this young lady being a "high maintenance woman."

I spent the night at Aunt Josephines, and the next day walked the mile to the depot and caught a train for the twenty-six mile trip to LaCrosse. The recruiting Sergeant met me at the station. The news was not good. He said he had tried to reach me before I left home. Apparently the quota for the area had been filled and I would have to wait a few more days before I could report for the enlistment process. Now I had to return home and explain why I was back. I was glad there were no formal good-byes on the previous leaving.

During this two or three day period before I was due to report again an event occurred that I still remember ever so clearly. In fact, although my nephew Mike has remodeled the old barn considerably I can still find the spot where my dad and I stood during this event. I was cleaning the area where we kept our four horses one morning when Dad approached me. Apparently he was now convinced of my intent to follow through on enlisting. He asked me not to do so, and in a plaintiff voice asked me to think of my brothers and sisters. I might have responded that my brothers and sisters would be in the same situation as they'd be in if he were to send me off to work for another farmer—as was mentioned from time to time. I knew he didn't want to lose this "horse" who knew the ins and outs of the farm quite well. Wisely I said nothing. I felt sorry for him, and guilty since I knew I was going all the way if I could. We had a subdued conversation wherein I deviously mentioned that at least I wanted to go as far as Milwaukee. Actual contract enlistment would not occur until I went on to Chicago. That cheered him and in a more confident voice he suggested this was a good idea since I would have the opportunity to visit Milwaukee—"But then come back home," he said.

I don't think I wavered in those few days as to whether or not to follow through. I do remember though being sick the night before I left home and throwing up from my upstairs bedroom window.

Again no remembered good byes upon leaving for my second attempt. This time no Aunt Lena along either. I walked to the Ebert farm that late January evening. As you proceed west from the home farm on what is now Kellogg Avenue you crest a hill. Look back and in January you can see right into the barn a couple of hundred yards away. Another one-fifth mile beyond was my own home standing out clearly in the stark winter countryside. I really felt empty looking at that well lit barn with the familiar evening milking operation going on, and the more distant lights from our house.

I suspect Leander Ebert had his doubts of my enlisting too, but he did take me to my Aunt Josephines in Sparta. No dropping off candy along the way this time. The next day I was off to LaCrosse where the recruiting Sergeant sent me on to Milwaukee. I arrived there around 4:30 p.m. Within an hour a group of five prospective Marines were on the train for Chicago and I was one of them.

Chicago! Loud, brassy, broad-shouldered Chicago! A really big city! We were right "down town." This farm boy was in awe of the noise, particularly of the elevated trains. I remember too the dirty snow, partially melted, and how eerily yellow it all looked under the lighting from adjacent buildings and what seemed like dim streetlights. We were fed at a downtown restaurant and put up for the night in what I assume was a YMCA. Now ten prospective Marines were assembled in this one large dormitory room. I found my roommates to be a pleasant and friendly bunch. I was particularly amused by one of them who, on several occasions said he was looking for the individual who *Began the Beguine* (a popular song at the time) so he could tell him to stop it.

The next day was the physical, and what a crushing disappointment when I was rejected because of a tooth cavity. Fix the cavity and all would be okay, but I had no money to cover this kind of expense. I saw myself going home once again—this time truly embarrassed and humiliated. A Marine Master Sergeant in the recruiting office took pity and made arrangements for me to see his dentist. This kindly dentist who treated me said he was happy to do the work at no charge under the circumstances. All this delayed my departure for Boot Camp by a day so I spent another night at the YMCA. The next day I was sworn into the Marine Corps for four years.* I was now a "salaried" man ($75.00 per month). My serial number was 643262. The date was 30 January 1947. That evening I was off by train for Parris Island, South Carolina and ten weeks of Boot Camp. I recall being quite happy to have been able to join the Marines—yet understandably apprehensive of what might lie ahead.

---

*The oath at the time was as follows: I (Joseph C. Hedrick) swear that I will bear true faith and allegiance to the United States of America; that I will serve them honestly and faithfully against all their enemies whomsoever; and that I will obey the orders of the President of the United States, and the orders of the officers appointed over me, according to the Rules and Articles for the government of the Army, Navy, and Marine Corps of the United States. So help me God.

PART 2

Military Service

CHAPTER 20

Parris Island and the First Day of Boot Camp

The train trip through Illinois, Indiana, Ohio, Pennsylvania and Maryland was thoroughly enjoyed by this geography buff. I arrived in Washington, D.C. around three p.m. the following day. A couple of us joined forces for a taxi tour of the nation's capital. When I mentioned in a letter home all the places I saw in those couple of hour tours, some in my family questioned how I could see so much in so little time.

Later that evening we started off for Parris Island. I remember the railroad passenger car being of a lower quality than the one we traveled in from Chicago to Washington, D.C. Perhaps a way of easing me into what lay ahead. I was increasingly apprehensive.

At first light the next morning I took note of the landscape as we rolled along. We were in the South—the Confederacy! But where were the plantations, the camellias and magnolias? Where were the Negroes playing banjos and strumming *Old Black Joe*? Nor was the Tara plantation to be seen so no Scarlet O'Hara or Rhett Butler. All I saw was mile after mile of piney woods and decrepit shacks.

Sometime that morning we rolled through Beaufort, S.C. and on to the railroad siding at Yemassee. This was the last civilian outpost and now the real world hit us. I remember the surroundings and atmosphere as being grim—very grim! The heavy cloud cover and intermittent mist did not help. We were not exactly cheered either by a group of recent Boot Camp graduates departing at the time who kept chanting, "You'll be sorreee!"

Parris Island is approximately four miles long and three miles wide. Of the 8000 acres of land, 4400 were usable for training and maintenance of the base. Most of the island was only a few feet above sea level—no point was above twenty feet. Before it became part of the United States; France, Spain and England owned the Island in that order. At one time the Island was called Port Royal and was the home port for pirate ships. Poisonous snakes such as copperheads, water moccasins, and coral snakes inhabited the Island. Most prevalent were the southeast diamondback rattlesnakes. Sharks were known to show up at the Island's boat dock and alligators occasionally visited the training area from their homes in the swamp. Those who wavered in the days ahead no doubt took all this into consideration before attempting to make a break back to civilian life by swimming off the Island. In summary, Marines considered Parris Island a combination of Alcatraz and Devil's Island. There was a second Marine Boot Camp at San Diego. This one was surrounded by the city of San Diego and was located next to the city's airport. The regimen there was just as tough as at Parris Island, but its citified location, pleasant climate, and no insects resulted in those of us who went through Parris Island to somewhat derisively refer to Marines who went through San Diego Boot Camp as "Hollywood Marines."

The term "Boot Camp" has its roots in the jargon of the U.S. Navy. It might be well to point out here that the Marine Corps is part of the Navy Department. Our vocabulary is based on Navy terms. We learned early on that a "Boot" was the lowest rank in the Corps. At one time the Navy issued rubber boots to be worn while cleaning decks of ships. Quickly discarded by veterans, new recruits reporting on board ship with their brand new boots were made all the more conspicuous. These new men were greeted by; "Here comes some more rubber boots." Over the years this was simplified to "Boot." In practice the term lingers in the military vocabulary long after Boot Camp. A Sergeant with twenty-seven years in the Marine Corps may refer to a friend with twenty-six years of service as a "Boot."

We had few precious seconds to reflect on what these departing graduates meant to infer by their chant of "You'll be sorreee." We were quickly hustled onto Marine Corps buses. Some of the brave souls were still hamming it up—or was it false bravado? Here we sighted for the first time the non-commissioned officers (Corporals and Sergeants) in field hats carrying menacing swagger sticks: the dreaded **Drill Instructors!**

The first thing this super sharp Marine Sergeant did upon entering the bus was just glare at us disdainfully for what seemed an unnecessary long period of time. One New York City boy was sitting near the front of the bus and he unwisely made a remark. Boom! This muscular Sergeant grabbed him and literally threw him off the bus. There a second Marine caught him and hoisted him back onto the bus. Then the Drill Instructor uttered his first words. He began nicely enough, "You shitheads," he screamed—but the language relative to personal references all went downhill from there.

At this point the Sergeant told us what he thought of us. "Never had such a load of trash, pond scum, etc. arrived at Parris Island." He strode up and down the aisle reminding us over and over how insignificant and absolutely disgusting we were. In less than thirty seconds he convinced us, at least many of us, that we were indeed nothings. "Okay, they may have accepted you back home, but this is the Marine Corps—BOOT— and you are now nothing, etc., etc. But damn it, I am stuck with you and from now on when I say jump, you jump, etc., etc. **Do you understand?**" We answered with a chorus of disjointed "yes's," and a few "yah's." That really infuriated him. He forcefully and convincingly informed us that from now on our response was to be a simultaneous **"Yes Sir!"** We were no longer individuals after all. **"Do you understand?"** I thought we gave him a coordinated and loud "Yes Sir" this time, but his response was something like, "You scum, you shitheads, I could not hear you: **DO YOU UNDERSTAND?"** This time our **"Yes Sir!"** proved we were reasonably fast learners.

As noted, it took less than thirty-seconds to completely convince us that we were indeed insignificant, if in fact even worthy of being called human beings. I am sure I didn't think of this at the time, but I still remember clearly another attempt to make me feel insignificant. The locale was what was then Sacred Heart Catholic Church in Pine Hollow. This was a small rural church a few miles east of Cashton. I recall a long—long Sunday afternoon of services involving many parishes. I suspect the Bishop was there as well. I was eight or nine at the time. I have three distinct memories from this event. The first was the perception that all those who graced the altar were unsmiling angry men. Another was the angry and long public tirade one of the priests made against one or more boys in a front pew who did something to provoke the ire of this man. Finally, there was the passionate attempt by another priest to convince us how insignificant we as humans were compared to the Almighty. He went on and on and on, working himself into frenzy as he searched for the right words, the right analogy to make his point. One of his analogies was to ask us to visualize ourselves as insects (ants) and compare ourselves to God. He hesitated a bit; decided we humans might still see ourselves as much too significant, then quickly went on to suggest we imagine ourselves even considerably smaller than an ant. I don't know how many of those in the pews he convinced—I know this Sergeant, with his more colorful vocabulary, made his point of our insignificance in a few seconds.

The routine for the next few hours was hectic and humiliating. It took twenty to twenty-five seconds to give each of us a haircut. The result—absolutely no hair left on our heads. At one point we stood in front of long steel tables where we surrendered the last reminders of civilian life. We stripped naked. Shorts, undershirts and socks went into the trash. The rest of our civilian clothes were folded and placed in a bag. Into the bag also went wristwatches, combs, keys, wallets, money, etc. Now the bag was sealed and stored. When you left Parris Island, either as a graduate or if you flunked out, your sealed bag was returned to you. Being suitably clothed (naked), we were routed, one by one, into a small office. Here a psychologist asked us one question; "Do you like girls?" Next we were issued a sea bag (duffel bag) along with the military clothes and footwear we needed over the next ten weeks. Quick, snap judgments were made relative to sizes. Actually the unsmiling people issuing clothing were quite astute at quickly sizing up a person and giving him what fit fairly well. More attention was paid to ensure we had the correct size shoes. Then we dressed in a military uniform and stuffed everything else in our sea bag.

At the next table we were issued what is called 782 gear: so called because the form you sign to obtain this equipment is so numbered. A Marine will sign many 782 forms as he goes from unit to unit over the years. Now we had a cartridge belt, entrenching tool, knapsack, haversack, poncho, shelter half, tent pole, tent pegs, canteen and a mess kit.

There remained one more table to walk by. Here there was a wire basket for each of us. As we passed down a line various items relating to personal hygiene were tossed in. Soap, tooth paste and brush, razor and blades, deodorant, towels, etc. Also a book that was to be our bible for the next ten weeks entitled *Guidebook for Marines*. Finally a tin pail and heavy hand brush. What in the world could these be for?

Late that afternoon sixty thoroughly confused and bewildered young men, loaded down with a heavy sea bag, were led to our new home—a nondescript two story barracks. We occupied the top floor. The Drill Instructor then informed us of what was to happen next. "When I say dismissed, I want you to double-time up those stairs. Then, two by two, I want you to stand in front of a bunk." He also told us not to put anything on the bunk. Not only was he kind enough to tell us what he wanted us to do, he also told us what he wanted to see when he said dismissed—"asses and elbows!"

The bunks were two high and naturally we all eyed the bottom bunk and wondered how we might win that coveted slot. The Drill Instructor took care of that. As he passed down the line, bunk by bunk, he pointed to one of us and said "top bunk." I was assigned a top bunk.

Next we were schooled on how to stow our newly issued clothing and equipment. Selected items in a footlocker, others in a wall locker, and 782 gear strapped to the end of the bottom bunk. Top bunk man's gear on starboard side; lower bunk man on port side. Next we were issued bed linens and two blankets—followed by practice in making up a bed. Many of us were introduced that night to a "hospital fold."

This tall, neat, and stern Sergeant who greeted us on the bus, and who bedeviled us during the entire checking in process was our new god, and he treated us with steadied contempt. He kept reminding us that we were not Marines, and from what he had already observed we were unlikely to ever make the grade. We were Boots, or Recruits, and often that most endearing of terms—**Shitheads**. I am sure most of us were in a state of shock, to varying degrees homesick, and scared stiff.

We then fell out for chow, on the double naturally. Darkness had fallen as our ragged and loose formation was led off for the evening meal. The relatively dark and spartan mess hall did not make us feel any better. When we returned to the barracks we practiced over and over making up our bunks. There would be no grace period as of tomorrow. Many times that day I asked myself why in the world did I chose to place myself in this situation? Mercifully it was then time for lights out.

CHAPTER 21

Boot Camp

I was punctual at getting up in the morning when called. I recall a neighbor discussing with my dad his problem in getting his son to "rise and shine." He looked towards me and said, "I suppose you have the same problem with Joe." "Oh no," my dad replied, "Joe gets up at first call." I really appreciated that statement. My fellow recruits used to joke that the first two sounds they heard in the morning was whatever method the Drill Instructor used to awaken us, followed by my feet hitting the floor (deck) as I bailed out of the upper bunk. As a result I was assured of a wash basin in the head (bathroom) while many others stood in line waiting for an opening. This gave me extra time to both make up my bunk to ensure a quarter bounced if tossed on the blanket, and otherwise square my gear away before "fall out for chow" was yelled.

The word to "fall out for chow" was always a welcome announcement and resulted in a prompt response. We marched as a platoon to the mess hall. Each platoon had a time slot they had to hit to ensure that the maximum number of men were fed in an allocated amount of time. On command we filed in and picked up a steel tray with five compartments along with flatware. Then we passed along a steam table for that meal's portion of the 3500 to 4000 calories we consumed daily. A platoon was allocated twenty minutes to move in and out of the mess hall for a given meal. Eight minutes to go through the mess line and twelve minutes to eat. This permitted 1000 men to be fed in one hour. I had no complaints about the food. I was particularly fond of what was called apple butter. Much like applesauce but smoother, and used as a spread on bread.

Other than the sixty minutes a day involved in eating three meals we were kept hopping from reveille at five a.m. to lights out at nine p.m. How quiet it became at nine p.m. No talking was allowed. We were all alone with our thoughts. Sleep came quickly given the physical exertion we were subjected to. The exceptions were those on firewatch, or those unfortunate few who had to sleep lying across eight rifles.

The second day at Parris Island we were introduced to what was to be our "best friend" from then on. This was the nine and one-half pound Garand M-1 semi-automatic rifle. For many of the recruits this was the first time in their lives they had held a firearm of any kind. God help the man who did not dedicate himself to taking the best of care of his rifle. In those days it was not unusual for a Drill Instructor to punch one forcefully in the chest with the butt of the rifle if the weapon was not absolutely spotless. And if you dropped your rifle you were not likely to sleep alone that night. As noted above, you slept, or tried to sleep lying across eight rifles.

After we were issued the rifle, along with a bayonet, we learned how to disassemble, clean, and then reassemble the rifle. On our own, in the short time before lights out that evening, we were expected to learn all the ballistic and mechanical characteristics of the rifle—and from the third day on we had better be able to know the answers when asked. Another stern requirement was to know our rifle's serial number. "Boot," the Drill Instructor said as he stood in front of you; "what is your rifle's serial number?" Heaven help the man who couldn't rattle it off. Another stern no-no was calling the rifle a gun. This was particularly tough for men to grasp who did not understand the difference between a rifle (rifling or grooves in the barrel) and a gun (smooth bore like a shotgun).

During the first week written tests of one kind or another were administered. We did not know it then, but the scores on these tests helped determine assignments out of Boot Camp. In fact these test scores determined assignments throughout your service in the military. The critical one was the general classification (IQ) test. There was also a surprise visit to the dentist. Apparently the folks at Parris Island were not convinced that all recruit's dental examinations were as thorough as the one I had in the Chicago recruiting station a few days before. I still had to see the dentist and since I needed no work he let me sleep during my allotted time slot. I recall dreaming of how pleasant it would be if only I could go back to working for my dad on the farm. When I awoke my first thought again was, "What had I gotten myself into?"

We also had to immediately learn a whole new vocabulary. A toilet was now a "head"; the floor or ground was the "deck" (like in parade deck); the ceiling was "overhead"; door a "hatch"; walls were "bulkheads"; and stairs a "ladder". No longer was it upstairs or downstairs; the terminology now was "topside" or "down below" (i.e. below decks). And for the smokers the word was either the smoking lamp is lit, or the smoking lamp is out. This goes back to those days in the Navy before intercom systems when actual lamps communicated a yes or no to smoking. If the lamp was out, it meant a fire or explosive danger existed aboard the ship. For example, when handling gunpowder. In a more mundane sense, at night it applied to sleeping compartments after lights out (taps). And no more did the word "rope" appear in our vocabulary; from now on it was "line." Topographic language changed as well. A swamp, and there was plenty of swampland at Parris Island, was termed the "boondocks." Our means of getting to and from the boondocks was via our legs—so our shoes were called "boondockers."

Another important lesson we learned early on in Boot Camp was the three ways of doing things. They were the right way, the wrong way, and the Marine Corps way.

In whatever free time we had before lights out, we were expected to study our new bible, the *Guidebook for Marines*, and work on squaring away our gear—and cleaning the rifle. For at least eight members of the platoon there was fire watch duty each night. Two of us at a time worked a two-hour shift. We patrolled the squad bay and adjacent passageways (hallways) to be on the alert for fire or any other disturbance. We also had to be alert for a surprise appearance by the Drill Instructor or his representative to check up on us.

Although there was some classroom time, a majority of our sixteen-hour waking day was spent outdoors in physical activity of one kind or another. A large part of the outdoor activity involved close-order drill, punctuated by frequent rifle inspections.

Parris Island is known for its sand fleas that loved to feast on recruits. We called them "flying teeth" or "no-see-ums." The Drill Instructors considered sand fleas as allies in the process of turning recruits into Marines. Picture this: you are standing at attention, perfectly still and you had better remain in that position until ordered to stand at ease. The sand fleas favorite target was your nostrils, although any part of your exposed body was fair game. Here are these sand fleas tormenting you, and yet you had better not move a muscle, to include a facial muscle. Is there a lesson here? You bet there is. Imagine yourself in a combat situation. You are out in front of your lines on listening post duty. Your life, and possibly that of your fellow Marines depends on your remaining absolutely still. So what if a leach or other annoyance attaches itself to you?

That sixteen-hour activity crammed day covered Monday through Saturday. On Sunday we still put in a sixteen-hour day, but a more relaxed sixteen hours. Those who desired to do so marched to their respective church services. Those who were not churchgoers remained in the barracks. But certain work details and other forms of harassment befell those who remained under the watchful eye of the Drill Instructor back at the barracks. As a result, everyone became a practicing churchgoer after that first Sunday. Approximately an hour was devoted to close-order drill on

Sunday. We were also allowed time for more personal matters. A time to write letters, study our *Guidebook for Marines*, etc. This was also the day to hand scrub our laundry. A new experience for most of us. So that's what the metal bucket and scrub brush were for!

By the end of two weeks the dropouts were gone to be replaced by men who for some reason had their training interrupted earlier—usually due to sickness. I think it took about two weeks for me to fully acclimate to military life. We were worked hard, belittled continuously, and purposely kept sleep deprived. Dangling out there in front of us was the possibility (with the odds being slim to none as the Drill Instructor emphasized) that a few of us might someday be allowed to wear the globe and anchor of a United States Marine.

In the first two weeks we learned how to march. Unless you have marched under the right kind of circumstances you cannot know what a thrill it is to be an integral part of a platoon of sixty men marching to the rhythmic, indeed melodic cadence of your Drill Instructor. "Thrip-faw-ya-leahft" translated to "three four your left." Another was "awn-owp-reep…reep-fawya-laf." All this punctuated in the early goings by a barrage of cursing that turned the air blue. I'll bet on the cursing issue alone that our neighbor Clarence Dittman would have made a great Drill Instructor.

Can I not make you hear it? The sound of sixty feet hitting the pavement (deck) at the same time to the rhythmic cadence called out by the Drill Instructor. Can't you see everyone of those sixty rifles carried at the prescribed forty-five degree angle, with elbows tucked close to the body? Now listen and watch as the Drill Instructor, in order to have the platoon move the rifles in unison from our right shoulder to our left shoulder commands, "Left shoulder—arms." The movement is executed in four counts with the precise point for each count occurring at exactly the same moment that sixty boots hit the deck. On the first count the rifle is lifted off the right shoulder, then rotated so it comes to the diagonal in front of the body on the second count. On count three the rifle is rotated to the left shoulder. On the count of four the right arm is dropped smartly away to begin its swinging motion while we march. Now the left hand and arm assumes the responsibility for carrying the rifle at the prescribed forty-five degrees with elbow close to the body. (Like Father Mechler must have been taught in the seminary to hold the censer during the Benediction service.) Nothing here out of line! My dad's rows of corn shocks should have looked as squared away as our platoon of Marines.

From time to time the Drill Instructor tried to catch us napping. Imagine marching at right shoulder arms and the Drill Instructor commands, "Right shoulder—arms." No mercy was shown the recruit(s) who was not paying attention and brought his rifle off the shoulder. "SHITBIRD," the Drill Instructor probably yelled, or he halted the platoon, then brought the guilty recruit(s) out in front of the platoon for "special" instruction.

Although the recruit who fouled up was often punished as an individual, in some cases his mistakes led to punishment for the entire platoon. For better or worse we had to learn that the unit; a platoon in this case, was indivisible. One man's carelessness in Boot Camp resulted in the entire platoon having to perform extra heavy-duty drill or other onerous tasks. In combat carelessness could result in casualties. Imagine that one recruit fails to have his footlocker squared away. The Drill Instructor yells, "Everybody outside with your rifles." So what if it happens to be just minutes before time for lights out? The entire platoon ends up running a mile as punishment. Let that happen a couple of times with the same individual responsible and there will be some persuasive discipline administrated by the platoon itself. Initially it may be verbal, but if this same individual continued getting the platoon in trouble the punishment could be physical. Cleanliness was also stressed. We were required to shower daily. This was something new for most of us. No excuses sufficed for a lack of personal cleanliness. Again, the reason was related to combat. Men who keep themselves clean will be able to ward off the dangers of diseases in a combat situation. Once again, it wasn't unusual for platoon members themselves to use one form or another of encouragement to bring along the careless member(s).

Was all this fussiness and harassment necessary? It must seem to be unnecessary to outsiders. Some might even call it sadism. Yet the basis of military discipline is the "unquestioned" and "meticulous" attention to orders, to personal cleanliness, and above all, to the care of weapons. By parade ground drill a recruit is trained to pay attention to orders. He learns that he is a member of a group, and that the group is indivisible. He learns above all that his weapons must be kept clean and ready for action. As an example of the value in keeping one's weapons ready for action were the English barmen (archers) who at Agincourt in 1415 defeated four times their number of Frenchmen by ensuring their bowstrings remained dry by keeping them inside their caps until ready to engage the enemy. The bottom-line was to instill "Esprit de corps;" to be ever faithful to oneself, to one's group, to his Corps, and to his country. It embraces pride, honor and a degree of selflessness deemed to be unique. Esprit de corps is the linchpin of the Marine Corps—an intense respect for traditions and perseverance established by our predecessors. Esprit de corps is the cement that holds together men facing a common danger.

One of the events we all looked forward to was the two weeks we would spend on the rifle range. After all, isn't that what the military is all about? For some it would be the first time they ever fired a weapon—for others a chance to show off. This break to the normal routine occurred during our seventh and eighth week in Boot Camp. After assembling our field transport packs we marched the three miles to the range. A field transport pack weighs fifty pounds and included all clothing and gear a Marine carried into a campaign. Add to that the weight of the rifle and you have a sixty-pound load. At the rifle range a separate camp awaited us with barracks, mess hall, dispensary, etc. The move was bittersweet. Yes, it was great to move along in the training cycle, but in the process we had to leave our old familiar barracks that had been home for the past six weeks.

Along the route of march we passed the camp's farm. Here was a scene right out of Wisconsin's dairyland. The barn, silos, cows and pigs were familiar reminders of home. I was surprised to learn of the farm. For the city boys it may have been, in addition to a surprise, a sight they had not seen before. I learned later of an interesting incident that occurred when President Franklin Roosevelt visited Parris Island in April of 1943. Moments before the President and the Marine General escorting him drove by the farm in an open convertible the pigs were slopped (fed) to ensure they were all aligned at the trough. A big grin spread across the President's face as he turned and commented to Brigadier General Emilo Moses how "delighted" and "impressed" he was by the pig's military bearing.

A large part of the first week at the rifle range was spent in classroom instruction related to weapon firing. We were reminded that all things considered, the Marine Corps preferred its recruits had not ever fired a weapon. That way no bad habits had to be overcome and a man could be taught from scratch the "Marine Corps way." Remember there are three ways to do things, the right way, the wrong way, and the Marine Corps way. For example, we were not allowed to use "Kentucky windage," where one estimated the velocity of the wind and aimed the weapon to the left or right of the target to compensate. We were taught to make adjustments on the sights to compensate for the effects of varying wind velocity from different directions. This permitted the rifle sites to remain locked in on the target. The same for elevation should your shots be going high or low.

We also did a great deal of "snapping" in. This we viewed as a hand-me-down from medieval torture techniques. Snapping in involved dry firing your rifle. Miniature black targets, approximately the same size as they appeared at the 100, 200, 300 and 500-yard range were displayed in the center of a circle. The platoon formed around the circle and went through the process of practicing sight alignment and sight picture while taking a deep breath, letting half of it out, and then s-q-u-e-e-z-e-ing the trigger. Rifle slings were drawn as tight as trip wires around the arm to better ensure a steady rifle. This tiresome routine went on for hours as we rotated through the standing, kneeling, sitting, and prone positions. Boring! Boring! We hated snapping in.

We also spent time doing maintenance work in the target pits (called the "butts"). This primarily involved repair of targets. On Thursday and Friday of our first week we pulled targets for those platoons, now in their last week on the range, who were firing for record.

During the second week we began firing the range, working up to pre-qualification on Thursday and qualification on Friday. For some, as noted earlier, this was the first time they fired a weapon. Monday, Tuesday and Wednesday mornings were spent in arriving at what was called the "true zero" of our rifles. This was the elevation and windage setting that served as the basis, at a given range, for any subsequent adjustments due to wind, etc. During the afternoon of those three days the routine involved working the butts and more snapping in.

As noted above, Thursday was pre-qualification day. We fired the full quota of fifty rounds from all positions just as we would the next day—but the next day would be for official record purposes. Those who did not do well were required to do heavy duty snapping in under steely-eyed instructors. The rest were required to snap in, but could work at the position they felt they needed to improve on.

Earlier mention was made of a psychologist asking us if we liked girls. We sure did, but we all wanted to avoid "Maggie's drawers." In the slow fire routine, after each shot the target was pulled down and a spotting marker is placed on the target where the shot struck. The target is then run back up and a disk mounted on a pole is raised up above the butts to let the shooter know the value of his shot. Depending on the disk used this could be a value of two, three, four, or five. The shooter then knew the value of his shot, and the spotting marker told the shooter where on the target his shot hit. From these non-verbal communications the shooter can readjust his sights. But if the shot was a clear miss, a red flag was waved slowly, **very slowly** across the entire target giving everyone a chance to see it. This red flag was affectionately referred to as "Maggie's drawers" and having it waved across his target was most embarrassing to the shooter. Further, his coach is not happy either. Maggie's drawers can make an appearance during rapid fire scoring as well. Rapid fire involves firing ten rounds in quick succession. But now everyone is busy watching their own score so in all likelihood only the shooter and his coach are witnesses to the miss (or misses).

Friday was the big day—rain or shine. An axiom at the time was that it "never rains on the rifle range." For all of us, whether or not we had ever fired a weapon before, this was exciting. The basic requirement was to accumulate enough points to make "marksman." If not, you were dropped from your platoon to join a platoon then in its first week on the rifle range. From then on this was your new platoon—not a pleasant happening to be separated from your familiar fellow platoon members, and at least a familiar Drill Instructor. I was one of those who thought my experience with rifles and shotguns might earn me an expert badge. I was lucky to have earned those few extra points moving me out of the marksman category into that of sharpshooter. And yes, many of those who had not ever fired a weapon before fired expert. They had been taught the "Marine Corps way" without any bad habits to be eliminated along the way.

That Friday afternoon, our last day on the range, we first fired the forty-five-caliber pistol. I had not ever fired a pistol before, which meant I could be taught the Marine Corps way. Again, there was time devoted to snapping in—perhaps an hour—but this was easy to do with the pistol. I adapted easily to the pistol and had no trouble firing expert. Later on that afternoon we each threw a live hand grenade. We did throw a few practice grenades beforehand. There was no "snapping in" with hand grenades.

"Every Marine a rifleman" is a vital maxim in the Marine Corps. Each year all Marines return to the rifle range for re-qualification. For the junior Marines, Sergeants and below, that still involved many hours of snapping in. The senior non-commissioned officers and junior officers are expected to do on their own whatever training they feel is necessary to ensure that they qualified. If not, a statement to that effect might appear in their fitness reports, not a desirable entry to have in your record for a career Marine. Field grade officers, Majors and above had only to fire the pistol.

During my early years in the Marine Corps, I was a radio operator and carried the forty-five caliber pistol. How envious were those who had to carry a cumbersome and relatively heavy rifle. The pistol was also a great deal easier to keep clean. But the maxim "every Marine a rifleman" meant I now had to fire both the rifle and pistol during my yearly visit to the range until I was promoted to Major. At this point, as noted above, I was only required to fire the pistol

But let me take you back to the pistol range at Parris Island. There was a Master Sergeant on the range resplendent in his green dress uniform and with a mass of red stripes on his sleeves. Six stripes denoted his top enlisted rank, and six diagonal stripes, called hash marks, were for his twenty-four years of honorable service (four years for each hash mark). I was thoroughly impressed! I thought it must be the absolute pinnacle of success to attain this man's standing. Dare I even hope that I might someday sport six stripes of a Marine Master Sergeant? I came close. I was one stripe away when commissioned a Second Lieutenant in 1953.

The following Saturday we marched back to the old barracks area, but this time we were assigned to a bottom deck (floor). No more running up and down those ladders (stairs) to the top deck.

The next week was spent being introduced to other aspects of military life. We spent a couple of days and nights in the "boondocks." First of all, there was the novel experience of living in a two-man "pup tent," along with an introduction to patrolling at night. Mines and booby traps were touched on, but only a hint of their complexities and dangers could be given in Boot Camp. The gas chamber was something else. We marched into the chamber and then put on our gas masks. Instructors ensured our masks were on tight and that the mask airways were clear. Then the instructor pulled the ring on a canister of CS riot gas. Next they ordered us to remove our masks and stand fast until told to move outside. There followed a long fifteen seconds of choking, weeping, and itching. Happiness was groping our way outside after we were told to do so.

Next was graduation week. We were to be inspected and tested by members of the Marine Corps we had seen little of—Marine officers! Our Drill Instructor did his best to frighten us with tales of how steely eyed and thorough these officers were, and that it would be tough to pass their inspections. If we fouled up as individuals we could be sent back through Boot Camp again. Not quite true—but what did we know? At any rate we drilled with intense fervor, studied our *Guidebook for Marines*, and dedicated hours to ensure our rifle, bayonet, and uniforms were spotless.

In the meantime we were also issued the rest of the clothing to complete our Marine Corps wardrobe. Of most importance to us were the dress khaki and green uniforms, along with dress shoes. We were also paid for the first time. There was strong pressure from the authorities to either bank our pay or send it home. Written tests were also administered in the final week measuring our knowledge of military subjects.

At one point during this last week our Drill Instructor, who was now observed to smile now and then, marched us to a small military exchange (store). Here we were allowed to "tank up" on ice cream and soft drinks. No pogey bait (candy)* though. I recall wolfing down a pint of ice cream—and of being quite happy.

Thursday was largely devoted to officers inspecting our clothing. All items of uniform were at first displayed in our foot and wall lockers (as dictated by examples in our Guidebook). Then we were given an hour to display these items on our bunk. "Junk on the bunk" was the non-of-

---

*The Marines in China before World War II were issued candy (Baby Ruths, Tootsie Rolls, etc.) as part of their ration supplements. At the time, sugar and other assorted sweets were rare commodities in China and much in demand by the Chinese. As a result the troops found the candy useful for barter in town. The Chinese word for prostitutes, roughly translated, is "pogey." Thus, Marines referred to candy as "Pogey Bait."

ficial title of this exercise. The clothing and equipment was displayed in a manner to ensure your name was clearly shown on each item of clothing, to include each sock. These inspections also provided us with an introduction to Marine Corps officers. We found them to be stern and thorough—exceptionally thorough. If they found something wrong they forcefully pointed it out—but they did not use foul language—unlike the Drill Instructors.

Friday, our last day was devoted to an inspection in close order drill, uniform appearance, cleanliness of our rifle and bayonet, and again our general knowledge of military subjects. All this was conducted by, or judged by four or five officers. First we went through all the military drill routines. That took at least an hour. Then the officers descended on us for inspections of our weapon, uniform, and personal cleanliness. In the process many questions were asked relative to military subjects. Then there was the parade with other graduating platoons. This was the first time we marched to the music of a band. Initially the music was a stirring John Philip Sousa march. As we approached the reviewing stand the band struck up the Marine Corps Hymn. Exhilarating—absolutely exhilarating! At the conclusion of the parade a Captain told us we had passed the inspections and we were now United States Marines. He assured us that following the graduation our Drill Instructor would hand out the globe and anchor emblems as proof of our newly won status.

One after another we stood in front of the man who had driven, ridiculed and tormented, but above all challenged and inspired us over the better part of ten weeks. He half smiled as he handed us the emblems and said, **"Congratulations Marine!"**

So how did we feel about the man who had been the center of our lives for ten long weeks? After all, he was now history. A day or two later most of us would be on our way to various duty stations and in all likelihood not ever see him again. The simple answer was that we thought the world of him! We would have followed this man through hell and high water under any and all circumstances.

Now Boot Camp for me is history. I am now a United States Marine. What high adventure lay ahead for me?

The following Monday morning I was on a garbage truck collecting refuse from the married personnel's housing areas.

CHAPTER 22

Camp Del Mar, California

I spent three or four extra days at Parris Island while waiting for transportation to the West Coast where I was being transferred to attend a field radio operator school. Each morning we so called "casual" troops were assigned to police (work) details. As noted, I was on garbage truck duty the first day. Two of us were involved. One lifted the garbage cans up to the truck and the other emptied them. We finished off the day by washing out the garbage truck. The following day I was assigned to the camp's gardening/landscaping section. A civilian employee dropped us off, one by one, at various job sites. He did not ask, and probably could have cared less whether or not we knew anything about gardening. He merely saw us as "raw" labor. I was dropped off at a rather large home in the married officer's living area. Given the size of the home it seemed likely that a senior officer lived here. I was handed a shovel and directed to spade several plots, then rake it smooth for follow-on flower planting by one of the civilian gardeners. This was much like helping Mother prepare the garden for planting. While I was working the lady of the house drove in. She disappeared into the house, but was back out in a few minutes with a glass of lemonade and cookies. A pleasant change to speak with someone, outside of my fellow recruits, who wasn't "barking" at me, or at best, practicing stern aloofness. After all these weeks I found it particularly enjoyable to have this contact, albeit tenuous contact, with a woman. She made a couple of trips out to the work place with refreshments over the morning hours.

When the gardener picked me up at noon he expressed amazement that I had finished and had the ground ready for planting. He decided to change my routine for the afternoon by having me plant the flowers in the space I had prepared. A sketch map he provided with easy to follow instructions made it a pleasant, yet an all afternoon job. The lady of the house was gone most of the afternoon, but returned after I had finished the job. Time enough for a friendly chat before the supervisor picked me up.

The day following I was assigned to the base farm. A herd of seventy milk cows was maintained there to support the base. A civilian employee sent me up into the silo and told me to toss out silage until he said to stop. When I came down from the silo he said, "You must be a farm boy. I had trouble making you hear me because there was the continual rattle of silage coming down the chute." That statement scared the dickens out of me. Was I now to be taken off the list for radio school on the West Coast and assigned to this farm?

Not to worry. A few days later I boarded a train in Yemassee. Although this was strictly a troop train we traveled in regular Pullman sleeping cars. Stewards handled the clean-up chores, making up the bunks at night and converting them back to coach seats for daytime travel, etc. We ate our meals in a dining car equipped with all the finery of that era. Cloth table coverings, china, multiple pieces of silverware/glasses, and solicitous waiters were quite a treat after the spartan mess halls in Boot Camp. We spent the better part of four days making this cross-country trek. Once again I delighted in the "reality" geography that I observed along the way. We headed south through Georgia, traveled for a while through the panhandle of Florida and on west. At Campo, California, approximately sixty miles east of San Diego we crossed into Mexico. Mexico—a foreign country! Pretty heady stuff for a guy whose "foreign" travel prior to 29 January 1947 involved crossing the Mississippi River in La Crosse, Wisconsin to enter Minnesota—all of forty miles from home.

A sergeant was in charge and all he asked was that we stay squared away and well behaved. No problem. On occasion, station stops along the way permitted us to exit the train and stretch our legs. An exception was at El Paso, Texas. There was a USO (United Service Organization) club near the station. We were invited to attend a late afternoon (i.e. around five p.m.) social that the USO had arranged for us. There was a small dance band and a number of local young women were present. Most of us were "cringing wallflowers" so we concentrated on the punch and cookies provided. The few extroverts took advantage of this arrangement to dance and get acquainted with the ladies. After an hour the party was over and most of us hustled back aboard the train. Others took their time. I had no idea a man and woman could become so well acquainted in so little time until I observed the passionate good-byes taking place on the platform. The rest of us stared in wide-eyed fascination. Never in a movie of that era had I observed this kind of long and passionate embrace. Summit Ridge girls were not likely to act like this. These now well acquainted couples ignored the whistle of the train and the conductor's urging. The sergeant though got the necessary response and we were once again on the move.

Camp Del Mar is part of the Marine Corps Base at Camp Pendleton, Oceanside, California. This is a strip of land approximately three-quarters of a mile wide and one-mile in length. It nestles next to and west of what was then Highway 101 (now Interstate Five) with its entire western boundary being the open Pacific Ocean. Our barracks was an easy stroll to what was then, and still is a golden ocean front beach. I recall one morning seeing something I had never seen before; a ship—and it was a large ship. It appeared to be stranded on the beach. This occurred on a Sunday morning so I was free to run to the beach and observe what

I thought was an accidental grounding. That was not the case, the ship moved along smartly, but it seemed to be close to shore.

Military life at Camp Del Mar was routine and pleasant. We were routinely issued a rifle and 782 gear. Frequent rifle inspections and some close order drill was conducted Monday through Saturday. As in Boot Camp we had to keep the barracks and head (bathroom) "squeaky" clean. The school itself was relatively easy—although I did not like learning Morse code.

On 30 July 1947 I reached the sixth month mark as a Marine. At the same time there came a routine promotion to private first class (PFC) if one's record was clean. The eager types sewed that treasured stripe on using their sewing kits. Others made the one-mile trip into Oceanside and had the work done at a tailor shop. Can you imagine what a difference that couple square inch of stripe did to the here-to-for bare sleeves of our uniforms—not to mention our egos? The red stripe on our green dress uniform was of particular joy. I suspect all of us promoted ended up in the head (bathroom) with its many mirrors where we turned this way and that to admire this treasured splash of red on our sleeves. As others entered the head we asked, "Does it look like the stripes are on straight?" No one wanted to admit that the viewing was strictly for ego purposes.

I joined the Marines on 30 January 1947. I arrived at Camp Del Mar in early May of 1947. Finally we were allowed to go out into the civilian world on liberty. Initially I made a couple of trips into the then sleepy town of Oceanside. One was to have my PFC stripes sown on; another was to buy an iron. No doubt my mother and sisters smiled when they heard about the iron. The big liberty though was up the road 100 miles to Los Angeles and Hollywood. One Saturday four of us teamed up for the bus trip from Oceanside. We were in uniform and the first thing we did in Los Angeles was to have steel heel clips put on our dress shoes. We were all country or small town boys and there probably wasn't a dime's worth of sophistication amongst the four of us. We strutted as we clomped down the street and no doubt thought we were kings of the hill. We either ignored, but more likely, we reveled in the amused stares of the locals.

In late morning or early afternoon we came across a burlesque theater. We had no trouble finding front row seats. Here was a new experience. I wondered if the strippers were the same women I had observed on that train platform in El Paso. I was glad my mother and Father Mechler were many miles away. What I remember most about this event was hearing two songs that the ladies performed to. One was *Cherry Pink and Apple Blossom White* played in a seductive manner, and the more mundane, yet pleasing *Stars Fell on Alabama*.

Having already sunk into the pits of depravity, we had nothing to lose so we visited one of the then infamous "dime-a-dance" ballrooms. I recall buying a long string of tickets, needed since a ten-cent ticket was valid for a minute. Our partners were friendly ladies—but you were unlikely to risk taking them home to meet your mother.

Next we caught a bus for Hollywood. At that time (1947), many open miles stretched between Los Angeles and Hollywood. We arrived in time to visit many of the tourist sights, then attended a stage show called *The Earl Carroll Follies*. We spent the night in a bunkroom at the Hollywood YMCA. Sunday we all four went to Catholic Mass—then headed back to camp.

I made a couple more trips to Los Angeles and Hollywood over the six months I was at Camp Del Mar. I also visited Tijuana, Mexico on one occasion. I was not a so called "liberty hound" who passed up no opportunity to leave the camp. I was quite content to laze around the barracks in off-duty hours, or participate in the many pick-up soft ball games. I was also a regular attendee at movies in the evening. The base library was also a favorite haunt. There was also a certain amount of studying I needed to do outside of the classroom.

As noted above, the camp was right next to Highway 101. In August horse racing season begins at Del Mar, a coastal community fifteen miles south of our base. The races attracted the then current crop of Hollywood stars, like Bing Crosby, Harry James, Betty Grable, Spencer Tracy, etc. On weekends we might spend time standing along side the highway trying to spot Hollywood stars as they drove past. If one was an observer at nine a.m. he might return to the barracks to tell the rest that he had seen Harry James and his wife Betty Grable drive by. Another man, who did not show up next to the highway until eleven a.m. swore he saw the same couple drive by. Not only that, but they slowed down and waved to him. Stars may have fallen on Alabama in that burlesque theater in Los Angeles, but they also drove by Camp Del Mar in large numbers during racing season on the way to the track, where, as the song goes, *The Turf Meets the Surf.*

In mid-October, a week before the end of our six month training session, we went into the hills of Camp Pendleton for field training. I was surprised at how cold it could get in the various canyons of the base. I was surprised too at how heavy some of the radio equipment was that we lugged from one location to another during this period. I was glad when that last week of training was over.

Graduation on 16 October 1947 was relatively low key, nothing as dramatic as graduation from Boot Camp. Yet we were proud of our new status as trained radio operators. Our military occupational specialty (MOS) numbers were 2533 for Morse code and 2531 for field radio operator. Now came one of those exciting events, played out over and over in the military, where will I be stationed next?

CHAPTER **23**

East Coast Duty

Second Marine Division

Those of us with orders to the 2nd Marine Division at Camp Lejeune, North Carolina were quite pleased. Not only was this the "real" Marine Corps in our eyes, but members of the division could wear a colorful red shoulder patch. In fact, this piece of cloth displayed more red material than did the private-first-class stripes on our dress green uniforms. We also liked the idea of being part of the Fleet Marine Force (FMF); we thought the term had a "gung ho" ring to it.

But first another four to five day cross-country train trip by pullman sleeper. No doubt we re-traced the same route we had traveled six months before. The Marine Corps had assembled enough men from the Southern California area to justify this being exclusively a troop train. I noted only a few familiar faces from the previous cross-country trip among the men now heading for duty stations on the East Coast.

Once again we stopped for about an hour to visit the serviceman's club (USO) in El Paso, Texas. Here again were several young women to dance or converse with. Most of us though did neither, pretending we preferred the cookies and punch. Actually we were still operating on the shy side despite having absorbed six-months worth of West Coast sophistication. I don't remember any amorous good-byes as the train pulled out of El Paso—but there must have been some.

An altogether pleasant trip, but how could it be otherwise? There was a Sergeant in charge, but all he asked was that we behave ourselves. We were free to read, play cards, eat, sleep, and best of all for me—watch the countryside as we rolled along.

Camp Lejeune is located near Jacksonville, North Carolina. We arrived around six p.m. after having our evening meal on the train. The checking in process took until nearly nine p.m. At this point I was assigned a bunk in my new unit's barracks. The unit was the 16th Marines, a regiment whose mission during an amphibious landing was to organize the beachhead. Teams from the regiment landed with the infantry assault waves and from then on, via radio, called in troops and supplies based on the ever-changing needs ashore. As the land operation continued, the bulk of the regiment's men and heavy equipment came ashore to handle the flow of men and supplies to support the operation. Causality evacuation was also an important part of the regiment's duties.

I remember as a low morale point in my military service to date, that late arrival at what was to be my new home. By the time the Duty NCO (non-commissioned-officer) had issued me my bed linen there was time to do little more than settle in with nothing but a barracks full of strangers around me. Arrival at Parris Island for Boot Camp was somewhat similar, but sixty of us were all in the same situation. My new barracks mates were much too busy settling in for the night themselves to pay anything but perfunctory attention to a newcomer.

The next morning, still feeling low, I made my way to the head (bathroom). There I crossed paths with a New Jersey boy, Jim Delaney who brightened up my life. Jim was one of those outgoing, entertaining, naturally friendly, and sincere individuals all too rare in our society. He was also a smiler, and in general one of those types whom everyone likes. He spotted me as a newcomer the moment I walked in the head. As I recall, his first words were, "Hey, you're a new man, right?" There followed some banter relative to the regiment and a quick and cursory review of our respective backgrounds. Luckily Jim was a member of the communication platoon. After breakfast he escorted me to the unit and introduced me around.

Apart from the necessary continuing military training, as best represented by close order drill and related military oriented subjects, I needed to learn the ropes as a radio operator in the regiment. This involved setting up the various man-pack and mobile radios along with learning a whole new vocabulary peculiar to radio communications in this particular regiment. Morse code fortunately was not part of my job and I was quite happy to end up as a voice radio operator and to carry and operate a SCR-300 radio.

In addition to the red Second Marine Division shoulder patch, we were required to wear another patch of red as a member of the 16th Marines. This was a one inch square red patch worn at knee level on our utility trousers, and on our cap or helmet. The idea behind this was to ensure men not authorized to be on the beach during a landing operation could be quickly identified and sent to wherever they should have been. Conversely, men with that red patch showing up anywhere but on the beach were in turn suspect.

Along with taking one's turn at barracks fire watch, there was guard duty of a more demanding kind. As a private first class my turn at this chore came up every ten days. The regiment had a great deal of heavy equipment needed to handle the flow of supplies coming across the beach. The inventory included bulldozers, cranes, forklifts, cherry pickers, backhoes, front-end loaders, fuel tankers and a fleet of cargo trucks to move supplies to inland supply dumps. In addition, warehouses contained other smaller miscellaneous mission related equipment. The equipment pool and related warehouses were located approximately ten miles from our barracks area. This relatively remote area was near the beach where mission-related training could best be carried out.

After normal working hours and on weekends and holidays the equipment and warehouses had to be guarded. There was both the threat of fire, and as we were led to believe, thievery. We were not told this officially, but word spread among the troops that the criminal element in the area on occasion would sneak onto the base to steal expensive equipment from either the outside parking area, or break into the warehouse where portable equipment was kept. Whether this was true or not, we rear-rank privates who walked the posts believed all this, and were as a result keyed up to that possibility. That may have been precisely what the authorities wanted us to believe.

Twelve of us were involved in the guard detail on a given day. We stood guard for four hours, then had eight hours off. On weekdays we started with an early evening meal (three p.m.), then were taken by truck to the site. We arrived shortly before the men who worked there day-by-day left for the barracks area.

My stint on guard duty started in late October and it can get cold, windy wet cold in the coastal regions of North Carolina at this time of year. We dutifully walked our posts during our four-hour shifts, bundling up as necessary to ward off the cold and wearing a poncho to ward off the rain. We had better dutifully walk our post since three inspections took place during your four-hour stint. Three different individuals, the Corporal and Sergeant-of-the-guard, along with the Officer-of-the-day conducted these inspections. We did not want to be surprised by any of these characters. This alone served to keep us alert. Once aware someone was approaching your post there was the customary, "Halt, who goes there?" A response could be, "Officer-of-the-day." "Advance Officer-of-the-day and be recognized." Once recognized the Officer-of-the-day was saluted by presenting arms with the rifle. Then the obligatory report; "Sir, Private-First-Class Hedrick reports my post all secure, my post and orders remain the same." Then questions were asked relative to my knowledge of the post, and at least one question along the line of what is this or that general order? If the inspection were by the Corporal or Sergeant-of-the-guard you could disperse with the "sir" and saluting.

I like the story about an inspection by the Officer-of-the-day that allegedly took place in the 16th Marines equipment park at around three a.m. The night was particularly dark and stormy. As a result the area was covered with rain filled puddles. The Officer-of-the-day was challenged, and just as he was ready to identify himself he stumbled into one of the puddles. Involuntarily the words "Jesus Christ" came from his lips. The sentry, without a moments hesitation yelled, "It's Jesus Christ, fall out the apostles." Fact or fiction? Certainly the weather and terrain conditions sound right. If someone like Jim Delaney were the sentry at the time he possessed the aplomb and audacity to respond in the way this sentry allegedly did.

Around midnight a truck arrived from the mess hall with what we called mid-rats (midnight rations—coffee and sandwiches). Our previous meal, as noted, had been around three p.m. that day. This was a highlight of our otherwise boring, and during inclement weather, uncomfortable duty.

As noted, guard duty is generally an unpleasant yet a necessary chore. Even if the weather was pleasant, I found it boring. What could make it really unpleasant, in fact downright miserable, was foul weather. We seemed to have our share of that when I was doing my duty as a sentry in the fall and winter of 1947/48. Imagine being awakened at 11:30 p.m. for your four-hour watch from midnight to 4 a.m. (the mid-watch). You hear the wind driven rain bouncing off our tin quonset hut, and since it's winter, you know its going to be a cold rain. We questioned whether the bad guys were likely to come out on a night like this to steal whatever they wanted—yet had to admit that this might be ideal conditions for them. So out we went, and for protection from the rain a poncho was draped over our rifle and body. However, our head was not covered since this would interfere with hearing and peripheral vision.

On one occasion weather conditions were so bad the Officer-of-the-day mercifully exercised his prerogative to cancel the guard. I was awakened at approximately 11:30 p.m. for the 12-4 a.m. mid-watch. The wind, rain, and wind driven debris were beating against the tin hut and I suspect everyone awake had to feel sorry for the two of us about to go out into that storm. Not a hurricane, but heavy weather none-the-less. Then the phone rang—and in a moment the Corporal of the guard said, "They canceled the mid-watch." Wow, the mid-watch cancelled; now I could climb back into a warm bunk. To this day, when the call of nature dictates a need to get up in the middle of the night, I invariably reflect back on those then magic words, "They canceled the mid-watch" as I climb back into my comfortable bed.

Sometime in November of 1947, a sharp-eyed company clerk noted that up to now I had not been assigned to mess duty. This is a usual assignment for all privates, and the term private includes privates-first-class. Radio school and travel associated with the school had kept me from that chore up to now. In retrospect all Marines should have in their memory bank the experience of mess duty. The hours involved were the worst part. The fire watch woke us up at four a.m., and it wasn't until around nine p.m. that we were through for the day. This was an everyday routine—weekends included—to include in my case Christmas and New Years day. Time off was allowed to go to Sunday church services. I rotated through several chores, ending up running the scullery. Here all the dirty trays, cups, and silverware accumulated. After the necessary preliminary scraping they were run through a steam cleaning apparatus. I did not peel a single potato, but I can't think of another chore I missed.

I remember being impressed by the cleanliness of the mess hall. It seems we were continually being sent to the head to wash our hands if we left a food handling assignment to do something that did not appear to be all that unsanitary. I have to wonder how many times a day I washed my hands until I was assigned to the scullery. Understandably, cleanliness and hygiene becomes significantly important where so many men could be affected by tainted food. If the work and hours were a negative, access to additional food was a distinct plus.

My mother wrote me about this time and mentioned that it seemed a shame I would be on mess duty over the holidays. I recall writing back and saying I didn't really mind at all—and I really meant it too.

Caribbean Maneuvers

Right after New Years Day in 1948 word reached us rear-rank privates of spring maneuvers in the Caribbean. We thought this was great! Preliminary training began in earnest to learn about shipboard life and practice climbing up and down rope ladders. The rope ladder training involved a wooden platform built to approximate the deck level of an amphibious troop ship. At the bottom of the platform was a mock-up of a landing craft (LCVP—landing craft vehicle, personnel).* It could carry thirty-six combat loaded troops or a jeep and trailer along with a few men. Up and down the ladder we went, four abreast and separated by just enough vertical space to ensure we didn't trample on each other. The routine called for us to fill the landing craft quickly so the next boat could come in for its load of troops. First the four of us needed to coordinate our move as we climbed over the rail of the pretend ship. This was as simple as ensuring all four of us swung the left leg over the rail first, then the right. Also emphasized was the need to grasp the vertical strands of the rope ladder as you went up or down. This prevented the man above you from stepping on your hand if you were slow or he fast in coming down or going up the ladder. Another stern rule was not to look down. We later learned that it was one thing to climb up and down the ladder from a ship and landing craft mock-up; quite another to do so as the vessels bounced up and down on the open seas. As training progressed the load we carried up and down the ladder increased. There was also a routine for what we did when we entered the boat. The first two on either side held the rope ladder steady for the rest. The other two helped those who were carrying

---

*Thirty-six feet long, ten feet wide; made of plywood with a metal ramp. It had a powerful diesel engine that could drive the boat up on the beach and pull it off again. Twenty thousand LCVPs were built during WWII.

USS Okanagan

equipment other than our packs; like PFC Hedrick who would be carrying a thirty-pound radio and a spare battery. Finally there was the need to position men so they balanced out the boat and could disembark as a unit. For example, a four-man fire team needed to be together, etc

The big day came when we were transported to the docks at Moorhead City, North Carolina. For the first time I was standing right next to an ocean-going vessel and was in awe of her size. This was the USS Okanagan,* officially called an APA (amphibious personnel assault), but in simple terms—a troopship. APAs were designed to carry a 1500 man infantry battalion, which included its supporting units. We were led up the gangplank, across an open deck and then down several steep metal ladders to a troop compartment deep in the bowels of the ship. The most remembered feature of these barn-like sized enclosures was the twelve-foot deck (floor) to overhead (ceiling) of the compartment. Access/egress was, as noted, via a ladder (stairs) set at a step angle. This was not the place for one with claustrophobia. Our sleeping accommodations consisted of heavy canvas, laced by rope to metal frames. The racks (bunks) were

*Named after the county of Okanagan in central Washington (state).

approximately eighteen inches wide with sixteen inches of vertical space between racks. The racks were stacked eight high in our compartment. I didn't know it on this first occasion, but in the future I remembered the top bunk was best. First of all, one had a few more inches of vertical space between the top bunk and the overhead (ceiling). Then too, you climbed to the upper racks by using the lower ones as a ladder. Can you imagine heavy boots hitting your rack as those above you climbed up and down? Finally, if others became ill you were "above it all." Chains held the racks upright and also permitted the whole array to be raised 180 degrees for cleaning and/or additional storage space. Not the best living conditions—but what an experience.

More spartan still were the heads (bathrooms). The toilet consisted of two long parallel planks over a metal trough with adequate separation of the planks to permit support while sitting. The planks and trough were on an incline to permit a stream of salt water to run steadily down the trough. Talk about zero privacy. Since the ship could not distill enough fresh water to meet the needs of nearly 2000 men we were introduced to salt water showers* and salt water soap. The skin did not feel all that great after showering—but the combination met personal cleanliness needs.

Eating was quite an adventure as well. Usually three, but at times only two meals a day were served. The Marines and the Navy crew used the same eating facility. Naturally the Navy crew ate first. The Marines were issued colored passes by compartment and we took our place in line when called. Even then the lines were quite long—but there was not much else to do, so what did it matter? The ship's policemen are those sailors designated as Master at Arms. We first met these men on the mess deck where they enforced the rule of "take all you want but eat all you take." Don't try to leave your tray on the table and sneak out; these men had eyes in the back of their heads. .

On our first day aboard we participated in abandon ship drill. We

---

*Even the salt water available was limited. Those who spent what was considered too much time in the process of showering were accused of taking a "Hollywood shower."

mustered at the same location topside (open decks) from which we would leave when we actually went ashore in the landing craft. The ship's LCVPs, nestled in their cradles along side the ship's rail were our lifeboats if needed.

Another new experience once we set sail was overcoming seasickness. I was lucky. Other than a bit of queasiness the first day we were out on the open sea I was from then on immune. For others it took days, and others never really felt their best while sailing.

A large number of men were assigned to cleaning details, with emphasis on the living compartments and heads. Most of our waking time, if not involved in a cleaning detail or mess duty was spent topside. It did not take long for cigarette butts and other debris to accumulate. On the half-hour we heard over the intercom system, "Now hear this—now hear this—sweepers man your brooms —clean sweep down fore and aft." This meant from the very front of the open decks to the very rear—wherever troops could gather. I took my turn doing all these clean-up chores, but luckily I escaped working on the mess deck. The mess deck was hot and there was no let-up in the workload from dawn to late evening. In addition to the unpleasant working conditions, and hard work, you were kept below decks for the better part of the day.

There was also daily physical fitness and classes related to the upcoming landing. These classes were usually conducted topside. Then too there was the continuing need to keep our weapons and other gear clean, and inspections to ensure this was done. On balance there was still much free time if not on mess duty. Card games were going on in every nook and cranny of the ship, both topside and below decks. Others were reading, writing letters, chatting, sun bathing, or leaning on the ship's rails daydreaming.

Once we entered tropical waters we were fascinated and entertained by schools of porpoises and flying fish. From time to time boxing matches were staged and enough musically inclined men were aboard to form a swing band. Musical instruments were provided either by the ship or from those brought aboard by our (Marines) special services. Listening to them was a welcome break in the routine. After dark, if we were not sailing under blackout conditions, there was a movie on the open deck. No chairs or benches were provided. We sat, sprawled, or stood wherever we could find a space. Uncomfortable, but the price was right. Generally we stayed out of the warm interior of the ship—there was no air conditioning on Navy ships in that era. Catholic and Protestant Chaplains were on board. For us Catholics there was a daily mass, and I was a regular attendee.

Usually once each day an announcement came over the intercom that the "ship's store is now open for troop personnel." What long lines as we waited our turn to purchase ersatz ice cream or honest to goodness candy bars (pogey bait as candy was called). More often than not the day's supply was sold out before you reached this closet sized store.

It's approximately 1800 miles from Moorhead City, North Carolina to the landing beaches on the Caribbean Island of Vieques. We didn't sail directly to the objective area. The Navy took advantage of this assemblage of ships to conduct a series of maneuvers as we sailed south-eastward. One of the most demanding was anti-submarine zigzagging while in the approximately twenty-ship convoy. At land speed we were moving about twenty miles an hour and often under blackout conditions. Blackout curtains at the hatches (doors) permitted us to go out on deck where we watched in awe as these ships maneuvered, insofar as we could see them in the darkness. Man overboard drills were conducted, along with gunnery practice and numerous other drills of one kind or another. All the Navy asked of us troops was that we stay out of their way as sailors hastened to various stations for this or that drill. We were interested observers of what to most of us was a whole series of new experiences.

From time to time the ship conducted debarkation drills. We were all sent to our compartments and then called away, boat team by boat team, to our debarkation stations. During drills and actual debarkation one ladder in our troop compartment was used for going up—the other for going down. In successive drills we showed up with more and more equipment—which made it more and more difficult to move in the crowd and on those steep ladders. The troops scheduled to disembark first were located in the upper compartments. This took care of the crowd on the day for landing, but we were in each other's way during these practice drills.

At one point, at a remote location off a beach, we carried this practice to the point of actually going over the side of the ship and into the boats. I was surprised and apprehensive when I looked down from the deck of the ship and noticed how that little landing craft bounced about. In the process of those five to ten feet bounces it slammed against the mother ship at one moment, then a large gap opened as the landing craft was shoved away from the ship by wave action. Before we went over the side we were reminded once again to not look down as we descended the rope ladder. Timing was everything! I was happy when we were loaded and could pull away from the ship, if for no other reason than to get away from continually bouncing off the hull of the ship. We then joined other boats circling as one by one a given landing wave was assembled. Then we proceeded in a column towards the beach. At some point we formed a line abreast for an abbreviated run towards the beach. Since this was a practice run we did not actually land. Then back to the troopship and more high adventure in climbing back up the rope ladder. Excellent training, not only for us troops and the two-man Navy crews in the landing craft, but for the planners as well. The rehearsal also convinced me that I was indeed immune to seasickness. Unfortunately, for others bouncing in the small boat was torture.

One morning, about a week after first boarding ship, we came out on deck to an amazing sight. We were riding at anchor off Vieques. Here we teamed up with the firepower of the United States Navy. Present were aircraft carriers, battleships, cruisers, destroyers, and submarines. Additionally, a variety of smaller vessels that controlled the ship-to-shore movement of men and supplies were also present. This was the day before the landing and small boats criss-crossed the anchorage as they carried officers to meetings. While the leadership was involved in all these meetings we troops watched the show as we basked in the tropical sun.

That evening we set sail, and once again the many troop and cargo transports sailed on their own. This time we had supporting cruisers and destroyers with us as the Navy assumed a full tactical stance. No movie that night either—we were under strict blackout conditions. We were now following the script for an amphibious landing. The script would have called for the warships and aircraft to be pounding the objective area for weeks. In conjunction with D-day and H-hour* this pounding would have been particularly savage. We were back in the objective area by dawn of the day for the landing. Since a naval gunnery range existed on Vieques the warships and aircraft were able to put on their full fire-power show. These gunnery ships were relatively close to shore—we in the transports were approximately eight miles out from the beach.

The day of the landing we were awakened and fed before dawn. Even though this was a peacetime maneuver the sound of heavy navy guns and aircraft ordnance made one think of another time, only a few years be-fore, when during World War II combat landings were frequent. While we were eating and preparing our gear to go ashore, minesweepers and underwater demolition teams worked at clearing away mines and beach obstacles in the shallow water. Boat team by boat team, we were called away to our debarkation stations. The sea around us was filled with small landing craft of one type or another. I was loaded much as in the rehears-al, except now I also had the radio. I observed during the rehearsal that no matter where you were positioned in the landing craft you were going to end up soaked as this flat-bottomed craft bounced on, or plowed into the waves. Before going down the rope ladder I removed the rain poncho from my pack and positioned it where I could easily reach it as soon as I was in the boat. Before the boat pulled away from the ship I double fold-ed the poncho and put it over the radio for protection. I wish I could say

*D-day is the day (date) for the landing; H-hour is that moment when the first as-sault wave hits the beach.

that I was thinking of the English archers who at Aginourt in 1415 won a battle against the French. As noted earlier, they did so by ensuring their bowstrings were dry by keeping them in their hats until ready to engage the enemy. I only recall being quite concerned that the radio wouldn't work for one reason or another. I felt deeply my responsibility to provide the communication needed. I knew I would be mortified if for any reason the radio failed. Any number of things could go wrong with radios of that era; I didn't want salt water to be the reason for potential failure.

After loading, we circled near the mother ship to wait for all the boats in our wave to join up. Then we formed in column and were led by a control boat to our line of departure. I was with the same men as on the rehearsal a few days before—but I didn't pay much attention to them. This was perhaps understandable since my level of excitement and apprehension was considerably higher during the rehearsal. After all, I was now an "old salt" relative to riding in and climbing in and out of a small bouncing landing craft. Since I was in the third wave, the boat team was made up for the most part of infantrymen. A platoon leader was checking his men relative to equipment and their placement in the craft since he wanted his fire teams and squads to hit the beach and immediately work as teams.

At this point I noticed a Marine Captain with that distinctive one-inch square red patch on his trouser legs and helmet. I don't think he participated in the rehearsal, but I could have missed him in the excitement of that first time experience. All I knew was that I was to provide radio communication for a shore party function. That was all I needed to know. I saw him eyeing me, unsmiling; stern I thought. Was this the man I was to work for? I feared he was saying to himself, "Damn you private, that radio had better work or you are going to be in deep trouble." Having subsequently been in that Captain's position I know now he was in all likelihood thinking: "Please private, make sure that radio works. My career to some extent depends on your being able to transmit information back to the control ships. **You are the man!**"

The relatively flat-bottomed LCVP has a powerful diesel engine that permits in most cases driving itself right up on the beach. The hinged bow (front) door drops and with luck one might step or drive onto dry land. The rule was for men to exit to the side of the now lowered ramp to avoid the possibility of a leg being caught between the ramp and the beach since the ramp kept moving as wave action moved the boat. I remember the landing, unlike some future ones, as a comfortable dry one. The time was around seven a.m. and the weather was delightful.

I carried both a long and short wire antennae for the radio. The short wire, three feet in length and flexible was used if communicating while on the move. The long wire, nine feet in length and rigid gave the radio the increased range we needed in this situation. As a result I could not accompany the Captain as he moved about the beach. He positioned me in the center of our beach area under one of the largest coconut palm trees fronting the beach where he could easily find me as his need to communicate arose.

This beautiful beach, located in a sheltered lagoon was lined with palm trees extending in a graceful arc for a quarter mile on each side of my central location. The sand was stark white, and when not disturbed by boat traffic the water was colored a pleasant azure blue. Absolutely idyllic! This former Wisconsin farm boy was quite pleased. If back on the farm on this February morning I might be thawing out after finishing spreading that day's accumulation of barn manure. Instead, here I was lolling in temperatures in the mid-seventies under a clear sunlit sky on a tropical beach. I believe the next twelve hours were among the pleasantest and most rewarding of my time in the Marine Corps.

Apart from the idyllic conditions under which I was currently working, the job itself was easy and interesting. The Captain's job was to assess the needs on the beach. He could change the routine for landing men and supplies as necessary. We landed in the third wave, at H-hour plus a few minutes. This put the Captain on the spot for decision making when the umpires introduced situations to which he had to respond. On one occasion there was a need for an emergency supply of thirty-caliber machine gun ammo, another was an unexpected armored threat, then a need to evacuate unexpected heavy casualties, etc. The planners anticipated emergencies and had several LCVPs with a jeep and trailer on board loaded with various types of ammunition floating roughly a mile off shore. The same was true for tanks aboard what was called a LSM (landing ship medium). Upon receiving a request these elements could be sent ashore out of the order originally planned to meet the emergency needs on the beach and the immediate front.

My job was simply to transmit and receive messages as related to this procedure. The battery for the radio, depending on the ratio of transmitting to receiving, lasted for six to eight hours. I carried a spare battery and at the six-hour level, without waiting for the old one to die, I checked out of the net for less than a minute to change the battery. At one point the Navy Beachmaster's radio(s) failed. They needed to be in contact with their own control vessel as related to boat traffic. When their communication failed my Captain directed me to handle their traffic via a relay set-up. Runners from the Beachmaster unit carried messages back and forth. I think both the Captain and I felt quite smug about our reliable communication link.

And so it went throughout the day. I was not all that busy as I sat under this palm tree with a panoramic view of all that equipment and men coming ashore. Nothing quite equaled the sight of those 4000 ton LSTs (landing ship tank) that came ashore later that morning and throughout the afternoon. The giant bow doors opened as the ship neared the shore and once beached a ramp dropped to permit unloading as many as forty-five tanks on its tank deck and a similar number of wheeled vehicles on its weather deck. Since the tanks, trucks, jeeps etc. were all loaded facing forward it took but minutes for one of these ships to discharge its complete load. I watched in wide-eyed wonder. My food and water needs were met by what I carried ashore. The menu was enhanced by the plentiful supply of ripened coconuts lying on the ground. I found both the milk and meat of the coconut tasty—and easy to open with my bayonet. If a head

Landing Ship Tank (LST) on the beach with bow doors open and ramp down.

call were necessary the Captain manned the radio for the few minutes involved. We were a good team.

Later in the day scattered clouds drifted by. When a cloud covered the sun the water turned a slate blue, but changed back to turquoise as soon as the sun came out again. Around eight p.m. my radio link with the control ship was no longer needed. I turned the radio in and went right to work helping to load fifty-five gallon drums of fuel into trucks to be hauled to supply dumps inland. I never did see the Captain I worked for again.

The rest of the few days on the island were routine. We lived in two man pup tents while providing communications for the regiment. This was a tropical island inhabited by all sorts of creepy crawly "things." These things were most active at night while we lay on the ground trying to sleep. Actually, it wasn't the creepy, crawly things that kept us awake as the one man who objected vociferously in a constant tirade, and with colorful language about these invaders of his pup tent. The rest of us found his performance downright entertaining. My friend Jim Delaney was clearly no friend of these insect inhabitants of the island. On our last day ashore we went on liberty to the only town on the island, the rather tawdry village of Isabelle Segundo. About all it had to offer was lukewarm Coca-Cola and inexpensive souvenirs.

The next day we re-embarked over the beaches to our familiar troop ship. I was amazed at the power of these small landing craft capable of pulling themselves off the beach from a standing start while fully loaded. Once back aboard ship, the salt-water showers and hot food were a pleasant change from life ashore. I had to admit though, I was a bit sad to be sailing away from this pleasant island.

The ships went their separate ways to various liberty ports in the Caribbean area. Our first stop was San Juan, Puerto Rico; then to Santiago, Cuba. As we proceeded slowly to our berthing dock, small boats crowded around the ship. Most had attractive young women aboard who waved and held up signs indicating where they could be found ashore. If not before, we now realized why on the way to these liberty ports we had those stern lectures on how to behave around the native women. The long lines outside sick bay on the voyage home indicated that not all remembered what they had been warned about in these lectures.

There was a popular song at the time sung by the Andrew's sisters titled *Rum and Coca-Cola*. Here on the one hand were all these young men, most under twenty-one, and on the other, the bars dispensing rum and Coca-Cola for ten cents a drink. Combine this with a warm sun and perhaps for most men, the major sin committed ashore was drinking more than they should have. I was surprised at how understanding the military authorities were as Sailors and Marines arrived back at the ship drunk, boisterous, and disheveled. Many were delivered back to the ship by the Shore Patrol. As long as an individual had not hurt anyone or destroyed any property all was forgiven.

I took my turn with liberty ashore and enjoyed my fair quota of rum and coke. Those of my ilk also found that if you avoided the bars and drifted around to the side streets you found friendly and curious people who greeted you warmly. On one occasion, three or four of us were strolling down a narrow residential street. An elderly woman beckoned us to enter her home. We hesitated, a bit surprised I suppose. After reflecting on the fact that we had not been warned about elderly women beckoning us into their home, we entered. She pointed to a corner where a piano sat. Via sign language she indicated one of us should play it. How fortunate that one of our group was a pianist. As he played this lady sat in a chair, eyes closed, a soft smile on her face. Just like my Grandmother Hedrick did when we sang *You Are My Sunshine* for her. But the exciting liberty, liberty in the "fast lane," was pitched in the bars and bordellos. I think we spent three days in each liberty port.

The Naval base at Quatanama Bay, Cuba was about fifty miles east of Santiago. We stopped here on a Sunday. After Santiago, not many viewed going ashore at a Naval base as all that exciting. Besides, we were at anchor and had to travel by small boats. A friend and I went ashore after breakfast. We would not be able to return to the ship until mid-afternoon. Noontime came and since this was a Sunday, nothing on the base was open in the way of food sales. At last, with hunger driving us, we overcame our fear and walked up to the base mess hall and asked if we could have something, anything at all to eat. We knew military mess halls received "X" amount of money per-day for each man they were responsible for feeding—and this mess hall was certainly not responsible for feeding a couple of itinerant Marines. A Navy Chief was summoned and with absolutely no hesitation at all, complemented by a warm smile, said, "Sure!" How lucky could we be? Gracing the menu was fried chicken with all the trimmings plus all the ice cream we could eat. I suspect my friend and I will not forget that episode in our lives—and the Navy Chief who so cheerfully allowed us to eat in his mess hall.

Later that Sunday afternoon we were off for Camp Lejeune, North Carolina. No more time consuming maneuvers at sea. Apparently everyone was eager to return home. I found it entirely satisfactory getting back to the more civilized living in barracks and the all-together better food without having to stand in long lines.

Barracks Routine and First Military Leave

We slipped easily back into the routine after returning from the Caribbean area.. I had arrived at Camp Lejeune in late October of 1947. A little over three months later we were off for Caribbean maneuvers. I really had little time to become fully acquainted with the camp or the neighboring civilian community. The civilian community was easy for most of us to ignore. For one reason, Jacksonville was a sleepy small southern town with little to recommend it for liberty. A second reason was the remoteness of Jacksonville from our living area (ten miles) and the lack of convenient transportation. Then too, Camp Lejeune was a large base with a variety of recreational and commercial activities much as could be found in a typical mid-sized city. Enlisted men's clubs were sprinkled throughout the camp. They sold beer and snack food. As I recall, age did not restrict one from imbibing, and as a result these were lively places in the evenings and on weekends. Many enjoyed having access to food other than that served in the mess halls. George Hedrick's son was reluctant to waste his money on snack bar type food when he had access to free meals in the mess hall. Besides, I rated the food provided as very good.

The daily routine itself was enjoyable. It involved time spent in military type training, but much more in maintaining our communication equipment and skills. There was still guard duty out at the equipment park but the weather was much better at this time of year. Our barracks housed approximately sixty men in one communal squad bay. Bunks separated by approximately four-feet of space lined the outside walls. We were fortunate that at the time there was enough barracks space at Camp Lejeune so as not to require double bunks. Wall lockers ran down the center to separate the two rows of bunks. A footlocker stood neatly in front of each bunk. Our 782 gear (pack, etc.) was strapped to the end of our bunk. Rifles were kept in racks interspersed with the wall lockers. Monday through Friday, before breakfast, we thoroughly cleaned the squad bay and head. Each morning before we left for our assigned work/

training station all was clean and squared away. The cleanliness was complemented by each bunk, each footlocker, etc. being lined up like troops in formation (or as Dad liked having his corn shocks lined up). Shortly after we left the barracks our living area was inspected. We knew that if it didn't pass inspection repercussions were likely. Each evening before lights out there was also a light clean up of our living area. Saturdays, Sundays and holidays were more relaxed, but the duty NCO (non-commissioned-officer) could order a clean-up at any time if in his judgment it was needed.

Friday evenings we routinely held an event called a "field day" at which time we more than thoroughly cleaned the barracks. There was no liberty until this event was over. We started right after the evening meal. One crew cleaned the head, passage ways and ladders. The bulk of the men cleaned the barracks proper, and we did do windows! First we moved every piece of furniture to one end of the squad bay so that one-half was wide open. This open half was subjected to the full treatment with scrub brushes and soapy water—followed by dry mopping. Then all the furniture was moved into the part just cleaned so the remaining half could be similarly cleaned. Bunks, wall lockers, footlockers and rifle racks were wiped down in the process. The chore reminded me of threshing—hard work but fun as well. We were a noisy, happy group as we worked together on this weekly project. The result was like moving into a house after the annual spring-cleaning. The place looked bright and squeaky clean. We finished up around eight or nine p.m. After a responsible Sergeant gave the place a white glove inspection, and found it satisfactory, liberty call was sounded. Only the true die-hard liberty hounds took advantage of the offer—the rest of us were happy to turn in, many before lights out at ten p.m.

Three other housekeeping type functions occurred at regular intervals. On Monday mornings we exchanged our old bed linen for new. At the same time we turned in our personal laundry. The cost was one dollar up front for twenty-five pieces. A pair of socks was considered one piece;

the laundry bag the clothes were in was not counted. That dollar up front was a problem for the liberty hounds and those who otherwise found ways to spend all their money. A Minnesota boy, Clarence Leikam and I were known as the "mid-west bankers" since we were usually hit up for dollar loans. No interest was ever charged. Periodically on a sunny day, ideally with a complimentary breeze, we aired our mattresses outdoors. We folded them length ways in a "U" and let them bask in the sun.

One morning I was singled out from the formation and told to report to the company office. No one ever wanted to report to the company office; that usually meant you were in trouble. I could sense that the rest of the platoon was wondering what I had done wrong—and were thankful it wasn't them. I reported to an unsmiling First Sergeant who told me to wait and the Captain would see me shortly. When ushered in by the First Sergeant I made all the necessary military movements to position myself in front of the Captain's desk, then reported, "Private-First-Class Hedrick reporting as ordered Sir!" He looked up and then did something surprising for an officer—he smiled. It seems that the unsmiling and stern Captain I had worked for on the beach on Vieques had written a complimentary letter relative to the job I had done for him. He even mentioned that I had used my poncho to protect the radio from water spray instead of myself on the eight-mile ride to the beach. The Company commander seemed pleased and even the First Sergeant smiled when he shook my hand. Private-First-Class Hedrick: well, he was on cloud nine. I sure hoped the Captain I had worked for on that beach was, or would soon be promoted to Major.

In April 1948 I took my first military leave. I was to be best man at my sister Dorothy's wedding. It had been nearly fifteen months since I left home. Four of us, all in uniform, started off as a group early one morning. To save money we began by hitchhiking. Three of us were heading for the train station in Washington, D.C. We had 380 miles to cover and we hoped to catch a late afternoon train to Chicago. Hitchhiking was not frowned upon in those days. Both the recent depression and World War

II gas rationing resulted in thumbing a ride being a common and accept-able means of travel. One member of our foursome split off at some point to continue on to his home in Kentucky. The rest of us ended up at a point about 100 miles south of Washington by early afternoon. We were doing well catching rides, but obviously it was going to be touch and go relative to catching that afternoon train. Then a big luxury sedan stopped to pick us up. The driver was an older man who looked a bit familiar to me. In a friendly fashion he inquired as to our experiences as Marines. Having just returned from maneuvers we went on and on enlightening this gentleman on all the details relative to amphibious warfare, and life in general in the Marine Corps. He mentioned that he was returning to his home in Virginia from a speaking engagement. This kind gentleman took us out of his way to drop us off at the Washington railroad station. As we exited we each shook his hand, thanked him, and mentioned our names. He said, "I'm Ralph Mitchell." As he drove off it hit me that this was a man I knew from my history books—specifically Marine Corps history. The workload at Camp Lejeune was relatively relaxed. That left ample time for watching Marine combat films from World War II. These films, in addition to the "gung-ho" combat footage highlighted the generals who played principal roles in whatever battle sequence was being shown. General Mitchell (USMC) was one of the generals so depicted in battle scenes shot in the Solomon Island (Southwest Pacific). He had retired since the end of the war. I'll bet when he arrived home that evening he told his wife that after thirty plus years in the Marine Corps he had finally been educated about amphibious landings by three crusty "old salts."

If the good news was that we made it to the railroad station without paying for transportation, the bad news was that we missed the train to Chicago by an hour. We teamed up with a sailor, also heading for Chi-cago, and rented a cab that took us to Pittsburgh where we arrived well ahead of the train we had missed in Washington, D.C. The reduced train fare from Pittsburgh to Chicago paid for the taxi fare. In Chicago we all four went our separate way—for me a train trip to Sparta. I arrived there at four a.m. and took a taxi to the farm. The house was unlocked (houses were generally left unlocked on Summit Ridge) and my initial reaction was one of shock at how small the rooms seemed. For nearly fifteen months I had lived in large barracks, ate in equally large mess halls, or lived in equally large compartments aboard ship.

My leave generally centered around Dorothy's marriage where I had my first opportunity to wear dress blues in public. These had been issued after returning from spring maneuvers and just before going home on leave. This was also a chance to get reacquainted with younger siblings, especially Mary who was not yet three years old when I left home in 1947. It seemed strange to be in a pew and not on the altar at St. John's Catholic Church. I also enjoyed eating at my grandmother's table again. Enjoyed too was the reunion with Grandfathers Hedrick and Berendes, and Clarence Dittman, along with other members of the extended family and neighbors. I also dated the young lady in whom I had invested the cost for costume jewelry and a box of chocolates. I enjoyed as well pitching in to help with all the familiar farm chores, from spreading manure to tooling along on that old familiar John Deere tractor. My leave flew by and I was soon on my way back to Camp Lejeune. I took the train from Sparta to Milwaukee, then my first commercial airplane flight from Milwaukee to Washington, D.C. No hitchhiking now, I took a bus the rest of the way to Camp Lejeune.

More Maneuvers

It seems we were usually off on maneuvers while I was with the 16th Marines. Then again, I was single and always ready and eager for more adventure. Each summer the Navy conducted four amphibious training exercises involving students from military schools. There was one each involving the upper classmen from the military academies at West Point and Annapolis. Another two involved were the Junior School (Majors) and Senior School (Lieutenant Colonels) at Marine Corps Schools, Quantico, Virginia. Apart from the students themselves, the only need for troops was for communication personnel since these officers were only executing plans for an amphibious landing they had devised.

We began the operations by traveling via rail from Camp Lejeune to either Quantico or Norfolk, Virginia. After about a week we boarded ship and made the amphibious landing at Camp Lejeune's Onslow Beach. Since only a small number of communication troops were involved there was no need for troop transports. We usually sailed on what became my favorite amphibious ship to ride, the landing ship tank (LST). The ship at 327 feet in length was the approximate length of a football field. She was 50 feet wide and could carry 2100 tons of cargo. Her best speed was eight and one-half knots, around ten miles per hour land speed. The flat bottom resulted in her bouncing all over the place and we "old salts," who were immune to seasickness thought of it as a wild bronco. This was particularly true while sailing around the rough

Landing Ship Tank (LST). Note pontoons on each side of the ship. If the beach gradient does not permit getting all the way to the beach these pontoons can be used to make a causeway for tanks, vehicles, etc.

passage off Cape Hatteras, North Carolina. The ship was also troop friendly in other ways. Instead of 1500 troops, we numbered about 200. Sleeping racks were three high with about eighteen bunks in a compartment. The compartments were only one deck below the main weather deck. The food line was correspondingly short and with jeeps and trucks covering the weather deck we found many comfortable spots to lounge or enjoy a movie. The ship had rope ladders, similar to those on troopships, to permit boarding small boats. In the many times I participated in landing exercises on LSTs I never disembarked over the side but went off the bow ramp in some type of vehicle. Finally, we found it much easier to mingle with the Navy crew on this relatively small ship.

Amphibious Cold Weather Training

There was one other amphibious exercise conducted in the late fall. This was cold weather training on beaches in the vicinity of Argentia, Newfoundland. Since an infantry regiment was involved several troop transports were needed, and I ended up on one of them. This time I did not escape mess duty. If that was bad news, the good news was that one other Marine and I were assigned to the Chief's mess. Navy Chiefs are the backbone of the Navy, as are other military service's staff non-commissioned officers. What makes the Chief unique is that he stands at the top of the heap—no one else in the enlisted ranks of the Navy shares their mess, their uniform, or their prestige. The selection process ensures that only the best men are promoted to Chief. As a result, the Navy takes good care of its Chiefs, as well they should. In the Marine Corps; Staff Sergeants, Gunnery (Technical Sergeants), and Master Sergeants were lumped together. These three pay grades, when ashore, have a combined mess, club system, and billeting area. While aboard ship, only Marine Master Sergeants, who are equivalent to Navy Chiefs in pay grade, could eat in the Chief's mess or sleep in their compartments.

This might be the time to mention that the Marines have no medical or chaplaincy departments. This need is met by the Navy. Chaplains and doctors are commissioned officers. Navy corpsman of the rank of E-5s (second class) and E-6s (first class) were equivalent to Marine Staff-non-commissioned officers and could use the more up-scale facilities provided for Staff-non-commissioned officers while serving with Marines ashore. In other words, they rubbed elbows with Navy Chiefs while ashore. But when aboard ship or at Navy bases they lost this privilege and were accorded whatever perks were available to their naval contemporaries. As a general rule, Navy corpsmen assigned to Marine units are quite satisfied. In addition to Staff-non-commissioned officer privileges being accorded to many of them, Marines think the world of their "Docs," as Navy corpsman are collectively referred to. As a result, the Marines place their corpsmen and doctors on a pedestal. In combat the yell "corpsman" is often heard, and like their contemporaries, Army medics, their casualty rate is high as they move under fire to care for the wounded.

But now back to the Chief's mess on this particular troopship, which as I recall was the USS Cambria. She was older than the USS Okanagan with even more austere troop accommodations. Since we carried "X" number of Master Sergeants who ate in the Chief's mess, thus increasing the workload for their assigned mess personnel, two of us Marines were assigned to help out. Since there were only about thirty Chiefs and Master Sergeants the workload was relatively light. The working conditions were excellent and the Chief's mess was located in an altogether more favorable location than the general mess. There was good food, and plenty of it. In fact, at the end of the workday we were reluctant to leave. Desserts, coffee, and other foodstuff were made available on a round-the-clock basis and we too had access to these delicacies while on the job. A further benefit of the job was that we were billeted in an all-together more desirable compartment with access to more modern bathroom facilities. I'm sure I went out of my way to do a good job. I had not forgotten that Navy Chief who ten months before had cheerfully allowed this ravishingly hungry person to eat a big Sunday meal of fried chicken in his mess hall—and at his expense in a sense. I volunteered for mess duty in the Chief's mess on the way home, and luckily I was accepted.

For those not assigned to a cushy job like I had aboard ship, life was not all that pleasant. This was not the sunny Caribbean where you could enjoy the sun on open decks; now there was cold wind and rain in the waters northeast of Maine that usually drove everyone below decks.

At this point, I had graduated to driving a radio jeep. My jeep and trailer were loaded first in a LCVP landing craft and then a couple Marines and I followed down the rope ladder. The day was dark and dreary with intermittent showers. Since we were not in the assault waves, the ship moved closer to the beach before we disembarked. Earlier troop assault waves had secured the beach and moved inland. The trip from ship to shore was about a mile this time. The jeep had a side curtain that provided protection from the usual spray and foul weather. The concern was whether the beach gradient would permit the coxswain to drive the boat up on the beach enabling me to drive off easily. As in all amphibious landings, motor vehicles were provided with the necessary modifications that permitted them to operate while completely submerged—at least for a few minutes. Basically it consisted of a water proof compound (goop) covering electrical components and a vertical pipe extending approximately six feet above the engine. This pipe permitted the carburetor to draw in pure outside air. There was no such device for the driver or passengers. We were told to hold our breath as long as we could and hope for the best. Not to worry though, we splashed ashore in a foot of water. The jeep was positioned next to the message center tent in a small command post for our unit. My co-worker and I set up our pup tent, but in practice we slept, or tried to sleep in the comparatively warmer jeep while the other maintained the radio watch.

A day or so later we re-embarked and were supposed to stop at a Canadian or New England liberty port on the way home. I am not sure of the reason, weather conditions possibly, but we did not stop at any port.

I don't recall being at all disappointed, given the weather—and besides, I was quite happy to be back working in the Chief's mess. We arrived back at Camp Lejeune via yet another over the beach landing at Onslow Beach in mid-November 1948.

A warrant promoting me to Corporal (E3) was waiting when I returned. The increase in pay was much appreciated, as was that added splash of red on my sleeve. I also enjoyed letting the family know of the promotion. What really pleased me was now I could wear that red stripe down the trouser legs of my dress blue uniform. Only Corporals and above could wear this stripe. The reason for this distinction from privates was based on the battle of Chaputepec fought during the Mexican American War on 12 September 1846. This hill mass on the outskirts of Mexico City was taken after heavy casualties by a Marine unit made up of Corporals or above. Lieutenant Ulysses S. Grant commanded the forty-six Marines of this detachment along with twenty soldiers. This group was the first to fight their way into Mexico City.

If promotion to Corporal was good news, the bad news was that the Marine Corps had directed removal of all shoulder patches. Previously only those Marines in divisions and air wings were authorized to wear the shoulder patch. That left out those many Marines in various support activities, i.e. schools, ship's companies, and higher headquarters, etc. The theory was that a Marine is a Marine and shoulder patches serve no useful purpose in that context.

The military routine for me changed somewhat as a result of this promotion. I still took my turn at guard duty, but not as often. Now as Corporal-of-the-guard I no longer had to walk a post. I also took my turn supervising a crew in the daily clean up chores in the barracks area. These were the barracks proper, ladders and passageways, outside area, and head. The four of us stayed behind a few minutes after the rest of the troops left for their work stations until the Company First Sergeant or his representative inspected the areas we were responsible for. I especially liked the head detail. In conjunction with the job we used a pine scent to swab (mop) the deck. The combination of clean and gleaming porcelain fixtures, mirrors, and deck, all complemented by that pleasant smelling pine oil scent might have earned us the "Good Housekeeping award."

Sometime in November of 1948 I returned to Wisconsin on leave. The highlight of the trip would be deer hunting. Once again one other Marine and I started out hitch hiking. This time we tried catching a flight from Camp Lejeune's airfield (Peterfield Point). We were in luck. A Navy Beechcraft was headed for Anacostia Naval Air Station just outside of Washington, D.C. The Beechcraft was a relatively small two engine utility plane that carried approximately five passengers. Only the pilot, the other Marine and myself were aboard—and I was allowed to sit in the co-pilot's seat. We were flying along and my eyes were wandering from the aircraft's instrument panel to the ground. No doubt I was daydreaming as well of flying a plane someday. Then, one or both of the engines started sputtering. The pilot instantly put the plane in a steep dive while flipping a couple of switches on an overhead control panel. The engines quickly came back to full power. The pilot turned to me, smiled broadly, and said something along the line of, "These birds fly a lot better if the pilot remembers to switch gas tanks in time."

Back to the Caribbean (Vieques)

February 1949 rolled around and we were happy to hear that spring maneuvers in the Caribbean with landings once again on the island of Vieques were planned. There was the routine preparatory training, which we old salts had to undergo along with the new men. This time I sailed on my favorite amphibious ship, an LST. We again loaded at Moorhead City while the ship was beached with bow doors open and the ramp down. The main deck was wide enough to permit me to drive the radio jeep and trailer up the ramp, proceed down the deck as directed, then make a U-turn to arrive at my designated parking spot. I then assisted a deck hand in chaining the vehicle to tie downs on the deck.

We sailed in a slow convoy this time. The lumbering LSTs and LSMs were escorted by a couple of destroyers. We did not participate in the rehearsal, permitting us troops to relax while the ships conducted various exercises until time for the landing. We were scheduled to land around noon on D-day. As we approached the beach I couldn't believe my eyes. All those beautiful palm trees that once lined the beach were gone. None of us knew why, but there were theories. One was that egress from the beach was much too restricted for mechanized equipment. This meant removing the palm trees. A more likely reason was that a palm-lined beach was not what you expected to see in an assault landing. Naval gunfire and aircraft ordinance would have shredded every tree before the troops landed. The reasoning may have been why not make the beach look more realistic?

Our ship routinely dropped its stern anchor about one-quarter mile out from the beach and began stringing out a connecting cable. When she backed off the beach a winch in the back of the ship served to assist the screws in moving the flat-bottomed ship back to open water. After dropping the stern anchor the next function was to open the bow doors before hitting the beach. (The hinged ramp still kept water out of the ship.) Oh! Oh! The doors only opened part way. This was most embarrassing for the Captain. As a result, we were sent to the Naval base at Roosevelt Roads on the island of Puerto Rico for repairs.

We returned to Vieques the next day and made a routine landing across the beach and belatedly joined up with our unit. We spent another day on the island with liberty in exciting Isabelle Segunda. The next day we boarded the LST for the trip home. This time our liberty ports were St. Thomas and St. Croix in the Virgin Islands east of Vieques. We would have gladly volunteered for these spring maneuvers even if enjoyable and exotic liberty posts had not been on the menu. These liberty ports were like a tasty dessert after a full and satisfying meal. We could count on many different sights to see, and young women in small boats of one kind or another could be relied on to greet the ship.

Last Months with the 16th Marines

Once again we slipped back into the routine at Camp Lejeune. This routine was pleasantly interrupted by promotion to Sergeant (E4). There was the additional splash of color on dress uniforms, more money, and also the pride in letting the folks at home know of the promotion. I found it quite pleasing to acknowledge that I was now a "Sergeant in the Marines." Operationally there was an added responsibility within our communication platoon. Also, on a rotating basis with other Sergeants in the unit I was responsible for all housekeeping functions in our barracks area. No more guard duty at the equipment park, but I was not off the hook in that regard. I took my turn as Sergeant-of-the-guard in the headquarters area of the 2nd Marine division (in which my 16th Marines was one of five regiments). This assignment was more comfortable than at the equipment park, but there was more pressure since the Sergeant-of-the-guard was responsible for raising and lowering the colors on the flagpole in front of division headquarters. Not only were we under pressure to do the job smartly, but to never, ever let the flag touch the ground! Then there was the audience. At evening colors the Officer-of-the-day was required to be present. The Division Duty-Officer (a Major or Lieutenant Colonel) also often observed the ceremony. In the morning, especially on weekdays, the audience included those coming and going in conjunction with the normal routine at the headquarters

Anglico, Fleet Marine Force (FMF)

In early July 1949 my name showed up on a list for transfer to a new unit being formed at Camp Lejeune. The transfer was held up for a couple of hours when my unit learned that another man named Hedrick had been in some kind of trouble in Jacksonville the night before. (You didn't transfer someone involved with a disciplinary problem to another unit.) But this was soon cleared up and I left the regiment that had been my home for the past twenty months. A bit sad? Yes! Physically the move was not all that distant—about three blocks to the new barracks area.

My new unit was titled Air Naval Gunfire Liaison Company (AN-GLICO) FMF (Fleet Marine Force). Transfer to this unit stands out as a cardinal event in my military career. I found my niche, and using farm analogy, I found fertile soil in which to grow. But first something about the unit. The Marine Corps is part of the Navy. Marines in that era served on major warships, provided security at Naval bases, but their primary mission was to seize and hold land areas that the Navy could then develop as forward operating bases. The best example of this teamwork between the Marines and Navy took place during World War II; specifically the Pacific Island hopping campaigns. The Marines landed across the beach and could be supported by naval gunfire. Spotting teams headed by Naval officers came ashore with the Marines to call in naval gunfire via radio communication links. The Marines, unlike the Army, also have their own air arm. Pilots were assigned to Marine ground units ashore to call in aircraft for close air support as needed via air-ground radio communications. The Marines are now all set, but how about an Army unit, or a military unit from an allied nation that the Marines might be working with? This then was the mission of ANGLICO (FMF), to work with these units by providing them with air and naval gunfire support. To identify this new ANGLICO's mission the term "Fleet Marine Force" was appended to the title of ANGLICO. That portion of ANGLICO involved in naval gunfire had both Naval officers and Marine artillery officers supported by enlisted communication personnel. The air unit had only Marine aviation officers (pilots) and communication personnel. I suspect ANGLICO numbered around thirty officers and three hundred men—with the naval gunfire contingents being the largest.

When the dust had settled on assignments I ended up as the senior non-commissioned officer (NCO) in the air support element. The more senior NCOs had an artillery background and were slotted for the naval gunfire element. The air section numbered approximately sixty men. First of all, I found my voice—literally. I found myself endowed with a strong voice and could call cadence like a Drill Instructor. We still did a certain amount of drilling. Quite frankly it was a thrill to have a large group of men respond to your drill commands. I also enjoyed and thrived in the role of an administrator as related to the operational and housekeeping chores. The job also came with a semi-private room in the barracks.

I thoroughly enjoyed working for and with Marine flyers. They had no problem smiling and yet were every inch a Marine Officer. There's a reason for this difference in demeanor. Aviators, particularly Captains and Lieutenants have as their primary job flying airplanes. The pilots as a result are usually involved with only a small number of enlisted men that service their aircraft. The primary enlisted man in that group is the Plane Captain. Ground officers by comparison are woven into the fabric of organizations with a large number of junior enlisted men. Thus the need for ground officers to maintain a certain aloofness from the men. This not only applied to officers/enlisted relations, but also to senior non-commissioned officer and junior enlisted men. How often we heard the term "familiarity breeds contempt."

I enjoyed my association with the aviators who were happy to leave one alone as long as the job was done. The two pilots I knew best were Lieutenant Norm Gourley, who became a Major General, and Lieutenant Dan Holland, who took our air team to Korea in August of 1950. I found it interesting work as well. We communicators operated the radios with which aircraft could be requested (ground-to-ground communications) and other radios used to actually direct the aircraft (ground-to-air). We had both vehicular and portable radios for both tasks. Our aviators knew most of the men actually flying the planes, which resulted in frequent low level buzzing when we worked in the field. At this point we became familiar with the F-4U Corsair, a Marine close support aircraft. This plane made a significant contribution to getting us out of the Chosin Reservoir of North Korea in December of 1950.

Sometime around mid-October of 1949 most of the unit boarded a Pullman train for the long ride to Fort Lewis (Tacoma), Washington.

We were to work with the 2nd Army division in an amphibious landing exercise in Hawaii. This was my third cross-country trip by troop train. An altogether different route this time. There was a chance we might be routed over the Chicago and Northwestern tracks running through our farm—but that didn't happen.

It seemed strange that first morning at Fort Lewis as we stood in an Army formation for muster. It must have been strange too for the soldiers who heard our leader report the presence of a Marine unit. We meshed easily with the Army personnel of the unit to which we were attached. A healthy camaraderie developed in the weeks we worked together. We spent approximately three weeks at Fort Lewis before shipping out. Enough time to visit Tacoma, Seattle, and Vancouver in Canada. The ship we boarded in Seattle was my old friend the USS Okanagan. Nothing had changed aboard the ship—except she was now older.

We sailed first to the beaches off Camp Pendleton, California where we made a practice landing. Once back aboard ship we traveled the few miles south to San Diego for liberty. Since a friend of mine had not been to the West Coast, I escorted him to Hollywood. While there we visited a nightclub and during the floorshow we were taken on stage by two of the showgirls. The next evening, while walking past a studio in Hollywood, we were accosted by ushers urging us to come in to be part of the audience for a radio show about to go on. The performer was Frank Sinatra. This

Hollywood (1949). The best duty I had while in the military.

was at a time when Frank was experiencing a low point in his career. We passed up his show to catch one involving Fred MacMurray.

Then we were off for Hawaii. The Army troops went to Scolfield Barracks and the Marines to Camp Catlin. Scolfield Barracks is still an active Army base. Camp Catlin, at the time out in the middle of nowhere between Honolulu and Pearl Harbor, has long since been swallowed up by development. We were there ten days, plenty of time to enjoy the Island of Oahu. We then went back aboard the troop ship for the landing exercise itself. As the script for the landing unfolded, umpires introduced certain situations to which the Army commanders needed to react. Now the commanders had two additional powerful tools, naval gunfire and aircraft ordinance under their direct control with which to respond.

Then we headed back to the mainland. The Army division sailed separately for Seattle while our group of approximately 200 sailed for Camp Lejeune, North Carolina via the Panama Canal. The troop ship, possibly the USS Okanagan, was equipped to handle 1500 troops so we had space aplenty—with a delightful absence of long lines for meals and for ice cream and candy in the ship's store. I remember it as being a smooth passage with a brilliant moon that turned night into day as the light reflected from the water. After all these years I still remember that scene, and how great it would have been to share the magic of the moment in the company of a woman.

Late in the afternoon on our first day out from Honolulu, a couple of Marine Corsairs buzzed us. One did not pull up, or did not pull up in time and splashed. We circled the spot until dark but could find only small pieces of the aircraft. The mood was quite somber; for our pilots especially since this was what they normally did for a living, and some of them learned later they knew the pilot. For me this was the first time to have witnessed an accident taking the life of a man.

Somewhere between Hawaii and the Panama Canal word reached us that some in our organization were to be trained as paratroopers. This would permit us to support Army paratroop units as we had supported the 2nd Army division in the just completed amphibious training exercise. Training was scheduled to take place at the Army's paratroop training base at Fort Benning, Georgia. I suspect we volunteered for the paratroop training to a man. Implementation of the program was not intended to begin for another six months.

Naturally we were gawkers as we proceeded through the locks of the Panama Canal. But first there was a day of liberty at Balboa, located near the capital city of Panama on the Pacific side of the canal. I remember especially the lush greenery of the area as we passed through.

Back at Camp Lejeune we were reunited with those of the unit who did not make the trip and therefore had to listen to all our sea stories. I was looking forward to military leave coming up in late December of 1949. This would be a big one since I planned to cash in the profits from my earlier pig raising venture by purchasing a new car.

My Pontiac

Choices in cars at the time were generally restricted to basic two and four door sedans, with the color choice either black or dark blue. I don't recall if I visited any other show room than Rasmussen's Auto Sales in Sparta. The date was 31 December 1949 when I drove away in a dark blue 1950 Pontiac two door sedan. The cost was approximately $1900.

Ernie Ziegler, with contacts in the area from his recent high school days arranged for two young ladies to join us in christening the car and welcoming in the New Year. My plan was to leave the next day for St. Louis. Somewhere along the way I had developed a pen-pal relationship with the sister of a fellow Marine. She was from Scottsbluff, Nebraska and worked in St. Louis. I had also made arrangements with my roommate, who was on leave at his home in Hutchinson, Kansas to meet in St. Louis for the trip back to Camp Lejeune. Ernie Ziegler was planning to travel with me as far as Madison, Wisconsin the next day. He was on his way to join the Air Force. At one point during our New Year's eve outing, Ernie asked me if his cousin, Betty Goetz could ride back to Madison with us. He would be staying with her in Madison in conjunction with enlisting. Betty was six months out of high school at the time and was working at the state capital in Madison. Around noon the next day we all met at Schaller's store. Ernie came the mile from his home and Fred Goetz showed up with his daughter—and we were off. Betty came prepared; she had the evening meal along, to include pie.

This was one of those sickeningly dreary days that can occur at that time of year in Wisconsin. Rain, that could not decide whether to turn to snow or not kept the windshield wipers working. As a testimonial to quality control in the automobile industry at the time, the driver's side windshield wiper popped off at one point. Luckily traffic was light and we were able to find and re-attach it. We arrived in Madison at dusk with the same scruffy weather condition prevailing. I was invited to dinner, but still had about 400 miles to go to St. Louis. I was foolish to drive so far without rest to begin with, more foolish still to do so in such foul weather—but I had this date the following evening. My memory says I declined the dinner invitation. Betty Goetz remembers my stopping for dinner. Since Betty Goetz is now my wife we have plenty of opportunities to resolve the "Yes" or "No" of this issue.

As I headed out of Madison the rain stopped and a heavy fog set in. Somewhere along the way I picked up a hitchhiker. An agreeable young man I thought, and I found it refreshing to have someone to talk with. He mentioned that he often hitchhiked. I asked him if he wasn't concerned that the wrong type people might pick him up. "I have no worry about that," he said, and pulled out a revolver for me to see. We drove on for a while, the fog getting thicker and I was a bit concerned about my passenger and his weapon. At last a truck stop—and I took the opportunity to say, "This is it for me. I'm not driving any further in this fog." He said he didn't blame me and quickly caught a ride with a trucker. After a meal I drove on to St. Louis arriving there early in the morning. I had plenty of time to catch up on sleep and that evening enjoyed a date with my pen pal. We both grew up on farms so had that in common. We continued as pen pals and I dated her again after returning from Korea. The next morning my roommate, Bob Kinsey and I teamed up for the 1000-mile shared driving trek back to Camp Lejeune.

To say the least it was most unusual for a junior enlisted man to have any kind of a car, but a brand new one—that was unbelievable. I explained over and over how I came about having enough money to buy a new car and it was generally agreed I deserved the car. One day I was gassing up at the station aboard the base. The attendant said, "Would you mind if I asked you something?" "No, not at all," I replied. "Where did you find the money to buy a new car?" I happily told him of my gold strike raising pigs.

I had many invitations to go on liberty with the liberty hounds. No more busses for them if I could provide the wheels. As mentioned earlier, I was not much for liberty off the base. I was entirely satisfied hanging around the barracks, going to movies, the library, and participating in the endless games of softball or basketball. Now I also had an additional duty; keeping my Pontiac clean and shined. I'll bet I owned the best looking vehicle in the south-eastern part of the United States.

Despite having been at Camp Lejeune for two years my contact with southern women was close to nil. Rarely did I ever exchange any but a few brief words with a woman, perhaps in the process of making a purchase at the Marine exchange (PX). Most of the time that lady was from a northern state and married to a Marine. But the Pontiac and an aggressive roommate combined to change all that.

One of the first weekend trips made with the car was to the neighboring community of Wrightsville Beach. My new roommate, Elmer Larsen, was along. As we approached the outskirts of town I caught a sideways glimpse of four or five ladies waving. Elmer spun around in the seat and practically shouted, **"Joe, they're waving at us—turn around—turn around—lets go back!"** I objected, "Why did we want to embarrass ourselves?" Despite my misgivings, I did turn around and drove into the driveway of a children's hospital. The young ladies, now "charmingly" shy and reserved, were student nurses. I'm sure Elmer did the negotiating, but we made arrangements for dates the next weekend with two of the ladies whose schedule permitted. They could only date on Saturday and Sunday, if not on duty, and had to be back at the hospital by midnight.

The Beach Boys have a popular song entitled *I Wish They All Could Be California Girls*. Relative to southern girls they sing: *...and the southern girls with the way they talk, they knock me out when I'm down there.* How true! How true! Those pleasing to the ear soft "you-awls" were delight-ful, as was that drawn out and melodic "awl-raht!" From then on Elmer and I were at Wrightsville Beach as often as the nurse's and our sched-ule permitted. These young ladies introduced both Elmer and me to the beach. Both he and I, having grown up in Minnesota and Wisconsin re-spectively were strangers to this recreational activity. During the six sum-mer months of 1947 when I lived practically on the beach at Camp Del Mar in California, I pretty much ignored this attraction. I must say that the beach became much more interesting when in the company of these southern belles.

The Pontiac also introduced me to the "Big Apple." It didn't take long for the New York City boys to suggest that I might enjoy visiting their city. They paid me seven or eight dollars each to cover my expenses for providing the taxi service. One Friday evening, around four-thirty p.m., five New Yorkers and I began the trek. The distance from our bar-racks parking lot to the subway station at Times Square was precisely 585 miles. It took twelve hours to make the trip, and I drove all the way. At the time this was a two-lane highway all the way with a third passing lane here and there. At Pennsville, New Jersey, twenty miles south of Philadel-phia, we took a ferry across the Delaware River. What a welcome break. Time too for a hot dog and a coke. It took us about twenty minutes to cross the river. I had trouble with a traffic circle in the Philadelphia area. This was my fist experience with a traffic circle. A police officer on the alert for a stolen car spotted my aimless circling and a car with no license plate. I had no trouble proving the car was new and that the Wisconsin license plates had not yet arrived. The officer understood too how I could be confused on a traffic circle. After letting us know he too had served in the Marines, he put us on track for New York City.

Dawn was approaching as the skyline of the city loomed in the distance. My five passengers were all sleeping. One awoke and when he spotted the skyline he roused the others. In an exaggerated voice he exclaimed, **"Hey, there she is—there she is!"** The rest quickly in turn paid homage, verbally and with waving hands. This farm boy was amused—but obviously these men loved their city. We ducked into the Holland Tunnel and on to Times Square. Times Square was all but deserted at five a.m. on this Saturday morning in January 1950. We pulled up to the curb and got out of the car. My passengers were quietly removing their gear from the trunk. Then I heard the first words uttered in New York City. A young lady speaking to a young man said, "I'm not f _ _ _ _ g for a ham sandwich." Foolish girl I thought, but she hadn't been driving since four p.m. the day before without eating anything to speak of. Tony Tinelli, the man who had organized the trip, could only give me a sick grin.

I had declined an earlier offer to spend the weekend with one of my passengers. I wanted to see the center of the city. The five New Yorkers ducked quickly into the subway for their homes. The father of one worked in a hotel near Times Square and had made arrangements for a room for me. I was concerned about leaving the car curb parked without a license plate. I checked in with a nearby police station where they agreed this could be a problem. The solution—parking the car in their lot.

I slept for about ten hours and finally ducked out for my close look of the city around five p.m. First stop was the then famous automat where food was dispensed automatically via coins. Not at all unusual now, but the talk of the country at the time. One began the experience by approaching the so-called "nickel throwers." These were cashiers who gave you five-cent pieces for your larger coins or bills. The nickels were then slipped into slots in the automat and a knob turned. In a few seconds the compartment next to the slot revolved into place to present the desired cold food through a small glass door that then opened. Hot food was picked up at a buffet-style steam table. You could either sit at a table, or if in a hurry, consume the meal at a stand-up counter. Then I went to a movie at Radio City Music Hall, which included a live stage performance by the Rockettes.

Since I had a twelve-hour drive ahead of me on Sunday I turned in early. Sunday morning I attended Mass at St. Patrick's Cathedral. Around noon the five New Yorkers met me in Times Square, and we retraced our route back to Camp Lejeune. I was not a great fan of this trip. On balance I preferred dating the student nurses I had met in the local area. I did make at least two more trips to New York City. But in each of my next trips one of my passengers was a non-New Yorker who went along to see the city—and catch a live performance of his favorite band. Dick West was a fan of the Stan Kenton band; another companion liked the Gene Krupa's band with its emphasis on drums. I enjoyed having a friend to share the New York experience with.

Now that I had wheels for getting me to the local civilian airport I decided to take flying lessons. A fellow Marine, Guy Roark joined me. We decided that for so frivolous an undertaking we would not use our military pay. To earn enough money for flight lessons we set pins in the base bowling alley. We each handled two lanes. Hard work to jump from one alley to another, but the money rolled in faster. After the first ball had hit the pins, assuming no strike, we cleared the pins and jumped back out of the way. If a strike, or after the second ball we stepped on a lever that raised ten steel pins about two inches above floor level. Each bowling pin had a hole in the bottom and we set a pin over each protruding floor pin and again jumped out of the way. We were busy working two lanes, but the pay per-line along with tips usually paid the ten dollars per hour needed for that weekend's flight instructions.

I suspect most everyone who takes flying lessons enjoys the training—even if at times making lazy "S" turns over a straight stretch of highway becomes boring. The challenge was for the wings to be perfectly level at the point where you crossed the highway after completing one-half of the "S" turn, all the while maintaining 1000 feet of altitude. "Fly the airplane," the instructor reminded me as necessary, "don't let the airplane fly you." More fun were full power stalls and recovering from various spins. The adrenaline flowed too while making landings. On the day I soloed, the initial flight was with the instructor. We taxied back to the hanger area where he climbed out and said, "It's all yours." I don't recall being all that excited. There was a routine to follow, much practiced, and all went well. Initially I made three quick takeoffs and landings, followed by a more relaxed half-hour flight just for fun.

I flew about an hour a week after soloing. I did not venture far from the airfield. The Marines had a busy air station at Cherry Point, approximately thirty miles as the crow flies from my airport. I did not want to be anywhere near their traffic pattern. One day I was about twenty miles north of my airport when I saw what looked like a formation of approximately ten planes coming right at me. Before I could react a flight of sea gulls or crows flew past while giving me plenty of room.

On 17 January 1950, while steaming out of Norfolk, Virginia through Hampton Roads the USS Missouri went aground on Thimble Shoals.* Momentum carried the ship 2500 feet onto a mud flat. Freeing the ship involved off-loading ammunition, supplies, and fuel plus the concentrated efforts of many tugs, dredges, and divers. Four attempts were made to free her. Tugs pushing from alongside and pulling from astern could not do the trick. The ship was finally re-floated on 1 February 1950 after dredging alongside and astern opened a path for her to return to the shipping channel.

A few of us were sent aboard with portable radios for what turned out to be one of the unsuccessful attempts. We were in the Norfolk area in conjunction with upcoming spring maneuvers. Our job on the USS Missouri was to provide radio communication from the ship to the many

---

*On 2 September 1945 the Japanese surrendered in a ceremony aboard the USS Missouri in Tokyo Bay. Today she is a museum ship located next to the USS Arizona memorial in Pearl Harbor, Hawaii.

tugs involved in the attempt to free the ship. We were each assigned to a Naval officer who needed to be in touch with a given tug. During the one or two attempts on the day we were aboard, at the point where the pulling tugs applied maximum power, we ran from one side of the ship to the other as directed by a whistle. No doubt this movement was also synchronized with those tugs pushing on either side of the ship. The idea was that it might take only a fraction of an inch of movement to break the hold of the mud. Who could say but that this might occur as "X" number of men topside moved quickly back and forth from port to starboard as the tugs alongside pushed or backed-off in sync with our running.

The grounding was a keen embarrassment for the Navy, as is the accidental grounding of any ship. What made the situation all the worse was the heated competition for dollars between the Air Force and the Navy at the time. The Air Force suggested that aviation should be expanded to meet future defense needs at the expense of other services. The Navy would have been the big loser here. When the Missouri went aground certain Air Force adherents suggested leaving the Missouri on the mud flat for the Air Force to use for high altitude bombing practice. That did not go over well with the Navy.

Back to the Caribbean Yet Again

Word reached us in late January of 1950 that we were once again going to the Caribbean for maneuvers. This was my third straight year to visit the island of Vieques. This time we worked with an Army Division based on the East Coast. In February those of us involved moved to Fort Lee, an Army post near Richmond, Virginia. We were temporarily stationed here until we boarded ship. I was allowed to drive my car to Fort Lee from Camp Lejeune.

Fort Lee was a recruit training base for women in the Woman's Army Corps (WAC). The ladies greeted the arrival of two hundred Marines rather enthusiastically. WW II had seen the Marines doing much of their initial fighting in the jungles of the southwest Pacific. This led to the ladies referring to us, mischievously, as "jungle bunnies." I was reminded of the comic strip titled *Li'l Abner* and the annual Sadie Hawkins day race depicted in the then popular comic strip. Since it's likely many never heard of author Al Capp's entertaining and lovable hillbillies, a quick introduction is in order.

The locale was Dogpatch, a mountain community somewhere in Appalachia. Most folks here were dumber than dumb—poorer than poor. The main occupation was raising turnips, which were ravaged year after year by "turnip termites." People in our country at this time were suffering under an economic depression. They could smile as they read about people worse off than they were. Li'l Abner Yokum was a naïve man-child and a paragon of virtue. He was also tall, dark and handsome. Let's also mention bashful and lovable. He was pursued by a voluptuous blonde bombshell named Daisy Mae. Mammy (Pansy) and Pappy (Lucifer) Yokum played supporting roles, as did the likes of Big Barnsmell, Joe Btfsplk, and Senator Jack "S" Phogbound (who could be found in April of every year investigating un-American activities on the French Riviera). Lonesome Polecat was every bit as loyal an Indian sidekick to Hairless Joe as Tonto was to the Lone Ranger. (Both Hairless Joe and Lonesome Polecat worked in the one industry outside of turnip farming in Dogpatch, the Skunk Works.) The "heavy" amongst these otherwise likable characters was a man named "Earthquake McGoon." And who could forget that ravishingly beautiful brunette, Moonbeam McSwine, who was usually depicted happily sitting amongst the hogs in a pigsty smoking a corncob pipe?* Then there was Sadie Hawkins.

Sadie was the homeliest gal in the hills. Her father, Hekzehiah Hawkins did not want Sadie living at his home for the rest of his life. He was also a power in the community. On 15 November 1937 he decreed the first annual Sadie Hawkin's day race. Unmarried women who wanted to could pursue bachelors who had no choice but to run. If the ladies

---

*Moonbeam's modern day counterpart is "Pig Pen," the Peanuts' cartoon character who walks around in a cloud of dust.

caught a bachelor, "Marrying Sam" tied the knot then and there. The men were given a ten-second head start. Sadie Hawkins caught her man that year, but it took several more years before Daisy Mae caught Li'l Abner. A son named "Honest Abe" came along to round out the family. The 1960's feminist movement was no fan of Al Capp's depiction of women or of Sadie Hawkins day. But back in 1950 the event was much re-enacted, usually at dances, and usually on college campuses.

Now here we were at Fort Lee with all these healthy young women who were somewhat isolated from the world at this point while in basic training. Their sheer numbers gave them a license to act aggressively, and some, in Sadie Hawkins fashion, played it out in a humorous way. All in all it was a happy hunting ground, especially for one with a car. Most of the ladies could not leave the base while they were in training, but were free after normal training hours to use the Camp's recreational facilities. Those in their last couple weeks of training could leave the Camp on weekends, but had to be back by midnight. I remember taking one young lady to a movie titled *Sands of Iwo Jima* starring John Wayne as a Marine Sergeant. My date kept touching my arm and saying, "Aren't you proud? Aren't you proud?" I thought to myself that being a Marine in this environment was absolutely great! We spent about two weeks at this Army post, and I did meet a young lady I came ever so close to marrying two years later.

In the meantime, we worked with our respective Army units regarding naval gunfire and air support. As was the case with the soldiers at Fort Lewis, Washington, I found it enjoyable working with the Army. This time we left from Norfolk, Virginia on the troopship U.S.S. Bayfield.

In the previous two trips to the Caribbean we sailed directly from the port of embarkation (Moorehead City, North Carolina) to the objective area. This time we stopped enroute for a day at the historical and altogether beautiful city of Charleston, South Carolina. Charleston is famous for its preservation of buildings and other historic landmarks of the 1700s and 1800s. This was my first visit to a southern city that combined sophistication, charm—and above all, "Southern Hospitality." From my school history books I was also aware that Charleston was the "Cradle of the Confederacy," and that the Civil War began on the Charleston waterfront in April 1861 with the attack on Fort Sumpter.

No doubt through a church or civic organization, those of us interested were invited to be guests for a day of a local family. A buddy and I were picked up around 9 a.m. on this particular Saturday. Our host family consisted of Dad, Mom, and two early school age children. They provided us with a day-long automobile tour of the historic sites of Charleston. Noon lunch was at their home, served by a maid. If their home was not a mansion in the southern sense of the word, it seemed like one to me. They returned us to the ship around 5 p.m. We sailed from Charleston the following Sunday morning. I will always have a warm spot in my heart for Charleston, South Carolina.

The usual time was spent for naval maneuvers and operations ashore. The island of Vieques looked the same to me as it did the year before. I still yearned for the beach as it had looked two years earlier in 1948.* Caribbean liberty ports were Bridgetown on the island of Barbados and Martinique. I was assigned to a four-hour shift of shore patrol duty while in Bridgetown. This was during the exciting eight p.m. to midnight shift. A Bridgetown police officer and I teamed up to patrol the bars and bordellos. I remember that it took until two p.m. before we cleared the bars and I finally returned back to the ship.

At the completion of liberty in Martinique I was assigned to a detachment from ANGLICO that teamed up with an Army reconnaissance unit. We made a night landing on some remote island in the area. We sailed on a destroyer modified to carry approximately 200 troops. This was known as an APD (Amphibious Personnel Destroyer). This relatively small but fast ship provided an altogether different ride from a troop ship

---

*Citizen protests led to the Navy abandoning Vieques as a training site in 2003. Today tourists can stay at guesthouses that dot the beach, or the new Bravo Beach Hotel (bravobeachhotel.com). Resorts are in the process of being developed.

or LST. At its faster speed the destroyer "sliced" through the water which resulted in faster and much more pronounced rolling. After the landing, we headed back to Norfolk. Since I had left my car in Norfolk I had the opportunity to visit my favorite WAC at Fort Lee before driving back to Camp Lejeune. At Lejeune I slipped back into the usual garrison routine.

Sometime after returning from this cruise another weekend trip opportunity came along, this one closer to Camp Lejeune. A fellow Marine from North Carolina convinced me it could be worth my time to visit Greensboro, North Carolina, a city about 200 miles west of Camp Lejeune. Four of us took off one Friday and ended up that evening on the ground floor of a girl's college dormitory. Here the housemother spoke with us: interviewed us might be a better way of putting it. At one point she sent word upstairs that four young men downstairs appeared to meet her standards. I am not sure how I ended up with this attractive blonde. Her demeanor and personality suggested to me this was the kind of girl you would like to take home to meet your folks. The ladies could not leave the campus area. There was a movie theater on the campus, also a small restaurant and pleasant grounds to stroll around. I believe the curfew was eleven p.m. We dated again the following Saturday night under the same rules. Plans for future dating was tentatively agreed on, but this was early June 1950 and before I could return, the Korean War had broken out.

There was one keen embarrassing moment in the dating game. A friend and I took two ladies to a small nightclub in Washington, DC. The singing group was either the Ink Spots or the Ames Brothers. We were not aware of the entertainment cover charge that resulted in a bill of over forty dollars for a few drinks. My friend and I had the forty dollars between us, but the ladies had to help us out by contributing a few of their own dollars. Embarrassing!

Norm Gourley, now a Captain and the officer I worked most closely with took note of my interest in aviation. One day in mid-June 1950 he and I flew the thirty miles in a small observation plane to the Marine

Corps Air Station at Cherry Point, North Carolina. I was informally interviewed by the Commanding Officer of a F7F night fighter squadron. The planes in this squadron were called "Black Widows," so termed since its primary mission was to shoot down enemy planes—thus producing widows on the enemy side. Others claimed the term related to the plane's color (dark black) and its dangerous night fighting mission that resulted in widows for our side. The F7F was a two-engine fighter-bomber manned by the pilot and a radar operator. I climbed in the radar operator's seat and was asked if I felt comfortable there? My answer was an enthusiastic, **"Yes Sir!"** "Okay," Captain Gourley said, "we'll start the paperwork to have you transferred to the squadron." The idea was that if I prospered as a radar operator, in time I could apply for pilot's training. I couldn't believe my good luck. But this was not to be. Events in a remote corner of the world on 25 June 1950 negated this well laid plan.

One Last Stateside Fling

On Saturday night, 25 June 1950 Ole Larson and I were out on a date with our Wrightsville Beach "Cinderella" nurses (so termed because they had to be back at their hospital school by midnight). Early Sunday morning, as we drove back to Camp Lejeune, the radio informed us of North Korea invading South Korea. I recall hearing the report, but it meant absolutely nothing to me at the time. I don't recall that we commented to each other on what I at least had heard.

That same week Ole and I, now on military leave, put the Pontiac on the road to Wisconsin. Ole spent a few days at my home, then the two of us, along with my folks and two youngest sisters headed for Minnesota. Ole lived in St. Cloud and my dad's aunt and cousins lived in Avon, a community nearby. While the rest of my family spent their time visiting relatives, Ole and I roamed the countryside.

On one occasion Ole and I arrived at a recreational area called Pelican Lake. About fifty yards offshore there was a moored float on which three attractive young women were sunbathing. Ole suggested we take a rowboat and go out there. I was flabbergasted! Doing something like that was completely foreign to my nature. But I suppose I remembered Ole and those Wrightsville Beach nurses, and with great reluctance, I went along on this quest for romance. I was far from optimistic!

I wish I could remember the small talk that took place. Ole naturally carried the load for our side. I do recall an initial "cold" and "stern" aloofness on the part of the ladies that embarrassed me. These were altogether different ladies than the WACs at Fort Lee, Virginia or the nurses at Wrightsville Beach, North Carolina. Yet, the result of the encounter was that Ole and I took two of the ladies to a dance that evening.

The young lady I dated turned out to be as Catholic as my mother. She was also from a large family of seven or eight children. Her family, to include her parents, was vacationing at Pelican Lake at the time. Another thread of commonality was that her brother, a navy pilot, had lost his life in World War II flying a Corsair fighter. I was at the time in an organization whose pilots had flown the Corsair in World War II, and who were still flying it. This lady worked in Minneapolis and I made a round trip from Wisconsin to date her again before ending my leave. She was destined to influence me a year later in what turned out to be a major military career decision.

While still at home on this particular military leave, I once again teamed up with Ernie Ziegler. Ernie, now in the Air Force, was also home on leave. One evening we made a fifty-mile liberty run to Wisconsin Dells. This was at the time, and still is, a well-known summer vacation spot in South Central Wisconsin with an emphasis on water attractions (something of a wet Disneyland). In 1950, young working women from Chicago found it to be a favorite vacation spot. Ernie and I met and dated two ladies. My date and I made arrangements for me to visit her in Chicago on my way back to Camp Lejeune. It so happened that the "chance" day I passed through Chicago coincided with a wedding in her family. I was treated warmly by the assembled guests. The party was well underway and was at this point a boisterous and lively affair—unlike any wedding I had previously attended. But what did I know about receptions following an Italian wedding? We eventually broke from the wedding festivities for our date.

I do not recall at any time while on leave hearing on the radio, or of talking with anyone about our country's then unfolding involvement in the Korean conflict. Nor do I recall the involvement catching my ear on the long drive back to North Carolina—but surely it must have. Had I heard about the conflict, the likely feeling on my part would have been that the Army and Air Force stationed in Japan could surely take care of the North Koreans. Then too, if the Marines were to be involved, it would logically be the 1st Marine Division on the West Coast at Camp Pendleton, California. The 2nd Division at Camp Lejeune in North Carolina was after all oriented to the Mediterranean area.

I returned around the middle of July to find a transformed Camp Lejeune. The 2nd Marine Division at Lejeune had been hit hard to augment the 1st Provisional Marine Brigade leaving for Korea from Camp Pendleton on the West Coast. The Marine Corps may have had a Marine Division by title on each coast, but both were severely under strength.*

At the time I enlisted, the Marine recruiting posters proclaimed that only "100,000 could serve." When the Korean War broke out, the Marine Corps numbered approximately 74,000 officers and men. These 74,000 were spread out over two Divisions, two Air Wings, as Marine detachments on Navy capital ships, as security forces at various locations around the world, and in training establishments. Drastic cutbacks were made in the military in the years after World War II. Few expected a war where ground forces, and particular amphibious forces, would again be involved in large numbers. For that matter, few expected a war less then five years after the end of World War II in August of 1945.

---

*It says something about the state of the nation's military strength at the time that there were not enough Marines in the division at Camp Pendleton's three regiments to fully flesh out a brigade composed of one full strength reinforced regiment plus a small brigade headquarters staff.

Although the draw down of Camp Lejeune personnel had stabilized, major decisions were still being made at a higher level. In addition to the brigade of approximately 6500 men (ground and air components), the decision was made to increase the force in Korea to a Marine division. This meant two more regiments plus all the combat support elements, e.g. tanks, artillery, engineers, etc. The need now was for approximately 27,000 men.* In addition, a Marine Air Wing of approximately 15,000 men to support the Division had to be fleshed out. That required calling up the Reserves, and drawing down on all available active duty Marines. Now our ANGLICO was called upon to provide most of its men to help flesh out the division. I returned to Camp Lejeune from leave right in the middle of all this.

My four-year enlistment was up in January of 1951. Although I did not mention this to anyone, my choices, had their been no Korean War, was first of all to stay in the Marine Corps—and I indeed loved the Marine Corps. With a chance to be transferred into aviation it would have been an easy decision. On the other hand, I did "flirt" from time-to-time with the idea of getting out and using my GI bill benefits. If that were the decision, I considered becoming a pediatrician, or more likely, a Catholic priest. I certainly was very Catholic and I suspect I wanted to fulfill my mother's dream for one of her sons to be a priest. At this point none of her four sons had made this commitment. But forget all that; there was no more leaving the Marines at the end of my enlistment, not until the emergency was over at the earliest. I am all but certain that even if there had been no Korean War, I would still have re-enlisted in January of 1951.

To say the least, we were excited and pleased that now we too would have a chance to test our mettle in combat. No more living the thrill of combat vicariously through those old war time combat films we saw over and over.

---

*For those interested in a breakdown of a Marine Division see Appendix D.

Then for me a keen disappointment arose. I was removed from the list of those destined for Korea. The reason—instructors were needed to train the influx of Marine Reservist in a field where I had considerable experience, and had demonstrated my ability to impart that knowledge to others. Perhaps a logical decision on the part of my seniors—but I wanted to go to Korea. Imagine what it was like to have been in the military for over three years and now to miss out on a chance to apply my training in a combat situation. I served with and looked up to the officers and senior non-commissioned officers who had served in World War II. How I longed to have the chance to show them that I too could carry the ball. Then too, most all my comrades were leaving on this great adventure.

Had I bothered to look at the other side of the coin I might have taken note of factors that all but screamed, **"Take this training job they are offering you and hug it tightly."** Here I was at age twenty-two, single with this still brand new Pontiac to tool around in. I knew my way to New York City and Ole Larsen, (who was not going to Korea) and I were still dating our Southern nurses. Then too there was this developing relationship with the college student in Greensboro, N.C. and the lady I had met at Fort Lee. Among the many Reserve Marines reporting to Camp Lejeune were women Marines. I had met two of them; sisters from Philadelphia, through a get-acquainted event set up by the Catholic chaplain. Finally, there was this new found friend in Chicago. Although my transfer to the night fighter squadron would likely be delayed, I could reasonably expect the transfer to occur in a few months if I stayed at Camp Lejeune. After all, my mentor in this projected transfer, Captain Gourley, was also remaining at Camp Lejeune. Finally, the mark of a well-disciplined military man is to accept the decisions of your seniors in the military and go about your job. So what did this well disciplined Marine and high school graduate with a fairly decent IQ do? He re-enlisted for six years in order to be put back on the list for Korea.

Later I had reason to recall how I felt my first day at Parris Island, when I asked myself why in the world did I choose to put myself into this situation? I asked myself the same question when that first North Korean mortar round landed in our neighborhood outside of Seoul.

We had only a few days from the time I returned from leave and our departure for the West Coast. We were used to packing up and shipping out, so the time element for packing under these hurried conditions was no problem. From a personal point of view this was a major problem for the married men. Imagine the many details to take care of under the most trying of emotional times and on such short notice. First Sergeant McCormick, who was staying behind took care of storing my car for me. The Pontiac spent the next year moth-balled in a storage garage in Wilmington, N.C. On my last night at Camp Lejeune I called home to let the family know where I was headed. I spoke with my mother who said what most mothers say in one way or another under the circumstances, "Be careful."

CHAPTER 24

Movement to Korea

Once again we traveled cross-country to the West Coast by train along that familiar southern route. This was my fourth cross-country trip by troop train. We traveled in comfortable Pullman cars with a typical fancy diner.

At Camp Pendleton we were sent to one of the sub-camps known as Tent Camp Two (now San Onofre). Here we learned that our air team was to be part of the 1st Battalion, 7th Marine Regiment. Our air team consisted of one officer (aviator) and ten men. I was a Sergeant (E-4) and senior enlisted man with the title of "Team Chief." We had been together as a team for over a year training to provide the communication means that permitted control of air strikes in support of front line rifle companies. As noted earlier, we operated radios both for ground-to-ground communications to request aircraft, but more important, from air-to-ground for controlling aircraft while making their firing runs.

The great majority of the men in our battalion were Marine Reservist who came hurriedly and unexpectedly from their civilian pursuits. We were pleased to learn that the Commanding Officer was an active duty officer, Lieutenant Colonel Raymond Davis. He was a much decorated

Tactical Air Control Party (TACP) for 1st Bn. 7th Marines. Picture taken in August 1950 prior to leaving Camp Pendleton for Korea. Back row left to right: Corporal Thomas, Pfc. Romp, Pfc Pozega, Corporal Wright, Sergeant Hedrick, Pfc. Burns, First Lieutenant Holland. Front row from left: Pfc. Rice, Corporal Tinelli, Pfc Tebo. (Not shown Corporal Wilkerson.)

veteran of Pacific battles in World War II, to include the Navy Cross for actions at Peleliu. He was destined to earn the nation's highest decoration, the Congressional Medal of Honor, for his exploits leading us in the rescue of a surrounded unit in North Korea.

Training went on night and day as we regulars and the reservist trained to work as a team. Remembered during this period were the punishing night marches. Once we were out of the boondocks and on our way back to the billeting area, we invariably began singing. What we really sang with gusto was the popular song of the time *Goodnight Irene.** The flip side of *Good Night Irene* was another seventy-eight RPM record

---

*Last Saturday night I got married
Me and my wife settled down
Now me and wife are parted
Going to take another trip down town.

Chorus:
Irene good night, Irene good night
Good night Irene, good night Irene
I'll see you in my dreams

hit song entitled *Harbor Lights*. This one did not lend itself to our type of singing. *You are my Sunshine* certainly did, and we sang this one with gusto as well. Although the last song brought back tender memories of home and my grandmother, I was where I wanted to be. We usually finished up with a rousing chorus or two of the *Marine Corps Hymn*. I'm sure the officers had to smile as they listened to this audible testimonial to high morale. This was true even though there was no chance to go on liberty while we were at Camp Pendleton.

We boarded ship in San Diego in late August 1950. The troopship was my old friend the USS Okanagan. She was the first Naval ship on which I had sailed in the spring of 1948. On this trip the ship carried close to the full 1500 troops she was designed to carry. This was the entire 1st Battalion, 7th Marines reinforced, i.e. artillery, engineers, shore party, etc.

We sailed under combat conditions since we could not be sure, at this early point in the war, of Russia's involvement and thus the threat from her submarines. That meant a darkened ship at night with no access to the open decks for the troops. We spent eighteen days at sea. Fortunately we had this much time since many of the Marine Reservist were in need of additional weapons training. Training with rifles, machine guns, rocket launchers, mortars and dummy grenades took place off the fantail (back) of the ship. Targets were every piece of trash the Navy could give us to toss overboard.

We stopped briefly in Kobe, Japan. We unloaded and stored our sea bags here. We carried only our field uniforms to Korea and a minimum of personal articles. At this time we were cautioned to take with us only what we absolutely needed for field duty. For a moment I wondered about my old but dependable Argus C-3 camera. But for only a moment. In reading World War II history I remembered what I had read of the German soldiers when they victoriously entered Paris in July 1940. Their officers were amazed at how many of them had been carrying personal cameras in their packs. I decided if the German soldier could—so could I. I took a great many pictures when the situation permitted. In order to remember when and where I took pictures I began keeping something akin to a journal. Before long I was jotting down notes of occurrences unrelated to picture taking. These old notes have served me well over the years.

There was time for one night of liberty in the city of Kobe, Japan. A fleet of rickshaws waited for us at the head of the pier. Smallish but powerful Japanese men whisked us to and from downtown in these one-or-two man passenger vehicles. Liberty was up at midnight and as usual the "liberty hounds" played it as close as they could. There was a Japanese manned checkpoint at the head of the pier to keep the rickshaws from getting in the way of traffic around the ships. What the Japanese guards were not prepared for was that many of these last to arrive rickshaws were powered by Marines or Sailors with the Japanese operator a probable reluctant and worried passenger. These Marines and Sailors blissfully ignored the checkpoint and rolled up whooping and hollering at the gangplank. No one seemed to mind, and no one as far as I know was ever subjected to disciplinary action. If anything, the scene brought a smile to all our faces. No doubt the rickshaw drivers experienced the ride of their life and were well paid as well. In all likelihood they marveled at having survived this "kamikaze" experience with these crazy Americans.

The next morning when we came out on deck the ship was headed for Korea.

Author's Travels in Conjunction with Korean War

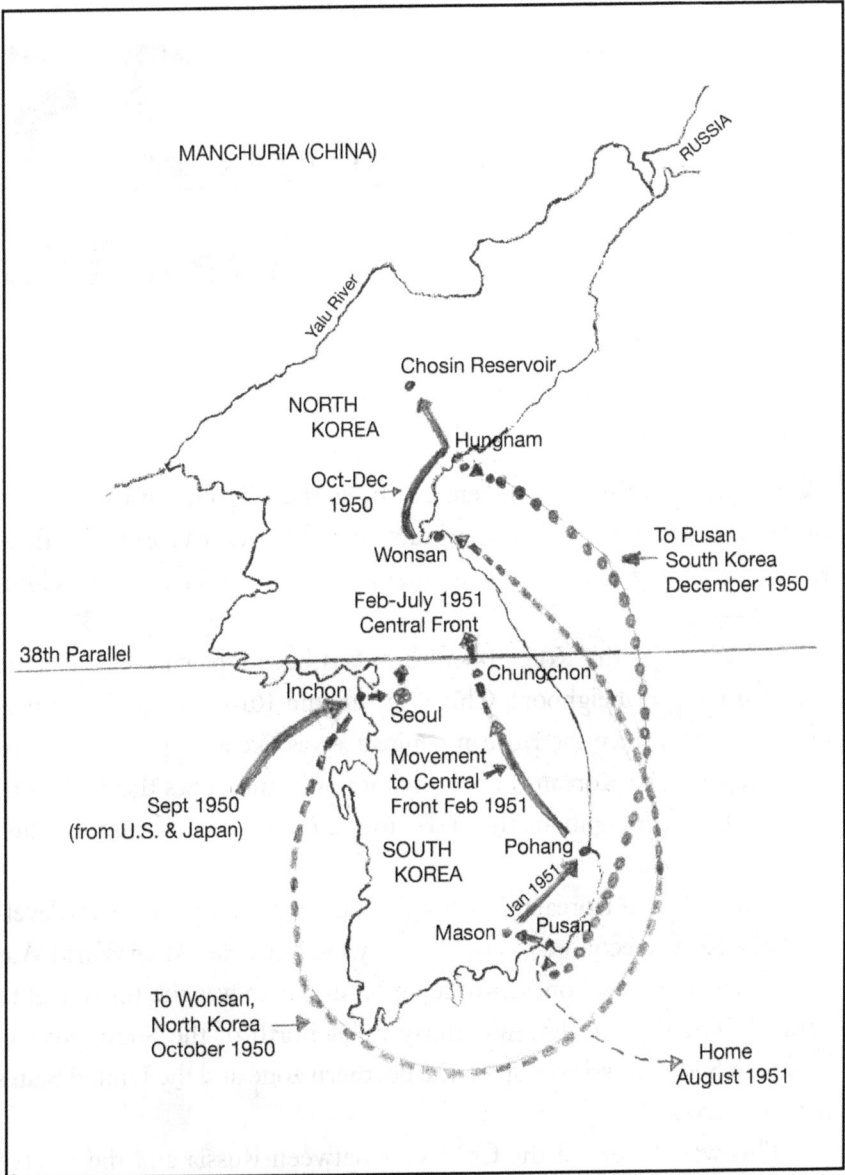

MANCHURIA (CHINA)

RUSSIA

Yalu River

Chosin Reservoir

NORTH
KOREA

Hungnam

Oct-Dec
1950

Wonsan

To Pusan
South Korea
December 1950

Feb-July 1951
Central Front

38th Parallel

Inchon

Chungchon

Seoul

Movement
to Central
Front Feb 1951

Sept 1950
(from U.S. & Japan)

SOUTH
KOREA

Pohang

Jan 1951

Mason

Pusan

To Wonsan,
North Korea
October 1950

Home
August 1951

CHAPTER 25

Korean War

Background

The Korean War is often referred to as the forgotten war. As noted earlier, it broke out less than five years after the end of World War II. In Korea we were challenged for the first time by the military of the Communist World.

For centuries the Korean peninsula has been a pawn in the dispute between its giant neighbors; China, Japan, and Russia. Japan had a particular concern since the Korean peninsula was like a dagger pointed towards Japan. The Koreans have a saying that summarizes their relationships with these neighbors; they refer to themselves as "a shrimp crushed in a battle of whales."

Japan annexed Korea in 1910, and for the next thirty-five years developed the Korean economy to benefit only the Japanese. After World War II, the separation for zones of occupation in Korea was the thirty-eighth parallel. The dividing line was thirty miles north of the South Korean capital of Seoul. Russia occupied the northern zone and the United States the southern zone

This was the era of the Cold War between Russia and the United

States. More accurately, this involved the Communist bloc of nations against the world's democracies. Under Russia's protective shield, and with their help, the North Koreans developed an efficient Army that struck without warning on 25 June 1950. On 27 June, President Truman ordered United States air and naval forces to help defend South Korea. On 30 June, he ordered United States ground troops to the aid of the South Koreans. The situation remained touch and go through the middle of September 1950 as to whether we could hold on. The United States and South Korean forces were pushed into a pocket in the southeastern tip of Korea called the Pusan Perimeter (see map page 336). General MacArthur's brilliant strategic move to land behind the North Korean lines at Inchon on 15 September 1950 turned the tide dramatically in our favor.

Nearly all the amphibious experts, including the Marines, advised General MacArthur to abandon his idea for a landing at Inchon. No ship-to-shore assault faced more hazardous difficulties. If the combination of tides, mud flats and narrow channels were not enough, now add the need to capture a fortified island flanking the landing site before the actual beach landing could take place. This proved to be a planner's nightmare, and a tough nut to crack for the 1st and 5th Marine Regiments who made the assault.

My involvement in the Korean War began with the landing at Inchon. Less than a month later we were back on a ship heading for North Korea and the Chosin Reservoir campaign.* This campaign generally covers the period from when we landed at Wonsan in mid-October 1950 through the evacuation from Hungnam in mid-December 1950. In Marine Corps annals this campaign ranks along with those of Guadacanal and Iwo Jima in terms of casualties and difficulties.

The Chosin Reservoir campaign was unique in that it was fought in the bitter cold of a Siberian winter on a high mountain plateau. What

---

*The historic name, and one preferred by Korea was "Changjin Reservoir." The Japanese named it Chosin, and since we used Japanese maps this was the place name used.

made it even more unique was that our Marine division was spread out along twenty-five miles of a primitive mountain dirt road with our flanks wide open to attack. Seventy-eight miles separated the two Marine regiments at Yudam-ni from the seaport and supply base at Hungnam. When the Chinese struck in force on 27 November 1950, they isolated and surrounded our forces located in six outposts, five of which were located on the plateau itself.* All were separated by five to ten miles from each other. Of the five outposts, only one was close enough to another to benefit from the latter's artillery. Each had to fight for its life since the distance between outposts, with the one exception noted, precluded their being able to support each other. The outpost east of the reservoir was overrun and lost. The other four had to survive, for the loss of one or the other could spell disaster for the rest of our forces in the area.

Approximately 20,000 Allied ground troops were involved at the Chosin Reservoir. Of these, 17,000 were Marines, 3000 Army (which figure included 700 South Koreans) and a force of approximately 250 British Royal Marine Commandos.

Mention should be made of our adversary and how he was organized and employed during the Chosin Reservoir campaign. The Chinese deployed their Fourth Field Army against our forces in and around the Chosin Reservoir. Each field Army contained four armies, each army having three divisions for a total of twelve divisions. A Chinese division normally numbered 10,000 men. But most of the artillery battalions of the divisions were not fully deployed with the division, leaving the best estimate strength of a given Chinese division at 9000 men. The artillery was left behind for sound tactical reasons. The Chinese moved through mountainous terrain during hours of darkness, making movement of artillery difficult. The lack of motor transport and danger of our air strikes were also factors in this decision. As a result, many of the artillery person-

*The 1st Bn, 1st Marine Regiment was located at Chinhung-ni. This was at the foot of the pass leading to the high mountain plateau where the remainder of the division was located.

nel were available to be employed as infantry or as cargo carriers. The total strength of the Chinese force in the Chosin Reservoir campaign was approximately 110,000 men.*

Appendix C lists five books for those interested in reading more on the Korean War. The first one listed, *Korea, The Untold Story of the War* by Joseph Goulden provides both a historical basis of the war and an account of the entire war. The next four deal exclusively with the Chosin Reservoir campaign.

Since military terminology and units appear often in this chapter the reader might benefit from this breakdown of units and unit strength.**

1. When you see "1st, 5th, or 7th Marines" keep in mind the term "Marines" used in this context refers to a regiment. The aforementioned are infantry regiments and when at full strength, numbered approximately 3500 men. The only other regiment in the 1st Marine Division was the 11th Marines. This was an artillery regiment with its individual battalions usually in direct support of an infantry regiment.

2. Battalions (1st, 2nd, and 3rd). Each infantry regiment has three battalions: each battalion numbered approximately 1000 men. My battalion was the 1st Battalion, 7th Marines.

3. Infantry rifle companies. Each battalion has three rifle companies plus a weapons company. A company numbered approximately 200 men.

4. Infantry platoons. Each company has three platoons, plus a 60mm mortar platoon. Each platoon numbered approximately forty-four men. To carry this trilogy on further, three squads (thirteen men) are in each infantry platoon and three fire teams (four men) are in each squad.

---

*At one of our Chosin Reservoir Veteran reunions we were officially welcomed by the Commanding General of a neaby military base. "You were surrounded by one-million Chinese," he said. The man next to me leaned over and said, "It gets better all the time, doesn't it?"

**For a block diagram breakdown of a Marine Division see Appendix D.

334 <small>ONE OUT OF LINE</small>

5. Sprinkled throughout the approximately 25,000 men in a reinforced Marine division were 1145 Naval personnel.* Twenty to twenty five were chaplains, the rest doctors and corpsmen. At the Infantry Company level eight Navy corpsman responded to the call of "corpsman" as casualties occurred.
6. A separate Marine organization in Korea was the 1st Marine Air Wing. It numbered approximately 15,000 men.

Inchon/Seoul

The 7th Marines landed at Inchon as the division's reserve regiment. We heard gunfire ashore and were concerned that the war might be over before we could get in the midst of it. Our first job after making a routine landing was to sort out equipment. In order to get underway quickly from San Diego the ship was not loaded tactically. Bulk loading, as was done in San Diego, permitted the ship to carry more cargo. Not to worry, the plan was to off-load all cargo in Kobe, Japan and reload tactically. Tactical loading permitted unloading pre-planned serial by pre-planned serial, like we did on the beach at Vieques during spring maneuvers. But there was a hurry-up need for troops in Korea so we ended up on the beach at Inchon identifying our equipment as it came ashore in bulk form.

Over the next year we spent all but sixteen nights sleeping in the open or in tents. The sixteen nights aboard ships were spent in conjunction with operations in North Korea. Over this same period we ate mostly pre-packaged C-rations, although at times the battalion mess was setup to serve hot meals concocted from what was termed A-rations. I preferred the C-rations.

Initially we took up a blocking position to the north of Seoul to protect the division's left flank. The next few days were relatively quiet for us. A few incoming mortar rounds resulted in our becoming experts at dig-

---

*The Secretary of the Navy is a "political" appointee made by the President. In 1950 the incumbent to that top Navy post, while visiting Korea, expressed surprise when he learned of the Marine's dependence on Naval medical and chaplaincy personnel.

ging deep foxholes. We had only limited contact with the people. From time to time we were assigned to search their oxen powered two-wheeled farm carts looking for weapons. I remember the people we did have contact with as being curious and friendly.

Next we crossed the Han River north of Seoul to take up the attack. As the North Koreans moved north out of Seoul our regiment (7th Marines) received its baptism by fire. Our eleven-man air team was quickly introduced to the realities of combat as well. Corporal Bob Wright was shot through his forearm and Private First Class Ken Burns took a round through his side. Both were evacuated to a hospital ship off-shore. For the next five days we fought pitched battles that made us realize combat is anything but glamorous. Lieutenant Dan Holland, our air officer had many occasions to run air strikes. On one occasion he had me run an air strike. The target was a hill mass about one-quarter mile to our front where enemy troops had been spotted. South of the small village of Uijongbu, and a few miles south of the thirty-eighth parallel, the Army's Seventh Cavalry Division relieved us. We Marines were thoroughly impressed by this division's rolling stock of trucks. For good reason the Army was so equipped. Their role was the long and fast pursuit when conditions permitted. This meant moving troops quickly, and more importantly, keeping units supplied. The Marines expected to operate near a beachhead, relatively close to supply dumps located a short distance from the beach, backed up by supply ships close offshore.

In the three weeks our division was in action in the Inchon-Seoul area we suffered 2430 casualties. Of this number 414 were killed in action or died from their injuries.

The rumor was that the war was over for the Marines. The Reserves were going back to their families, jobs, and schools. We Regulars were headed for continental U.S. duty stations. Well, if it had to be, I could certainly handle being sent back to Camp Lejeune. But it turned out to be only a rumor. Whatever disappointment, if any, we as individuals were exhilarated to learn that our battalion was slated to be in the assault waves

North Korean Advances
and Withdrawals June - Oct. 1950

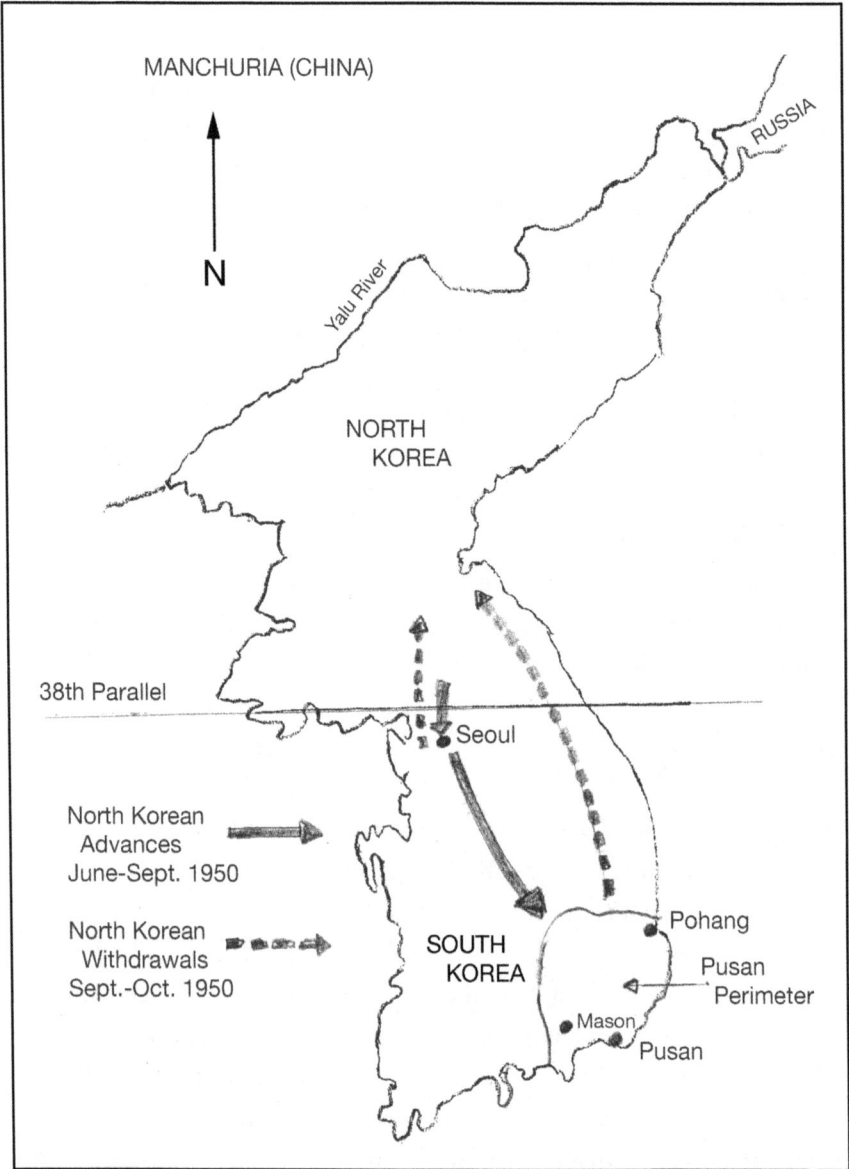

MANCHURIA (CHINA)

N

RUSSIA

Yalu River

NORTH
KOREA

38th Parallel

Seoul

North Korean
 Advances
June-Sept. 1950

North Korean
 Withdrawals
Sept.-Oct. 1950

SOUTH
KOREA

Pohang

Pusan
Perimeter

Mason

Pusan

on some still unknown (to us troops) North Korean beach. This was it for us. All those World War II amphibious landings were on our minds, and this was our chance to show those veterans of that war what we could do.

We were scheduled to land in amphibious tractors (AMTRACS)* which were carried on my favorite ship to sail on, a LST (landing ship tank). We gathered back at the Inchon beachhead to observe the loading operation until our time came to go aboard. A peculiarly unique feature of Inchon harbor was the tide, which rose and fell on the average of twenty-one feet in a twenty-four hour cycle. This is one of the greatest tidal variations in the world. At low tide, as the water moved back into the Yellow Sea over the relatively gentle gradient of the beach, it left two miles of slimy mud-covered sea floor jutting into the harbor. LSTs came in at high tide, and unless they could unload in less than two hours they sat high and dry on the mud until high tide again, about twelve hours later. The two hour turn around was usually possible if the LST was unloading since the vessel normally carried only vehicles positioned so they could be run off quickly. If she were loading men and equipment off the beach, much more time was required since the tank deck loading required tracked and heavy vehicles to be backed in from the beach. At one point we were watching one of the LSTs being loaded as it sat high and dry on the mud with not a drop of seawater visible. Its big clamshell doors were open and the ramp was down on the beach. AMTRACS were being backed aboard. All of a sudden we noted a rearward movement, very slow at first, then at a faster speed. The vessel was slipping backward over the slippery mud. In the process it backed over its stern anchor that was dropped as the vessel came onto the beach as an assist when it backed off. The LST finally stopped a quarter-mile from its former position and waited for high tide

---

*The LVT-3 AMTRAC was at that time the final generation of armored amphibious troop-carrying landing vehicles developed during World War II. These vehicles propel themselves in water by using their tank treads. Troop capacity was twenty, or a jeep and trailer with a couple of men. In addition to end and side armor it had an overhead armored cover. Although there was an escape hatch in the overhead cover the AMTRAC was often morbidly referred to as an "iron coffin" by the troops.

before coming back in to finish loading.

About this time Lieutenant Bob Wilson joined us as a second forward air controller, as pilots serving with ground troops were called.

The Trip to North Korea

We sailed from Inchon on 11 October 1950 and were due to make the assault landing on 20 October. Our LST was one of many older vessels our Navy had turned over to the Japanese self-defense force and was manned by a Japanese crew. This was a bit disconcerting. The crew no doubt were men who had served in the Japanese Navy, our mortal enemy only five years ago. The U.S. had contracted for their service for the landing scheduled to take place at Wonsan on the East Coast of North Korea. As far as I know, not one of the Japanese, including the Captain could speak English on the LST we sailed on. The ship's galley was stocked with only enough American food to last us the nine days it took to sail around the Korean peninsula. Nestled on the tank deck were the amphibious tractors we were to make the assault landing in. The main deck was loaded with assorted trucks, jeeps and artillery pieces. These vehicles would be off-loaded when the LST itself beached later during the landing.

Our LST lumbered on, pitching and rolling as only a flat bottom vessel can do. We headed south, down the Yellow Sea, then around the southern tip of South Korea, then north up the Sea of Japan. LSTs and others like her sail in what is termed the slow group. We sailed in a convoy under combat conditions with the usual anti-submarine zigzagging and blackout at night. Warships escorted us. Conditions were as usual for an LST, relatively comfortable. We carried a rifle company (approximately 200 men) plus those of us whose mission it was to support this company in the landing. If we felt crowded in the troop compartment, any number of trucks and jeeps were available on the main deck to lounge in.

We had only a Protestant Chaplain aboard who conducted daily ecumenical services. He was brand new to the ministry and to the military.

1st Marine Division Area of Operations
October - December 1950
(Scale: 1" = 20 miles)

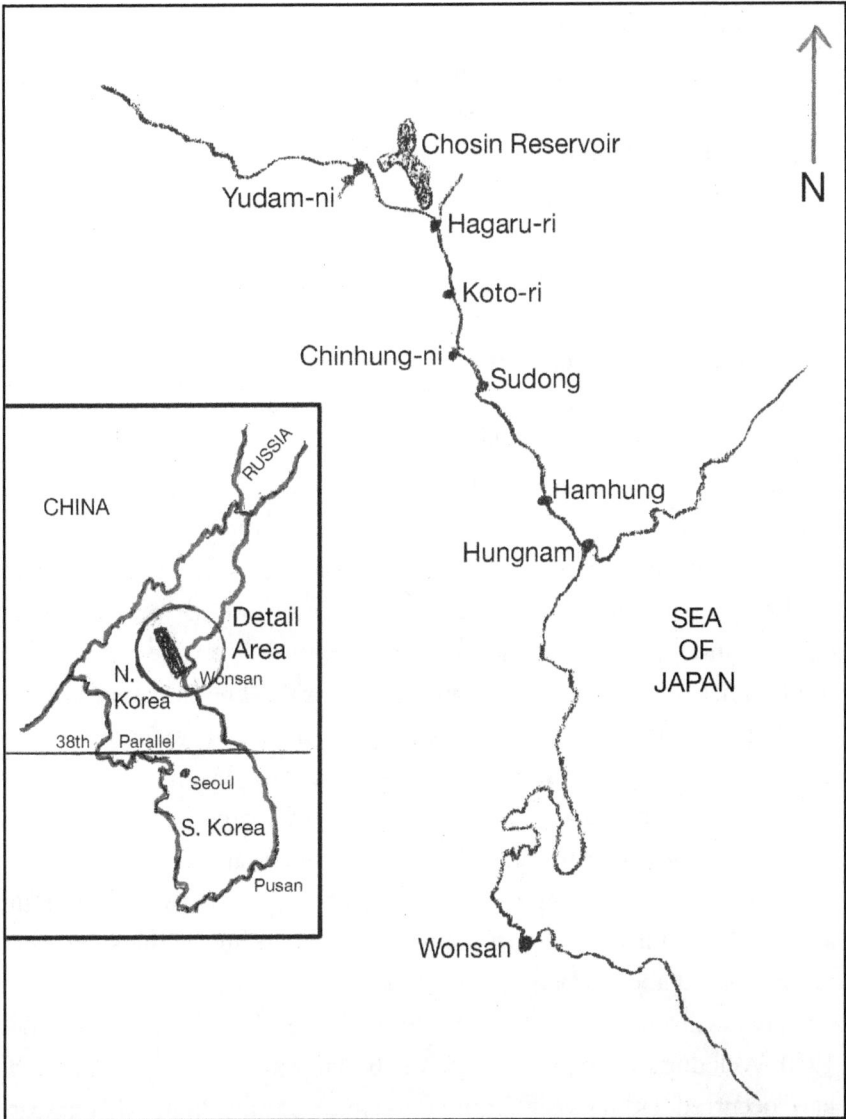

He had joined us from stateside a few days before we sailed from Inchon. One evening after services we were chatting when a group of men, completely independent of our group, began singing. I am reasonably certain they had no idea a Chaplain was within earshot. One of the songs sung went like this:

> I am Jesus' little lamb
> Yes by Jesus Christ I am
> I don't care if it rains or freezes
> I'll be safe in the arms of Jesus
> Etc., etc.

The Chaplain was visibly shocked and expressed wonderment that men about to go into combat could be so flippant with the Lord, who after all controlled their destiny.

As it turned out there was no combat amphibious landing. After being defeated in South Korea the North Korean retreat turned into a rout. While we were aboard ship, South Korean troops swept virtually unopposed into Wonsan and beyond. Even if Wonsan had remained to be assaulted, the landing could not have been made on the date scheduled.

After logically noting land on our left for several days after rounding the Korean peninsula we were surprised one morning when we came out on deck and noticed land on our right. Obviously we were now headed south. That evening we turned and sailed north. The next morning we were again heading south. I am not sure at what point we learned at the troop level that a large and well-laid minefield off Wonsan's beach was the reason for the delay. For six days we participated in what came to be called "Operation Yo-Yo." The only problem, apart from boredom, was food. We soon ran out of the galley prepared rations we had brought aboard. The simple answer to the problem was to invade the supplies of rations loaded aboard many of the trucks.

We finally landed at Wonsan via our AMTRACS on 26 October 1950. Well dug in gun positions on the beach reminded us of what might have occurred had we been required to land tactically. Somewhat embarrassing for us ground troops was having members of the Marine Air Wing watching us land. They had flown in to set up an airfield. Even more embarrassing was learning that Bob Hope and his troop had put on a show at Wonsan on 24 October while we were at sea participating in Operation Yo-Yo. Not only did we miss the legendary Bob Hope, but also Marilyn Maxwell and Les Brown's band. Although I do not recall seeing it, I heard there was a sign somewhere in the area saying, "Bob Hope welcomes the U.S. Marines."

About this time another rumor made the rounds. Two (of three) Marine regiments were moving back to the states with the third regiment to be stationed in Japan. This to occur as soon as the Army's Third Division relieved us. The rumor was believable, given the wild flight of North Korea's Army at this point in time. This rumor too proved to be false.

I suspect the days aboard ship had sapped our physical strength. I remember the miles of hiking with a field transport pack from the beach to a railhead station as one of the most fatiguing marches I made while in the military. We then moved by rail to Hamhung, then by truck to a position near Sudong occupied by a South Korean Army regiment we were to relieve. They were in contact with what they claimed were Chinese forces. The date was 1 November 1950.

Chosin Reservoir—The Campaign North

The actions of this Korean regiment made it quite clear they were anxious to leave the area. They pointed up to the hills and said, "Many Chinese up there." At the troop level we thought this was the nervous ranting of unsophisticated South Korean soldiers. Later we learned our officers had information that tended to support the South Korean claims.

At one point in mid-afternoon, a small team of Marines under Lieutenant Gene Hovatter, the executive officer of Able Company, accompanied a South Korean officer to the top of a hill to our right as we faced generally west. I and three members of the air team were assigned to accompany this small group. We carried the four-channel air-to-ground radio, that along with its wet cell battery, weighed in at eighty-five pounds. I don't recall thinking it at all unusual that I might be asked to call in an air strike. I ran an air strike on my own on this occasion, and again while leading an air team in a company-sized patrol on 24 November 1950, the day after Thanksgiving. Both were relatively simple to conduct and were run under non-threatening conditions. But a patrol on 27 November 1950 turned out to be neither routine nor non-threatening.

I didn't realize at the time that only pilots were authorized to run air strikes. My confidence in being able to run a strike was based on having observed air strikes being run in our training exercises for over a year, as well as those run by Lieutenant Holland against the North Koreans outside of Seoul. Lieutenant Holland was also aware of Captain Gourley's efforts to have me transferred to aviation. This policy of having only pilots control air strikes was not changed in the Marine Corps until after the Iraq war in 2003. Now a certain number of non-aviators are trained to run air strikes; no doubt with the proviso that this is done only in an emergency, and only when a pilot is not available. Lieutenant Holland was fifty-five years ahead of his time.

I don't recall Lieutenant Holland issuing any special instructions, nor was there a need to as far as I was concerned. I have to think, and will be forever thrilled that he had confidence in me. I suspect his thinking was that if I were to call in an air strike it would in all likelihood be a routine mission. Since the South Korean regiment was no longer deployed, and we Marines were not yet fully tactically deployed, no friendly troops were in position to be endangered

When we reached the top of hill the Korean officer pointed to a knob on the next hill mass, about a quarter-mile from where we lay on our stomachs. "Many Chinese observed there this morning," he said. Lt. Hovatter turned to me and asked that if any aircraft were available to run an air strike on that knob.

At this point we had all but abandoned the formalized method to request aircraft. This would have involved our first radioing an activity called a Direct Air Support Center (DASC) to request aircraft and indicate type of target, armament preferred, etc., etc. For this purpose we used a ground-to-ground high frequency radio. One set was jeep mounted; the other was portable and required three men to transport it. In the meantime higher headquarters, i.e. regiment and division, monitored this radio net at a center where artillery and mortars fire missions were also monitored. Logically this activity was called the "Fire Support Center (FSC)." This to ensure no conflicting missions with resultant dangers, especially to pilots, were run simultaneously. But the procedures were changing. In situations where air support might be needed, aircraft were kept on station and on call to be literally "plucked" from the sky.

On this, and the other two occasions where I ran air strikes, all I had to do was go to one of the four channels and say, "Any aircraft this net, this is Roughneck 14—over." If there was no answer I went to the next channel with the same request. On this particular occasion a flight of two aircraft responded on one of the channels, and an altogether routine air strike involving five-inch rockets and strafing was run on the target.

I am quite certain, that as a result of running this air strike, I was the first to run an air strike as a member of a Marine Tactical Air Control Party (TACP) against Communist Chinese Forces in the Korean War. Our 1st Battalion was in the vanguard of the division and our own regiment at the time. The other two battalions in our regiment were following us and were moving administratively, i.e. not deployed for combat. On this date the division's other two infantry regiments, the 1st and 5th Marines, were involved with North Korean guerrillas thirty miles to our rear.

November 1st was All Saint's Day. That evening at near dusk, Father Griffin said Mass. In his short homily I thought he sounded unusually serious and disheartened. To add to this rather gloomy atmosphere was his granting "general absolution" for all our sins. This meant no need for a formal Confession before receiving Holy Communion. That assumes one had on his spiritual record sins serious enough to preclude receiving Holy Communion. The combination of Confession and Holy Communion put you on the freeway to heaven. We troops were not aware of it at the time, but apparently the officers were convinced of danger on the road ahead.

Speaking of the road ahead: at this point we were thirty-seven miles from the seaport and supply base at Hungnam (see map page 346). The road was two lanes and was in reasonably good condition as it passed through relatively flat terrain. A narrow gauge railroad also ran parallel to the highway. A few miles north of our location both the two-lane road and the railroad ended at the base of a mountain. From here on the road narrowed to a one-lane dirt road, perhaps better termed an ox-path. This one-lane road climbed a 2500-foot pass over eight miles of zigzagging road that clung to the side of the mountain. The official history further described the road as "with a cliff on one side and a chasm on the other." This narrow and primitive road was to be our lifeline for supplies. Our engineers were kept busy in the days ahead improving the road to permit heavy vehicles and tanks to move forward.

The next day, 2 November 1950, our battalion relieved the Korean regiment by moving into position in the hills on either side of the road. The two pilots and all but four of the men in our team moved forward in vehicles. The rest of the team and I moved by foot. As daylight faded the four of us were making our way along the road with no other troops in sight. Mortar rounds started coming in. We quickly scurried off the road and up into a small gully. Rounds followed us as we worked our way up the gully. Our small group was obviously in the enemy's sights. The large rocks provided protection from the bursts, except for Corporal Tinelli who was hit and lightly wounded by a mortar fragment. He did not want the injury officially reported in order to spare his mother the telegram he knew would then be sent to her.

In the meantime, what to do? We were a small four-man group all by ourselves, and dusk was approaching. All we knew was that the rest of the battalion was down the road somewhere. I decided our best option was to spend the night in this now friendly gully and catch up with the rest of the unit in the morning. We were after all on the main road. Then a jeep tooled by. We merely watched it from our location a couple hundred feet off the road. I saw no need to flag it down. At the last moment the passenger's head turned slowly and casually to his right; then the jeep came to a sudden halt. The observant passenger was our Battalion Commander, Colonel Raymond Davis. He seemed surprised and shocked that we were out here by ourselves and told us to move down the road to the battalion command post. But for Colonel Davis' last second casual glance our small group might have had a rough time that night. Given what occurred it's doubtful we could have survived that night's action.

We settled into our newly dug foxholes that evening a mile south of Sudong. We expected it to be a cold but peaceful night and were on a fifty-percent alert status. The rifle companies were in the hills to our right and left. We were at the head of a narrow valley, probably less than the length of a football field in width. The road, to use the term loosely, ran through the middle of the valley. A few minutes prior to midnight on 2 November, bugles, shepherd horns, whistles, and grenades signaled the start of a wild and woolly night. Our rifle companies were soon heavily engaged. (We learned later that two regiments of the Chinese 124th Division hit us.)

Shortly after midnight we heard the clanking sound of a piece of heavy equipment. Most of us thought this was one of our bulldozers. But why is a bulldozer coming from the direction of the enemy lines? It turned out to be a tank with its searchlight on. The tank came rumbling into our command post. Now we all thought it had to be one of our tanks. A sergeant yelled, "Turn that god damn light off." The answer was a burst of machine gun fire from a Chinese T-34 tank.* The Chinese crew finally realized where they were. The tank passed through our area and went on to do mischief in an 81mm mortar unit to our rear. In a few minutes the tank rumbled back. Unfortunately armor piercing 3.5-inch rocket

---

*The T-34 tank was of Russian design and manufacture, and was Russia's mainstay tank in operations against the Germans in World War II.

Main Supply Route (MSR)
Hungnam to Yudam-ni (78 miles)

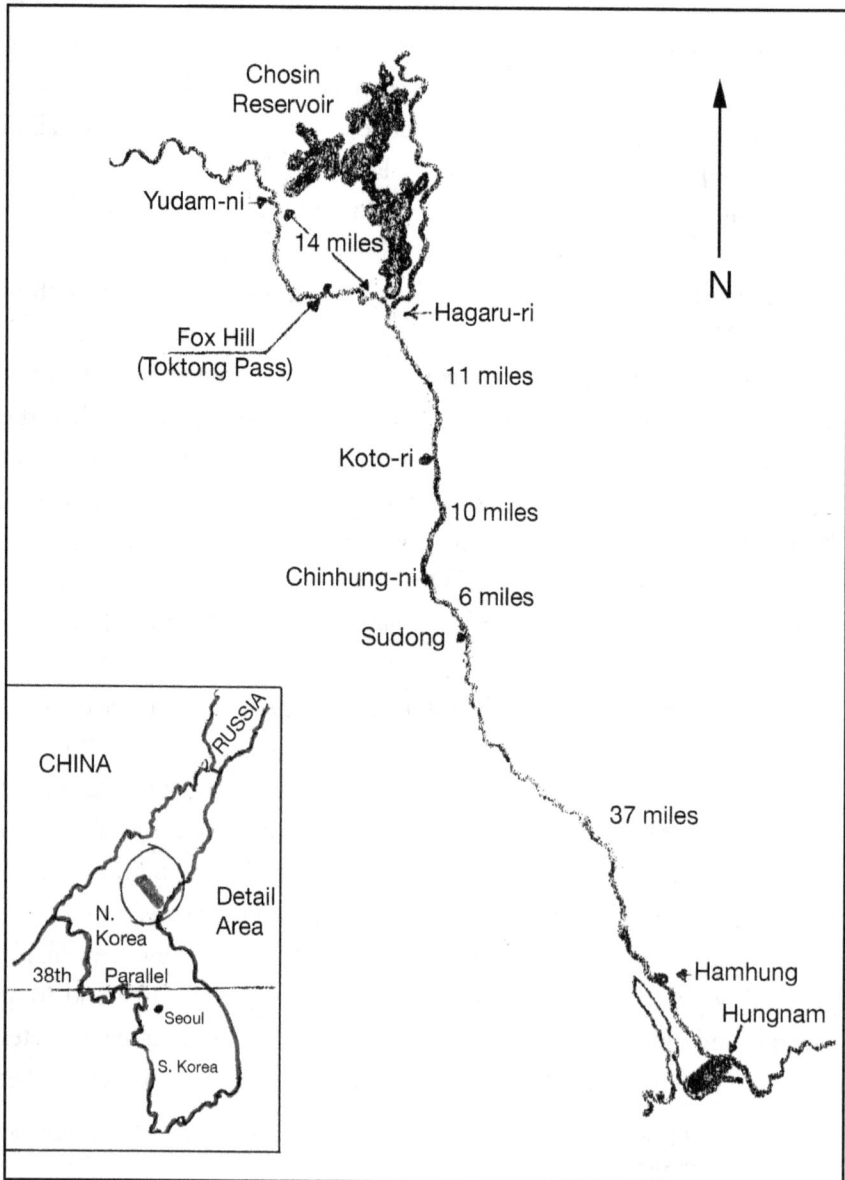

Chosin
Reservoir

Yudam-ni

14 miles

Fox Hill
(Toktong Pass)

Hagaru-ri

11 miles

Koto-ri

10 miles

Chinhung-ni

6 miles

Sudong

N

37 miles

CHINA

RUSSIA

Detail
Area

N.
Korea

38th   Parallel

Seoul

S. Korea

Hamhung

Hungnam

ammunition had not reached our area and the high explosive rounds did not stop the tank, which rumbled on back towards its own lines. From a tactical viewpoint, not a good idea to send a tank(s) into enemy territory without infantry support—especially at night. The usual culprit in mistakes like this is mis-communications. The Chinese were lucky on this occasion—but their tanks were not so lucky a day later. About an hour or two after the tank incident, Chinese infantry did attack through the valley but were repulsed. This might not have been so easily done had they accompanied their tank.

As a result of the night action we were cut off from the 2nd Battalion 7th Marines to our rear, and they from the 3rd Battalion 7th Marines following them. Early in the morning we were air dropped ammunition and medical supplies. At one point in the morning I helped carry ammunition up to Able Company on the hill to our right. While on the ridge a couple of small caliber mortar rounds drove us to ground. One round landed in our midst as we lay among large rocks. It exploded, but did no physical harm to any of us.

The remainder of that day was spent clearing up roadblocks the Chinese had set up during the night. When this was accomplished more supplies rolled in and we were able to evacuate the dead and wounded. The Chinese were at their best in night attacks when our air, artillery and other supporting arms fire were restricted. We soon learned that if you held through the night, daylight brought into play our heavy supporting arms that drove the Chinese back into the hills. As the morning wore on the surviving Chinese started to withdraw. In order for many of them in our sector to escape they had to cross a railroad embankment before reaching a ravine that provided protection. This embankment was approximately 100 yards from our location. Although two heavy machine guns did most of the work, many of us joined in on what we called a "turkey shoot" as these hapless Chinese ran the gauntlet. By nightfall on 3 November, the battle was essentially over with the two regiments of Chinese who had attacked us soundly defeated. Our 1st

Battalion counted 662 enemy dead; the 2nd Battalion did not conduct a physical count, but probably exacted a similar toll. The number of Chinese wounded could not be determined. Our casualties were 61 dead, 283 wounded and 1 missing. This was our regiment's first nighttime live fire defense action; there would be more to follow.

Our adversary impressed us. They were brave soldiers and well led. But they were seriously hampered by poor communications. Whistles and trumpets used by the Chinese created a definite psychological effect, but this was not an efficient way for them to communicate.

The next day, 4 November 1950, we moved north towards Sudong. Approximately one mile from where we experienced the night attack we came across four enemy tanks cleverly camouflaged. Before the tanks could fire a round, 3.5-inch rockets (we now had armor piercing ammunition) knocked out two tanks and two were knocked out by an air strike run by Lieutenant Holland. All of these tank kills occurred within a couple of minutes.

The tanks had entered South Korea via the relatively good roads in the Seoul corridor in June 1950. From there they moved south towards Pusan leading the North Korean thrust. When the North Koreans retreated, their tanks' route back through Seoul was blocked. This forced them to move over the central and eastern South Korean roads to where we encountered them. The road North, up the steep and narrow pass leading to the Taebek Plateau was impassable for tanks. Simply put; the tanks were trapped. The tank crewmen were either very brave, or very foolish since they had been abandoned by their foot soldiers, yet they stuck with their tanks.

All was quiet after this angry and noisy engagement. I broke out my camera and took pictures. One was of a Chinese crewman, halfway out the hatch of his tank with his body on fire. The color film was later sent off to a Kodak processing laboratory in Honolulu, Hawaii. Later a letter arrived from the laboratory saying some of the pictures were of such a graphic nature that they could not be sent through the U.S. mail. The

Father Griffin celebrating Mass for 1st Bn. 7th Marines one day after action at Sudong on 3 and 4 November 1950. (Photo credit George Dukat)

pictures would be held for thirty days during which time I could pick them up in Honolulu. Not a chance of that.

On 5 November 1950 the 2nd Battalion of our 7th Marines moved through our lines to take the lead. We remained at Chinhung-ni for at least five days. At this point a young sailor, Jay Skidmore, joined our air team. He was a Navy combat photographer who belonged to a unit* whose commanding officer was John Ford, the legendary movie director. Jay came along just in time to replenish my supply of film.

In the process of clearing the high ground around a power station on 5 and 6 November 1950, the 2nd Battalion, along with artillery support all but destroyed the remaining regiment of the Chinese 124th Division. At this point the Chinese pulled back and left only small groups behind to delay our advance. They generally offered only token resistance. Our objective was the Yalu River on the North Korea/Chinese border, approxi-

---

*Pacific Fleet Combat Camera Group.

mately 130 air miles to the north of the seaport at Hungnam. Once on the Yalu our Marine Division was to be allotted a forty-mile stretch as our area of responsibility. Despite all this action with the Chinese, both in our area and with the Army west of us, General MacArthur's headquarters in Tokyo saw the Chinese involvement as involving only a "few volunteers."

While we were in reserve at Chinhung-ni, the engineers improved the road up the mountain to where heavy trucks and tracked vehicles could make the ascent. This involved straightening and widening the eight miles of road leading up and over the Funchilin Pass. As noted, for some distance up the pass the road was on a one-way shelf with cliffs on one side dropping off at times 400 to 1000 feet to the bottom of a gorge. In addition to the steep drops, hairpin curves were so tight that sometimes trucks with trailers had to unhitch to make the turns.

We moved by truck the ten miles from Chinhung-ni to Koto-ri,* arriving there on 10 November 1950, the 175th birthday of the Marine Corps. That night we were introduced to Asia's old man winter. It had been cool ever since landing at Wonsan in late October, but I don't recall it being uncomfortably cold. On this particular night in mid-November we were far enough behind the lines that we were not required to dig foxholes. Perhaps we should have, but on this occasion we did not. We slept in our sleeping bags with our poncho either underneath the bag or used as a cover. I awoke first in our area and had to break through a blanket of snow. How eerie to look around and see this unbroken field of white, with man sized lumps here and there emitting little volcanic puffs of steam. And it was cold! The Siberian winds were blowing with the temperature minus sixteen degrees, plus whatever the wind chill factor was as measured today. For those men not familiar with snow or cold weather this had to be somewhat frightening. Later that day we marched the eleven miles to Hagaru-ri. I remember the hike was done under cold

---

*The Korean language suffix "ni" refers to a small village. The suffix "ri" applies to a larger village. The suffix "ri" also relates to what in our country we would call a county administrative unit.

but sunny conditions on a reasonably pleasant day. I remember too the Protestant Regimental Chaplain (John Craven) leading us in a series of Christian hymns as we marched along. Morale was high.

In mid-November 1950 we were issued our winter gear. It consisted of a mountain sleeping bag along with a heavy alpaca-lined knee-length hooded parka and wool cap. We were also issued winter weight cold weather trousers, a flannel shirt, long johns, heavy wool socks, an alpaca vest, wool gloves and leather and canvas mittens (some with an ingenious trigger finger sewn in). Most of us also kept our old reliable M-1943 field jackets. Finally, heavy shoe-paks, twice as heavy as the field shoes we were wearing, along with two pair of felt insoles completed our winter wardrobe. The shoe-paks were the cause of many cases of frostbite. When laced up no air circulated in these boots. Even limited exertion caused the feet to sweat. When we stopped moving the felt inserts and socks froze. During reasonably quiet times frequent change of socks and pads prevented frostbite injury. The pads and socks removed were tucked next to the body to dry. As the action quickened, and as it turned colder many could not find the time, or chose not to go through this ritual.*

The Chinese too suffered from the cold, no doubt to a far greater extent than we did. They wore a two piece reversible uniform of quilted cotton; white on one side, mustard-yellow on the other along with a cotton cap and fur lined earflaps. The Chinese we met at Sudong in early November wore a canvas shoe with crepe soles. Later arrivals wore a half-leather shoe and others a full-leather boot.

Something of a highlight of each day was the evening distribution of C-rations. They came in a cardboard box about the size of an adult shoebox. Each box contained six cylindrical cans, three heavies and three lights. The heavies contained the protein needs. At the top of my list was hamburger and gravy, followed by beans and franks, chicken and vegetables, and sausage patties. At the bottom of my list were corned beef

---

*Despite all that cold weather gear, there were times I yearned for the heavy horse blanket that kept me warm while in bed on cold winter nights in Wisconsin.

and hash, and ham and lima beans in that order. The "luck of the draw" determined what three were in your box. As a result there was heavy duty trading among us troops. If one of my heavies were ham and lima beans or corned beef and hash I might swap for one I liked, but I probably had to throw in the packet of eight cigarettes or some other delicacy in the daily rations to swing the deal. Since I did not smoke, and others needed more than eight cigarettes each day, I found it easy to trade up. The heavies tasted best when heated. At this point small cans of sterno were often available to heat the food. As an alternate, we mixed dirt with gasoline (not encouraged), or built a fire to heat a large can or pan of water. We then tossed in our food selection to warm it up. On occasion, if conditions and human compatibility were in sync, we made mulligan stew.

Then there were the three cans of lights. At least one can was fruit; my favorite was fruit cocktail. The other two were bread units, sort of a blend of cracker and heavier bread—a direct descendant of Civil War hardtack. They were tasty alone, but much enhanced when small packets of jam appeared in the rations. To round out the goodies there was chocolate candy in the form of a disc, salt, pepper, packets of soluble coffee and cocoa, and something resembling cake. Finally, there was a simple yet effective can opener and a packet containing a day's supply of toilet paper.

Our battalion once again took the lead from Hagru-ri to Yudam-ni, a distance of fourteen miles. The first day on the road was Thanksgiving Day, 23 November 1950. Baker Company fought a brisk action at a place called Toktong Pass. Our Lieutenant Bob Wilson ran a text book air strike in this action. Toktong Pass was destined to be a critical location as the saga of the Chosin Reservoir campaign developed. We set up camp that evening three miles south of Yudam-ni.

Our battalion celebrated Thanksgiving Day dinner the next day, 24 November, except for approximately 200 of us who went out on patrol. This was my second time to take an air team out on my own. This time we accompanied Charlie Company. We left shortly after daylight for what we knew was to be an all day patrol. We fully expected our hot turkey dinner would be waiting for us when we returned.

Our route took us into the hills west of the command post, then north along a ridge overlooking a valley leading into Yudam-ni. We were underway for less than an hour when we had a man killed by what was probably a small delaying force left behind by the Chinese. As a result of this minor action it was dusk before we reached the northern limit of our patrol. I was called on to run an air strike at this location. In the valley below several Chinese soldiers were seen by the lead element of the patrol running into an enclosure that appeared to be made from tree limbs and branches. The napalm bomb appeared to obliterate the enclosure, but the gathering darkness precluded a firm assessment. An interesting side light to the action was that Jay Skidmore, our Navy combat cameraman, was grinding away with his movie camera. Unfortunately much of Jay's footage from his time with us was lost in the ensuing breakout.

It was pitch dark by the time the command post came into view as we marched back over the spine of the hill mass. Other than the firefight at the start of the patrol it had been time consuming, but not all that tiring or dangerous. Our mouths watered as we thought of that hot turkey dinner waiting for us in the valley below. But alas, this was not to be. The battalion had forgotten all about one third of its fighting strength, a rifle company, being out on patrol. Not surprisingly, for those who were present when the meal was served at noon, there was left over food dished out as seconds.

We settled into our foxholes on what was an absolutely beautiful night. A bright moon along with the pure white snow turned night into day. I couldn't help but think of the many "white" Christmases I had experienced in Wisconsin. The command post was blacked out so that from any distance we must have appeared as part of the landscape. At one point during the night a mortar barrage lasting several minutes fell in a ravine next to us. The Chinese had the right idea, but either faulty map coordinates or their observer's inability to see us under blackout conditions saved us much grief.

The next day, 25 November 1950, we moved without opposition into

Yudam-ni. I recall climbing one of the hills along with Tony Tinelli and Jay Skidmore to view the Chosin Reservoir and take pictures. We acted much like tourists on this day. Remembered too was the extra bountiful mail call that day with many food packages from our families. I especially warmed to Tony Tinelli's package. This was my first taste of Italian sausage and pepperoni—and I thought it delicious. Someone else in the air team received several cans of Spam. It tasted like filet mignon when fried on a makeshift stove.

We did not know this at the time, but Yudam-ni was as far north as our division was destined to go. The next day, with the exception of our Able Company, we remained in a defensive position along with the 2nd (less Fox Company) and 3rd Battalion of our regiment. In the meantime, the 5th Marines moved through our lines to take up attack positions northwest of Yudam-ni. Our battalion's Able Company was sent out on patrol in the hills to the southwest of the command post. They returned that evening with several wounded. Two men were killed but their bodies could not be recovered. One of those killed was Lieutenant Frank Mitchell who was awarded the Congressional Medal of Honor for his actions during this patrol. There was no air team along with Able company on this patrol.

Baker Company went out the next day, 27 November to generally retrace the route taken by Able Company the day before (see map page 371). They were to recover the two bodies and determine if the enemy force that engaged Able Company was still in the area. I led an air team on this patrol. The thinking likely was that since this appeared to be one of those necessary, yet routine patrols, we can risk sending Hedrick out with the air team. Based on the previous encounters with the Chinese over the past weeks, the expectation probably was that those enemy soldiers Able Company engaged the day before had, in all likelihood, faded away.

The day was cloudy when we started out. We in the air team wondered if aircraft could be called in if needed. A further concern to us in the air team was the relatively short shelf life of the radio's wet cell battery. Although fully charged when we started out, the stored power dissipated in direct proportion to the outside temperature. This was the case even though the radio was off and thus consuming no power.

On this cold morning the combination of ice and a soft mantle of dry snow resulted in a "squeaking" sound as our boots slipped a bit as we moved over the ground. Nothing new for us northerners, but others had fun moving their feet to create this new sound. This was also the day we heard of General MacArthur's home for Christmas statement.* Between our elation at this news and having fun making all those squeaking sounds we were a pretty happy crew.

In addition to the eighty-five pound air-to-ground radio, our heavy winter clothing and a light pack further encumbered us. As noted, we were not fans of the boots, but we did appreciate the heavy parka. Around noon the clouds cleared and we were now in bright sunshine—yet it was still quite cold. The patrol was routine up to this point. Around four p.m. the company halted. The air team was well in the rear of the company that stretched out in a single file column about the length of two football fields. Just before halting we passed through a small saucer shaped depression that sloped to the west. Boulders and scrub pine abounded in this one to two acre area. As we came out of this depression we again began to gradually ascend the west side of a much larger saucer shaped depression with a high ridge line dominating its eastern side. This geographic feature also opened to the west. This area was pretty much devoid of surface features except for isolated locations. Our air team's tail near end location at the time placed us less than fifty yards from the small depression we had just passed through.

When the halt was called we all sprawled on the ground to rest. All was quiet except for the quiet murmuring of the men. Then the word

---

*While on an inspection trip to Korea in late November 1950 General MacArthur made a statement, possibly in jest, relative to the troops being home by Christmas. By the time the press and the rumor mill finished mangling whatever he said, and word filtered down to us troops, it was accepted as gospel that we would be home by Christmas.

came down the line for "air control to the front." I left the air team and ran in a crouch up the line of troops. As I approached Captain Myron Wilcox he motioned for me to get down. There to our immediate front was a large group of Chinese. I estimated the nearest Chinese to be fifty to one hundred yards away. They were obviously unaware of our presence and were busily engaged in cooking, chatting with each other, and still others in the process of meeting their biological needs. Although there was a wooded area to their immediate rear most of the Chinese I could see were out in the open, no doubt enjoying the last rays of the afternoon sun. At this point too a platoon from our company was quietly deploying to the right in a line facing the Chinese. Our Company now resembled an inverted "L" with the point of intersection being where Captain Wilcox and I were located. The deploying platoon formed the short line of the "L". Captain Wilcox asked if I could bring an air strike in on the target. I raced back down the line of troops to join the rest of the air team. My hope, and I'm sure Captain Wilcox hoped too that we could remain unobserved and an air strike, if planes were available, could hit the Chinese before they had time to scatter or deploy to any great extent. But before I covered half the distance firing broke out and the action was joined.

The few troops in our vicinity at the tail end of the column were quickly called up front to join in the action. Two members of the air team not needed moved up with the rest of the company while Private First Class Sam Rice remained with me.

I took off my helmet, pushed back the parka hood, and removed my cap; then fumbled barehanded in the cold to hook up the microphone and headset. Then I turned on the radio. My plan was to first check to see if aircraft were available, and if so to move back up to Captain Wilcox. As I pressed the mike switch and looked up to see if I could spot any aircraft I noted approximately ten Chinese dash across our right flank, abreast of me, and on to the rear of our company front. One of them was carrying an automatic rifle by an elevated handle. At this point the attention of the company was understandably to the front as it deployed and returned fire.

Only by accident did I catch a glimpse of the Chinese troop movement in the brief seconds when they had to expose themselves as they otherwise moved under cover to that small saucer shaped depression to our rear. I envisioned our being caught in a deadly crossfire. Further, large rocks and other cover would serve to protect and conceal them from our return direct fire once they made themselves known by firing into our exposed rear on the open slope. I don't believe anyone else, with the possible exception of Sam Rice saw them.

My priorities changed on a dime. Obviously we were not going to catch the Chinese by surprise—they were now either fully deployed or in the process of deploying. The greater danger appeared to be the enemy setting up in our rear. I did not know it at the time, but in the first exchange of fire Captain Wilcox had been wounded and incapacitated by a bullet through his jaw.

I don't recall how many of the four channels I went to with the standard "any aircraft this net" routine. I believe I was on the second channel when I heard in reply, "Roughneck one-four this is Lovelace two-one—over." The two Corsairs* came into view within seconds flying from south to north at what I judged to be 500 feet altitude, and approximately 300-500 yards off our right flank (east of our position). They both dipped their wings smartly in our direction when told our location was off their left wing. In addition to the Hollywood-like script, with the cavalry (aircraft) arriving at the dramatic moment they were needed, we were also blessed with excellent visibility conditions for the pilots. The sun was still shining but was low in the west. Apparently with the sun in the right position for his maximum visibility, and with our backdrop being patchy snow, it is understandable why the flight leader was able to inform me that he had us clearly in sight. I then pointed out what I judged to be the immediate threat from en-

---

*The planes were from VMF-312, the Checkerboard" squadron with the distinctive checkerboard patterns on the rudder and engine cowling. Lieutenant Colonel "J" Frank Cole commanded the squadron.

F-4U Corsairs from the "Checkerboard Squadron." (USMC photo)

emy troops setting up in our rear, and identification features of the
target area. The flight leader confirmed with his wingman that he too
was satisfied with friendly troop disposition and that of target location.
The flight leader informed me that they would be making their attack
run down the long axis of our "L" shaped position.* These verbal exchanges, time wise much shortened by the cryptic jargon we used, took
place in the few seconds that elapsed while the planes were lining up for
their firing runs which necessitated there making two ninety degree left
turns. The two turns brought the planes, now at approximately 100 feet
altitude, generally down the long axis, yet a bit to the west of us troops
on that long arm of the inverted "L". The pilots dipped over on their
left wing, this time sharply, for one last quick look at our position before
leveling off for the strike.

---

*This is generally against the rules. For troop safety air strikes are required to be run
at right angles to friendly troops, but this was judged to be an emergency where one is allowed to deviate from "the book."

The first aircraft released its canister of napalm. These canisters are not designed aerodynamically so they tumble end over end as they fall. (Fuses at both ends of the canister insure detonation.) Sam Rice and my proximity to the target necessitated that the napalm be released before the plane all but passed over our heads. Eerie! The second Corsair fired one or two of its five-inch rockets into the target area, likewise while all but over our heads. I told the pilots they had scored what looked like direct hits. The planes had expended their heavy armaments but were asked to strafe the target area with their fifty-caliber guns. As they were coming back down the inverted "L" for their second run our wet cell battery went out. (Later on I had reason to smile when I thought of my dad's experience with a wet cell battery during that 1936 Joe Lewis-Max Smealing fight. By a critical small margin I had better luck.) The pilots, apparently still comfortable with target identification and our position made additional runs in the process of expending their ammo load.

I could only hope that the air strike had eliminated the threat to our rear. I took some comfort from there being no enemy fire from the target area—at least for the moment.

While running the air strike it was necessary to stay in place. As a result, Sam and I, along with another Marine who was nearby, but further up the slope, became physically separated from the rest of the company by about fifty yards. As I removed the headset and microphone from the radio I accidentally kicked my helmet and it rolled a few feet off to one side. As I went to retrieve it, Sam left with the radio while I put my cap, helmet, and gloves back on. As I picked up my rifle a shot rang out on this "lonesome" end of the battlefield. The Marine who was a few yards up the slope let out a yell and hunched over. Looking to my left I saw the Chinese soldier, down on one knee and in the process of attempting to put another round in the chamber of his rifle. He was probably armed with what many of the Chinese at this time carried, a Japanese 25-caliber bolt action rifle. Approximately 40,000 military men, Chinese and American, were within the immediate valley and hills around Yudam-

ni, and here the two of us have a one-on-one confrontation. I was carrying a thirty-caliber carbine with a banana clip holding thirty rounds. I quickly removed the glove from my right hand—but I had a problem. It had been necessary to remove the gloves in the process of hooking up the radio's headsets and microphone—then to operate the radio. As a result, instead of a trigger finger all I felt was a cold mass of fingers—not one distinguishable from another. So here we were, he having to clear a jammed rifle (I suspect) and I'm trying to force a finger or fingers in the trigger guard. I won the encounter, but I am not proud to say I fired all thirty rounds in the process.* Apart from what I call near panic firing I found the encounter somewhat unsettling and not something easy to talk about. Running air strikes where men were in all likelihood killed or wounded was one thing, but you are not pulling the trigger in those cases. The same might be said for other occasions, like the shooting gallery at Sudong where as a group we fired at the Chinese as they ran in the open over a railroad embankment. Who knows where one's rounds went under those conditions?

Fear of being accidentally hit by aircraft ordinance was always a nagging concern for front line troops. I learned later from conversations with participants on that patrol, or in their being quoted in written accounts, that apparently only Captain Wilcox at the officer level was aware of the air team's presence on the patrol. Imagine how those two Corsairs making firing runs practically over their heads had to appear to the rest of the company. At least to those who could take time out from the hot firefight to take note of the air strike. Captain Wilcox, having been shot through the jaw was unable to speak. I suspect that only the Captain and the four of us in the air team were aware that the aircraft were being directed from the ground. As noted above, Sam Rice of our air team was the only person with me at the time of the strike. If he heard my side of the conversation he could not have known what the pilots were saying in reply. Later writ-

---

*At this point those of us who carried carbines taped two thirty-round clips together so we could remove the empty clip, flip it over, and insert a second thirty-round clip.

ten accounts of this action mention Sam standing and waving brightly colored air panels as the planes made their runs. We carried air panels and Sam would have had the good sense and initiative to wave them, and the courage to stand while doing so. Standing was not a good idea under the conditions prevailing, and if Sam was standing he was in all likelihood the only one doing so at the time.

As a corollary to this patrol action was a December 1980 issue of the *Marine Corps Gazette*, the Marine Corp's professional magazine. In that issue was an article written by Joe Owens.* Joe, a Lieutenant at the time led the company's 60mm mortar platoon. He was one of the officers on the patrol, and the only surviving officer of that action. His article was entitled *Chosin Reservoir Remembered*. In discussing this patrol he writes:

> "Baker Company is alone today, and with limited visibility, there is no air support. Radio communications is not effective enough to give us artillery." Later on in his article he states, "Now we are fully surrounded and the Chinese fire is intense." Relative to the air strike, and in referring to the pilots, he states, "They show an excellent understanding of our situation…the Chinese at our end of the perimeter are silenced." (Reprinted by permission from Lieutenant Owens.)

After reading the article I wrote to Lieutenant Owens. I began my letter by saying, "Hey there Lieutenant Owens; there was too an air team on that 27 November 1950 combat patrol."

In subsequent meetings with Lieutenant Owens at reunions we often discussed our shared experiences while in Korea, with emphasis on that 27 November patrol. Naturally we talked about what might have occurred had we remained surrounded and found it impossible to break

---

*Lieutenant Owens authored one of the five books listed in Appendix "C" (*Colder Than Hell*). Lieutenant Owens fought at the "blood and guts level" while in Korea. His book, in my opinion, should be a must read for young officers and non-commissioned officers in the military. That point made, all readers with a sense of history and feel for the human side of war will enjoy the book. The war and Lieutenant Owens' career as a Marine ended about ten days later during the fighting withdrawal from the Chosin Reservoir area. A burp gun put a round in his left shoulder with two more tearing into his right arm, disabling him from further military duty.

out. Lieutenant Owens told me he had the word from Lieutenant Kur-caba, who assumed command after Captain Wilcox was wounded that we would form a circle and fight it out, i.e., no surrender. In retrospect, an analogy could be drawn to Custer's last stand on a ridge at the Little Big Horn on 26 June 1836. Every man in Custer's group was killed. Approximately 200 bodies were counted, including Custers when this battle was over. Baker Company as constituted on 27 November 1950 numbered around that same number of men.

Now back to the scene of the action. The wounded Marine who I had observed being hit apparently had moved forward under his own power. I worked my way up to where the rest of the air team was located. This was a lively and noisy encounter with bullets whizzing continuously overhead, seemingly just clearing us as we lay on the ground. Exploding enemy mortar rounds added to the noise and danger. I honestly thought it was all over for us. We were miles from our lines and had obviously run into a hornet's nest. I said to myself, "This is it! You will either be dead or dying within the next couple of hours." One thing I knew for sure; we would fight it out to the bitter end.

It was Sam Rice who came up with a method to destroy the radio. He first used the butt of his rifle to knock the channel selector knob off. Then he fired several rounds into the exposed chamber to destroy the frequency crystals, and otherwise damage the circuitry.

We began our withdrawal under cover of darkness. The company slowly made its way back out through that small depression where the air strike hit, then worked its way towards the road on the valley floor.* The Chinese did not pursue us aggressively, and there was nothing to be heard from those Chinese who had raced to that shallow saucer shaped depression to our rear we were now passing through. When the battalion was informed of our situation they dispatched Charlie Company, less one platoon left to guard the regimental command post, to assist us. This

---

*We were unable to recover the bodies of the two men from Able Company killed the day before.

involved their moving back down the road the three miles we in Baker Company had covered that morning before heading up into the hills. When they arrived at this point it was pitch dark. Before ascending the hill they fired 60mm white phosphorous rounds to help guide us back off the hill mass to the road. Before they attempted to ascend the hill we were disengaged and on our way down. Charlie Company took up a position that night three miles south of Yudam-ni. Charlie Company was destined to be in deep trouble in the hours ahead; probably from the same force we had tangled with.

We were safely out of harm's way at this point, but I still had a concern. I felt like a teenager who had to tell his father that he wrecked the family car. In this case it was that we lost the radio. Despite my personal concerns about the radio, the four of us in the air team were now looking forward to telling the other air team members of our "wild ride" while on this patrol. As we came down from the hills we were surprised to see many vehicles lined up on the road facing south. All us troops knew when we reached the road was that they were waiting to pick up our casualties. We learned later that it had been a troublesome day at Yudam-ni. The trucks, after delivering supplies and troops were routinely heading back to Hagaru-ri carrying the casualties of that day's action at Yudam-ni. As a result our patrol experience was no big deal to the rest of the team given the overall deteriorating tactical situation at Yudam-ni.

The first thing I blurted out when I saw Captain Holland (promoted to that rank just a few days earlier) was that we lost the radio. Captain Holland said he understood. It was then that I noted the somber mood of those who had stayed behind, and it was obvious that the tactical situation had worsened.

Other than Baker Company's patrol this was supposed to have been a quiet day for our battalion. Able Company rested after its harrowing experience while on patrol the day before. Charlie Company was deployed to guard the regimental command post, a comfortable enough job. Our regiment's 2nd Battalion plus two companies of the 3rd Battalion were deployed or deploying on the hills around Yudam-ni to support the 5th Marines. On that same date one battalion of the 5th Marines began the attack to the west of Yudam-ni. The idea of heading for the Korean-Chinese border on the Yalu River was temporarily shelved. Two days earlier, on 25 November 1950 our Eighth Army, approximately sixty miles west of our location had been hit and overwhelmed by the Chinese. The mission of our Marine Division now was to strike due west and relieve pressure on the Eighth Army by hitting the Chinese on their presumed open left flank.

It turned out not to be a good day for either the attacking units of the 5th Marines or for our 7th Marines deploying on the hills to support the 5th Marines attack. The hills we had run up and down like tourists the day before were now hotly contested. No longer were the Chinese shrinking from the battlefield after fighting small delaying actions. Every foot of ground and every hill to the west, north, and east of Yudam-ni were bitterly contested. This despite air strikes and artillery fire. Our Baker Company patrol had been operating in the hill mass to the southwest of Yudam-ni. The Chinese in that area, some of whom we tangled with, were heard from later that evening and in the early morning hours of 28 November. In later years we learned that hidden in the forested hills around Yudam-ni were three divisions of Chinese, 28,000 to 30,000 men. We numbered approximately 7000. Our two regiments, minus two isolated companies, were spread out in the hills and lowlands around the little village of Yudam-ni. One of those isolated companies was our own battalion's Charlie Company. As noted above, after meeting our patrol late on the 27th, they were left in position three miles south of Yudam-ni. The other was Fox Company, 2nd Battalion, 7th Marines.

If we in Baker Company in our patrol action could draw an analogy to the plight of Custer, how about Fox Company? The company reinforced numbered 240 men. They were assigned to hold Toktong Pass, a potential choke point midway between Hagaru-ri and Yudam-ni (see map page 371). The dominating height was Toktong-san at an elevation of 4700 feet. The company arrived at the pass around five p.m. on 27 November. By this time it was dark. This was about the time we in Baker Company were coming down off the hills after our firefight. Fox Company's new Company Commander, Captain Bill Barber had joined the company from the states only the week before. He ordered them to dig in. The troops wondered why? After all, other than the action at Sudong on 2 and 3 November there had been no heavy fighting for any of the Marine units. A number of the troops grumbled about their new commander, who being fresh from the states, was in their opinion not clued in to what was really going on. None knew that Bill Barber had won a Silver Star on Iwo Jima during World War II. He was destined to earn the Congressional Medal of Honor for his role in holding Toktong Pass in the days ahead.

By nine p.m. Fox Company was dug in. Half the men were on alert. A bright moon illuminated the landscape—and it was bitter cold. A convoy from Yudam-ni passed by about that time. The convoy, which was destined to be the last one out or into Yudam-ni was carrying the casualties of that day's action around Yudam-ni plus those we suffered in our patrol action. No one knew it until the next morning, but about this time (nine p.m.) Fox Company was surrounded, as were we at Yudam-ni. Also Charlie Company, those good men who came to the aid of Baker Company that afternoon, was surrounded in their position three miles south of Yudam-ni. Further south, the trap was closing at Hagaru-ri and for the Army units east of the reservoir. Fox Company was hit, and hit hard a little before 2:30 a.m. on the 28th, just a little over seven hours after they arrived at Toklong Pass. They remained surrounded and besieged until our battalion, after a nighttime passage through enemy lines, reached their position around noon on 2 December.

Back at Yudam-ni, we settled in for the night. The temperature was minus twenty below at sunset. Our officers were suspicious and concerned after that day's action, but had no solid proof that so many Chinese were assembled in the hills surrounding Yudam-ni. The Chinese announced their presence early that evening. The first light Chinese probes were made around nine p.m. on 27 November. The first major assault occurred a little after ten p.m. when approximately 300 Chinese hit a company of the 5th Marines west of Yudam-ni. Within hours nearly the entire perimeter was involved in heavy fighting. Our own position, in the southwestern quadrant of the perimeter was reasonably quiet. From our foxholes in this sector we were apprehensive witnesses to the fireworks on this wild and wooly night. This was reminiscent of the Chinese night attack at Sudong on 2 November 1950.

Historical accounts credit the patrol action of Able and Baker Company on 26 and 27 November as the probable reason for the relative quiet on the southwest quadrant of the perimeter. The enemy forces we clashed with could have otherwise easily moved into an attack position, permitting them to strike the southwest portion of the Yudam-ni perimeter simultaneously with their forces hitting the rest of the perimeter. The sharp firefights with Able and Baker Company may have weakened the Chinese so as to preclude an attack. They may also have been thrown off balance and not have had time to re-organize and move into an attack position southwest of the Yudam-ni perimeter. Another obstacle could have been our Charlie Company, upon whom they may have stumbled on the road to Yudam-ni.

Like isolated Fox Company, our Charlie Company was also hit and surrounded around 2:30 a.m. on the 28th. The men in Fox and Charlie Companies must have wondered what was going on as they observed the flashes of light and sound of guns as they looked north towards Yudam-ni between ten p.m. and when they were hit four hours later.

The action on the night of 27 and 28 November at Yudam-ni resulted in our medical personnel being overwhelmed. Sick bay tents were quickly filled with wounded. Those not severely wounded were left outside and covered with canvas and straw. The conditions under which medical personnel worked further hampered their efforts. Blood plasma was frozen and could not be used. Morphine syrettes had to be warmed in the mouth before they could be used. Add to that the need for medical personnel to wear gloves as much as possible to ward off the freezing cold. There was a benefit resulting from the freezing temperature. Blood froze saving many men from bleeding to death.

The morning of 28 November 1950 confirmed that we were in dire straits. While the rest of the units at Yudam-ni hung on, what remained of our battalion headed south out of Yudam-ni to rescue Charlie Company. In all likelihood the same large Chinese force our patrol tangled with the evening before now surrounded Charlie Company. If time permitted after the relief of Charlie Company we were authorized to continue south down the road the additional five miles to rescue Fox Company. The proviso though was that we had to be back at Yudam-ni by dusk to take our place in the 360-degree defensive ring. The risk that was taken during the day in vacating the entire southwest sector of the perimeter was not acceptable at night. As it turned out, we were fortunate that we were able to rescue Charlie Company after hard fighting; Fox Company's lonesome ordeal had to continue.

In the meantime, back at Yudam-ni that same day, there was a consolidation of units and adjustment of lines as more defensible positions were established. There was no noticeable pulling back of the Chinese during daylight now; they hung in there and even attacked in some locations despite our preponderance in artillery and air power. Artillery was much hampered by the freezing weather. Once a round was fired it took minutes for the recoil mechanism to bring the guns back to battery to permit another round to be loaded and fired. The four artillery battalions of the 11th Marines maintained the best documented temperatures since they needed to factor the temperature in as an element of gunnery. They routinely recorded temperatures of minus twenty to twenty-five degrees. The frigid cold effected small caliber weapons as well. In Boot Camp our Drill Instructors "drilled" into our thinking the need to always keep a thin coat of oil on our weapons. In the freezing cold even a thin coat tended to congeal and freeze the weapon's action. The official solution was no oil at all, but some still preferred a razor thin coat; perhaps just a hint of oil was a better idea.

Although heavy fighting erupted throughout the hours of darkness on 28 November it did not compare with the ferocity of the night before. Not surprising since the Chinese too suffered heavy casualties in the prior fighting and no doubt also needed to move up men and supplies to their front line units. Speaking of supplies, on 29 November we received our first air drop at Yudam-ni. Airdrops were the only way we received supplies, for the most part emergency supplies in the days ahead. Most deliveries were made by U.S. Air Force transports. Critical was the need for ammunition, medical supplies and food. A medal should be given to the person who decided to drop Tootsie Roll candy as a substitute for C-rations.* What a truly great idea. We marched and fought our way out of the Chosin Reservoir nourished by this high-energy candy. Not only did C-rations require more air transport space than was available, but frozen cans of food were close to useless under the weather conditions we operated in. The Tootsie Rolls, although frozen solid as well, melted in your mouth. Our water needs were met in one of two ways. A canteen could be carried close to the body so the water didn't freeze, or we gulped snow.

While we were having our difficulties at Yudam-ni, other units at locations in the reservoir area were also having their own problems. Their problems were our problems since the way out could only be made if these outposts held their critical choke points on the one road leading to the seaport at Hungnam. Fox Company, holding the critical Toktong Pass midway between Yudam-ni and Hagaru-ri was like us, cut off and besieged. Fortunately they were within artillery range of the outpost at Hagaru-ri. Two Army infantry and one artillery battalion (3000 men) were cut off from Hagaru-ri by seven tortuous miles on the eastern side

---

*An unconfirmed story has evolved over the years that suggests the words "Tootsie Roll" were a code name for 81 mm mortar ammunition. When air delivery personnel in Japan saw the words "Tootsie Roll" they interpreted it literally. More on the role played by Tootsie Rolls at the Chosin Reservoir can be found in the *Unofficial Dictionary for Marines* at www.4mermarine.com. Then click on Marine Dictionary.

of the Chosin Reservoir and were fighting for their lives. The same was true of forces at Hagaru-ri, and to a lesser extent, at Koto-ri, eleven miles south of Hagaru-ri at the top of the Funchilin Pass.

Back at Yudam-ni, the night of 29/30 of November was, with the exception of occasional flash points, relatively quiet. On 30 November the inevitable was acknowledged. Plans were developed that day for fighting our way out. Captain Holland briefed the air team that evening. He was not strident, or theatrical, but made it quite clear we were destined to have the fight of our lives ahead, but that we were coming out as Marines. I know I was impressed at the time, and in retrospect I might add how typical of a good leader. Of course Captain Holland knew a great deal more about the overall situation then we at the troop level did, i.e. how serious the situation really was. One of the senior officers at Yudam-ni, who had fought in some of the bloodiest Pacific Island battles of World War II, was quoted later as saying, "I thought my life would end at Yudam-ni." On the other hand, I was so happy to have made it back from that 27 November patrol that what Captain Holland had to say was digested with calm acceptance.

My battalion's part in the plan was to move overland to the relief of Fox Company. In addition to the need to rescue the company was the absolute necessity of holding open Toktong Pass so men, and especially vehicles could move through this critical choke point during the breakout. Perhaps some of the able bodied men could have fought their way out, but what then of the many wounded? Although four and one-half air miles separated us from Fox Company, we moved nine miles in traveling overland through the hill masses by night. We would have the element of surprise on our side insofar as the Chinese, in all likelihood, assumed that any breakout attempt would have to be made by road, and certainly not at night. To guide us, the plan was for the artillery at Yudam-ni to fire artillery starburst shells every three minutes on the compass reading (azimuth) we were to travel through enemy territory.

Breakout

We were up shortly after dawn on 1 December 1950. The 500 of us traveling the overland route carried only our sleeping bag, weapons, and food we could eat on the move, i.e. Tootsie Rolls for the most part. The rest of our personal gear was loaded aboard our battalion vehicles that would hopefully make it through with the main body by road. There was no need for all members of the air team to function as a unit so a number of us were assigned as riflemen/ammunition carriers. I carried 60mm mortar ammunition. Our Battalion Commander, Lieutenant Colonel Davis, as noted earlier, earned the Congressional Medal of Honor for his role in leading us in this rescue mission.

The first hill mass we had to take was called "Turkey Hill" (see map page 371). This was where our battalion celebrated Thanksgiving a few days earlier. As a result the area was littered with turkey bones, hence the name. I remember before starting up Turkey Hill observing Lieutenant Joe Owens, the 60mm mortar Platoon Commander, joshing good naturedly with his men. I knew he was a good officer from both my limited observation and what I heard from his men. At any rate, here was the Lieutenant, smiling, joking and seemingly 100 percent confident we would accomplish what we all knew was likely to be a difficult task.

It turned out to be an all day battle as we clawed our way up the hill mass that positioned us behind enemy lines and gave us access to the planned overland route to Fox Company. By this time it was dark. We knew it would be necessary to move quietly. As a preliminary to moving out we were directed to jump up and down to ensure our equipment made no noise. At approximately nine p.m. the column started moving towards Fox Company. We stretched out one-half mile as we laboriously crossed slopes, ridges, valleys, and saddles of this rocky wilderness. About this time a measured minus twenty degrees was recorded at Yudam-ni. Colonel Davis, in a later account of the march said the temperature, with the harsh Siberian wind chill factored in, was minus

Yudam-Ni Area

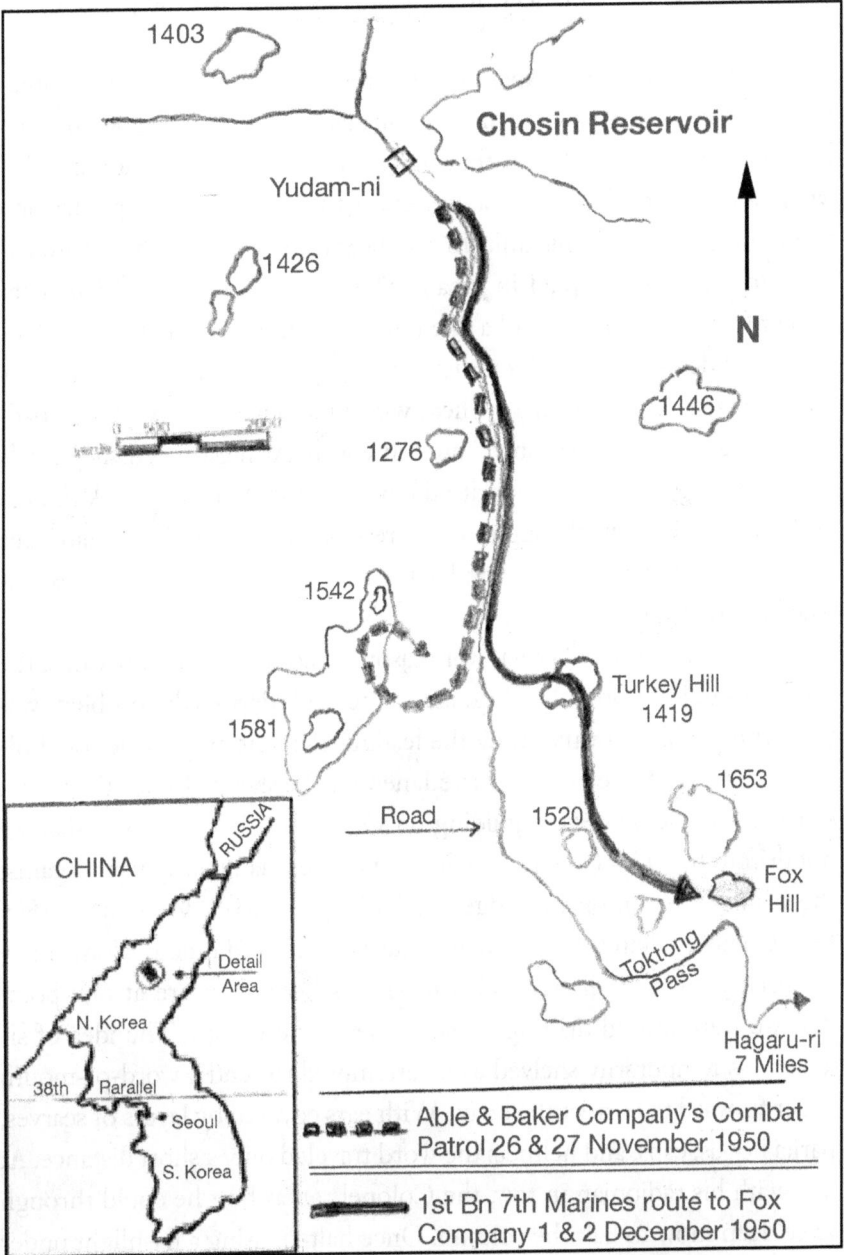

1403

Chosin Reservoir

Yudam-ni

N

1426

1446

1276

1542

Turkey Hill
1419

1581

1653

Road →   1520

Fox
Hill

CHINA

RUSSIA

Toktong
Pass

Detail
Area

N. Korea

Hagaru-ri
7 Miles

38th   Parallel

Seoul

Able & Baker Company's Combat
Patrol 26 & 27 November 1950

S. Korea

1st Bn 7th Marines route to Fox
Company 1 & 2 December 1950

fifty degrees. First Lieutenant Chew-Een Lee, probably one of the best rifle platoon commanders at the Chosin Reservoir, led the point at this stage of the breakout.

Lieutenant Lee had experience in breaking out of undesirable situations. He suffered a broken arm when struck by a bullet in the Sudong action on 3 November. He was transported to an Army evacuation hospital where a doctor told him to plan on at least thirty days of hospitalization before he could rejoin his unit. In the meantime he was slated for evacuation to an Army hospital in Japan. This was not what the Lieutenant came to Korea for. He found a like minded wounded man from our battalion and devised a plan. First they found weapons and web gear to fully outfit themselves for combat. Then, with Lieutenant Lee waving a loaded carbine they "requisitioned" an Army jeep. At high speed they made their breakout and were back with the battalion within an hour. Although bothered by the arm throughout the rest of the action, Lieutenant Lee was a stalwart platoon commander until seriously wounded and evacuated later on in the breakout.

In the meantime, for whatever reason, or combination of reasons, the star shells did not provide the guidance needed. Part of the problem was the terrain, which at times took the leading element into ravines or similar depressions. When this occurred, neither the star shells nor the bright star the lead element were guiding on was visible. It was critical that we not drift to the right (west) since this would eventually bring us up against the Chinese dug in on the ridge overlooking the road. We could in fact hear Chinese talking from time to time as we moved quietly along a few hundred yards to their rear. Colonel Davis became aware at one point that we were indeed drifting towards the Chinese lines. The idea of silence was temporarily shelved as he attempted to send a word-of-mouth order forward to correct the error. With ears covered by layers of scarves, parka hoods, caps, and helmets the word traveled only a short distance. At last, with his radioman in tow, the Colonel ran as best he could through knee deep snow to halt the column. Once halted, using a flashlight under a poncho, he took a compass reading to put us back on the right track.

Just before midnight Lieutenant Lee's point ran into a squad of Chinese and a firefight erupted. Those Chinese not killed or wounded scampered away. There was little doubt but that the Chinese now knew something was going on behind their lines, but without radio communications it would take time for them to pass the word and organize a response. Colonel Davis, taking note, as he said later, of the troops being in a near virtual state of collapse decided it best to risk all and give us a rest. After setting a twenty-five percent watch we dropped where we were to sit, kneel, or sprawl in the snow. As tired as we were sleeping was possible in any position.

We were on our way again before dawn. Before long we were traveling in daylight. Around ten a.m. we came under long range machine gun and small arms fire from four directions. We were at the time traveling across an open meadow. The long range resulted in the rounds being largely spent by the time they reached us, but we didn't know that at the time. It was nightmarish knowing that any round might hit you, and yet being able to move so slowly through the deep snow. But this was to be our last ordeal on the march to Fox Company.

We moved into Fox Company's perimeter at 11:25 a.m. on 2 December 1950. As we approached, the survivors stood and waved, smiling broadly. Air supply had been crucial for Fox Company as well and some waved strips of colored parachute fabric. The area in front of their lines, through which we moved, was littered with enemy dead. Lieutenant Joe Owens is quoted in the book *Breakout** as follows:

> The bodies got thicker as you got closer to Fox Company. I swear to God you could have walked all the way around Fox Company's position without touching the ground, using those bodies as a carpet. Every one of them died a brave soldier, facing the enemy. When you're a young Marine you never think such thoughts, but I think of them now.

---

*By Martin Russ (see Appendix C). Permission to reprint granted by Mr. Russ and Lieutenant Owens.

The rough estimate of enemy dead around the perimeter of Fox Company was 2000.

As we entered Fox Company's perimeter two things caught my eye. The first was that many of the Marine positions had been fortified with barricades made of frozen Chinese bodies. The second was that of the twenty-six dead Marines of Fox Company stacked up like cordwood, their bodies in many cases contorted in the position they had been in when they died. Three missing Marines were never accounted for. Another eighty-nine were wounded, to include all but one officer. Sadly this young officer, First Lieutenant John Dunne, was killed a few days later as he led the remnants of his platoon in the breakout. All in all, the original 240 men had been reduced to 122 fit for duty. A couple of tents were full of those severely wounded. Those that were ambulatory huddled outside the medical tents or lay outside in their sleeping bags.

That night I was in a group assigned to a defensive position on the northern rim of the perimeter. I had no problem whatsoever taking over an unused foxhole with two Chinese bodies serving as a parapet. One of the bodies served as a convenient table for the meal I had that evening. Before starting off on the rescue attempt I had placed a C-ration can of fruit cocktail next to my body to keep it from freezing. There had been no chance to eat anything but candy while on the march. The fruit cocktail, along with crackers that could be eaten under the frigid conditions that prevailed was the evening meal. Water needs were met by gulping snow. The night was quiet, other than for the long-range fire plunging into the area from time to time. When not on watch I slept comfortably in my sleeping bag.

The next day was largely spent waiting for what we expected to be the momentary arrival of the main body from Yudam-ni by road. At one point in mid-morning Corporal Tony Tinelli and I, along with others, answered a call for assistance to bring in some wounded Marines who had been on patrol in the vicinity of the dominating height in the area (Toktsong-san). We took the wounded man we were carrying to the medical tent. As we walked away a shot rang out and at the same time someone shouted, "The doctor is hit." We turned to see Doctor Peter Arioli, who had been on his knees working on a wounded man, pitch slowly forward. Death apparently was instantaneous from a bullet in the back. I wasn't aware of it at the time, but Doctor Arioli had accompanied us through the hills on the march to the relief of Fox Company. Fox Company had no doctor during their long ordeal, with Navy Corpsman doing their typical valiant job in caring for the wounded. As a result the doctor was a busy man from the time he entered the perimeter of Fox Company, a little less than twenty-four hours earlier.

Now yet another bizarre event. Right after the doctor's death and while we were still in the area, a helicopter came into view flying at about 500 feet. The helicopter was almost directly overhead when it started making strange noises. The noise was in part due to the machine going into crazy arcs as it whirled out of control. Here again was another of those scenes common in a bad dream. Tony Tinelli and I ran first one way; then another as the plunging machine seemed to follow our moves. It hit 100 feet from us, and within 250 feet of the medical tents. The area was sparsely wooded and it came down between the trees. It did not hit the ground real hard—apparently the blades were still providing a degree of lift. There was no fire or explosion, only steam from that hot machine's contact with the cold ground and snow. We approached the chopper, which had crashed on its belly and was tilted slightly towards Tony Tinelli and me as we approached. I can still see in my mind's eye that small blue hole over the pilot's right eye—and noted too that he was wearing a leather Marine flight jacket. Other than the barely noticeable head wound his body was not in anyway disfigured. His body was removed to join five others, to include Doctor Arioli, who had been killed over the past few hours. All but three were buried in a mass grave dug by a bulldozer before the last of our troops left Fox Hill. Room was found on vehicles for three bodies. At this point many of our wounded that should have been riding were walking and there was no way we could bring out most of the dead, as was also the case at Yudam-ni.

A sentimental postscript came along relative to the helicopter crash. In 1997 a letter appeared in our Chosin Veteran's newsletter from a Jim Westendorf. Jim was in the observation squadron that included this helicopter, one of three in its fleet. Helicopters were new to the military at this time. He mentioned that mid-morning on 3 December one of their choppers came "barreling" in to their base. The pilot, making a hasty landing near him, motioned him over and shouted at him above the roar of the engine and whirling rotor blades, "Get me two cans of mo-gas, there's a truck holding up traffic, out of fuel on the road, full of wounded, etc." Jim rushed to get two five gallon cans and placed them in the passenger space behind the pilot. With his M1 rifle slung over his shoulder Jim was getting in when Lieutenant Robert Longstaff turned and yelled at Jim to, "Get out; I don't need you along on this trip." No more than twenty to thrity minutes elapsed before his outfit received word that the chopper had been shot down as it flew low over Toktong Pass. Jim's letter went on to say, "Whether he was shot dead immediately upon being hit we don't know, but the chopper went out of control, crashed, exploded and burned upon impact with the ground. To the best of my (Jim's) knowledge we were unable to recover his body." He closed by mentioning that but for the pilot's "Get out, I don't need you" he (Jim) might not be here today. I hustled a letter off to Jim giving him the particulars as mentioned above. Jim in turn was quick to write me back, expressing relief that the anguish he had imposed on himself over the years for his erroneous belief that the chopper had exploded and burned upon crashing was cleared up.

About the same time we started our march to the relief of Fox Company, the main body began moving south from Yudam-ni by road. From our positions in the hills, we could see clouds of billowing black smoke from the fires our troops set to burn supplies and equipment. Anything not needed that could possibly be used by the Chinese was destroyed. I suspect at the top of the list was every tent at Yudam-ni. The first priority after loading the necessary ammunition in vehicles were the non-ambulatory wounded who were placed in sleeping bags in vehicles. Those with leg injuries rode on fenders or any other reasonably flat area where they could grab hold. Others, the walking wounded, marched along with the vehicle column. Room was found for some of the dead on trucks. Many more were secured to fenders and hoods of vehicles. The eighty-five for whom there was no room were buried at Yudam-ni in a mass grave dug by a bulldozer. During the many firefights that erupted along the way, those wounded not stacked in vehicles could, some with difficulty, make it to a protective ditch. Those stretched out on litters in the vehicles had in all too many cases endured additional wounds, some fatal. As noted above, one blessing as a result of the frigid cold was that men who might otherwise have bled to death did not due to their blood freezing as it flowed from wounds.

The attack down the main road was led by the only tank that made it to Yudam-ni, an M-26 Sherman. It had been sent up from Hagaru-ri to test the roadbed for tanks. Before other tanks could make the trip the road was closed. Two bulldozers followed the tank. The bulldozers removed the debris from roadblocks once the tank, infantry, and engineers had cleared them of enemy troops and supporting enemy fire. The bulldozer was prepared to push the tank aside if disabled in order to keep the road clear for vehicles. The process was excruciatingly slow and it wasn't until noon on 3 December that we at Toktong Pass heard the welcoming sound of our clanking tank coming up the pass into Fox Company's position.

With the arrival of the main body my battalion took off to lead the way into Hagaru-ri, seven miles to the south. Scattered firefights erupted along the way, but generally the Chinese kept their distance. Our aircraft were given free rein to hit anything they saw moving on distant hills. From time to time we observed long columns of Chinese moving on distant hills and watched as napalm bombs hit the columns. Most lay still, others ran about, their clothing and bodies on fire.

Around seven p.m. on 3 December we approached the perimeter at Hagaru-ri. Colonel Davis halted the column about 500 yards from the perimeter. His words were along the line of, "Shape up; look sharp; we are going in like United States Marines." Soon after we began trudging along, someone began calling cadence. Most likely a former Drill Instructor. I'll be darned if that didn't serve to straighten us up. Then someone began singing the Marine Corps hymn. We all joined in and before long we were "strutting" a bit.*

We found an unheated tent to call home that night; at least we were out of the cold wind. More important, we found hot food. Pancakes were the piece-de-resistance, but hot coffee and stew of some kind were a welcome treat as well. There were no security watches for us that night. Sometime in the early morning hours of 4 December our tent shook as four explosions, seemingly close by woke us up. Much later we learned one of our B26 bombers had dropped its four bombs in error. We also learned later that no one was injured, but it was tough on our nerves none-the-less.

Our battalion was the first unit of those once at Yudam-ni to enter the comparative safety of Hagaru-ri. With our arrival, and the steady stream of men that followed us, Hagaru-ri's chance of being over-run was much reduced. Despite the steady flow of men and equipment it took until early afternoon of 4 December before the last of the rear guard from Yudam-ni entered Hagaru-ri. Speaking of the rear guard, this dangerous mission was accomplished by the 5th Marines. Their experiences in holding back the Chinese as they successively covered the rear of our column at Yudam-ni, Fox Hill, and Hagaru-ri is described in the books listed in Appendix C. Their exploits in this role make for exciting reading.

December 4th and 5th were spent in organizing for the next push, the eleven miles of open space between Hagaru-ri and Koto-ri. There

---

*The colorful term "Magnificent Bastards" was coined as we marched into Hagaru-ri. It originated with Navy Doctor Robert Harvey, a quiet and soft-spoken man, when he observed our battalion passing by his medical company's encampment at Hagaru-ri. He was as moved as he had ever been. Turning to a stranger beside him he exclaimed, "Look at those bastards! Those magnificent bastards!" From that statement there evolved any number of memorabilia items such as "T" shirts, coffee mugs, etc.

was no time to waste. We were well aware of many Chinese in the area, some 40,000 as we later learned, around Hagaru-ri and Chinhung-ni. More were moving south from Yudam-ni.

There was also a need at this point to take note of casualties. The 5th and 7th Marines entered Hagaru-ri with approximately 1000 wounded on trucks; another 800 were walking wounded. With the exception of less than ten carried on vehicles, our dead were buried at Yudam-ni or at what we now reverently referred to as Fox Hill. The Army forces to the east of Chosin reservoir once numbered 3000 men, 700 of whom were South Korean Army recruits. Only 385 able bodied men made it to Hagaru-ri. Approximately 900 were air evacuated from Hagaru-ri. The remainder, approximately 1500 men, were either killed in action (KIA), missing in action (MIA), or made prisoners of war (POW).

One of the first projects undertaken when the division engineers moved into Hagaru-ri was to develop an airstrip. Not an easy job, given the frozen ground and enemy attacks. The job was not yet completed when the need for evacuation of wounded and emergency supplies dictated use of the strip in advance of completion. After dark, when planes could no longer fly, the engineers went back to work on the strip. Over a four-day period, ending at dark on 5 December, a total of 4312 Marine, Navy, and Army wounded were evacuated from Hagaru-ri. Room was also found on some of the last departing transports to fly out the bodies of 137 dead. This along with several hundred tons of ammunition, fuel, and medical supplies flown in rounded out the effort.

Although Marines and Navy air transports did their large part, Air Force pilots and aircraft made the major contribution to this medical evacuation effort. At one point Air Force General William Turner flew into Hagaru-ri to confer with General Oliver Smith, the 1st Marine Division Commander. The Marines were great fans of General Turner's Combat Cargo Command who were doing sterling work providing us with air dropped supplies and casualty evacuation. General Turner offered to evacuate all the troops he possibly could from Hagaru-ri via a massive airlift. General Smith declined this generous, indeed heroic offer. First of all, now having two and one third of his infantry regiments at Hagaru-ri he was probably feeling a bit optimistic relative to our chances of getting out by road. Then too, there was a problem of holding the airstrip as troops were flown out. A sizeable force, those needed to hold the perimeter, would have to be sacrificed. Finally, over 1000 motor and tracked vehicles would have had to be abandoned.

Marine transport aircraft flying into Hagaru-ri brought in 537 replacements. Some of these were men returning to duty after having recovered from earlier wounds. Even with these new men, infantry units were at best operating at half strength. Most though were young men who were brand new to the war. They were but recently removed from their homes and families, and were now parceled out among what for the moment were strangers. These strangers in turn had no time to adequately welcome the new man into their ranks. A particularly poignant episode concerns a young Navy corpsman who flew in around noon one day during the siege at Hagaru-ri. He was hastily shuffled to a unit on the line. He was killed in late afternoon on his day of arrival. More than likely he never got to know a soul in his new unit.

On the bright side at Hagaru-ri was the abundance of Tootsie Rolls.* No longer did we have to depend on airdrops. Apparently the candy had been delivered by the truckload during those days when convoys were still getting through from the rear area supply dumps.

We began the breakout from Hagaru-ri to Kotoro-ri on the morning of 6 December. During the day most of our battalion moved along the high ground west of the road. I was assigned to the vehicle train. It turned out to be a stop and go slugfest as one roadblock after another was eliminated. From time to time the convoy of vehicles were split with one

---

*At our "Chosin Few" organization's fiftieth anniversary reunion in December 2000 (in San Diego) the President, Mrs. Ellen Gordon and CEO, Mr. Melvin Gordon of the Tootsie Roll Corporation were guests of honor. They were made honorary members of the Chosin Few. They in turn presented everyone present with a cylindrical package, the size of a rolled-up Sunday newspaper, loaded with Tootsie Rolls.

Marines resting amidst a snowstorm on the way out of the Chosin Reservoir.
(USMC photo)

segment temporarily stopped as groups of Chinese, striking out of the surrounding hills to our left (east) attacked the convoy.

Halfway between Hagaru-ri and Koto-ri we came to the scene of the ambush that took place on 29 November 1950 and the early morning hours of the 30th. At this point in time Hagaru-ri was hanging on by its fingernails and reinforcements were desperately needed. An attempt was made to break through from Koto-ri to Hagaru-ri, a distance of eleven miles. What was assumed to be an adequate force of 922 men, 29 tanks, and 141 vehicles was assembled at Koto-ri. British Royal Marine Colonel Douglas Drysdale led the force. They ran into a hornet's nest of opposition from the start. By midnight of the 29th, fully a third of these men were dead or prisoners of war. Only a few hundred made it into Hagaru-ri, a few hundred more found their way back to Koto-ri. The survivors of the ambush termed one segment of the route "hell fire valley." The scores of vehicles that had been destroyed, many with their drivers frozen at the wheel, lined this mile long corridor. Here and there were clusters of American and Chinese dead. Some of the vehicles were carrying mail and Christmas packages. The Chinese had six days to pillage the packages and whatever else the cargo trucks were carrying. Empty Christmas packages; bright red and green wrapping paper and ribbons were blowing about. Time and circumstances did not permit us to retrieve the letters also blowing about in the wind.

As darkness closed in, these attacks became more frequent and more violent as more Chinese joined the fray. They were no longer plagued by our air attacks and only to a limited extent by our artillery. I recall how eerie it seemed with our red and their green tracers providing a backdrop to this hellish scene. A nightmare scenario occurred around two a.m. on 7 December. A group of Chinese, who had worked their way down from the hills to the east of the road, again temporarily interrupted our convoy. A gap of approximately fifty yards opened along the line of vehicles. Somehow Tony Tinnelli and I ended up in the middle of that gap. If we were not alone it certainly seemed that we were. Tracers from both sides made the scene hellishly surreal. Tony and I hustled to join the rearward segment of the forward string of vehicles. We sprawled in the ditch next to a couple of jeeps. Several huts along side (east side) of the road had now burst into flames lighting up the entire area. About this time we heard the distinct splat of a bullet hitting flesh. Colonel Daucett, the Executive Officer of the 7th Marines was hit. Understandingly, troops find it unnerving to note the wounding of a senior commander who is leading them in a tough situation. A few yards ahead Father Griffin was seriously wounded as he administered the last rites to a Marine in an ambulance. His clerical assistant, Sergeant Matthew Caruso was killed when he threw himself between the priest and the side of the ambulance from which bullets were entering. His last words were, "Look out Father, look out!"*

From time to time halts occurred in the forward movement for one reason or another and there was no enemy action at your location. During these breaks we tried to catch some sleep. Ideally there was a vehicle or trailer to lean against while napping. Better yet we found a spot near the hood of a vehicle so we could benefit from engine warmth. Often we just sprawled out on the roadway since the road was fairly clear of snow. On one occasion while I lay on the road I must have fallen into a deep sleep. I awoke as someone shoved me with his boot and said gently, "I think this one's dead." I objected in a flash, and the person I objected to was Warrant Officer Stanley Novak, a communication officer I had once worked for.

I reached Koto-ri at daylight on 7 December. The last of the division's 10,000 men and vehicles were all in the Koto-ri perimeter by midnight on the 7th. It had taken a total of forty hours for all our forces to make the eleven-mile trek from Hagaru-ri. I recall only a brief stop in a tent and hot food of some kind, no doubt pancakes, before moving on to a position south of the main encampment area. I was at the time with Baker Company of our battalion. The Koto-ri perimeter was crammed with 14,000 souls. Again there was the need to move out of there quickly. I recall watching Air Force C-119 flying boxcars dropping unusual shaped objects by parachute mid-morning on the 7th, but had no idea at the time what they were dropping. That delivery, combined with an engineering miracle was vital to our getting the rest of the way out.

Another miracle of medical evacuation occurred at Koto-ri. Here as at Hagaru-ri the rough dirt runway actually extended out into no-mans' land. It became operational on 6 December. That same day 700 wounded were flown out. Initially only obsolete Navy torpedo planes (TBM) and small Piper Cub observation aircraft (OE) could be used. The TBMs

---

*A plaque honoring the memory of Sergeant Caruso has been placed in the School of Infantry Chapel at Camp Pendleton, California.

could carry up to seven men, the OEs two. Later C-47 two engine transports used the strip to carry twenty-five to forty men. Throughout the day on 7 December an additional 600 casualties incurred in the move from Hagaru-ri to Koto-ri arrived. On that day, under spotty weather conditions 200 were evacuated. A heavy snowfall on 8 December put an end to the evacuation for the moment, leaving about 400 remaining wounded, most of whom eventually came out by vehicle.

While in this area I was introduced to the refugee problem. Older men, women and children thronged the road in an attempt to flee the Chinese and a return of North Korea Communist rule. A pitiful sight to see these shabbily clothed and shod people trudging unsmiling and uncomplaining along the road. Many were loaded down with bundles and pushing or pulling carts. Farm animals and dogs were also mixed in. A small pup trotting along caught my eye. It appeared that he was trying to keep all four paws off the cold ground at the same time. A total of 91,000 refugees were eventually evacuated from Hungnam seaport and carried to South Korea.

On the night of 8/9 December, the temperature hit minus thirty degrees. This was the coldest night of the campaign. I slept on the ground a few miles southeast of Koto-ri. At one point during the night a small animal tried to burrow its way into my sleeping bag. I thought it a small pig, but it could have been a small dog. It would have been a much better night to have gone to bed with a Virgin.*

Three miles south of Koto-ri on the Funchilin Pass an estimated twenty-four foot section of a one-way concrete bridge had been destroyed. The bridge spanned a 2900-foot chasm, and given the terrain,

---

*Virgin: In colonial days a stone heated and wrapped in cloth to assist in the transition from a cold bed to one warmed by body heat. Later a hot water bottle was so termed. When the man who was to be our second President, John Adams, was Minister to Great Britain (1785), his wife Abigail wrote him to say, mischievously, that in view of those cold and damp London nights it was fine with her if he took a "virgin" to bed with him. John wrote back to thank her, and in an equally mischievous manner, noting that since it was cold in Massachusetts as well, he was authorizing her to sleep with the woman's equivalent code word for the warmer, which was "abbe" i.e., priest.

Treadway bridge construction area looking North (USMC photo)

there was no way to construct a by-pass. At this location an underground tunnel fed water from the Chosin Reservoir into large pipes called penstocks. From there the water was carried to a power plant at Chinhung-ni in the valley below. A sub-station containing the valves that controlled the transfer to the penstock was built into the rock facing of the cliff. The twenty-four foot section of the concrete bridge was in front of this small enclosure. After all the fighting were we destined to be stopped by this twenty-four foot gap in the roadway? The solution, if it could be made to work was to span the gap with a treadway bridge. The delivery would have to be made by air. But a treadway bridge had never been dropped by parachute before. A test drop of the 2500 pound section was conducted in Japan with promising possibilities.

The "unusual shaped objects" I saw parachuting to earth on 7 December were four sections of a treadway bridge. One section fell into enemy territory and one other was badly damaged, the other two were usable. Also lost to the enemy were two of the four plywood center sections needed to play their part in final construction. One miracle that made using a treadway bridge a possibility was the presence of the Army's 58th Treadway Bridge Company in Koto-ri. They had been destined to join Army units at Hagaru-ri. They had luckily reached Koto-ri before the Chinese cut-off travel in all directions. The company consisted of four treadway bridge trucks and a few men commanded by Lieutenant Charles Ward. The trucks were loaded with prefabricated building material for building an Army Command Headquarters at Hagaru-ri.

Moving the bridge sections down that narrow and icy mountain road, in a snowstorm no less, was a challenge itself. Along the way the Chinese had blown holes in the road, one a monster ten feet deep. There was no way a bulldozer could dig enough dirt from the frozen ground on that narrow road to fill the gap. In forty-five minutes the hole was filled using what there was an abundance of—snow. We did not worry about what was likely to happen when the thoroughly packed snow melted that spring.

The first necessary step in installing the bridge was to clear the bridge site of enemy. Our battalion's much depleted Baker and Charlie companies combined to do the job. It turned out to be a relatively easy job. A few shots were exchanged and about a dozen severely frost bitten, but ambulatory prisoners were taken. Another fifty were found dead, or near dead in their fighting holes around the site. One Chinese soldier interrogated on the spot said he was part of a 1000 man unit that had raced on foot across the hills the night before to get into position to defend the bridge site. A sudden drop in temperature had caused nearly all to freeze in their own sweat. The sixty in and around the bridge site were apparently lucky enough to find a cave where they could remain alive during those cold early morning hours before they moved into po-sition around the site.*

---

*The Chinese soldier was a ferocious fighter, but amazingly docile, indeed cooper-ative when captured. Our intelligence people were continually amazed at how well in-formed the average soldier was relative to the size, disposition and intent of units in their sector. As implied, they seemed at ease in giving us this information.

Marines on the march coming out of the Chosin Reservoir—and down the Fun-chilin Pass . (USMC photo)

The engineers with their heavy equipment reached the bridge site at a little after noon on 9 December. Now an accurate measurement of the gap revealed the startling fact that the actual gap was in fact seven feet more than the length of the treadway bridge sections carried to the site. But how lucky could we be? At one end of the gap there was a shelf eight-foot below the road surface and a full ten feet long, termed a "purchase" by the engineers. Using a combination of sandbags and timbers found in the area, the shelf was built up to where the bridge could be installed. The Chinese prisoners were enlisted in the project. Approximately six hours after arriving at the bridge site the first vehicles rolled across the bridge. In the vanguard were the heavy engineer bulldozers and other engineer vehicles needed to perform additional road clearing along the way. Nothing though as formidable as the installation of the treadway bridge. Not until midnight on 9 November did the first of the division's vehicle trains cross the bridge.

Time out here to acknowledge what a debt of gratitude we owe our engineers for improving the roads, hacking out air strips, doing their large part in destroying roadblocks, and above all, bridging that thirty-one foot gap on the otherwise impassable mountain road. Noteworthy too was the support given us on the ground by aviation. If there was one aircraft to be singled out as having made the major contribution the gull-winged F-4U Corsair was the one. It's most unlikely we could have made it out in the manner we did without this plane and the men who flew it.*

I reached the valley floor and relative safety of Chinhung-ni around midnight on 9 November. Chinhung-ni was in the vicinity of where our battalion knocked out four enemy tanks on the way up to the Chosin Reservoir. The next day the forty-three mile trip to the seaport at Hungnam was made by truck.

In the meantime the tail end of our division was still back at Koto-ri. Before pulling out on 10 December two bulldozers dug a pit to bury those

Burial at Koto-ri (USMC photo)

---

*More than 12000 Corsairs were produced for the Navy and Marine Corps during World War II and the Korean War. Today, less than thirty are still in existence. One of those is on display at the Flying Leatherneck Aviation Museum at Mira Mar Marine Corps Air Station, San Diego, California. This Corsair flew combat missions during the Korean War.

dead we could not carry out. The pit was sloped at one end to permit trucks to drive down and unload. A Chaplain said a few words for the 117 Marines, Soldiers, Sailors and British Commandos buried there. Colonel (Chesty) Puller,* Commanding Officer of the 1st Marines was among the last to leave. He came out with a dead Marine strapped to the bumper of his jeep and two others on the hood. At 2:30 a.m. on the morning of 11 December our engineers destroyed the treadway bridge.

Casualties among the Chinese have never been revealed. Estimated Chinese causalities for those in the Chosin Reservoir campaign from 15 October through 15 December were 25,000 killed and 12,500 wounded. Unlike our casualties, wounded Chinese were likely to die given their primitive medical support and difficulty in evacuating casualties. Marine casualties numbered 916 dead, 163 more died of wounds, 199 were missing in action and 5517 wounded. An additional 8900 men were non-battle casualties. Most of these were frostbite victims, with more than one-fourth of this number soon returning to duty.

Late on 11 December a landing craft took us from the beach at Hungnam to a transport in the harbor. By this time darkness had fallen. The ship was already fairly crowded, but I did find a bunk and then headed for the mess deck. No doubt the early birds dined on something better, but I was quite happy to eat my full of hot food. Hot dogs were the main attraction. Next a hot shower, the first scrub down since late October. The entire experience aboard ship was at the time, a little bit of heaven.

We sailed for Pusan, a seaport on the southern tip of South Korea that same evening. I think this 400-mile trip was made in record time. We then went into a tent city in a field that had once been a bean farm. This was at Mason, forty miles west of Pusan. We camped here for the next month to absorb and train the many replacements needed to flesh out the division. Equipment lost or damaged in the north also had to be replaced or repaired

---

*For more on the legendary "Chesty" Puller see footnote on page 460.

Postscript to the Chosin Reservoir Campaign

The battle of the Chosin Reservoir involved thirteen days of fighting over the entire first half of the seventy-eight mile route back to Hungnam. One can easily draw parallels to other military events, e.g. the oft-used Custer's Last Stand. On a larger scale than Custer, the breakout was somewhat akin to the march of Xenophon and *The Ten Thousand*.* They cut their way to the sea through a vastly superior Asiatic foe in 401 B.C. In both Korea and the march of Xenophon it was found necessary to set up moving 360-degree perimeters. Vehicles (carts for Xenophon) and wounded in both cases were protected by infantry positioned in the rear, on their flanks, and at the front of the column.

Naturally enough we veterans of the Chosin Reservoir campaign have

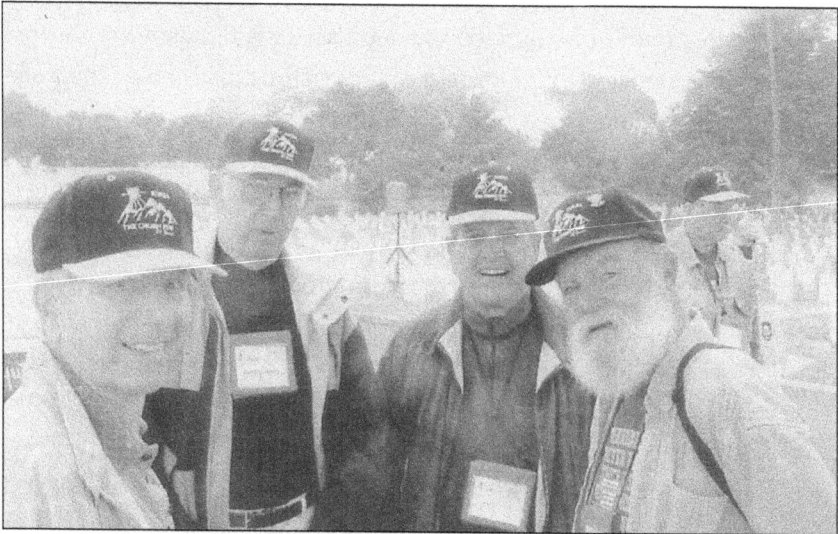

Chosin Reservoir 50th Reunion (2000) Air Team members. Left to right: John Romp, Author, Tony Tinelli, Bob Wright. (Photo by John Burke)

---

*Xenophon was the leader as well as historian of a fifth century A.D. military force called the "Ten Thousand." In his literary classic, the *Anabasis*, he wrote about tactics he evolved and tested in the heat of action. These tactics proved so effective that after a terrible 4000 mile retreat his Greek Army cut its way out of Persia (Iran), though only half of them lived to cry, "The Sea! The Sea!"

formed an organization. Naturally too we have reunions.* I regularly see
Tony Tinelli, John Romp, Bob Wright and Bob Wilson, all members of
our air team. Joe Owens and Chew-Een Lee, both from Baker Company,
1st Battalion 7th Marines, mentioned in this account, are also usual attendees. So is Jay Skidmore, the Navy combat cameraman who accompanied
us during this campaign. Lt. Colonel Ray Davis, our battalion commander, who went on to become a four star general was also a regular attendee,
but we lost him in 2003. The organization is named The Chosin Few. I
consider that to be a relatively "wimpy" title for an organization of military
veterans. In what I intended to be good-humored satire, I wrote an article
on the issue of our less than macho title. It appeared in the November—
December 1998 issue of our Chosin Few Digest. It read as follows:

> **Yes Virginia, we really are a military related organization.**
>
> Oh, I know—the term "Chosin Few" does have strong re-
> ligious overtones. And yes, Virginia, I know what occurred in
> Orlando, Florida during the 1988 reunion. No doubt you are
> referring to the visit our group made to the Kennedy Space
> Center. Let me retell the story; after all, I was an "ear" witness
> to the occurrence. At one point an announcement was made
> that all Chosin Few members were to assemble at a certain
> point. A lady in front of me turned to her husband and said,
> "Who are the Chosin Few?" "I dunno," he said with a shrug of
> the shoulders, "must be some fundamentalist religious group."
>
> I must say Virginia, I was surprised and pleased that one as
> young as you should be a student of warfare, and specifically—
> the Korean War. I'm sure all of us in the Chosin Few agree
> that you picked the "big battle" of that war to concentrate on.
>
> I appreciate Virginia that you are concerned about the im-
> age we project as currently titled. You are right too in saying
> that the title is otherwise appropriate both as relates to geog-
> raphy (Chosin Reservoir) and number of survivors (few). You
> didn't mention this, but I believe the founders of the Chosin
> Few took their cue from Eric Hammel's book entitled *Chosin*.
> Unfortunately, you may also be right in saying that as memo-

---

*We can count on Tootsie Rolls being lavished on us by the Tootsie Roll Corporation
at these reunions.

ries of the total population dims, few will see the title as an association of military warriors.

I enjoyed the analogy you drew of the winter 1944 battle in the Ardennes forest of Belgium—better known as the Battle of the Bulge, or the Battle of Bastogne. Our own battle six years later does indeed have many parallels to the Bastogne event. And how right you are that the term "Battling Bastards of Bastogne" conveys the macho image of John Wayne striding into a western saloon, with sawdust on the floor and ordering a double whiskey straight up. It hurts a bit though to have you suggest that the term "Chosin Few" suggests a warm glass of milk in a convent garden or quiet monastery.

Let me digress for a moment Virginia. I must say that I was surprised, amused, and a bit shocked at your frequent use of the term "bastard" by one of such tender age. The world is changing I guess, and I just have not caught up yet. But my, you are precocious! I do appreciate that you are trying to give us a more macho image and the term "bastard" does that—I guess.

You apparently did some deep research on the term bastard as used in a military connotation. As you pointed out, the troops on Bataan and Corregidor in 1942 certainly felt the term bastard applied to them. I was surprised that you did not mention Wake Island. The date is late December 1941 and the troops on Wake have done a near miraculous job in fending off the first attack by the Japanese. A large and powerful task force sails from Pearl Harbor in relief of Wake. On 20 December a Navy PBY (patrol aircraft) lands in the lagoon at beleaguered Wake Island bearing the news that the relief force is due off Wake Island on the morning of 23 December. Now note the timing Virginia. At 2:15 a.m., 23 December, a Japanese assault force is spotted off Wake. By 2:50 a.m. Wake Island tells the world the enemy is landing. In the meantime, the Wake Island relief task force turns around and heads back to Hawaii. In justice to the task force commander, he was concerned about risking a precious aircraft carrier at this point in the war. If the term abandonment relates to the word bastard, I would suggest the troops on Wake Island also had some justification in viewing themselves as such.

I know we of the Chosin bandy about the term "magnificent bastards" and derivatives thereof. In fact, one of our members here in California regularly runs 26.2-mile marathons. His running attire depicted parka clad Marines marching through the snow—and emblazoned across the top in bold letters are the words "Magnificent Bastards." No problem really—but we were certainly not abandoned. In fact Army, Air, and Navy forces literally held the door open like anxious parents so that we could once again enjoy the benefits of life and liberty in this great country of ours.

So what do we do about changing our title? Your suggestion of "Reservoir Raiders" has a certain "Rambo" ring to it—but military purists could fault us here since the operation wasn't a raid as such. We could ignore the purist in the happy thought that if so titled we could be viewed, at worst, as a macho professional football team.

Perhaps in the grand sweep of time it really doesn't matter, Virginia. As long as the term "Chosin Few" electrifies those of us who were there it shouldn't concern us as to how the rest of the world reacts to the term. One wonders too what Dixon Poole, our national quartermaster would do with all the PX memorabilia he has in stock emblazoned with the term "Chosin Few." And just think of all those letterheads having to be changed.

You suggested my wife or I might have some ideas relative to a "warrior" sounding term. No way Virginia, we are not at all good at coming up with names, as our children Morganlelia, Artinuous and Lastarious could attest to.

I will send your letter on to our Chosin Few President and let him decide whether to pursue the idea of a more "gung-ho" title for the organization. In the meantime Virginia, treasure these youthful years of yours—junior high school can wait.

Respectfully,
Joseph C. Hedrick USMC
ANGLICO-H&S/1/7"

Guerrilla Hunt

The replacements arriving at Mason brought us news from home. We were largely ignorant of what was going on as it related to the national scene. We couldn't believe the song *Mocking Bird Hill* had replaced *Good Night Irene*, the song we sang so lustily in the hills of Camp Pendleton.

Fuel oil heaters kept our tent warm. The food was plentiful and tasty. We even had cots to sleep on. I consider this one of the most pleasant

Christmases I ever enjoyed. Safe for the moment, warm, well fed and in the company of other men with whom I had a shared a common experience at the reservoir. This was "camaraderie" at its best. I also found time to break the camera out again, and in general bring my notes (journal if you will) up to date. At this point Captain Holland left the air team to go back to flying the gull-winged Corsair. First Lieutenant Lawrence Haynes joined us as his replacement. Also leaving us was our battalion commander, Lieutenant Colonel Davis. He moved up as Executive Officer of our regiment as a replacement for Lieutenant Colonel Dawcett who was wounded during the Chosin Reservoir campaign.

In the meantime the Chinese and newly rejuvenated North Koreans pushed United Nations troops well south of the former dividing line between North and South Korea, the thirty-eighth parallel. They also recaptured the capital, Seoul.

In mid-January 1951, we moved to a large rural mountainous area near Pohang, forty miles north of Pusan and along the coastal eastern side of South Korea (see map page 396). That area still had a large number of North Korean soldiers who had been by-passed in our rapid advance north in September and October of the year before. They were now operating as guerrillas. We tried to hunt them down. This gave the new men in the division quasi-combat experience, and the entire division once again became accustomed to field duty. I recall endless trips in trucks as we scurried from one reported guerrilla sighting to another. From my standpoint it did not appear all that productive in terms of enemy casualties or prisoners. I also recall on one occasion being hungrier than I had ever been before or since. Somehow we ended up out in the sticks where the supply chain did not reach us with rations. I kept conjuring up the image in my mind of two eggs, sunny side up.

On the lighter side, we in the air team had a chance to meet the legendary Hollywood producer John Ford. Jay Skidmore, the Navy combat photographer was still traveling with our air team. His boss, Navy Captain John Ford was also located at Pohang. One quiet day Jay took us over to meet him. We soon said good-bye to our good friend Jay Skidmore who had traveled with our air team throughout the Chosin Reservoir campaign. He left us in early February of 1951.

Korean Central Front

In mid-February we began our move to the Central Front (see map page 396). No longer was the military involved in two independent thrusts as occurred in late 1950 in North Korea. Now we had a near continuous front across the width of Korea. As fighting progressed we passed through the towns of Wonju, Hoengchon, Hongchon, Chunchon and Hwachon. A few miles north of Chunchon we re-crossed the thirty-eighth parallel.

First of all we had to travel to the Central Front from our position on the East Coast of Korea. Pohang was approximately 200 miles from our assigned sector on the Central Front. We traveled for two days by what the military calls a "motor march." We troops sat on the wooden seats in the cargo bed of a two-and-one half-ton truck. To add to the discomfort, cargo was stowed down the center of the truck bed. Hot meals were served at the appropriate times. The first night we camped in what started out as a dry streambed. I believe we pitched our two-man shelter tents, but then again we may have slept in the open. It wouldn't have mattered; a cold rainfall around one a.m. turned the creek bed into a small lake. We were back on the trucks by three a.m. and underway in a pelting cold rain. From our open-air seats in the trucks we viewed the desolate countryside. The poverty of the people was so apparent, especially as we drove through towns where ragged children ran alongside the trucks begging.

This was an altogether different war than we experienced in North Korea, completely apart from the cold. In North Korea we were employed as independent spearheads at critically dangerous distances from our supply base. As noted above, on the Central Front in South Korea our divisions were abreast, forming a continuous front across the entire waist of Korea. Something of a routine evolved. We pushed north along the entire front; then the enemy, striking in force at this or that point drove

Guerrilla Hunt and
Korean Central Front

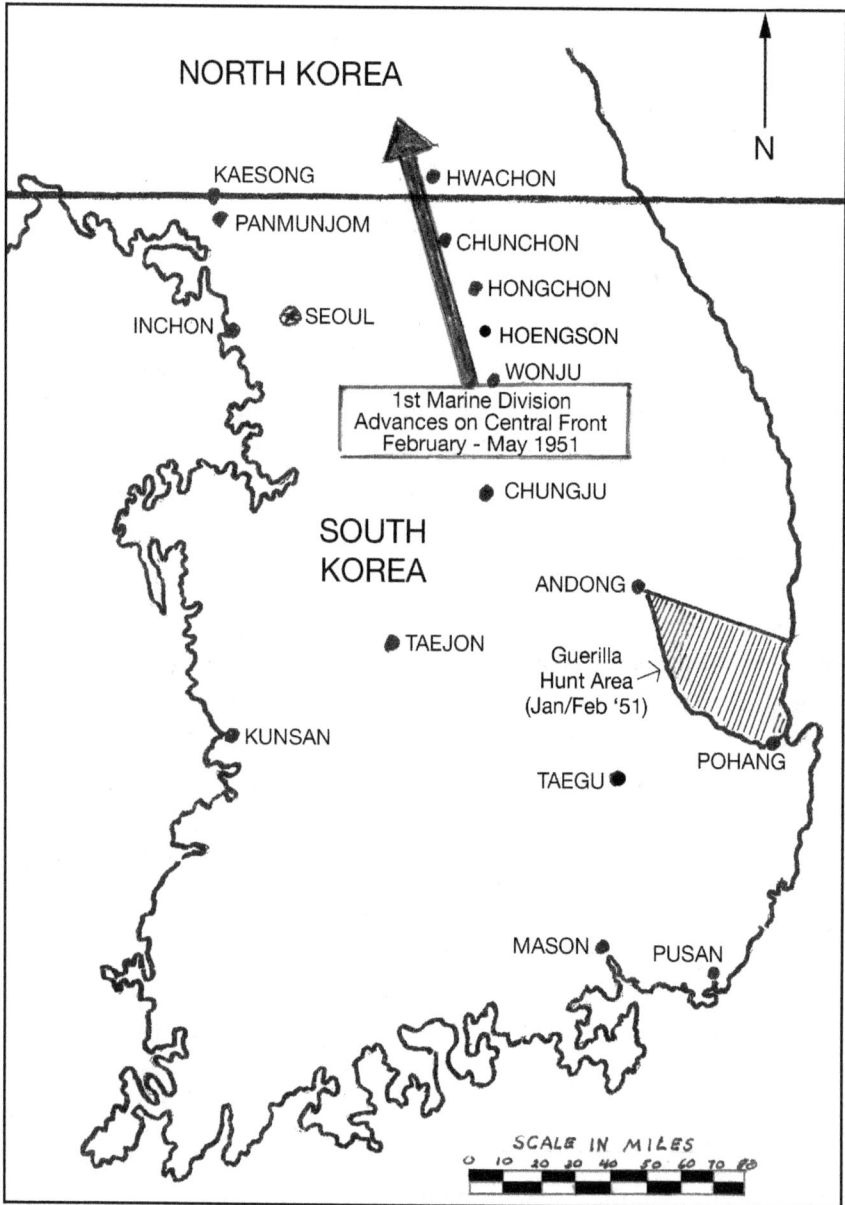

NORTH KOREA

N

KAESONG
HWACHON

PANMUNJOM
CHUNCHON

HONGCHON

INCHON
SEOUL
HOENGSON

WONJU

1st Marine Division
Advances on Central Front
February - May 1951

CHUNGJU

SOUTH
KOREA

ANDONG

TAEJON
Guerilla
Hunt Area
(Jan/Feb '51)

KUNSAN
POHANG

TAEGU

MASON
PUSAN

SCALE IN MILES
0 10 20 30 40 50 60 70 80

a wedge in the line. This invariably caused neighboring units to move back along with the unit(s) that had been hit. After a few miles the enemy, now including revitalized North Korean Army units, advanced beyond their supporting artillery, and in general lost communications with their higher headquarters. If we could move fast enough with the right forces we could hit their open flanks. This pattern was repeated over and over. Some referred to this routine in the same fashion as we did while heading for North Korea by ship, i.e. "Operation Yo-Yo."

The war had changed in other ways too. We had to leave the cots behind when we left Mason, but we were issued inflatable air mattresses. The combination of the mattress and a sleeping bag made life a bit more comfortable. At one point in early summer we swapped our winter sleeping bags for lighter summer ones. If we were in reserve, or if the situation otherwise permitted, the battalion "fired up" its field kitchen equipment and served hot meals. From a supply and labor standpoint it was much more economical to provide food from a battalion mess than by issuing C-rations. The former arrived in bulk form, most in five-gallon cans or large bulk boxes. The pancakes with syrup, canned fruit and beef stew were generally quite tasty: less applause for the dehydrated corn beef and hash, diced potatoes, chipped beef on toast and what passed for scrambled eggs. The coffee was okay, but it heated up our aluminum cups to where one had to sip carefully to avoid burned lips.

Apart from the quality of the food, which I found acceptable, was the regimentation now involved with a meal. Instead of eating C-rations at our own leisure, we had to show up when our unit's time to do so came along. The rifle companies, assuming the front was quiet, took one-third of their troops off the line at a time in the process. Then there was the necessary rigidity of precautions taken to prevent dysentery. Before going through the food line we dipped our mess gear into a fifty-gallon can of boiling water. The water was heated by a temperamental immersion heater having an annoying tendency to explode. Now where to eat? Only a limited number of vehicle fenders or hoods were available to serve as a table. Those inclined to be supple could sit on the ground and cradle their mess gear in their laps. Others had to assume a more clumsy position. A person had to be careful that one side of the mess kit did not flip as he moved about. When we finished eating we had three more cans to parade by. In the first we emptied our left over food. The next two were once again drums of boiling water that rounded out the necessary sanitation requirements. The weather could not be counted on to cooperate with these al-fresco-dining experiences.

Now too we had access, infrequent as it turned out to be, to what was called a fumigation and bath unit. The under and outerwear we were wearing was tossed in a bin before entering the shower. The clothing surrendered was eventually recycled, but in all likelihood you did not see your own again. After showering you literally "rummaged" through bins of clean recycled clothing for an outer uniform that came reasonably close to fitting. Most of us emerged in uniforms that did not fit. Provisions were made for reclaiming your original footwear. I don't recall using this facility more than a couple of times. We had access to this facility only when we were in reserve, and we were rarely in reserve. There was enough quiet time while on the line when we could wash our own clothing, or pay a Korean women to do the job. Bathing in a stream or from a pail or helmet was a common and effective enough method for keeping the body clean.

Another pleasant re-introduction to civilization was the lavish distribution of the Army's newspaper *Stars and Stripes*. The paper was of tabloid size and reflected the Army's version of news events—but it was more creditable than its civilian counterparts. The paper was comprehensive in scope, to include an *Advice to the Lovelorn* column. We eagerly read the paper from cover to cover. Not as lavishly distributed as the newspaper was beer. Once again, if available at all, it would be only when we were in reserve. I remember one such occasion for sure—two at the most. The limit was two cans per man, and we didn't mind at all that it wasn't refrigerated.

Another change from the past was how front line companies were supplied. Our line companies operated for the most part in the hills. Food, water, ammunition, and medical supplies were manually hauled from valley floor roads to where the troops were dug in. In North Korea, the line companies sent working parties to the battalion command post to haul supplies back up. Now an organization called the "Korean Civil Transport Corps" was organized using Korean men too old for military service. Using an "A" frame riding high on their back they routinely muscled loads of 100 pounds or more up the steep hill masses we were operating in. In the process of climbing the steep slopes they bent forward until their noses came close to touching the ground. Each infantry battalion was assigned approximately 100 of these men, but more could be made available if needed. Officially they were called "Cargadors." We referred to them as "Chiggy Bears." They often suffered casualties, as a rule from artillery or mortar fire, but those not wounded invariably kept on moving. They were highly respected and appreciated; and we lavished candy, cigarettes, and rations on them.

Another innovation was the use of searchlights to create artificial moonlight. All that was needed to make it work was a low hanging overcast to reflect the light. Since the enemy usually attacked at night he had to wait for conditions that did not permit this artificial lighting. In the meantime a measure of relaxation for us.

There was a religious ritual that evolved around our day-by-day routine at this time. When weather and the tactical situation permitted, the Catholic chaplain and a few of us gathered for an outdoor rosary service. This was usually after dark, and at some distance from others for the sake of their and our privacy. More often than not the artillery, logically located behind us, was firing interdiction (harassing) rounds over our heads as service proceeded.* At the completion of the rosary a few of us stayed

---

*Our artillery at the time was using proximity fuses. A radar impulse transmitted from the fuse bounced back from the ground to a receiver also in the fuse. The fuse could be set to explode at varying distances from the ground. This resulted in shell fragments covering a wider area. On occasion heavy cloud cells caused these rounds to explode in flight. As a result, we were always a bit nervous when they fired, especially on cloudy nights.

around to sing. I think we sang only one song, *I Don't See Me in Your Eyes Anymore*.* I suspect our voices were anchored in distinctly separate keys, but we viewed ourselves as quite talented. The Chaplain, being a man of refinement, left quickly to seek more elevated company.

While I'm on the subject of religion: mentioned earlier was Father Griffin granting general absolution the day before we first tangled with the Chinese on 2 November 1950. General absolution now became common and was the usual ritual before Mass in the field. As noted, this permitted those absolved of all sins to be able to receive Holy Communion. This in turn assured one their right to enter heaven—assuming the grim reaper caught you along the way. To think of how I used to plot and plan as to when to get in line for confession with Father Mechler. As noted earlier, one method was to avoid following sweet older ladies who might leave Father Mechler with the idea that his parishioners were saints. Better to follow the younger men, or maybe one of the attractive younger women. In other words, play the odds. And here we have general absolution and with no way to take advantage of it. I suspect the Catholic chaplains in our division got together and decided that rather than stand out there in public, and have us come by one by one for confession, to make it easy on the men and themselves by granting general absolution.

Over the next few months we participated in several offenses, all with macho sounding names. For example, there was Operation "Killer" (21 February—3 March 1951); and "Ripper" (7 March—22 March 1951). Now the Chinese were able to bring up their artillery and heavy mortars. This added considerably to our discomfiture. My pictures and related notes show us as constantly moving in the hills, initially snow and ice covered, and often in cold and foul weather. On one occasion we were

---

*I Don't See Me in Your Eyes Anymore
Oh why can't I make them shine as before?
There was a time love was new – life was ecstasy
But now I doubt what the future will be
I hope and I pray – I'll be the one you adore
Then I'll see me – in your eyes as before

moving single file along a knife-edged ridge with a near shear drop-off on both sides. When two in our party slipped they could not stop themselves on the icy slope until they hit a patch of scrub trees in what I estimated to be a hundred yards down the near vertical slope. Bruised and battered they must have been, but after traveling parallel with us for a while, grasping trees as they went along, they were finally able to join up with the column.

The most concentrated loss of American lives in the entire Korean War occurred during Operation Killer. An Army artillery battery, supported by an infantry guard, was moving along a narrow road three or four miles northwest of Hoengsong. They were moving north to support a Republic of Korea (ROK) unit on the front lines. The Army unit bedded down for the night, apparently without establishing a perimeter watch, or an "adequate" perimeter watch. The Chinese attacked the Korean Army unit who broke and ran. Around two a.m. the Chinese swarmed over the artillery men. Of approximately 530 men, only two survived—a corporal and a private. We had just arrived from Pohang and were quickly rushed into the breach. Later that same day our battalion, moving tactically, came upon the ambush site. Moving tactically on this occasion involved two of our rifle companies securing the high ground on either side of the road, while the other rifle company and the battalion headquarters section, which included our vehicles moved along the road. I was with this road bound group on this occasion. I did not see any bodies on the road, but bodies abounded in and around the vehicles right next to the road. I was glad that the segment of the group I was in passed quickly through the area.

One day we passed through what at one time must have been a fair sized city called Chunchon. The city center through which we passed had been totally destroyed. A few miles north of Chunchon our division recrossed the thirty-eighth parallel into North Korea.

Somewhere in the Chunchon area occurred one of those experiences that seems to be indelibly stamped in my memory. This occurred in late February; it was cold—it was dark—and it was raining. The prospects for a decent meal and a reasonably comfortable night's rest did not look promising. We were moving in single file along a crude footpath that angled off a dirt road. We then entered a narrow side valley. The column moved in fits and jerks, which added to our discomfiture. We were all tired so there was no banter—we just trudged along, each lost in his own thoughts. Melancholy might be the word to describe my mood at the time. We came to a farmer's house, a hut really, only a couple of feet off the path. I suspect our passing was a complete surprise to them. The family, numbering about five, stood on what I judged to be a small narrow porch; seemingly completely unafraid as they watched us pass by. The only light was cast by the home's cooking fire. One family member caught my eye; I thought she was an absolutely beautiful young woman. Her perceived beauty seemed completely out of place in this war-ravaged country, and in this remote location. This was a deeply poignant moment for me, and served to further deepen my gloom as I reflected on what deep down most of us yearn for—a home and family of one's own.

In April 1951 I was promoted to Staff Sergeant. A few days later, while kidding around with the rest of our crew I let the "F" word slip out. It surprised and embarrassed me to had done so. I was not at all in the habit of using profanity of any kind, and particularly that inflammatory word. I immediately resolved not to let it happen again. A little later, maybe an hour, maybe a day, Lieutenant Wilson found a private moment to bring this matter up. In a quiet, yet convincing way he delivered a humbling, instructive, and never to be forgotten sermon on the use of profanity. His presentation was short and to the point. He made two points: the first was that having been promoted to the Staff non-commissioned-officer ranks it was now especially incumbent on me not to use foul language in front of juniors: the second was more profound. He suggested that as a Staff NCO, the Marine Corps assumed I could express myself without using profanity. Profound advice! I haven't forgotten that occasion insofar as my own choice of words is concerned, and have used this experience as an example to others when the occasion and relationships permitted me to do so.

In early May of 1951 our regiment (7th Marines), heavily reinforced with tanks, established what was called a patrol base (outpost) approximately six miles in front of our own front lines. A Chinese offensive was expected and this base blocked a likely avenue of approach, in addition to providing early warning of an attack. The Chinese did not seriously molest us, but our own round-the-clock bombardment with the tank's 90mm guns made sleeping difficult. One day we noted smoke covering the hills to our front, a strong indication that the enemy was hiding his movement from air observation by setting fire to woodland. The regimental commander suspected the Chinese were preparing to attack our front lines and would move around our strong outpost. After dark he pulled the 3rd Battalion, reinforced with tanks, back a few miles to a pass. The Chinese plans were in place and they were not aware of this repositioning of our troops at what had been an open pass and logical route to our main lines. That night they wisely passed around what they knew was our strong heavily reinforced regimental outpost. The result was they hit the 3rd battalion lying in ambush. The Chinese were stopped cold, leaving 112 counted dead and 82 prisoners taken. We lost seven killed and nineteen wounded. Two of our tanks were disabled, and a third tank had a close call when the Chinese made an unsuccessful attempt to roll a fifty-five gallon drum of gas against the tank and ignite it. That afternoon the rest of regiment moved back through the carnage to take up a position on the front lines.

Going Home

At about this time Lieutenant Wilson, who had been with us since right after Inchon returned to flying. A Lieutenant Barnhardt was his replacement. Starting in May of 1951 the eight remaining original members of the air team who had landed at Inchon in September of 1950 were replaced by new arrivals. The one exception was PFC Ken

Burns who had his tour in Korea interrupted by a convalescent period in Japan following his being wounded outside of Seoul in September of 1950. These reliefs occurred one by one, week by week, as replacements worked their way down through the division and its needs for communication personnel. A Sergeant, who was my designated relief finally arrived. After a week of his familiarizing himself with the routine, I started my trek home, passing through various administrative headquarters in the process.

The first leg was by truck to division headquarters. After a few days here the group I was in was transported to a rough airstrip where we waited nearly all day for a flight to the Mason area (where I had spent Christmas in 1950). The day was unusually warm, but knowing I was on the way home made the wait acceptable. Again, a few days of administrative processing and I was on my way to Pusan where I would board a ship for home. The few days before boarding ship were spent in "perfect leisure." I remember the food, clearly excellent and all one could eat. Nothing was more pleasing than walking up to the cook at breakfast to order "three fried eggs, sunny side up."

While I was being processed for returning to the states a tragedy befell our air team. The team, along with the rest of the battalion was moving administratively; that is, not under fire or expecting to be under fire. Under these semi-relaxed conditions three men were in the air team's radio jeep, and one on each fender. During a halt the jeep pulled off the road to come alongside another jeep for the assumed purpose of a conversation. The jeep hit a reinforced tank land mine killing all five men. Captain Haynes was killed, along with PFC Ken Burns, who was in all likelihood but days from being detached and sent on his way home. This tragic event took the shine off the joy of my leaving Korea.

So ended my war in Korea—a momentous experience in my life. The old saying, "I wouldn't do it over for a million dollars nor would I take a million dollars for the experience" can be applied here. I had followed the battles of World War II closely from the time the war broke out in

September 1939 through its end in August 1945. Naturally I wondered how I would fare if thrust in the middle of the battles I had read about. My chance came and I am satisfied that I did my job. As it turned out, I marched with rifle companys, to include reconnaissance and combat patrols outside our own lines. Nothing I have ever experienced compares with that of the Chosin Reservoir, and nothing at the Chosin Reservoir can compare to that patrol with Baker Company on 27 November 1950.

CHAPTER **26**

Stateside Duty (1951-1956)

I sailed for home on the USS Black in late August of 1951. This ship was considerably more comfortable than the typical troop ship. We stopped briefly in Kobe, Japan where I was reunited with an old friend. This was my sea bag that had been turned in for storage a year earlier on the way to Korea. It was comforting to once again be in possession of all my military clothing and personal effects.

The trip was otherwise routine, which means boring, but I was happy to be going home. A few hundred miles west of San Diego we began picking up commercial radio stations. One of the songs we heard for the first time, and really liked was Nat King Cole's rendition of *They Tried To Tell Us We're Too Young*. We were given a warm greeting when we docked in San Diego. The Mayor made a welcoming speech and a band played a number of stirring melodies. We were then transported to the Marine Corps Recruit Depot (MCRD) in San Diego to await assignments. What I remember best from those few days in San Diego was a great steak dinner in a downtown restaurant.

Quantico, Virginia

My next assignment was Quantico, Virginia, thirty miles south of Washington, D.C. The combination of unused leave and travel time added up to around sixty days of leave. With all that time I decided to travel by rail. Wisconsin was my ultimate destination, but my first priority was to pick up my Pontiac sitting in a storage garage in Wilmington, North Carolina. Here is yet another cross-country trip by rail. This time though not a troop train. All things considered, I preferred the mixed population to the all males found on a troop train. On the other hand, this was pay your own way coach accommodations for me on this trip, not a more comfortable Pullman berth with meals furnished as was the case on previous troop train cross-country trips.

I found my car all ready for me and then stopped briefly at Camp LeJeune. In my earlier days at Camp LeJeune the population was relatively light. Now its population had exploded, and in that condition the camp was not to my liking. From there I traveled to Greensboro, North Carolina where one of the nurses I had dated before leaving for Korea was working in a hospital. No longer did that "Cinderella" mid-night curfew apply as it did when she was a student nurse. From there I stopped to visit a buddy who was also just back from Korea and on leave in Ohio. In the meantime my family was waiting for me in Wisconsin. As far as they were concerned, I was long overdue. I remain embarrassed for having dawdled along the way.

Time passed quickly, as it usually does when you are on vacation, or as was the case here, on military leave. First of all were the many relatives and neighbors to check in with. High on the list of neighbors was Clarence Dittman. My paternal grandfather Isadore Hedrick, the man who introduced me to the world at a tender age, had passed away while I was in Korea. I would have especially enjoyed having the opportunity to visit with him at this point in my life. I also visited Father Mechler who had been transferred to another parish. My paternal cousin Jim Muehlenkamp, my partner in thirteen years of serving Mass at St. Johns and I spent a pleasant couple of hours with the good Father. I recall spending many days pitching in with the field farm chores, and enjoyed doing so. Evenings seldom found me at home, not surprising given my age and having my own car. I also found time to visit, on two occasions, the young lady I had met the past summer at Pelican Lake in Minnesota.

Somewhere near the end of my tour in Korea I was encouraged to apply for a commission as a Second Lieutenant. I was quite content in my role as a Staff Sergeant, and at the time found it an offer easy to decline. When I mentioned this to my Minnesota date she encouraged me to go for a commission. I was not entirely convinced—but it started me thinking.

On one of my trips to Minneapolis I visited the family of Captain Haynes, one of the men killed when our air radio jeep hit a tank land mine. His was one of those poignant stories that crop up in the course of life in the military.

Captain Haynes served in the Pacific Theater during World War II as a fighter pilot. After the war he settled in Minneapolis, Minnesota where he married and started a self-owned small construction business. His love of flying, and no doubt the additional income, prompted him to stay in the Marine Corps Reserves. He was called back to active duty in 1950. In addition to the sadness of leaving his wife and children, he found it necessary to close down his business as well.

Captain Haynes was a devoted family man. It seems that whenever he had the opportunity to do so he would take out a couple pictures of his family and gaze at them. On those occasions when we were sleeping in a so called "perimeter tent" (designed for eight, but could hold twelve) he would use a flashlight to illuminate the pictures. At times he spoke movingly of his children, a boy aged four and girl two. But for the most part, these were private moments he stole from his busy days. His audience during these private moments was the rest of the air team, to include Lieutenant Wilson. The ten enlisted men of the team were all single, and we were to a man left in respectful awe of his quiet devotion to his family.

I suspect we all learned something about fatherhood and family values from this man.

Naturally I passed on this information to Mrs. Haynes. I would like to think she was comforted to a degree, and that she passed this information along to her children as they grew up.

I am deeply saddened to this day when circumstances arise to remind me of this good and decent man, who hailed originally from McPherson, Kansas. In September of 2002 I visited the McPherson Memorial Park at the County Courthouse in McPherson, Kansas. There on a monument to McPherson's fallen heroes of past wars is the name "Lawrence Haynes" as one who died during the Korean War.

The day arrived when I had to leave home for Quantico. I left myself enough time to visit my pen pal in St. Louis and the Army WAC I had met at Fort Lee, Virginia. She was now on recruiting duty in Fort Wayne, Indiana. I reported in to my new duty station sometime in October of 1951.

I was assigned to a communication unit in Quantico. Our job was to provide communication for field exercises conducted in conjunction with the several military schools for officers at Quantico. Here for the first time since being promoted to Staff non-commissioned officer rank I was able to enjoy the perks that came with this rank. Although there was a separate club for Staff NCOs I was not one for drinking and saw no need to buy my meals at the club. A separate dining area for Staff NCOs was provided in the regular mess hall. After less than three months at Quantico, I had orders to a Navy Radio Technicians school at Treasure Island (San Francisco), California.

Treasure Island (San Francisco, California)

Treasure Island is man made and is connected by a narrow causeway to the "natural" island of Yerba Buena. This latter island of 147 acres serves as a land anchor for the bridge connecting San Francisco and Oakland. Treasure Island's 403 acres was created as the site for the 1939-1940

Golden Gate International Exposition. Construction of the island took place between February 1926 and January 1939. Twenty-nine million cubic yards of sand and gravel were used in creating the island. Some of this material came from dredging the bay; others transported from the Sacramento River delta. The name "Treasure Island" refers to the gold-laden fill dirt that washed down from the Sierra Mountains into the bay. This fill was then dredged and transported to create the Island. At the start of World War II, the Navy leased the Island from the City of San Francisco and remained in control until 1993 when the base was selected for closure and returned to the City and County of San Francisco.

I drove to San Francisco with stops in Fort Wayne (Indiana), Wisconsin, Minneapolis (Minnesota), St. Louis (Missouri), and Tucson (Arizona). Tucson was added since my sister Elaine and her husband had moved there a few months before. My Minneapolis date once again encouraged me to apply for a commission. I have no doubt but that her logical encouragement persuaded me to eventually take that step. Assuming her encouragement was the catalysts for my eventually being commissioned, my family and I have much to thank this young lady for. But there was no time for the necessary academic testing and other administrative process involved until I finished the year of school that lay ahead.

While on this drive across the Western states I was introduced to the Burma Shave brushless shaving cream signs. I don't believe they exist anymore, but in the 1940s and 1950s, before Interstate highways, they could be found frequently along the old two lane well traveled routes—like "Route 66." They were small red signs with white letters. Five signs were spaced about 100 feet apart. Each sign contained one line. For example:

Sign 1	Soap may do
Sign 2	For lads with fuzz
Sign 3	But Sir you ain't
Sign 4	The lad you wuz
Sign 5	BURMA SHAVE

or

Sign 1	If you think
Sign 2	she likes your bristles
Sign 3	walk barefoot
Sign 4	through some thistles
Sign 5	BURMA SHAVE

And how could you not but smile at this one?

Sign 1	My job is
Sign 2	Keeping faces clean
Sign 3	and nobody knows
Sign 4	De stubble I've seen
Sign 5	BURMA SHAVE

These popped up quite frequently along the highways and were helpful in keeping you alert and entertained on long drives.

I found Treasure Island to be resort-like. The clear emphasis was on school, not the military. San Francisco was a mile away across the Bay—and how beautiful it glowed at night. Oakland could be viewed from the eastern side of the Island. Finally, there was Alcatraz Island looming out of the Bay to the northwest.

The Navy portion of the training lasted six months. I found the curriculum tough. I had taken no math courses in high school and this school required a great deal of applied trigonometry. As a result, I stayed close to my barracks home and studied—even though those bright lights of San Francisco beckoned from only one mile away. But it was not all study. I am not sure what prompted me to do so, but shortly after arriving I started taking dance lessons on Friday nights in San Francisco. This was an organization much like Arthur Murray with dance studios throughout the country at the time. This firm operated their chain of studios under the name of "Velez and Yolanda." Not surprising, given their name, they specialized in teaching Latin dances. My favorite was the tango. Once each month the studio held a social for its entire staff and students at a downtown hotel. I found this event increasingly enjoyable as my dancing skill improved.

Shortly after I arrived at Treasure Island I was promoted to Technical (Gunnery) Sergeant (E-6). This was in March of 1952. I had been at Treasure Island about two months when the young lady who had been on recruiting duty in Fort Wayne, Indiana was transferred to the Presidio, an old and picturesque Army post in San Francisco. I maintained my stern regimen relative to study, but did dedicate Saturday nights to dating. Her arrival also ended the dance lessons and the once a month Velez and Yolanda socials. Our relationship blossomed to the point where our marriage had been formally announced. A small wedding was planned. No one from Wisconsin would be able to attend, nor her family members from Pennsylvania. I am not sure of the exact timing, but within days of the planned marriage the Army made an announcement that served to put everything on hold. The Army was planning to develop a helicopter fleet. They were planning to recruit volunteers from all military services for their first batch of pilots. Successful aspirants were to be commissioned Warrant Officers. As much as I loved the Marine Corps, the idea of flying was a temptation I couldn't resist. One "stern" requirement was that applicants be single. I was much too interested in flying to pass this up—and the lady, being Army herself, understood.

As a postscript to this I should mention that it wasn't until nearly sixteen months later that the Army started its helicopter-training program. By this time, I had been accepted for the Marine's Officer training program. Along the way the young lady married a Marine. While stationed in Washington, D. C. they bought a modest three-bedroom home on a couple of acres in Manasses, Virginia. A year later a dam was built—and presto, they ended up with lake front property and riches beyond their wildest dreams.

Marine students who finished the class at Treasure Island were sent to a six-month follow-on technician school at the Marine Corps Recruit Depot in San Diego. The Navy school was primarily devoted to teaching theory as it relates to electronics. The follow-on course in San Diego involved training in trouble shooting and repair of Marine Corps field radios and related communication equipment.

San Diego, California

In July 1952 I journeyed to San Diego via a side trip to my sister Elaine's home in Tucson. The curriculum at this school involved more practical work, but I still felt obligated to hit the books at night and as a rule on weekends too. I rather enjoyed studying and the satisfying feeling that resulted from being all caught up when I launched into the next day of classes. Much to the disappointment of my fellow classmates, who did not have cars, I was not available to provide wheels for liberty runs. But I liked to drive, and on occasion made a weekend trip to Tucson, Arizona.

The Marine base in San Diego is located on the north side of the City's international airport (Lindbergh Field). Initially we lived in Quonset huts at the western end of the runway. Takeoffs were right over our living area since the prevailing wind was from the west. The normal passenger and cargo traffic was noisy enough—but then the super-noisy Convair B-36 bomber arrived. Called the "Peacemaker," this was the largest bomber ever built. Its 230-foot wingspan was just 70-feet shorter than a football field. Six reciprocating engines, all mounted on the back of the wing, powered the bomber.

In 1941, during World War II, it appeared that Germany would soon defeat Great Britain. Development was started on a bomber that could fly from the United States to Europe, drop its bombs, then return. The prototype first flew after the war ended, in August of 1946. Now the big bomber was modified to meet the need for a bomber that could "keep the peace" during the Cold War. To enhance mission capabilities, two jet engines were added to each wing to augment the power delivered by the six "pusher" engines organic to the aircraft.

The Convair plant in San Diego modified the Air Force's fleet of 388 bombers, with the addition of the jet engines representing the major modification. Naturally there were many test flights. Naturally too, takeoffs were right over our Quonset huts. The noise was made somewhat bearable by the thrill of watching those bombers take off. One weekend the school set up a tour of the Convair plant and we were permitted to tour one of the bombers. Here we were, training to be radio technicians where we might have five to ten vacuum tubes in a field radio. It blew our minds to learn that a single B-36 bomber had over 10,000 vacuum tubes to meet its electronic needs.

Living was pleasant at this base, the routine close to strictly academic, and the food at the staff NCO mess is remembered as being excellent. Despite being a "meat and potatoes" farm boy, I sure did develop a fondness for the frog legs served on Friday evenings at the mess.

I finished the class in February of 1953 and was assigned to the Marine Corps Air Wing at El Toro, California. El Toro is located approximately thirty miles south of Los Angeles and less than ten miles from what was soon to be Disneyland. Communication personnel move easily between the ground and air components of the Marine Corps. After my experiences with pilots in ANGLICO, I was quite pleased to be assigned to the Air Wing.

My 1950 Pontiac was now three years old and still running nicely, but I wanted to upgrade. At the time, freight for shipping a new car was charged so much per mile from the factory. If you lived ten miles from the factory the shipping charges were minimal. If you lived in California, the cost was considerably more. As a result, a used car in California commanded a comparable increase in value. I took advantage of this economic bonanza to sell the car before I left California to go on leave to Wisconsin. Another feature of car buying at the time (1953), at least for Pontiac, was that you could order from a dealer and pick the car up at the factory in Pontiac, Michigan thereby saving all the shipping charge. I set the deal up by mail with Rasmussen Auto Sales in Sparta, Wisconsin, the same folks who sold me the 1950 Pontiac.

Cars had grown a bit fancier over the past three years. I might have purchased a convertible had they been making them at the time. Instead, the car I ordered was what was called a hardtop convertible. The two tone color, cream colored bottom and avocado top gave the illusion of it being a convertible, as did the preponderance of glass around the top. It had leather seats and an automatic transmission. The cost was around $3200, and I ordered it sight unseen. My feeling was that if it were a Pontiac, I couldn't go wrong. The vehicle went on to serve as the family car through 1965, and in the process met the transportation needs of five Hedricks.

I had to fly home since I had but a limited amount of leave on the books. When I calculated in the time needed to pick up the new car in Michigan and then travel back to California I was left with only three nights at home, only two after picking up the car. I flew from Los Angeles to Chicago on a rickety, nondescript aircraft run by a charter company. The condition of the seats alone made one wonder how long the aircraft had been in service, and what kind of operators maintained an aircraft in this manner. We made an unscheduled stop at a remote airport in Western Kansas or Nebraska for some maintenance reason. This didn't add to my confidence. Dawn was breaking when we finally arrived at one of Chicago's airports.

As soon as I arrived home I picked up the necessary papers from the dealership. Along with a fellow Summit Ridge friend, Paul Ziegler, we headed for Pontiac, Michigan by rail. We had no problem picking up the car, and after a brief stop to visit Paul's uncle and aunt, we headed back to our homes in Wisconsin. While on the road Paul and I discussed dating. I am not sure who mentioned Paul's cousin, Betty Goetz, but Paul agreed to set up a double date. As noted earlier, Betty was a fellow member of St. John the Baptist Catholic Church. Also mentioned earlier was that a remote corner of her family's farm bordered an equally remote border of our farm which honestly made her "the girl next door." The double date went well and on the next night, my last night at home, Betty and I soloed. Her cousin, my friend Paul Ziegler, had done his duty and could now bow out.

On the trip back to the West Coast my brother Noel accompanied me as far as Tucson where sister Elaine and her husband still lived. I was looking forward to introducing Noel to those Burma Shave signs. We were well west of the Mississippi River when the first one showed up:

> She kissed the hairbrush
> By mistake
> She thought it was
> Her husband Jake
> BURMA SHAVE

Followed by:

> Passing school zone
> Take it slow
> Let our little
> Shaver grow
> BURMA SHAVE

After spending one night in Tucson I hustled off to my new duty station at El Toro, California.

El Toro, California

I was assigned to a Marine Air Support Squadron (MASS). Their mission was to track aircraft by radar and then, via ground-to-air radio, direct pilots on headings that permitted intercept of enemy aircraft. This was the unit's primary mission, but they could also assist friendly aircraft, especially in bad weather or at night. In the case of enemy aircraft, the vector given the pilot placed him on a course where the shorter range radar in his own plane could pick up the target. But for the Korean War I might have been the radar operator in one of those planes, glued to a radar set. More optimistically, I could be piloting the plane.

The rules had changed since the time I was invited to apply for a commission in Korea, especially the education requirement. For the first time in a year I was not involved in military schooling where I had felt the necessity of studying in my free time. I now dedicated my time to studying for a two-year college equivalency test I had to pass as the first step in applying for Officer's Candidate School. There I was, stationed at El Toro, considered one of the best locations from the standpoint of liberty. We were just a few miles from Los Angeles and Hollywood, and here I was holed up during my free time with college level textbooks. In the meantime my brand new Pontiac hardtop convertible sat in the parking lot. Once again, as in San Diego, I had to resist the pleadings of my contemporaries who thought the car should be on liberty runs. For a break in the routine, I occasionally visited my sister Elaine in Tucson on weekends.

In the meantime I was carrying on a lively letter exchange with the "girl next door" back in Wisconsin. I was quite certain that she was the one for me. That was another reason, perhaps the major reason why I found it easy to dedicate my free time to studying.

I took the four-hour long college equivalency test sometime in early May of 1953. In late May the results came back. I was pleased not only to have passed at the two-year level, but also at the four-year level. This turned out to be of major importance since the rules changed while I was in the process of applying to require a four-year college equivalency-passing grade for the officer-training program.

Around the end of May (1953), Betty and I made arrangements to meet in Minneapolis. We were seriously contemplating marriage and as well as we knew each other, and each other's family, it seemed like a good idea to expand on what we could cover in letters. She traveled by train—I by air. One of the benefits of being with an air wing was the availability of flights on weekends. Those pilots who were desk bound during the week did their necessary flying time on weekends. In the process they flew all over the country. I made arrangements for a weekend flight to Minneapolis. The plane was one of those old reliable C-47s (DC-3 in the civilian world). The aircraft was not outfitted for comfort, but the price was right. We left El Toro around noon on Friday, stayed Friday and Saturday night in Minneapolis and then flew back to El Toro on Sunday.*

---

*One of our daughters, in the process of proof reading this script, practicaly screamed in a margin note: "Well??? What happened?"

One of the duties of our communication unit was to set up and maintain the air-to-ground radios. These four channel radios with their heat-producing vacuum tubes had a tendency to drift off frequency after two to three hours. When this happened communication initially became ragged, then stopped. At this point, unless a spare was ready to come on line, a technician had to go through a five to ten minute process to re-tune the set.

On my first field problem with the unit I was something of an observer, yet responsible and embarrassed at the amount of down time. The solution in future field exercises was simple. We took a given radio off the line when it had been operating for two hours, and without the air controllers being aware of it, switched to a fresh radio. A technician then re-tuned the radio taken off the line. The radio was now ready when we rotated back to it later. This system worked like a charm in the next field problem. At a subsequent critique of this particular field problem, the Officer-in-Charge of the Control Center commented that he had never experienced better radio communication. That statement was music to my ears. My boss, the Communications Officer, was particularly pleased. Communications Officers, as I learned later, are rarely patted on the back when it comes to field communications.

As one of the senior non-commissioned officers I also had troop leading administrative type duties, both in the Communication Platoon, and the Headquarters and Service Squadron. Much as in ANGLICO in 1949, I thoroughly enjoyed the role, and in particular the task of conducting close order drill. Once each year a team from Headquarters Marine Corps showed up for an inspection. Part of the inspection involved troops displaying their clothing and equipment, a personnel and weapons inspection, and for selected units, close order drill. Time did not permit the inspectors to observe all the units drilling so they arbitrarily selected one platoon and assumed the rest of the unit was on a par with the one selected. I was hoping my platoon would be selected, so confident was I that they would make a favorable impression. They were selected—and the platoon earned us a high grade.

The next hurdles in the road towards a commission were two appearances before selection committees. The first was at the squadron level, the second at the wing level. A squadron is the administrative equivalent of an infantry battalion, the wing the equivalent of a division.

I felt I had a good reputation in the squadron, but I was not about to take anything for granted when I went up before the squadron personnel interview committee. Nothing was ever said as to how one did on an interview so I had no choice but to sweat it out. About a week after the squadron interview I went before the wing's interview committee. That was the end of the application process as far as my part was concerned. The positives were that I knew my IQ score was high enough, I was within the age limits, and I had passed the necessary four years college equivalency test. Now it was in the hands of the gods, i.e. Headquarters Marine Corps. I knew I had given it my best shot, and if I were selected for the program—great! If not, I was happy in my job and happy to be a Marine Staff NCO as well.

During this period in our history the military was busy testing atomic munitions in the Nevada desert. I remember how disappointed I was at the time at not being able to participate in any of these tests. The tests involving troops called for them to walk among the fallout of nuclear detonations at varying time intervals after detonations. In retrospect, how lucky I was not to have been involved. Many of those who did participate were plagued with twenty-one types of cancer believed linked to exposure to nuclear radiation.

Marriage

Relations between Betty and me had progressed to where a diamond had entered the scene, and the wedding was scheduled for 1 August 1953. Prior to going on leave I had made arrangements to assume the lease of an apartment in Santa Ana, California from a fellow Marine who was being transferred. Three other Marines traveled home with me and were dropped off at various locations along the way. As we traveled along I luxuriated in thinking of how enjoyable the return trip was likely to be with my bride. I arrived home in late July to find a telegram waiting for me. It said in so many words, "Terminate your leave and report to Camp Pendleton immediately."

In July 1953 the French were in the process of losing their war with the North Vietnamese Communist. The 3rd Marine Division, then at Camp Pendleton, was alerted for deployment in conjunction with supporting the French. (At least that is what we were told.) Once again, as occurred during the start of the Korean War, the Marine Corps had to dig deep into its resources to flesh out the division at Camp Pendleton. I was at this point home from Korea close to two years and possessed a military skill needed in the division. With a wedding scheduled for 1 August I gambled on there being a degree of leeway in the word "immediately" as used in the telegram. There was as it turned out, but I needed to report by midnight July 30th. This necessitated moving the wedding day up to July 29th.

This sent the wedding planners into high gear to make arrangements for the new date. The big job was notifying the guests. As it turned out only one couple was unable to attend, and a professional photographer was either overlooked in the frenetic process or was not available on such short notice. Not overlooked was the need for kegs of beer (along with surreptitiously introduced "harder" liquor) and plenty of food. Home movies of the al fresco reception indicate a pretty happy crowd, with many seemingly auditioning for St. John's choir.

The next morning (July 30th), I flew off to California from La Crosse, Wisconsin. What a hell of a way to begin a marriage! Since Betty did not drive at that time, the Pontiac went into the garage on the home farm. Coincidentally, the car was six months old, the same age as the 1950 Pontiac when garaged in conjunction with my going to Korea. I was both proud and saddened by these events. Betty's and my adopted song was *No Other Love*, a popular tune sung by Perry Como. Naturally the song was often played on disc jockey shows and had the effect of dispensing "sweet sorrow" each time I heard it.

Camp Pendleton was once again a very busy place as it juggled people and equipment into place. One morning, a couple of days after I arrived at Camp Pendleton the word was passed that we were to board ship the next day. That same afternoon my unit's First Sergeant sent for me. He had been reviewing service records and noted an entry in mine relative to an application for an Officer's training program. The rule was that anyone awaiting action on this program was not to be sent overseas. I was immediately taken off the unit's list. I don't recall my exact emotion— other than surprise, but I had to be pleased. All this occurred within three or four days of our marriage. But it took a couple of weeks before the dust settled at Camp Pendleton and I could fly home and reclaim my bride.

As a postscript to all this: while underway, presumably for Vietnam, orders were changed and the division was diverted to Japan, and then eventually to Okinawa. The French lost their battle for Vietnam sometime in 1954 with Vietnam ending up a divided country—north and south. But that did not end the saga of Vietnam. In 1965 United States organized combat units entered the country. As for my own personal involvement, I was lucky to have had this conscientious First Sergeant catch that entry in my service record book. But damn, it would have been so much better if someone had caught the entry before I was called back from leave.

After reclaiming my bride and car we "re-ignited" our interrupted honeymoon. We journeyed leisurely to California, stopping to visit my sister Elaine in Tucson, Arizona. Betty now had an opportunity to be introduced to the Burma Shave signs.

> Cautious rider
> To her reckless dear
> Let's have less bull
> And more steer
> BURMA SHAVE

Officer Candidate School (OCS)

Back at Camp Pendleton we rented a furnished apartment in Carls-
bad and I returned to my unit, a 155mm Artillery Battalion. Two weeks
later orders arrived assigning me to Officer's Candidate School at Quantico, Virginia. I have to wonder if I had shipped out with the division,
would I have been sent back to attend the school?

After a leave in Wisconsin we started out for Quantico. I was required to live in a barracks so Betty was dropped off in Madison, Wisconsin. She resumed her old job at the State Capitol while I spent the
next ten weeks in school. In school did I say? This was "Boot Camp" all
over again. Our class numbered approximately 650, about 30 of whom
were enlisted who had entered the program as I did. The rest were men
who had graduated from college that year. The thirty of us were equally
divided among the platoons of officer candidates. A Captain spoke to
those of us who were candidates from the enlisted ranks. He pointed
out that we had to be prepared to go through Boot Camp all over again.
Further, to forget all about our rank (pay for one's rank did continue).
Finally, and this might be the hardest; be prepared to take orders from
men junior to us. We now needed to view the Drill Instructors as we
did when we were privates in Boot Camp. Since we were now in effect
privates, it would have been logical to have us purchase new utility uniforms. The stenciled stripes on the sleeves of our current uniforms were
done with permanent ink. We could, if we chose, sew a patch over the
stripes of the uniforms. Then if we chose to drop out, or were flunked
out, we could remove the sewed on patches. Most of us sewed on patches rather than buy new utility uniforms.

And another Boot Camp experience it turned out to be. Despite
my nearly six years in the Marine Corps, and only one promotion shy
of the top enlisted rank, I had absolutely no problem assuming the role
of a private. The enlisted Drill Instructors were in turn told not to treat
the thirty of us with any deference. There was a change in the language

used by the Drill Instructors. No longer was it "shit birds;" we were now, in deference to all the college men involved, collectively called "educated idiots."

Graduation and commissioning took place on 12 December 1953. My wife and my sister Joan were there for the ceremony. My officer serial number was 063907. There was also a swearing in ceremony, but with a somewhat different oath than I took when I enlisted in January of 1947.* With 597 graduates, only one man from each platoon represented the rest of the platoon in accepting their commission from General Gerald Thomas. I was proud as punch to be that man in my platoon, and to have that honor with my wife and sister Joan in the audience. In a larger sense, I stood 6th out of 597 in the total class, somewhat better than my high school class standing.

When I graduated from enlisted Boot Camp our Drill Instructor shook our hand and presented us with a globe and anchor emblem. This simple ceremony symbolically made us "Marines." Now a different tradition prevailed. We newly commissioned officers stood in a line facing our Drill Instructor. As each of us reached the front of the line, the Drill Instructor rendered the "first salute" we received as officers. We returned the salute, shook hands, then handed him a dollar. I'm not sure what the dollar represented, other than that it was the "first dollar" we spent as officers, and it went to the "first man" who saluted us as brand new Second Lieutenants.

Betty and I rented an unfurnished apartment in Alexandra, Virginia where we lived while I attended a follow-on school for newly commissioned officers. While I finished up the last few days of school, Betty and Joan were furniture shopping in Washington, D.C. My shopping involved purchasing officer's uniforms and a sword.

---

*Officer Oath: I (Joseph C. Hedrick) do solemnly swear that I will support and defend the Constitution of the United States against all enemies foreign and domestic; that I will bear true faith and allegiance to the same; that I take this obligation freely, without any mental reservation or purpose of evasion; that I will well and faithfully discharge the duties of the office on which I am about to enter. So help me God.

After Christmas leave in Wisconsin, we returned to our apartment in Alexandria, Virginia. I began Basic School for newly commissioned Second Lieutenants. Gone was the hassle of the previous ten weeks, but the new regimen remained physically and mentally challenging. The curriculum involved an overview of the many combat arms of the Marine Corps, with a heavy emphasis on infantry tactics at the platoon and company level. In the meantime, Betty found employment with the Department of the Army's Transportation Corps. My transportation to and from Camp Geiger, a remote training camp at Quantico was in a five-man car pool. It took nearly an hour, given the best of road conditions, to make the trip to or from Alexandria. The training involved occasional overnight field problems and others that ran into the late evening hours. Although we all had a bunk in a Quonset hut, I don't recall ever using it in the latter situations. Given just a few hours off duty, we headed for our wives waiting for us in Alexandria.

Two of us came close to being pulled out of Basic School. On 1 March 1954, four Puerto Rican nationalists, sitting in the visitor's gallery, shot up the House of Representatives.* Five Congressmen were injured, one seriously. Apparently an early reaction was to assign Marines to guard the Congress. Another former enlisted man, Frank Frey and I were asked if we wanted to volunteer? I said, "Yes Sir!" However, nothing came of this, but I was pleased to know I had been considered for a job of that nature, and in the middle of Basic School at that.

We graduated in June of 1954. I stood 4th in the total class of 584, and was again my platoon's honor man. Once again I was able to "strut" in the presence of my wife in the role of Commander of Troops in the graduation parade.

---

*The group was angered by Puerto Rico's new commonwealth status with the United States. Lolita Lebron led the group. Shouting, "Long live a free Puerto Rico," she then unfurled a Puerto Rico flag and joined her comrades in firing thirty shots from their Lugers and automatic pistols. President Carter released the four in 1979 after they had served twenty-five years in prison.

Camp LeJeune, North Carolina

After nearly one year in close association with my fellow students, military orders now scattered us to the winds. Betty, now pregnant, and I headed for Camp LeJeune, North Carolina. Logically, given my enlisted communication experience, I was given the military occupation specialty number 2502 (Communications Officer). My assignment was to a communications battalion. If deployed, this battalion's mission was to provide communications for a corps headquarters. A corps commanded by a three-star General normally had two to three Marine divisions and associated air wings in its structure.

In late fall of 1954 we experienced a hurricane (Hazel) that went through Camp Lejeune. We were sent home early from work to ride out the storm with our families. Heavy weather yes, but no extensive damage.

Once again, now for the fourth time, I was slated to return to the Caribbean (Vieques) for maneuvers. Betty was due to deliver in January 1955; I was scheduled to leave in mid-February for maneuvers and be gone ten weeks. Diane Mary was born on January 17. I remember having an overwhelming feeling of responsibility when I learned the news.

A young lady named Eleanor DiMarco stayed with Betty while I was gone. Her husband was also going on maneuvers. This was comforting to me. Our battalion had many heavy communication vans, which all but dictated that we sail on an LST—my favorite ship. We sailed from Moorhead City, North Carolina on 18 February. This was also my first time to enjoy the more commodious officer living quarters, and meals in the wardroom mess (dining room) aboard ship. The maneuvers were routine. Betty and Diane were there to meet me when the LST dropped its ramp in Moorhead City, North Carolina. Betty's diary indicates the ramp of LST 1167 dropped at 10 a.m. on 5 May 1955.*

---

*Betty started a five-year diary on 11 September 1954. To date (December 2005), she has not failed to make a daily entry.

Quantico, Virginia

In late May of 1955, I received orders for a six months Communication Officer's class back in Quantico, Virginia. At about the same time these orders arrived I was promoted to First Lieutenant. We left Camp LeJeune in mid-July and took leave in Wisconsin before reporting to Quantico for school. I was a bit apprehensive about traveling with a six-month old baby, thinking her as being delicate and fragile. Here we were exposing her to the rigors of the road at such a tender age. When we arrived at Betty's home, one of those moments "frozen in time" occurred. Our daughter Diane was the first grandchild on Betty's side of the family. After Betty greeted her mother, Diane was brought from the back seat and presented to her grandmother. This was more than grandmother could handle. I saw the tears in her eyes as she quickly turned away, in embarrassment I suspect, to hug that little glob of protoplasm.

We arrived at Quantico in mid-August and found a comfortable upstairs apartment to live in for the next six months. The schooling too was comfortable. The curriculum involved communications to support the elements of a Marine division and air wing. One of my associates in the class was a First Lieutenant Al Gray. Al and I were assigned to the same unit after graduating from the school. Al became a four-star General and the Commandant of the Marine Corps from 1987-1990.

Graduation was in early March of 1956. Much to my surprise and pleasure, my orders permitted me to take the family to Japan. At that time a rare occurrence for a Marine to be able to take his family along on an overseas assignment. There was an initial one-month Navy school at Imperial Beach, California (San Diego area). From there we were assigned to the Naval Communication Station at Kami Seya, Japan. Kami Seya was located approximately ten miles west of Yokohama.

Our vagabond family traveled by car to California via our homes in Wisconsin. The mid-west was having heavy winter weather at the time so we were happy when we reached the warmer climes as we traveled southwest. The Burma Shave signs were still there:

>Trains don't wander
>All over the map
>'Cause nobody sits
>In the engineer's lap.
>BURMA SHAVE

We stopped in Tucson to introduce Diane to my sister Elaine and her husband Fran. Then we traveled to San Diego and four weeks of school at the Naval Communication Station (Imperial Beach).

CHAPTER 27

Japan with Family

While attending the one-month Navy school in the San Diego area, we lived in a small-furnished upstairs apartment on the beach in the city of Imperial Beach (the most southwestern city in the United States). Although the family could live in Japan, they had to wait for transportation while the unit and I went on ahead. In mid-May, Betty and Diane went to stay with my sister Elaine in Tucson until she was cleared to travel to Japan. My unit, titled the "First Special Communications Platoon," hitched a ride on a Navy Cargo ship out of Oakland, California to Japan. I took our car as far as Oakland and turned it over to the military for shipment. Like Betty and Diane, the car had to wait for travel space before joining me. The car arrived first, a blessing to have a vehicle when Betty and Diane arrived.

Our unit arrived at Kami Seya in early June. My previous exposure to Japan had been a one-day stopover while enroute to and from Korea in 1950 and 1951. Now I was able to see the real Japan; the farm fields, antiquated vehicles and roads, bomb damage, and the people of Japan. My general impression was that this was an impoverished country. Not surprising since the war had been over only eleven years ago and Japan was a devastated country in August 1945.

A pregnant Betty received her permission to travel to Japan in July. She and Diane flew. My sister Elaine escorted Betty and Diane to San Francisco to help out, and see them off on the flight. Their aircraft was one of those legendary commercial aircraft of the time, a TWA Constellation, called the "Super Connie." They arrived in Tokyo on 27 July 1956. The Pontiac and I met them at Tokyo's Haneda airport. We lived in a hotel apartment in Yokohama for ten days, (fifty-two dollars a week) then moved to a furnished rental home in the little community of Tsuruma, three miles from my duty station. This was a privately owned rental and we lived here until government housing became available.

The house in Tsuruma was part of a small complex of similar styled homes. The home was a single story ranch type having a living room, kitchen with eating area, bathroom and two bedrooms. A kerosene space heater sat in the living room. The rent was 216,000 yen (sixty dollars) per month. Although other military families lived in Tsuruma and the adjacent equally small town of Minami-Rienken, our immediate neighbors were all Japanese.

We settled in one day, and that night I went on duty at midnight for my eight hours watch in a communication center. Betty and Diane were spending the first night in the new community surrounded by complete strangers, and fairly recent former enemies. Her discomfort led to a fitful night that came to the attention of a Japanese night watchman. From the dirt road next to the house he said, "Oksan (wife) okay?" This brief statement by the watchman, said in a tone of voice that conveyed concern and sympathy, comforted her and now sleep came easily.

Now a new domestic experience for Betty. A maid! Yoko joined us within days of moving to Tsuruma. Betty had grown up as the oldest of five girls on a farm.* That meant a great deal of farm work along

---

*A brother, the baby of the family, was seventeen years younger than Betty.

with pitching in on housework. After high school she went to work full time, then marriage and a child. Now she and the other young military wives were relieved to a great extent of housework. Baby sitting also was taken care of. All this gave the ladies a great deal of free time for shopping and socializing. As a result, we enjoyed frequent get togethers with other military families who lived in these two small Japanese communities.

Differences between our culture and the Japanese often showed up—many times in humorous ways. The first time Yoko did our laundry Betty noticed the pants and shirts were hung on the clotheslines right side up—the way they were worn. We Americans usually hang them upside down (pant waist closest to the ground).

I often took our then eighteen month old daughter on walks around the neighborhood. All of the streets in Tsuruma were dirt. The Japanese women found this little "round-eyed" American to be something of a curiosity and smiled broadly as we exchanged pleasantries. If it were morning we greeted each other with "Ohayo Gozaimasu," "Konnichi wa" at midday; and "Kombau wa" if it were evening, ending up with "Sayonara" when we said goodbye. Diane and the little children her age we met had absolutely no problem at all with language. When Diane got a sandbox we often found like-aged Japanese children playing with her. The sand came from the beach at Kamakura. This was black sand, the result of volcanic action over the years in the area. A large quantity of sand was hauled from the beach at Kamakura to sand boxes in our yard over the next few years. Frequent festivals were held in the center of town, which was only a few blocks from our house. Little Japanese children in traditional garb tried to catch fish in a portable fishpond. Enjoyed too were the frequent mini-parades passing by our house. One man beating a drum we called the "bang-de-bang-bang man" led them. Little children in costumes and colorful banners marched in the entourage.

While we were living in Tsuruma (October 1956), Egypt seized control of the Suez Canal from the British and French owners precipitating an international crisis.* A nuclear exchange was a possibility had the Soviet Union intervened forcefully on the side of its Egyptian ally. Atsugi Naval Air Station, a couple of miles west of us was considered a prime target. I thought it prudent to show Betty where there was a dike in a nearby rice paddy that could at least provide blast protection should worse come to worse.

Kami Seya Naval Communication station was involved in what at the time was a "hush-hush" operation. All our wives knew was that we worked either in a building enclosed by a strong fence with controlled entry or in a tunnel equally well guarded. I can now say that we were involved in intercepting the then enemy's communications, breaking their codes, and analyzing their electronic traffic. Not all intercept was performed at Kami Seya. Some took place aboard aircraft, surface ships, and submarines.

Our detachment of Marines, along with a similar detachment that went to Europe, was the Marine Corps re-introduction to a type of clandestine work not seen since World War II. My first job was as a Watch Officer in the Communication Center. The many chattering teletype machines and related communications equipment used for encrypting and decrypting messages initially overwhelmed me. I was apprehensive too about having an all Navy crew. Heretofore my association with sailors had for the most part involved staying out of their way when aboard ships. I quickly learned their names, and with their help, the routine. We soon became a proficient, indeed a spirited team. Then there came that sad day for me when after six months I was transferred to another department. I enjoyed my association with those young sailors, as well as the party they threw for me at a bar on "Cherry Hill" in Yokohama. (Cherry Hill is further described below.)

In December (1956) our name came up for government housing. Our new home was in Yokohama at a place called West Bluff. This was

---

*This led to Israel, France and Great Britain invading Egypt. The United Nations, with the "strong" support of Russia and the United States ended the fighting and arranged a peace agreement.

a small complex with five other military families. A Japanese girl's middle school was across the street and two foreign embassies bordered another side of our complex. The ridge we lived on overlooked the city of Yokohama. A Japanese Catholic Church was a few blocks away along the ridge. We had a two-bedroom two-story duplex home. We were allowed to ship by express a certain amount of personal items before we left the states. For the most part this was clothing and a limited amount of small kitchen appliances, dishes, etc. The express shipment was available when we moved into the rental unit in Tsuruma. Our final shipment of furniture and other household goods was delivered to our new quarters. This was a much larger home than we had in the past so there was the need for additional furniture. Not to worry; the Army administered military housing in Yokohama, and did so to most everyone's satisfaction. We visited a warehouse showroom of sorts where, based on our size home, we could select what was needed to completely furnish the new home.

The Army also functioned as a middleman in providing maids once we moved into government quarters. The Army ensured that maids employed by military families met security and health standards. We interviewed three applicants with the help of an interpreter. The lady we employed was Keiko, a middle-aged widow with a grown son. She arrived around seven a.m. six days a week. Unless needed for baby-sitting, she left around seven p.m. Keiko worked for us the next two and one-half years and became, in many ways, a member of the family (and a lifetime friend).

At this point in time the rubble of World War II bombing had been hauled away. Still, many open spaces were to be seen where buildings had once stood. We took frequent walks throughout our neighborhood. We lived within easy walking distance of a small zoo and a shopping center in what was called China Town. Carnivals and mini-street parades catering to children were also frequent occurrences here. As in Tsuruma, the Japanese women seemed to be particularly fascinated by our little "round-eyed" daughter. Naturally as parents we enjoyed their attention.

Another novel experience for us all was adapting to driving on the left side of the road. This was made all the more difficult since our American cars had steering wheels on the left side. We seemed to adjust with no problem to this change in our driving routine. We also had to adjust to the speed limits shown in kilometers on roadside signs. Something of a cultural shock, particularly for the American ladies, was the Japanese driver not hesitating for a moment to stop their vehicles in traffic if they had to urinate. It mattered not at all that vehicles stacked up behind them as they stood in the open on the side of the road to relieve themselves.

At the time we were in Japan the great majority of Japanese vehicles were basically motorcycles with a relatively large truck bed supported by two rear wheels on an axle. Naturally we called them "three wheelers." Like a motorcycle, they were steered by handlebars. They were grossly under powered and to end up behind one loaded down with cargo and/or while climbing any kind of a hill was torture for those of us on a schedule. The masses rode trains, busses, bicycles, or walked. On one occasion the wife of one of the Navy officers at Kama Seya had car trouble on her way to the base. The gate sentry could not believe his eyes when a "three wheeler" chugged up to the gate to drop off this young lady. Where she found a seat I don't know.

On one occasion Betty was making the ten-mile drive from our home in Yokohama to the base at Kami Seya where I worked. Along the way the car broke down and there she was alone on this stretch of highway. Helpful galleries of Japanese men pushed the car into one of the nondescript gas stations on the side of the road. Now a language problem came up as the Japanese mechanic attempted to tell Betty what was wrong. A telephone call, with some difficulty, was made to our maid Kieko who acted as an interpreter. What the Japanese mechanic was trying to explain to Betty was that a rod connecting the accelerator to the carburetor had disengaged and he reconnected it. Further, there was no charge—although Betty insisted on paying him something.

We moved into government quarters on 19 December 1956. We had hardly settled in when it came time for delivery of our second child. An Army ambulance was called at 5:30 a.m. on 24 December to transport Betty to the Camp Zama Army hospital at Sagami Hara. The twenty-mile trip over rough roads did not hasten the birth. Cathryn Ann was born around three p.m. that day. The telegram we sent home to unsuspecting family members said something along the line of "Cathryn Ann, weight seven pounds, three ounces was born on Christmas Eve and joins us to wish you a Merry Christmas." Two weeks later, on 8 January Betty developed an infection and spent the next ten days back in the hospital. That first night, with two children, one not yet two, the other two weeks old was a traumatic one for me. To add to my problems, both had colds. I doubt that I slept a wink during the night. I was one happy guy when Keiko showed up the next morning. Keiko made arrangements to stay full-time on the job until Betty came home from the hospital.

My new job was as an assistant to a Naval Officer-in-Charge of a department where men on watch worked around the clock intercepting target country communications. One of the four watch sections was made up of Marines from our detachment. I was now back on a regular daytime work schedule. Two of the Navy watch sections threw a party each calendar quarter at a bar they had adopted on "Cherry Hill." Cherry Hill was actually in the flat lands of Yokohama, notorious for its bars that doubled as houses of ill-repute. Betty and I were invited to the first of these parties that came along after I joined this department. The Navy Chief of this department, "Red" Carpenter, took me aside for a little counseling. He advised me that these parties were "bawdy" and that the bar's stable of prostitutes would be present at the party. The Chief didn't know whether or not this might be repulsive to Betty, and thought it best he warn me. I confirmed that the wife of the Naval Officer-in-Charge was also planning to attend.

We went to that first party and to other similar parties during the six months I was in this department. This was quite a series of experiences. The parties were indeed bawdy and lively. Betty had no complaints relative to how she was treated by the assemblage, to include the young Japanese women who were in awe of these two "round-eyed" women in their midst. This was the first time Betty had been introduced to the uni-sex toilet (benjo) facilities common in most bars and some restaurants in Japan. The toilets had no partitioned stalls or urinals as such. What you basically found was a floor level angled concrete trough. Men and women squatted or stood next to each other. It may have been embarrassing for some—but when nature calls! Perhaps those bumper stickers that read "Sailors have more fun" have some validity.

My next assignment was in the Operations Division. I was now back on a watch standing basis. This routine involved being on watch two days (eight a.m. to four p.m.), then two eves (four p.m. to midnight), followed by two mids (midnight to eight a.m.), then two days off. We found this to be a comfortable schedule domestically speaking. Plenty of time to meet our shopping needs with ample times to travel around Japan as well. A must was to visit the Great Buddha in Kamakura and the hot springs (baths) at Atami where both private and public facilities were available. Atami also had a reputation as a shopper's paradise. We men were ever ready to take our wives shopping in Atami. And what the heck, since we are here why don't the two of us visit the baths? Nightclub shows in To-kyo were popular too, especially for the men. The Japanese were not at all puritanical when it came to their nightclub acts "showing some skin," much like Las Vegas today. Then there was Mount Fuji, at 12,500 feet the highest mountain in Japan. The Japanese have a saying that there are two kinds of fools in Japan; "Those who climb Mount Fuji and those who do not." My friend Jesse Goldstein and I were two who did. We started out at dawn and reached the top around three p.m. The downward trek took about three hours.

Shopping was big time as well. The exchange rate was 360 yen to the dollar. The bargains were in clothing, china (dishes), pearls, crystal glassware, electronics, and a variety of other goods peculiar to the Orient. A twelve-piece place setting of Noritake China cost around nineteen dollars. Another ten dollars covered postage. Several members of Betty's and my family were recipients of these china shipments.

Around the two-year point of my tour, I was assigned as Officer-in-Charge of a detachment of sailors aboard the fleet air craft carrier U.S.S. Hancock (CVA 19). Our duties were along the same lines as those at Kami Seya. The Hancock was commissioned on 15 April 1944 and was hit by a kamikaze off Okinawa in 1945. In conjunction with her battle damage repair, she was given an angled flight deck to permit simultaneous take-offs and landings. As a history buff of World War II, I was keenly aware of the major contribution of aircraft carriers to winning the war in the Pacific. For that matter, carriers remain one of the better ways to show the flag today, and of delivering an offensive punch as well. I still marvel at the fact that we spend billions of dollars to build a modern aircraft carrier. We then put 5000 men and women on it. Then we employ a screen

USS Hancock (U.S. Navy photo)

of several ships and a submarine to provide protection. At this point how many billions of dollars have we invested? How many military personnel are involved? Next we send them all 7000 miles from home. The result after spending all those billions of dollars and employing all those personnel is that 100 young men; the pilots, will do the work for which this entire armada was launched—each of them is the "Captain" of his ship i.e. airplane. Quite a difference from the time when surface ships slugged it out with long range guns.

It pained me to leave the family, but what an experience this assignment was likely to be.

I left home on 15 May 1958 for my assignment on the Hancock. This was the first time since the days of World War II that a Marine officer was assigned as I was to a carrier group in this type of duty. The Hancock at the time was in Subic Bay in the Philippines. I flew to the Air Force's Clark field (near Manila) in the Philippines. From there a vehicle took me to Subic Bay where I boarded the ship. The Navy officer, with whom I shared a cabin, met me and did his best to orient me to this floating city of 5000 souls.

We were underway for only a few hours when the ship's aircraft arrived from the airfield at Cubi Point in the Philippines. This was Air Group Fifteen which sported an interesting mix of aircraft ranging from jets to the soon to be phased out AD propeller driven Skyraiders. I was an interested observer to this spectacle. A little later I was checking in with my new boss, Captain Fisher, who was the Intelligence Officer on the staff. While we were talking, the Captain was informed that a package of top secret classified material needed to be picked up back at Cubi Point. He knew I had the proper security clearance to serve as a courier, and how handy could I be? "Lieutenant" he said, "have you ever been catapulted off an aircraft carrier?" "Never Sir," I replied. "Would you like to be?" he said. "You bet I would Sir," I replied. The aircraft (C-2) was the standard two-engine propeller workhouse used for logistics purposes, i.e. mail, critical parts, personnel, etc. The plane was nicknamed "COD" for

Carrier Onboard Delivery. If the flight deck had been clear the aircraft could have taken off without the need for a catapult assist. But since the air group had just arrived their planes were still crowding the flight deck.

The catapult shot was a thrill to say the least. A short flight took us back to Cubi Point where another courier was waiting to deliver the package of classified material to me. We also picked up a young sailor who had returned too late from liberty to catch the ship when she sailed. He was still angry with his girlfriend for not waking him in time. He asked me if I thought he might be charged for being AWOL (absent without leave) for missing the sailing of his ship? "After all," he said, "I will be back so soon." I suppose an analogy here was like being just a little bit pregnant. He seemed to be an altogether decent young man and appropriately frightened at what might be in store for him. He confirmed that he had not been in trouble before. I don't know precisely how I replied. I had been observing Navy Chief's operating for over two years and I knew they handled many disciplinary problems at their level—many times in a "tough love" father-son like scenario. I mentioned that the Chief of his division might take care of the matter and his record would stay clear.

The day was bright and clear and the carrier came into my view from twenty miles out. The landing was smooth; the stop via the arresting wires was abrupt; the experience great for a non-aviator. I couldn't help but reflect again that but for the Korean War, I might be flying planes off a carrier. After all, Marine flyers are carrier qualified and Marine squadrons routinely are assigned to carriers.

This round trip took little more than two hours. After delivering the classified material I resumed my interview with Captain Fisher. He then took me up to meet Rear Admiral Paul Ramsay, who appropriately enough was on the Admiral's bridge.* He was the commander of a two-aircraft carrier group with supporting ships called "Carrier Divi-

---

*The Admiral's bridge is one level above the Captain's bridge from where the ship is controlled.

sion One." We were part of the Seventh Fleet. Our immediate job was to patrol the straits between Taiwan (Formosa) and the Chinese Mainland. At this point in world history, Communist China was threatening to take over two small islands, Matsu and Quemoy, a few miles off the Chinese mainland. A crisis developed and for a time it looked like the United States might have to come to the aid of the Nationalist Chinese in defense of these two islands. Our country was geared for a shoot out if necessary. President Eisenhower addressed the nation to warn us of what might happen if worse came to worse. Luckily the crisis blew over, but these were anxious days.

Up to this point I had not inter-related with flag rank officers. I had walked across a stage on a couple of occasions to shake hands with a General in conjunction with school graduations. While at Kami Seya, I formed an honor guard of our platoon of Marines from time to time and escorted an Admiral during his perfunctory inspection. Now I had close and relatively frequent contact. I don't recall being in awe of the Admiral's two stars, but I certainly was impressed.

This apparently was a quiet time for the Admiral as he led me along in a rather lengthy, altogether pleasant conversation. All the while he was puffing on a cigar. He commented on how unusual to have a Marine on his staff and had many questions about my experience on the ground at the Chosin Reservoir. (He had served on a carrier in the Korean area during the war.) At one point he reached for a tablet and had me sketch out certain geographic details related to the Chosin Reservoir campaign. He asked if I had ever been on an aircraft carrier before? I replied that I had not. (I suspect I was the only officer on his staff who wasn't a Naval Aviator.) He took a genuine interest at this point, and on later occasions to explain the intricacies of carrier flight operations. He suggested that his bridge was a great place to view flight operations, and when my duties permitted I was welcome to observe the action from this vantage point. I thought it considerate of him to extend the invitation, but thought it presumptuous of me to accept. A few days later, an officer from his bridge called my office to say that if I wasn't busy a certain event was about to take place that the Admiral thought I might like to observe. From then on when I visited, and after greeting the Admiral when he was present and not busy, I slipped into the background unless and until he beckoned me from my viewpoint in the shadows.

My primary official job related contact was with the Intelligence Officer, Captain Fisher who I met with several times each day. On occasion, I attended meetings in a conference room involving the Admiral. I missed my family, but what an experience for this former Wisconsin farm boy. In addition to having a great crew of hardworking sailors, my quarters were comfortable and the food excellent. Stewards took care of all the housekeeping duties. Then too I had this smooth working relationship with the boss. Apart from being away from the family, I was enjoying myself. Being on the ship twenty-four hours a day, with flight operations going day and night offered many opportunities to view the raw drama of takeoffs and landings. I remember only one occasion where I was present when an emergency developed. One of the jets was having trouble making a night landing. The jet had been waived off two or three times. After the last wave off I noted the crew readying the deck for what I assumed could be a crash landing. Luckily, on the next attempt the plane landed safely.

The ship's home port was in Yokosuka, approximately twenty miles from where we lived in Yokohama. We were back in Yokosuka two weeks after I had flown to Subic Bay to meet the ship. Betty was there to meet me. I remember waving to her from the end of the flight deck. It seemed like she was a mile away from the high vantage point I occupied. She had never been on a ship before. Imagine what an introduction the aircraft carrier was for her. I enjoyed escorting her to lunch that day in the wardroom of the ship. I took advantage of my official membership in the Officer's mess aboard ship to entertain our friends from the home base at Kami Seya while we were in port as well.

We were in port about a week and then back to sea for a six-week stint. I remember frequent VIP (very important people) demonstrations during this period. High ranking foreign officers and civilian leaders from the area were flown on board by helicopter. Then the Navy put on their show—all to impress the visitors with our firepower and what we were capable of doing. I was impressed as well.

From time to time I visited the mess deck to see how the men in our detachment were faring (there was rarely a complaint). One day while on a tour, the Duty Chief on the mess deck was escorting me when we heard someone yell, "Lieutenant." Here was a young sailor deeply involved in the food preparation business. "Remember me?" he said. I certainly did: I had not completely put out of my mind the young man who flew back to the ship with me after he had missed the ship's sailing at Subic Bay. With the Chief an amused observer, he went on to tell me that indeed the Chief of his division gave him a royal chewing out and put him on mess duty (rarely a desired chore)—but his record remained clear. While on mess duty he impressed the people he worked for and they invited him to transfer to the galley to be trained as a cook. He told me he thought he had found his niche. The Chief suggested that if I had a "cast iron stomach" I might be willing to try the dessert (cake) this man was involved in baking. I was properly complimentary in conjunction with the large piece of cake served. I saw this young sailor from time to time when I visited the mess deck and on each occasion made it a point to ask how he was doing. He was in turn always upbeat so apparently all worked out well for him.

Given the tense situation relative to the Quemoy-Matsu crisis, we did not make a scheduled liberty in Hong Kong. We generally patrolled the straits between Formosa and the China mainland. On several occasions we enjoyed welcome returns to our home port of Yokosuka for a few days.

The ship was in port and I was at home on 23 July 1958 when Japan was hit hard by a severe typhoon named Alice. We took the necessary precautions, as we did in 1954 during hurricane Hazel while stationed in North Carolina. We made sure we had candles, water, food, blankets, etc.

handy. We had a few tiles blow off our roof that damaged the car. Four homes at Kami Seya lost their entire roofs. Alice caused a great deal of damage as she swept through Japan.

Orders to Camp Pendleton, California arrived that would take us back to the U.S. in November 1958. Sometime in October I was detached from the ship. Naturally I was happy being home, but I did miss the routine of shipboard life and especially the people I worked with and for. This of course is a part of military life played over and over. Establishing roots and friendships over a period of months or a couple of years—then being uprooted to begin the process all over again. On balance, a healthy process since it forced one to make new friends and was an especially important ingredient in professional growth as one's job experience changed and responsibilities increased.

We both found it particularly hard to leave the friends and work associates at Kami Seya with whom we had lived and worked for close to three years. Since we all had a maid there was an active social scene, both at military clubs and with each other in our homes. The ladies especially were destined to miss those maids in the future. Our maid Keiko had been with us for nearly all the time we had been in Japan. She was in many ways a surrogate mother to our two daughters. Unfortunately, neither of them remembers Keiko.

We shipped our car home far enough in advance of our leaving to ensure its availability when we arrived in the states. Our mode of transportation home was by ship. In mid-November we boarded the USNS Barrett in Yokahama. Betty was pregnant. She had "smuggled" a child into Japan, now she "smuggled" one out. It turned out to be an unusually rough crossing along the great circle route in the North Pacific. I thought I had experienced rough rides on flat-bottomed LSTs around Cape Hatteras (North Carolina), but this was much worse. Betty, in part due to her pregnancy, experienced discomfort from seasickness. We had to lash Cathy's crib down to keep it from sailing on its own. Diane and I generally roamed the ship, catching all the activities appealing to a four-year-old.

We arrived in San Francisco on 15 November 1958. We were housed in quarters at the Army's Presidio* in San Francisco. I was required to check in with a Marine organization at 100 Harrison Street in the city. The person endorsing my orders, noting that I was a First Lieutenant, mentioned the selection list for Captain was out—and did I want to see it? Well, yes and no. One is usually a bit apprehensive when looking for your name on such an important document. No news sometimes is good news. But I did check—and my name was there.

The next day I picked up the Pontiac waiting for me in an Army dock side compound. After outfitting the car with four new tires from Sears, and spending one more night at the Presidio, we headed for Camp Pendleton. Our initial home was a rental unit in the neighboring town of Oceanside. We spent Thanksgiving and the Christmas holidays in this altogether comfortable little home at 1822 South Tremont Street.

*An old Army post established in 1846 during the Mexican-American War. The Presidio's 1000 acres is located on the south side of the Golden Gate Bridge. In the late 1890s coastal defense batteries were established on its western bluffs. The Presidio was turned over to the National Park Service in 1997.

CHAPTER 28

Military Duty Station 1958-1972

Camp Pendleton, California

My assignment at Camp Pendleton was to a Communication Battalion, a sister unit to the one I had been in during 1954 at Camp Lejeune, North Carolina. How logical this assignment was. For the past three years I had been part of a unit that "exploited" the other fellow's communications. Now I was in an organization whose mission it is to communicate via electronic means. Now the other fellow will in all likelihood be attempting to intercept and exploit our communications. The Marine Corps had every right to expect that I had learned something from my Kami Seya and USS Hancock experience as related to communication security.

My promotion to Captain came along and I became the Executive Officer of a Communication Company. To the uninitiated, the Executive Officer, whether on board ship, in an aircraft organization or a ground unit is second in command of the unit. He is much involved with the paperwork leaving the Commanding Officer (CO) free to command. He is also much involved with discipline, and in general, with ensuring that the CO's policies are carried out. In his role as disciplinarian he is often viewed by the troops as the "bad guy." He played this role too so that the Commanding Officer can be seen as "above it all" by the troops.

In January of 1959 we moved into quarters aboard the base at Camp Pendleton. The family as a whole spent four years in this home. With my overseas times, I spent fifteen months less.

About this time I began the process of earning a college degree. Although I had passed a four-year college equivalency test, military authorities recommended we earn a degree from an established college. The Marine Corps had a program to achieve this goal. If through night school classes and/or correspondence courses you worked your way through the junior year of college, you were eligible to at least be considered to attend a civilian college full-time for your senior year. This was titled "The Boot Strap Program" i.e., pull yourself up by your bootstraps. My first college level class was in accounting. This was a night school class sponsored by Palomar College and held in Oceanside, California.

On 8 July 1959 our third daughter, Joyce Lynn was born at the Naval Hospital at Camp Pendleton, less than a mile from our home.

In late 1959 our battalion participated in an amphibious landing exercise in Formosa (Taiwan). We were gone for three months. Our heavy communication equipment, much of it carried in two-and-one-half ton trucks, dictated that we sail on a LST. LSTs are slow. We spent thirty days, yes, thirty uninterrupted days sailing to Formosa. We did not see another ship or any land during the entire thirty-day trip. As far as I know we sailed in an absolutely straight line, given the necessary correction for the world being round. Day after day when one looked astern (back) all you saw was the ship's wake, straight as an arrow. I don't recall any foul weather, or that the swells (waves) were ever more than one to two feet wavelets. Betty should have been so lucky in 1958 on her trip home from Japan across the North Pacific.

I loaded myself down with college level correspondence courses from the University of Maryland, and in my free time I worked on these. A private stateroom made this task all the easier. We had well trained and well behaved troops in our unit. Troops do not as a rule get into much trouble while aboard ship. The temptations found in the cities while on liberty are far removed, as is the related possibility of coming in late from liberty. Then too, alcoholic beverages are not allowed aboard naval ships. I accompanied the ship's Executive Officer when he inspected the troop compartments, took care of a much reduced amount of paperwork, oversaw and participated in the physical exercise programs, and conducted or oversaw a certain amount of informal classes. My favorite to conduct was a weekly current events class. Otherwise the men busied themselves with card games and reading—a great deal of reading, and getting plenty of sleep. All in all a pleasant trip.

The landing exercise was routine, to include communication problems. As noted earlier, the Commanding Officer of a unit functions best when he is kept isolated from routine and time consuming paperwork, along with not having to handle minor disciplinary problems. If so—all goes well in his unit. But higher headquarters holds the Commanding Officer fully responsible for what his command does or fails to do. On this particular exercise the Commanding Officer took a great deal of flak for the communication difficulties that arose.

After the exercise we traveled from Formosa to Japan, and then back to San Diego on a Navy cargo ship known as an AKA (Amphibious Cargo Assault). These are in many ways sister ships to troop transports known as APAs (Amphibious Personnel Assault). The AKA's mission was to carry cargo, primarily bulk cargo to support a landing operation. We left much of our communication equipment in the Far East. This ended up on Okinawa and was used to equip a newly established Communication Battalion. The limited troop accommodations on the cargo ship were adequate to meet our Company's need to transport us home. A stopover in Japan provided another opportunity to stock up on bargains, and the cargo ship had plenty of room to carry them.

We arrived back on 29 April 1960. I was then transferred to the

Communication Company of the First Marine Division's* Communication Company. Initially I was the Radio Platoon Commander, then the Company's Executive Officer. Other than a few two or three day field problems this was a job complimentary to family life.

Iwakuni, Japan

I knew military orders for an unaccompanied (no family) overseas assignment was just around the corner, in fact overdue. My last unaccompanied one-year tour was in Korea from September 1950 through August of 1951—and I was single at the time. As noted earlier, all that saved me from an unaccompanied tour in July of 1953 was a last minute assignment to Officer's Candidate School. The orders arrived in early May of 1961 and I was on my way to Iwakuni, Japan by late June. I was pleased to be assigned to the First Marine Air Wing. The alternative was the Third Marine (Infantry) Division on Okinawa. Accommodations on Okinawa at the time were considerably more primitive than at Iwakuni. Mentioned earlier was that communication personnel could fill slots in either an infantry division or air wing. Thus the luck of the draw determined whether a "communicator" was assigned to one place or the other. My experience with aviators, to include a year in Korea, and my overall interest in aviation had resulted in a warm bond. Then too, how could I forget that I was serving in a Marine aviation unit when I went through the preliminaries leading to my being selected for officer training?

Luckily, Betty and the three girls were allowed to remain in government housing aboard the base at Camp Pendleton. What a relief to me to know they could remain in the home we had lived in for three years prior to my going overseas for a year. School for our oldest daughter was a two-block stroll through the housing area. The Hospital, Post Exchange and Commissary were all less than a mile away. A further blessing was that most of the neighbors remained in place during the year I was gone.

---

*This was my old Division from Korean War days.

Betty and the girls drove me to the Oceanside train depot. As she drove away the three girls, ages six, four and two waved merrily as they stood on the back seat looking out the rear window (these were the days before seat belts). I was absolutely overwhelmed with sadness—unlike anything I experienced before or since. Would I ever see any of them again? For sure I was going to miss out on a year's growing up for each of the three girls. I knew Betty could handle the job of caring for the family on her own; she had experience doing so after all—but I would miss her and worry none-the-less.

I flew from Travis Air Force Base near Sacramento, California to the familiar base of Tachikawa, Japan, and from there by vehicle to the even more familiar Naval Air Station at Atsugi. Both these bases were often visited while the family was stationed in Japan. My flight south to Iwakuni was scheduled for the next day. That evening I had the opportunity to visit Kieko, the lady who was our maid and who served us so well while the family was stationed in Japan a few years earlier.

My satisfaction level increased considerably when a friend and fellow communication officer, Dave Foster, met me at the Iwakuni airfield terminal. I was his relief and no doubt he wanted to be sure I was well taken care of so he could return home. My new home was really quite comfortable; a Quonset hut divided into three rooms and a head (bathroom). Maid service provided. I shared the hut with two pilots who I can only remember now as Joe and Ron. They were pleasant, lively, and most agreeable roommates.

If family separation was bad news the good news was that you could devote your full time to the job. Something has to be said too about the camaraderie that builds up in a group of men, all away from home and loved ones, and sharing a common experience. I quickly established a close relationship with both the Catholic and Protestant Chaplains along with two or three other compatible individuals. We routinely had lunch and dinner together at the Officer's mess. I looked forward to these get-togethers. This was the first time in my life that I socialized in this fashion with a Catholic priest. Other than squirrel hunting with Father Mechler on a couple of occasions, my association had been strictly priest on the one hand—layman on the other. I enjoyed participating in conversations embracing a wide range of activities. One evening Father Galland (in mock seriousness I suspect) told of an encounter he had with a prostitute in the city of Iwakuni (the city bordered the base). Apparently the lady came up to him and offered her favors for a price. Father Galland, who was in uniform, pointed to the cross Chaplains wore on their collar. This young lady brightened up, gave him a big smile, and said, "Okay, okay, me Christian girl!" Could it be a true story?

My job was as Officer-in-charge, Communication Section, Headquarters and Service Squadron. Behind this officious title I was responsible for the men and equipment providing communications for the Marine Air Wing when deployed in the field. Our job day by day was to keep the communication equipment we might someday take to a remote airfield ready to go, and that we remain proficient in operating the equipment. On balance, a rewarding job, and one I enjoyed. The job came with a jeep so I had wheels available for my use, to include to and from my living quarters. At times the jeep was in for maintenance and I walked to Mass. If General Condon, the 1st Marine Air Wing Commander, was at Mass on these occasions, he gave me a ride back to my quarters in his jeep. After a few pleasantries he might comment on this or that area not looking all that great with what I perceived was a degree of frustration. I made it a rule to pass those comments on to the office with responsibility for maintaining the buildings and grounds on the air station.

I quickly fell into the routine of an early Mass each morning followed by breakfast, then the work routine punctuated by lunch, and finally a relaxing dinner at the end of the day. Evenings I usually spent writing my daily letter to Betty and studying for the Japanese language class I was attending two nights each week. At the same time I was taking other college level correspondence courses. As previously mentioned, I was working to finish my junior year college work so I could apply for the Marine Corps's "Boot Strap" College Degree Program. If I was an indifferent student in high school I was sure making up for that now. Studying was a pleasant process for me at this point, given my separation from the family and free time on my hands. Our workweek went to Saturday noon and then I went back to the books.

I rarely left the base, but did on one occasion join a group to tour Hiroshima, located approximately thirty miles from Iwakuni. We had a Japanese guide who was both diplomatic and thorough as he described the devastation caused by the atomic bomb dropped on the city on 6 August 1945. I found it moving to stand at ground zero in Hiroshima and to imagine what happened there in August of 1945. An apt analogy is to visit Gettysburg and stand on the ground to view the wheat field across which Confederate General Pickett made his famous charge on 3 July 1863.

In early spring of 1962 the Air Wing took part in military maneuvers in the Philippines. Most all our equipment was loaded aboard various ships and off we went for about three weeks. We landed after the infantry of the Third Marine Division who were also participating in this exercise. Communication in the field is a frenetic and worrisome job. Invariably there are problems, usually multiple problems. This or that radio or radio relay link is down, land (wire) lines have been cut somewhere, and a backlog of messages are piling up in the message center. I envied the Chaplain, who as far as I knew had absolutely nothing to worry about. From what I observed he sat in his tent until time for church services. But time passed and the maneuvers ended. I was lucky to fly back in what was then the new C-130 Hercules, a plane still in wide use today (2005). Those of us having specific responsibility for certain functions were required to write up a critique. We were flown back so we could write up our reports in the relative comfort of the home base at Iwakuni. I hope the Chaplain had to come home on a slow ship.

Over the year Betty and I exchanged daily letters. Admittedly, I had to write a number of letters in advance while on maneuvers since obviously I could not mail them on a daily basis from the ship. A friend who did not make the Philippine trip fed my letters, one by one, into the postal system each day. I don't know about her, but mail call was really a big deal for me. We both had movie cameras, tape recorders, and still cameras which permitted us to stay in close touch. I also sent many packages of electronic toys and clothing home. The Japanese were at their best at this point in time in turning out gimmicky, but cute electronic toys. In addition I sent clothing, jewelry, and pottery for Betty and other family members. At the time bargains were still to be found in the Far East. Personally I succumbed to the latest in a stereo music system.

University of Nebraska (Omaha, Nebraska)

Orders came along in May assigning me to "precisely" where I wanted to go—the University of Nebraska (Omaha) to complete my college work. My trip home took me from Iwakuni back to Atsugi Naval Air Station, then by vehicle to Tachikawa Air Force Base, from there to March Air Force Base (Sacramento, California), then a plane to San Diego, and finally a train to Oceanside. Betty had hired a baby sitter and we spent two days on a second honeymoon. Second honeymoons were then and now common in the military—a serendipity benefit for those long separations.

Seven year old Diane and five year old Cathy greeted me, admittedly a bit shyly when I finally arrived home. Three year old Joyce took one look at this stranger in her life and set an all-time speed record for escaping down the hall.* That fear did not last long. While taking the baby sitter back to Oceanside, Joyce from her perch on the back seat leaned over the front seat and chatted continuously in my ear. Her perception may have been that this may be a stranger, but he listens.

After a trip to the then fairly new Disneyland and Knottsberry Farm theme parks we headed for Omaha, Nebraska. A lightweight metal shelf suspended from the front seat bridged the short gap to the back seat.

---

*I like the story of the military dad who returned home after a year's deployment. The children were asleep when he arrived home. The next morning he was awakened by his three-year-old son beating him furiously on his face with his little fists while shouting, "Get out of my mother's bed!"

A crib mattress then provided a place for the girls to romp (to some extent), play, and sleep. Two small turtles traveled in a bowl underneath the back seat array. Since this was July we started out from Camp Pendleton in mid-afternoon. This permitted crossing the California and Nevada desert during the cooler evening and early morning hours. We did wake the girls so they could enjoy the lights of Las Vegas. From then on we stopped at motels with a swimming pool at the end of a day's drive. A stop at Yellowstone National Park interrupted the otherwise routine trip. We stopped briefly in Omaha where we rented a house before driving on to Wisconsin.

This was our first long trip with the three girls—then ages, three, five, and seven. I was reminded as we drove along how often I had day dreamed over my single years of this scene, i.e. traveling with a wife and children. At one point in my single days I was amused by a story told by a married senior Marine. He was traveling cross-country with his family in a large station wagon. Two children, boys ages three and five were often misbehaving in the back of the wagon where they hung out so Mom couldn't reach them to ensure acceptable behavior. Somewhere along the way Dad stopped alongside the road to cut a stick from a growth of small trees—the stick long enough to reach the furthermost corner of the station wagon. The result, as you might expect, was a much better behaved couple of boys. Later, during a gas stop Mom went to the restroom while Dad settled the gas bill. When they returned the stick was in three pieces. The boys had "accidentally" broken it. In addition to amusing me, his story reminded me of my longing for a family of my own. Well, here we were with three children; good travelers all; playing, singing, and often sleeping in the limited confines of the back seat. Speaking of singing, a few years later I learned another way other than time to measure how long it takes to move from point "A" to point "B". On this occasion we were traveling the forty miles from San Diego to our home in Vista. Two children were with us at the time. At the start of the trip they began singing *101 bottles of beer on the wall.* They reached the *one bottle of beer on the wall* as we drove in the garage.

We were traveling to Wisconsin on a more northerly route than I had traveled by car before. But soon I saw some old friends:

> The midnight ride
> Of Paul for beer
> Led to a warmer
> Hemisphere
> BURMA SHAVE

Followed by:

> Car in ditch
> Driver in tree
> The moon was full
> And so was he
> BURMA SHAVE

It had been six years and five months since we had been home. Personal contact with our families back in Wisconsin was sporadic at best. Betty's Aunt Vera Cunitz visited us in Yokohama when her cruise ship made a port call. Betty's cousin Eugene Ziegler was deployed to the Japanese area while on the submarine U.S.S. Bugara, and he visited us as well. The only other family contact was with my brother Ronald, then an active duty Marine who visited us at Camp Pendleton, California in 1959. During this period six of our collective sisters were married (all four of Betty's). As a result we had six brother-in-laws along with ten nieces and nephews to meet for the first time.

Since school started in September I had the opportunity to use up all my accrued leave. I helped my dad thresh, the old fashioned way, with a threshing machine. No longer did a large group of neighbors come together since many now had combines. On this occasion we threshed using the Muehlenkamp's (maternal aunt) threshing machine and their family members for added labor. I also helped my father-in-law. It was my first experience with a combine. My job was to show up at the right time with a pick-up truck so the nearly full hopper on the combine could be emptied (by gravity) into the truck bed. From the field to the granary where a motor driven elevator carried the grain to a bin. Much less labor extensive than using a threshing machine as we did on our farm.

I reported into an Omaha, Nebraska Marine Reserve unit for the few weeks before college classes started. We enrolled Diane in a parochial school's second grade and Cathy in a public school kindergarten class. Our home was on a quiet tree-lined street in a quiet corner of northwest Omaha. College classes with the young crowd I was now associated with was a strange, but altogether pleasant experience. Unlike my high school days, I was now a disciplined student, without the typical distractions plaguing the younger students. I was pleased to earn straight "As" in that environment. I was pleased as well when later I learned that the college had forwarded that information to Headquarters Marine Corps for inclusion in my service records.

These were the "coldest" days of the Cold War. A key ingredient in keeping the all too fragile peace at the time was the Air Force's Strategic Air Command (SAC). The headquarters for the SAC was at Offut Air Force Base, a few miles southeast of Omaha. We often used the base for our shopping and medical needs. In October of 1962, the Cuban missile crisis occurred, where for a while, we were eyeball to eyeball with the Russians on the issue of a nuclear exchange of terror. In the event of a nuclear exchange, SAC headquarters was likely to be a primary target. If the Offut base were hit, Omaha would be affected in a major way as well. Unlike the Suez crisis when we were in Japan, there were no fields to go to or dikes in rice fields to hide behind. The best we could do would be to retreat to our walkout basement. In fact, many homes in Omaha did have basements with well-stocked fall-out shelters, understandable since folks in Omaha were well aware that the neighboring Air Force base was likely to be a primary target. Other than for a few nervous days the crisis passed and life went back to normal.

Back in 1956, when U.S. forces were stationed in Japan, we were led to believe that any American child born on a military reservation was automatically an American citizen. We found out much later that Cathryn and all others born in Japan at the time were dual citizens of Japan and the United States. This meant that we had to appear with Cathryn before a Federal judge in Omaha to have her declared a naturalized American citizen. Cathryn, now nearly six, had no problem coming up with the "I do" after the judge asked her if she would uphold the laws of the country, etc. At this point she truly became an American citizen, but because she was "naturalized" she could not become president of the United States.*

The college was only a couple of miles from our home and I invariably came home for lunch. One spring day I came home to be greeted by a wife exhibiting a serious demeanor. "The White House just called," she said, "they want you to fly to Washington." That was all the information she had. I searched my mind for a reason why the White House could possibly summon an obscure Captain in the Marines to Washington. The only possible reason I could think of was an event occurring late in my tour at Iwakuni. In May of 1960 Laos was threatened with a Communist takeover. President Kennedy responded by sending American forces to nearby Udorn, Thailand. A fighter squadron of our air wing's jets was sent to Udorn to meet this emergency. Unfortunately there was no fuel at the base—and there was supposed to be. Someone had dropped the ball and there sat those jets out of fuel. The top man, General Condon, had to take the heat for this goof-up. But I was in no way involved in this—yet that was all I could think of.

I did not have long to wonder. Within a few minutes of my arriving home a follow-up call from a Marine Captain in Washington, informed me that I was being considered for duty at the Presidential Mountain Retreat at Camp David in Maryland. I needed to fly to Washington, for a series of interviews. A few days later I flew out of Offutt Air Force Base

---

*On 5 October 2004 a group began a drive to amend Article II of the constitution so that a naturalized citizen could serve as President. This followed the success of Arnold Schwarzenegger being elected Governor of California in conjunction with a recall election of the sitting governor in 2003. Governor Schwarzenegger, a naturalized citizen, was born in Austria.

for Washington, D.C. After meetings in Washington, I went to Camp David to meet officials there. I was surprised by the remoteness of the Camp. The decision was made that I had the job before I left to go back to Omaha. As a result, I carried the house plans for the quarters we were to live in for Betty to study.

Graduation from college was in June of 1963 and then we were off to Wisconsin. Betty and the girls stayed in Wisconsin while I drove on to Washington, D.C. and Camp David. Betty and the girls joined me after I relieved the man I was replacing, at which time the quarters he was living in became available.

Camp David, Maryland

While stationed at Camp David, my normal administrative unit was Marine Barracks at Eighth and I Streets in Washington, D.C. I came down "off the mountain" twice each month for meetings at the barracks. Quarter's Number One at the barracks, the historic home of the Commandant of the Marine Corps, has the distinction of being the only public building in Washington not burned by the British during the War of 1812.

Prior to reporting to Camp David, Colonel Wheeler, the Commanding Officer of the Barracks discussed the job with me. He mentioned that I would be on my own since the White House strictly controlled access to the Camp. In other words, the Marine Corps had no way to conduct routine inspections so normal, and indeed so necessary in the military routine. "The Marine Corps will have to trust you Joe, so keep in mind what could go wrong in this sensitive assignment," he said. With this sobering reminder I journeyed to Camp David where in a few days I assumed the job of "Marine Corps Security and Liaison Officer." This equated to being responsible for the physical security of the Camp under the direction of the Camp's Commander, Navy Commander Charles Howe. A senior non-commissioned officer, Gunnery Sergeant Leo Spenla and I were the only two Marines permanently assigned to the Camp. The remainder of the Marine guard force rotated on a two-week basis from the Marine Barracks in Washington. These young Marines and their officers were the "spit and polish" ceremonial troops who performed the many highly public functions in the nation's capital. For the most part these men enjoyed the opportunity to break from the demanding ceremonial functions to the equally demanding, but more routine and comfortable duty at Camp David.

Camp David's location on a mountaintop in the Catoctin Mountains of Maryland is remote, rural, and beautiful. On one occasion I was returning from a Marine Barracks meeting with two young Marines. The passenger in the front seat mentioned that he was from the East Side of New York City. The other Marine from somewhere in the Mid-West. This was a seventy-mile drive and before long the chatter died away and we proceeded in silence. During the last few miles up the mountain, stately trees closely bordered the relatively narrow and winding two-lane road. On this occasion in early fall, and at this time of day, the mid-afternoon sun was producing magic with the colored leaves filtering sunlight to the roadway. I noted my New York City passenger looking from left to right, taking the beauty of the moment in. Finally he said, "You know Captain, this is what I always thought heaven would be like." That statement hit me like a ton of bricks. Why hadn't I noticed the splendor of the scene? No doubt being from rural Wisconsin where nature played its magic throughout the year I took nature's beauty here for granted.

Presidential visits to Camp David were good news, and in a minor way, bad news for those of us who worked there. The good news was that presidential visits were our reason for existence and I found it exciting when the presidential party was on-board. The downside, a minor downside, was that there went our weekend. Since the President was not required to book in advance, a decision to visit the Camp could occur at any time. As a result, we had two-way radios installed in our personal vehicles so we could let home base know where we were and how we could be reached if away from our quarters—and where we could be located if away from the car. Betty had her own call sign should she ever have an emergency while driving.

The world knows President Kennedy was assassinated on 22 November 1963. Those of us stationed at Camp David were privileged to have had a private opportunity to visit the East room of the White House where he initially lay in state.

Shortly after assuming the presidency, President Johnson visited Camp David. I recall that the Sunday evening the presidential party departed was relatively cold. A light rain was falling, but not enough to preclude the helicopter from taking the presidential party back to the White House. I received a call on the radio, and via a code we used, I was made aware that a sentry near the helicopter pad was detaining three people. Indeed he was. One was Jack Valenti,* at the time a presidential aide and two young women whom I assumed were secretaries. These folks had wondered too far away from the heliport and the sentry was doing his duty in detaining them. All three cheerfully understood why they were being detained, with the young women seemingly thrilled to have had this confrontation with an armed Marine.

On another presidential visit the Reverend Billy Graham was a guest and conducted Sunday services. Our families and those not on duty were invited to attend services, as was the case when Catholic services were held when either President or Mrs. Kennedy were aboard. At this point we all had been introduced to the presidential beagles named Him and Her. We were waiting in the small meeting room that served as a chapel for the President and Mrs. Johnson to arrive. Reverend Graham was standing with a bible or prayer book in his hands, wearing a soft smile and a most serene look. All of a sudden Him and Her bounded in barking up a storm. Reverend Graham's composure changed not a bit. We were embarrassed and after the dogs had been removed Reverend Graham said, "I could sense that you were embarrassed for me, but you should know that when I first started preaching in North Carolina dogs far outnumbered people in the audience."

---

*After President Johnson left office Mr. Valenti served as President of the Motion Picture Association of America. He served in that office from 1966 to 2004.

Another episode that evoked smiles occurred when President Johnson and Secretary of Defense Robert McNamara intercepted our Marine Sergeant-of-the-Guard on one of the pathways. This too took place during one of the President's first visits to the camp. The President stopped the Sergeant and in a friendly fashion asked, "How many acres here at Camp David Sergeant?" "I think two or three acres Mr. President," was his reply. The President put his hand on the Sergeant's shoulder, and with a big smile said, "Son, I'm from Texas, and I know this is considerably more than three acres." The Sergeant hastened to our office to report this encounter. His first statement was, "How many acres are there here at Camp David?" He was not pleased to hear the degree to which he underestimated the acreage.

We lived in a twenty unit military housing area with the living units forming a circle. The interior space was a playground for the children. A Navy bus took the children to school, dropping some off in Thurmont, Maryland at the base of the mountain. Others, to include our children continued on to Mother Seton's Catholic School in Emmitsburg, Maryland. In many ways we were like one of those small isolated cavalry posts Elizabeth Custer (General Custer's wife) wrote about in her book *Boots and Saddles*. We too were rather isolated and in large part dependent on each other in work and play.

In November of 1964 I flew back to Wisconsin to attend the ordination of my brother Noel. Our mother's prayers were answered. She now had a son who was a priest. I suspect to Mother this was the equivalent of finding the Holy Grail.* How proud we all were. This event resulted in most of the extended family gathering in Marathon, Wisconsin where the solemn ordination ceremony took place.

Sometime in December of 1964 the Camp Commander invited the Inspector General of the Marine Corps to visit Camp David. The Camp

---

*The Holy Grail was the cup or platter used by Jesus at the last supper and by Joseph of Arimathea to collect drops of Jesus' blood at the crucifixion. The vessel was lost—but the search for it goes on and on.

Commander and I briefed him, gave him a tour, and he conducted a personnel inspection of the Marines then at the Camp. All went well as far as I could tell, and since this was not an official inspection I did not expect to hear anything more. A few weeks later Betty and I were invited to a Christmas party at the quarters of the Commandant of the Marine Corps, General Wallace Green. At one point our paths crossed with that of the Commandant and I introduced Betty and myself. After an exchange of typical pleasantries he went on to say, "I was pleased to hear from General Ray Murray of the good job you are doing at Camp David." Wow! Here is the boss man, the top man in the Marine Corps coming out with this accolade, and with Betty an interested listener.

One of my responsibilities at Camp David was the wintertime care for the official mascot of the Marine Corps; a bulldog named "Chesty."* He joined us after the parade season in Washington, D.C. Chesty was the "crowd pleaser" when he performed at the Friday night parade. (With a smile and a wink Chesty received the proper clearance from the White House, Secret Service, and Camp Commander to live aboard the Camp.) Chesty was a popular member of the crew. His pen (with a heated house) was at a busy pedestrian crossroad so he received many friendly head pats from the many pedestrians who passed by.

When I arrived at Camp David in June of 1963 we had in our care a retired Chesty who was on his last legs. His replacement was at the time involved in the summer parade schedule at Eighth and I in Washington. On occasion old Chesty was allowed to roam about the Camp—but only if no visitors were onboard. Chesty was nearly blind and he waddled rather

---

*The moniker "Chesty" has a near religious significance in the Marine Corps and relates to Lieutenant General Lewis B. Puller. In the annals of military valor he is known as "Chesty" Puller, not only for his bull chest, but also for his absolute fearlessness and devotion to duty. He is the most decorated Marine in Marine Corps history. He was authorized to wear fifty-two ribbons. Fourteen were personal combat awards, headed by five Navy Crosses and one Army Distinguished Service Cross—the Army equivalent of the Navy Cross. The then Colonel Puller commanded the 1st Marine Regiment during the Chosin Reservoir Campaign in North Korea. He was awarded a Navy Cross and the Army Distinguished Service award for his service in that campaign.

than walked; and invariably used the middle of the road. In the process he was oblivious to traffic. When Chesty was turned loose the Camp personnel were mischievously alerted by a public address system. The word went something like this: "Now hear this, now hear this; Corporal Chesty is now involved in his morning workout. All hands will use due caution, etc., etc."

Naturally, foul ups occurred now and then. Remember Chesty was not supposed to be allowed to roam when guests were on board. On one occasion he was mistakenly let loose and Mrs. Kennedy called the guard shack to ask that he be removed from her social gathering of Cabinet members wives at Aspen Lodge.

The routine called for me to attend meetings at the Barracks the second and fourth week of the month. The man I relieved told me I was expected to render a report on "old Chesty" since the General's wives who lived in the quarters around the parade ground at the Barracks were quite interested in his welfare. I was somewhat concerned on the day I told Colonel Wheeler that the veterinarian had suggested we put old Chesty to sleep. I suppose I thought that given the General's wives interests this might have to be debated—but the Colonel simply said, "Okay."

After the 1963 parade season Private First Class Chesty II (as I recall his numerical designation) arrived for his first winter stay at Camp David. He stayed in 1964 and 1965 also. At one point during his winter stay we were informed by the Barracks that Chesty II had been promoted to Lance Corporal. We sent a letter back to the Barracks informing them that the custom at Camp David was for the promotee to set up a keg of beer for the crew. Colonel Robert Carney was now the Commanding Officer at the Barracks and he gave us a quick okay. This led to Chesty II sitting at the bar on a blanket, lapping up a saucer of milk, while the "all services" crew toasted his promotion, and his continuing success as the reigning official Marine Corps mascot.

I continued my flirtation with education at Shippensburg State College in Pennsylvania. I enrolled in graduate classes starting in September of the year I arrived at Camp David (1963). I attended one night each week. The College was twenty-two miles from Camp David over a series of mountain and valley highways. That could be a long twenty-two miles on some winter nights. I found this exposure to the formal education scene a pleasant and refreshing break from the military routine. I was awarded a Master's Degree in Education in August of 1965.

Also in 1965 we purchased a new Pontiac. This was a big four door Catalina sedan that said, "I am a family car" loud and clear! We also graduated to an air-conditioned vehicle as well. Our old faithful 1953 Pontiac hardtop convertible was relegated to being the family's second car.

Promotion to Major at Marine Barracks, Washington, D.C. Betty and Colonel Carney do the honors.

In August 1965 I was promoted to Major. Betty journeyed to Marine Barracks at Eighth and I Street to assist Colonel Carney in pinning on those oak leaves.

At about this point in time a Captain Chuck Robb assumed the duties of Adjutant at the Barracks. His duties were in the administrative realm, but no officer actually stationed at the Barracks escaped ceremonial functions. Captain Robb was a good looking and altogether "squared away" Marine. He was also single. Single officers like Captain Robb were routinely called upon to attend social functions at the White House. While carrying out these duties Captain Robb met President Johnson's oldest daughter Lynda. Their romance blossomed under these conditions.*

---

*They married in a White House ceremony on 9 December 1967. Captain Robb went on to be Governor of Virginia from 1982-1986 and U.S. Senator from Virginia from 1989-2001. In February 2004 he was appointed to co-chair the Iraq Intelligence Commission, an independent panel tasked with investigating U.S. intelligence surrounding the United States' 2003 invasion of Iraq, and Iraq's weapons of mass destruction.

I was a Major at the time and on occasion Captain Robb had a need to call me. When he called he followed the custom we all practiced when talking to a senior officer by using the third person. (Not at all unlike the deference we show to Judges in courtrooms.) I recall one such call in the fall of 1965. Captain Robb was at the time involved in planning the upcoming Marine Corps Birthday Ball. His end of the conversation went something like this:

"Would the Major and his Lady prefer (which main entrée)? Does the Major have need for a parking space?" "Does the Major... etc.?"

Now all this would have been of no significance but for Captain Robb being part of the presidential party that same weekend at Camp David. Now "the Major" could be viewed as part of the "hired help" at Camp David whose job it was to ensure that the President and his guests, like Captain Robb, had an enjoyable stay. The following Monday Captain Robb was back on duty, and being a thorough professional he once again assumed the role of Adjutant.

Three or four times each year we were invited to social functions at

Author and wife at White Hosue reception (1965)

the White House. One of these functions was at Christmas time when we also took the children. I have often suggested to Betty that having been invited to those bawdy parties the sailors threw while we were in Japan that she should write her own memoirs. With a great deal of accuracy she could title her book, *Partying From the Whorehouse to the White House.*

Somewhere along the way Commander Chuck Howe's tour of duty as Camp Commander came to an end. My new boss was Commander (later Admiral) John Paul Jones. At my current age, young people have a tendency to think twice when I mention that I once worked for a Naval officer whose name they might be familiar with, i.e. John Paul Jones

At this time the Vietnam War was at its height and it was now my turn to go. The Catholic Church in Thurmont, Maryland accelerated six year old Joyce ahead so she could make her First Holy Communion before we left the area. I flew to Wisconsin in late May to find a place for the family to stay while I was gone for the year. We found an ideal two-story home in Sparta, one block from the church and hospital. Our three daughters had one block to walk to Saint Patrick's Catholic school. Perhaps even more important, the house was but two blocks from my parents who were now retired and living in Sparta. Betty's family in turn was twelve miles away, still living on the family farm on Summit Ridge. The downtown shopping center for this city of 7000 was but a couple of blocks away as well. All in all, an ideal arrangement, and I was much comforted to know the family was to be living in the bosom of both our large extended families while I was gone for the year.

In early June, after selling the 1953 Pontiac, we drove to Wisconsin. Betty was once again pregnant, this time with our fourth child.

Vietnam

After settling the family in Sparta I was off for Vietnam, arriving there in July of 1966. I was engaged in the same work here as I was while

stationed with the Navy at Kami Seya, Japan earlier. This involved the
interception of enemy communication and its follow on analysis and de-
cryption. My title at the time was one of the most "officious" I ever held:
"Officer-in-Charge, Naval Administrative Unit and Commanding Officer Company L." We were located in an Army run camp at Phu Bai
that at one time had been a French military compound. Phu Bai is close
to the old provincial capital of Hue, and approximately ten miles south
of the demarcation line between North and South Vietnam. I and my
predecessors, and successors in the job all enjoyed the distinction of being the only Marines to be an Officer-in-Charge of a Naval unit at the
time we so served. I had three senior officers making out fitness reports
on me. At the head of the list was a Naval Officer in the Philippines who
reported on the operational performance as pertained to our unit's mission and administration of the Naval element. The Commanding Officer
of Marine Support Battalion, back in Washington, D.C. reported on the
administrative handling of Marine Company "L". Finally there was an
Army Colonel who was the host (landlord) for the camp where we were
stationed. He reported on such factors as cooperation and the manner in
which our unit met the responsibilities he levied on us for defense of the
compound, discipline, etc.

My association with the Communication Station at San Miguel in
the Philippines did provide for a break in the routine while in Vietnam.
At one point I flew back to San Miguel for a conference. On the flight to
the Philippines I was the only passenger on this cargo aircraft. Otherwise
the cargo hold was packed with derelict military equipment of one kind
or another being flown back for repair. The result—a whimsical feeling
of insignificance.

Unlike Korea, where I ended up all over the country, I was permanently stationed at Phu Bai during my year in Vietnam. In late November
I kept looking for a Red Cross telegram that would announce the arrival
of our fourth child. A garbled telegram finally arrived that basically told
me only that the baby was a boy. I had to wait for a letter to inform me

that David Joseph was born on Thanksgiving Day in the states, and that he was a healthy eight pound three ounce baby. I was keenly aware that after skating a bit, as fathers can do with daughters, I now had to gear myself up for the added involvement in raising a son.

Mid-way during my tour I took advantage of a program allowing those of us on one-year tours to take four days to travel to various liberty locations out of Vietnam. I chose Hong Kong. Betty provided me with a shopping list of what she wanted and I spent my time there involved in heavy shopping. I called her each morning, Hong Kong time, with questions I needed answered. Usually these questions involved additional items being ordered, sizes, etc. Several boxes entered the postal system from a U.S. Navy post office in Hong Kong. Some items were not ordered, like several wigs in many colors, to include platinum blonde.

I did award myself a half-day off from shopping to take a harbor cruise of Hong Kong. At the time literally thousands of poor Chinese, so called "Boat People," were living aboard nondescript boats in one section of the harbor to which they had been herded—and apparently then ignored. The smell of unwashed humanity and eastern food hung heavy in the air as we passed this point.

A couple of months before my tour was up, I was notified that my next duty station was to be with a Navy command in Norfolk, Virginia. Betty and I were pleased with this assignment. I was happy when that jet rolled down the runway at Danang (South Vietnam) taking me home. Betty met me in Saint Paul (Minnesota) for one of those "second honeymoons." Then we journeyed back to Sparta and a reunion with my daughters, and an introduction to our seven-month old son.

A few days before my leave in Wisconsin expired, we moved out of our rental house that had served the family so well over the past year. While the family camped with my sister Helen in Sparta, I drove on to Norfolk to find our new home. That done, I flew back to Wisconsin to escort the family back to Norfolk.

Norfolk, Virginia

Our new home in the suburbs of Norfolk permitted our three daughters to walk to a Catholic school. I joined a four-man car pool, permitting Betty to have the car three out of four days. We were settled in nicely, domestically speaking.

My job was on the staff of CINCLANTFLT.* The title of my position was "Marine Liaison Officer, Naval Security Group Detachment." This detachment was part of the same organization with which I had served in Kami Seya, Japan, and in Vietnam. I was involved in staff work, which is usually not a military officer's favorite type of duty, especially at this level. I was assigned a classified project and became the so-called "Action Officer" for this project. This meant digesting the data (documents and messages) that in anyway related to the project, and then drafting the responses, if a response was needed.

Assume the needed response was a routine message for eventual electronic transmission. First I had to obtain the signature of the Navy Captain who headed our department. His signature at this point indicated his approval of the "process" and no one subsequently contacted would look at the message without his authentication. (He needed to see the message one more time before electronic transmission.) Next I visited various offices getting senior officers to sign-off on the message. Depending on the subject, or nature of the message, this could be five or more departments that had to give an okay before the message could be transmitted. We action officers kept a list of buzzwords or phrases that we knew a given Admiral, or his office responded favorably to. Generally you had a choice as to the order in which a given message was routed. Here again you played the odds. We learned that if Admiral "X" (or his office) signed off on a message it influenced Admiral "Y" and "Z"

---

*CINCLANTFLT (Commander-in-Chief, Atlantic Fleet). That commands counterpart was CINCPACFLT (Commander-in-Chief, Pacific Fleet). These two naval commands divide the world between them with the foreign line of demarcation off the East Coast of Africa, with the Seychelles Islands in CINCLANTFLT's area of responsibility.

to do so as well. If a word or phrase were changed along the way the message might have to go back into the full routine of signatures again. Finally, when all interested officers had signed off on the message, my own Captain looked it over since in all likelihood it had changed from what he originally reviewed.

The aforementioned routine is not to belittle the system, but rather to praise it. At this high command level it was most important that outgoing messages reflect accurately, and in the proper diplomatic language, the view of that three star Admiral who was in effect talking to one half of the U.S. Naval World. That said, it was not all that exciting for those of us who at one time had been Commanding Officers of our admittedly small units, and had the authority to draft and transmit documents and messages over our own signatures. Here again though, excellent exposure to seeing how a senior command functions.

While stationed at CINCLANTFLT two events occurred that reached the level of being international crises. Both were related to my department at CINCLANTFLT. The first occurred on 8 June 1967 during the Six-Day War in the mid-east. The combatants were Egypt, Syria and Jordan; with Israel their opponent. Israel aircraft struck our electronic spy ship, the USS Liberty killing 34 and wounding 171. The "official" investigation termed it a case of mistaken identify—but there are still skeptics who think differently. This incident occurred in CINCLANTFLT's area of responsibility. A second, much more serious event occurred in CINCPACFLT's area. This was the capture of the electronic spy ship USS Pueblo off the coast of North Korea on 23 June 1968. This event hit the Navy like a ton of bricks. "How could the Captain of a Navy vessel surrender his ship without a fight?" was the incredulous question raised. At no time in the long history of the United States Navy had a Captain surrendered his ship without a fight. For the first and only time while at the headquarters I was aware of what I perceived as "red-hot anger" (directed at the Captain) punctuated by some profanity.

The dust has now settled on that event and history suggests that the Navy itself must share most of the blame for sending what was pretty much an unarmed ship into the dangerous enemy waters off what is still today the renegade country of North Korea. The ship's Captain, Lloyd Bucher and his crew of eighty-two, were subjected to eleven months of brutal captivity during which time they were beaten and tortured. Lloyd Bucher especially, and his crew too, are collectively now judged as heroes in this saga.*

Two other significant events occurred during this period. On 4 April 1968 I was driving home after attending an evening college night school class in downtown Norfolk. As I drove home I noted clusters of people gathered here and there along the downtown streets. They appeared to be angry and upset. It seemed strange, but I did not give it much thought. When I arrived home I learned that Martin Luther King had been assassinated that evening. Two months later, on 6 June Senator Robert Kennedy was assassinated. I remember the somber mood of our car pool as we pondered what was happening in our country.

Near the end of my two-year tour in Norfolk I was promoted to Lieutenant Colonel. That was followed by orders to the 5th Marine Brigade at Camp Pendleton, California. Betty was ecstatic; she a great fan of the climate in that area of the country. I was somewhat apprehensive. It had been seven years since I had been in a purely Marine Corps unit. One of the pluses for duty at Camp Pendleton was that my sister Elaine and her family were now living in San Diego. Their three children's ages roughly correlated with our four. The forty-mile distance between us was easily and often bridged. Both sets of children were fortunate to have cousins to grow up with.

---

*Lloyd Bucher died in January 2004. On 13 September 2004 the U.S. House of Representatives approved a resolution that posthumously praised Commander Bucher's "exemplary bravery and sacrifice."

Camp Pendleton, California

We put together a "family friendly" travel plan to make the move to Camp Pendleton. After all, our sedan was not the best mode of travel for a family of six, with children ranging in age from two to fourteen. Betty flew with the oldest and youngest to Wisconsin. I followed by vehicle with the two middle daughters. After leave in Wisconsin, I drove* on alone to California, again to find a home. We had tentatively decided to buy a home since military retirement was in all likelihood close at hand. I found my choices perplexing, so Betty flew out one weekend to help make the final choice; then flew right back to Wisconsin. After escrow had closed on the house, Betty and the children flew to San Diego.

This was the first home we owned. The five bedrooms permitted each of the children to have their own bedroom. A swimming pool provided "on-site" recreation. We also treated the family to two days at Disneyland before I reported in for duty at Camp Pendleton.

My job was Communication Electronics Officer (CEO) with the 5th Brigade, later redesignated the 1st Marine Division.** Once again a staff job, but one with wide latitude for initiating programs on my own. It also involved close work with Marines in the field. I worked for General Ross Dwyer, a demanding and hard-as-nails type Marine officer. The General was a tall man who towered over most of us who worked for him. That could be intimidating, but I thoroughly enjoyed working for the General. My three years at Camp Pendleton were probably the most enjoyable and most rewarding of my twenty-six years of service. As implied, working for General Dwyer had much to do for making it so.

One of my additional duties was as the senior member of a Bad Conduct Discharge Board. The five of us on this board met periodically as a final reviewing authority before an individual was discharged for bad con-

---

*Interstate highways resulted in the demise of those entertaining Burma Shave signs. I missed them.

**Once again my old outfit from Korea days.

Author and wife Betty ready for the Marine Corps Birthday Ball

duct. Usually this was merely a review of supporting documentation, but on occasion an individual appeared with his civilian attorney to plead his case. Since most cases involved only review of documents, we had to keep reminding ourselves that there was a "flesh and blood" human in the equation whose life would be affected in a major way via our action in his case.

I have commented on occasion of how frustrating the job of Communication Officer can be. Given twenty means of communication you can be sure that one or two, usually important ones, will be a problem. There was one system that usually gave us problems of one kind or another every time we set it up for use. That was a portable public address system. To make matters worse, they were set up for important occasions, i.e. award and retirement ceremonies, etc.*

On 30 April 1971 President Richard Nixon visited Camp Pendleton to welcome home the 1st Marine Division. There was a grand parade as part of the ceremony. We went into "high gear" to make sure everything came off okay. This meant making as sure as we could that the public address system worked. The Camp Pendleton Base Communication Officer was responsible for this system. But I was the General's "Communicator" so when something went wrong, I naturally heard about it. One of the back-up systems was a hard-wire hookup to a microphone to be cleverly

---

*Public address system problems occurred at the very top of the military hierarchy as well. The date was 29 August 1968. The event, held at the Pentagon, was a farewell ceremony for outgoing Secretary of Defense Robert McNamara. President Johnson and other dignitaries were in attendance. The public address system broke down so that the crowd heard only a few words of President Johnson's remarks.

hidden out where the Parade Commander issued orders to the assembled troop units. When the crew dug the trench to bury the wire they went in a straight line from the power source to that hidden microphone. That straight line turned out to be a diagonal line. General Dwyer called me to his upstairs office and pointed out the window. He was right; it would have looked much better if a couple of right angle adjustments had been used. In the intervening time before the President's arrival we watered, stomped, and dressed up this narrow strip so it was barely noticeable on the big day.

Lighter moments occurred in the field of communications as well. On one occasion we were going to have a satellite link during a field exercise. In 1970 this was an innovative and untested means of communication. A vehicle suitably equipped arrived for our use in the field. Prior to a field exercise all us staff officers briefed the rest of the staff and principal commanders in our area of expertise. I mentioned this innovative satellite link and that it would be in a position over our part of the country for use only four hours a day, and we were allocated only two hours of that time for our exclusive use. General Dwyer frowned, and his next question was along the line of "How come we only have two hours?" "Because General," I replied, "The National Fish and Wildlife Department has use of the other two hours to track a bull moose, outfitted with a transmitter to determine the migratory route of the animal." The General accepted this with a soft smile, but wondered where the animal was? I replied (without really knowing, but with a smile), "Currently in southeast Montana and generally heading northwest."

In April of 1971 my mother passed away suddenly. She was not quite sixty-seven. Her son Noel officiated at the Mass and delivered the eulogy. Someone once said that when you lose your mother you lose the only person in the world who you can count on to stick with you through thick and thin. I only recall feeling cheated that she died so young. On the day of the funeral, and before the casket was closed, Dad and I were alone at the casket. I said something along the line of, "She was really a good mother." He nodded. I am unlikely to ever forgive myself for not following through on what I wanted to say at this point. It revolves around an "inside joke" my parents shared, although it was invariably Dad who brought it up. Apparently during an impromptu baseball game a second baseman was needed. My then unmarried mother was drafted. She was given a glove she didn't quite know what to do with and told to stand near second base. What should have been an easy to handle ground ball headed towards her at second base. Then that easy to handle ground ball headed towards center field. Apparently this "rookie" second baseman made no move to field the ball.

As we stood by her casket I thought of saying something along the line of, "Heaven is getting a heck of a second baseman." He would have known instantly what I meant. No doubt he would have smiled, he might even have chuckled. Assuming this to have been his reaction, the next step logically would have been to suggest we include a fielder's glove in the casket. Two of her grandsons, then twelve year old John Sullivan and Kevin Riley both lived a few blocks from the funeral home. I'm quite certain one or both would have volunteered a glove and made a record breaking round trip to bring it to the funeral home. I assume celestial baseball teams have tryouts like we do here on earth—so how much better to show up with a glove.

Career military personnel are "keenly" aware that they can retire after twenty years of service. At this point I was at the twenty-six year level and seriously considering retirement. I knew my next tour would be a one-year unaccompanied (by family) tour in Okinawa or Japan. Our oldest daughter Diane was in high school and Cathy was in the eighth grade. Like most parents we saw them as vulnerable to the increasing drug problem in our society. Furthermore, with close to seven years of enlisted service I was, at a minimum, four years older than my contemporaries in the rank I held. Our overseas control date was made known to us so we could plan ahead. At one point I was planning to retire in July of 1971. Then my control date slipped a year. This permitted me to delay this big move until July of 1972. Never have I agonized over a decision more than that related to military retirement. The family and the need to establish one's self in a second career at some point had to be bounced against what to me was the joy of being an "active duty Marine!"*

Members of the division staff who were retiring had a choice of doing so at a parade in their honor, or if they preferred, a more subdued ceremony in the General's office. I chose the subdued ceremony (for one reason, no need to set up the public address system). Betty and the family, along with fellow division staff officers attended the mid-afternoon ceremony on 31 July 1972. I returned to the office for the remainder of the workday. That evening as I passed out the gate and returned the gate sentry's salute, I realized that this was in all likelihood the last salute I would render as an active duty Marine.

---

*The decision to retire was made all the more difficult since by law I could have remained on active duty seven more years. That would be extended yet another four years if promoted to the next higher rank.

PART 3

Post Military

CHAPTER 29

Post Military

I woke up feeling lost the next morning. I was no longer an active duty Marine. Once again the same question arose that I had asked myself during those first couple of days of Boot Camp, and again in Korea; what in the world had I now volunteered for? I know "once a Marine always a Marine" is a truism, but there's a big difference from being on active duty. Then too, here I was, forty-four years of age and it's most unlikely my military retirement pay could support a family of six. The children were ages five to seventeen. I was well aware there would have to be a post-retirement job, no matter when one left the military, but was it wise to accelerate that eventuality? It all turned out for the best I am happy to say.

Student Teaching

I found it enjoyable and relaxing being able to work full time on projects around the home. Luckily for my peace of mind I had only a month of leisure. In early September of 1972 I did my student teaching at Vista High School. I have to wonder what those two much younger teachers thought when they were told a middle-aged retired Marine Lieutenant Colonel was to be their subordinate for a semester. That was no problem for me. I was well aware they were my "Master Teachers" in this relationship. I viewed the upcoming semester as being the third Boot Camp experience in my life.

My subjects were U.S. History and Government. History for the juniors; government for the seniors. The seniors were in a remedial group that were having problems with the regular government curriculum. I knew from the start that the students, as a group, were not likely to resemble a platoon of trained Marines in terms of discipline or built in attention to their instructor. Amazing though what learning the names of all the students in the first few class meetings could do in terms of acceptance. In summary, the students and teachers could not have treated me better. I remember a comment from one of my master teachers. She relayed to me what a student had told her. "We like Mr. Hedrick, but wish he smiled more." That was a wake up call. I was immediately struck with the irony of my early days in the Marines when I viewed our officers as stern and unsmiling. I resolved to display a more pleasant demeanor in the future.

Job Search

In January of 1973 I was job hunting. Mid-semester is not the best time to find a teaching job, nor did I expect it to be. The job market in general was not all that great at the time. I learned that looking for a job can be one of the toughest jobs in the world. The most interesting flirtation was with Scripps Hospital in San Diego. The job was for an "Ombudsman."* The job announcement appeared in the help wanted column of the San Diego Union newspaper for the entire world to see. The salary was advertised as $12,000 annually. I was one of the lucky ones called for a one-on-one interview. A second interview involved four interviewers, two from management and two from what I will term labor. A week

---

*A Swedish term denoting one who functions as a trusted middleman between employer and employee. That person's job is to ensure communication channels are kept open and that a minimum of misunderstanding occurs between the two groups.

later I was called and informed that I and one other person had survived the selection process which had originally involved twenty-six who were called to appear for the initial one-on-one interview. Now an executive from the home office in Los Angeles came to San Diego for the final interview to determine whether my unknown fellow competitor or I was to be the person hired. On the big day I was ushered into a small room. My interviewer entered, we exchanged a few pleasantries, then got down to business.

He asked only one question: "Mr. Hedrick, imagine that you are to spend a weekend in a mountain cabin. You have absolutely no reading material, no radio, and no television. You can take one other person with you. Sex plays no part in this scenario. I need a one word answer; would you take an introvert or an extrovert?" I have no idea now what my one word answer was. In retrospect it seems that if the correct answer was important, extrovert was more than likely the best answer. Then again, the answer itself may not have been important. What might my body language have communicated to him? Did my eyes flicker in such a way as to suggest a dilemma? Did I hesitate for a critical split second? Was the question germane to begin with, or merely a cover while he made his call based on my appearance, demeanor, etc? I'll never know. What I do know is that I didn't get the job.

I took advantage of this slow period in my life to become active in a local Toastmaster Club. I suspect that in the back of my mind was my mother's disappointment in me for not participating in the extemporaneous speaking class while in high school.

Although the job of ombudsman did not come my way, I felt quite happy about having survived as long as I did in the selection process. I was next invited to teach a six-week summer school session at Vista High School. This was the first paycheck I had earned since military retirement. I rather enjoyed having my own classroom. I could see where a second career in teaching might be ideal if a job opening came my way.

Employment Agency

Along the way in my search for a job I had applied at a private employment agency. This firm, if successful in placing you in a job, collects a fee for their service. Subsequently the firm was sold and the new owner, Bob Wickens, ran across my application on file with the agency. He called to ask if I wanted to go to work for him. Bob was a retired Air Force pilot who was one of those unsung heroes of the Cold War. He along with his contemporaries maintained, on a twenty-four hour a day basis, the B-52 bombers and associated refueling tankers that so effectively played a major part in keeping our then mortal enemy, the Russians at bay.

In October 1973 I began my new job with Career Opportunity Employment Agency. The good news was multiple. I found a niche I turned out to be proficient at, and one I enjoyed. Then too the experience served me well in obtaining a follow-on job. Finally, our small three-person office was like family. Shortly after the secretary left, around four p.m., Bob broke out a bottle for an end of the day "camaraderie" drink. The bad news was my commissions did not suggest I was likely to ever be wealthy.

In June of 1974 a job came along that Bob could not pass up. He asked if I might be interested in buying the business? After discussing it at length with Betty we decided to do so. I seem to recall we paid around $12,000 for the business. The secretary, Judy Crouch and I kept the office running while Betty did the financial bookwork. A couple months later Judy exercised her open option to pluck off any plumb job that came to the attention of the agency. At this point our three children still at home were in school, leaving Betty approximately six hours each day to help out at the office. Ann Landers once said relative to husband and wives working together in the workplace, "Nose-to-nose at the work place all day long does not lead to cheek-to-cheek at night." We did not find that to be the case. I found it delightful seeing this new woman in my life coming to the office around nine a.m. each day, all dressed up in business attire. When she left around three p.m. I knew this same attractive lady would be waiting for me when I arrived home. While on the job I found it delightful to be able to dedicate nearly all our time to nothing but office business.

Betty enjoyed this exposure to the world outside of the home as well. It had after all been twenty years since the Department of the Army had employed her in Washington, D.C. One afternoon, as Betty walked towards her car, one of our clients intercepted her and asked for a date. One of her emotions was of pleasure to think that she might still be attractive enough for a man to ask her for a date.

Like Bob Wickens the former owner, and Judy Crouch the former secretary, I too kept my eyes open for a job with a stable income. My application was out there with several school districts, the two community colleges in our area, the State of California's Employment Development Department (EDD), and other miscellaneous private employers. The State of California job related closely to what I was doing day-by-day in the private employment agency.

The employer I really wanted to work for was Palomar Community College. So did a hundred or more other people, all with the proper education credentials. I had been interviewed for jobs there on a couple of occasions. At one point my supporters on the interviewing committee told me to be patient—it was not yet my day. I did not know what this meant at the time, but it sounded encouraging.

Palomar College

Then it happened, after all this time, three job offers came along at the same time. One from where I had done my student teaching, Vista high school; another from the state of California, and the third from Palomar College. I knew to the dollar the salary with the high school and approximately what the California job paid. I knew Palomar College had a known base starting salary, but this was usually increased based on one's life experiences. When the Chairman of the College Interview Committee suggested I might be interested to know what my approximate salary was to be if hired. I recall replying, "I know it will be fair." Imagine my pleasant surprise when the salary, after credit for military service, was twice what Vista high school, and presumably the State of California would have paid.*

The job my supporters at the College had envisioned for me, but couldn't inform me of in advance, was a new position titled "Job Placement Coordinator" for a vocational job training program. The job was close to a mirror image of what I had been doing in the employment agency. This vocational program was titled the "Regional Occupational Program (ROP)." A somewhat bureaucratic title that embraced a down-to-earth job training program. The 150 plus courses taught countywide at the time were open to all residents of San Diego County, sixteen years of age and older, on a first-come first-served basis. It did not matter where you lived in the county, or for how long you had been a resident of the county relative to eligibility to enroll. For example, if you lived in the city of San Diego and the class you wanted was forty miles away in Vista, and you enrolled before the class filled, the slot was yours.

The courses were intended to teach entry-level skills for the jobs available in the area. Ideally these skills could be taught in a semester. Nurses aid, electronics assembly, auto mechanic, office skills and bank teller serve as good examples. Approximately sixty-five percent of our students were adults, with so called "displaced homemakers"** making up a large percentage of the adult students. There was no charge for the classes, or for any books or materials needed in the class. The idea was to put people to work, with payment back to the state coming in large part from the taxes these new wage earners paid.

The ROP center I worked in had three principle functions. The first

---

*Betty ran the employment agency for a few weeks, along with a lady who eventually purchased the business.

**A term common at the time used to identify those women, who up to this point in their lives had been for the most part involved as homemakers. Some needed jobs for financial reasons, either to help support the family or as single mothers after a divorce. Others were interested in breaking out of the routine they felt themselves locked into.

was enrollment, where the first come—first served right to a class slot was assured. Two vocational counselors provided a second service. They were there for those not quite sure what they wanted to do, or might be best suited for. Through certain diagnostic tests and/or "talking it out" decisions were made. The final function was that of job placement/development.

I particularly enjoyed this latter job. It involved visiting potential employers to promote our graduates, liaison with the vocational teachers in our area, publicity for the programs, and perhaps most important, the interaction with graduates who came to our office for job referral. The process was much like that which occurred in the previous job. The person filled out a form listing their employment history (if any); was then interviewed; and if openings were available and the person was qualified and interested, a referral was made to the potential employer. If no job was immediately available, their applications, appropriately annotated and coded, was kept in a file and the person was contacted when and if a job came along they were qualified for.

I was proud not only of my association with the ROP program, but also to be working for a five star employer, as was Palomar College. Part of the joy was setting my own schedule. My duties involved a pleasant mix of placing students in jobs, visiting classes in San Diego's North County, making presentations to service clubs and other organizations, and working with potential employers of our students. This latter process began with a one-page letter mentioning briefly the highlights of the job-training program pertaining to that employer's business. We ensured the letter went to an identified person, either the boss or personnel director. The letter also said I would visit, and I did so. I found it a comfortable process since the letters sent to potential employers of our students came on Palomar College letterhead, and I in turn was able to function as representing the college on my follow-on visits. This was much more comfortable than being from a private employment agency where the employer knew you were charging the potential employee a fee. On occasion I set up visits for our teachers to employers who in the future might employ their students. Conversely, on occasion I escorted employers to the training sites.

This routine permitted on many occasions my being a conduit for employer suggestions to reach the classroom. For example, several of our classes involved teaching basic automotive mechanics. At the time small gas stations were able to do considerable basic automotive repair work, and our training programs were geared to this. At the time self-service gas pumping was not all that prevalent so persons employed as mechanics often had to pump gas as well. One gas station owner asked me to carry a message back to our instructors. "Tell them," he said, "to stress salesmanship along with being skillful mechanics. When pumping gas, take the time to observe the condition of the vehicle. People are busy and often overlook defects, especially safety defects relating to their cars. Tires grow bald, fan belts fray, windshield wipers wear, mufflers may need replacing, etc. By all means be honest, but be alert to this potential sales opportunity by pointing out potential problems. After all, a large part of my income comes from selling parts, tires, etc. and installing them." I carried the message back to our instructors who agreed to include instructions along this line.

Another corollary of the job was in the area of public relations. We belonged to the Chambers of Commerce in the five largest cities in San Diego's North County. I regularly attended their monthly happy hours. My job was to promote our vocational training program at these so-called "Sundowner", "Mixer", "Attitude Adjustment", or whatever other gimmicky title a given Chamber of Commerce could come up with. In another role I made presentations at meetings of the area's service clubs and other civic or fraternal groups. A final chore in this arena was to place advertisements for the program and/or specific classes.

In addition to the responsibilities mentioned above, I also managed the office for the College's Dean of Vocational Education, and later for a representative from the San Diego County Office of Education. We were a relatively small operation, employed approximately ten people for all functions; enrollment, counseling, and job placement.

In March of 1981 I made the trip back to Wisconsin for my dad's funeral. Like my mother ten years earlier, he died suddenly. Unlike her death at age sixty-seven, he had reached the age of eighty-three. Naturally a flood of memories hit me as I stood at the casket, gazing at the man who not only raised me, but with whom I worked so closely, as is the case with fathers and sons on a farm.

I continued my after working hours involvement in higher education while employed by Palomar College. This resulted in the award of a second Masters degree from San Diego State University. This degree was appropriately in Vocational Education Administration. Interspersed also at this time with the work routine were two trips of significance for Betty and me; one back to the Orient; the other a first time trip to Europe.

Trip to the Orient

In 1982 a new bank came to Escondido, California: Mitsubishi Bank with its home base in Japan. As one method in public relations and to introduce itself to the community, the bank involved itself in the annual membership drive for the Escondido Chamber of Commerce. The bank made available an all expense trip for two to the Orient for the lucky person whose name was drawn at the end of the membership drive. To have your name in the drawing you had to bring another business into the chamber. For each business you signed up you had your name entered, as did the business that joined the Chamber. One Saturday morning, after the drive was over, the drawing was held. I had brought in one new member, Toyota of Escondido. Betty and I were at the drawing. As the card came out of the box I saw thereon the name "Joe Hedrick."

The trip turned out to be a twenty-three day odyssey that began in Japan. While in Tokyo the lady who had worked for us twenty-five years ago visited us in our Tokyo Hotel. Her daughter-in-law accompanied Kieko. Betty and Kieko were both aware that when Kieko worked for us she was the same age as Betty was currently. We were pleased that this unexpected trip resulted in our meeting Kieko once again.

From Tokyo we took the bullet train to Osaka. Next came the part of the trip that promised to be, especially for this history buff, the highlight—a visit to Red China. We flew in a Chinese aircraft from Osaka, Japan to Shanghai, China. Remembered from the trip were a delicious box lunch and the charmingly polite and ever smiling flight attendants. If the plane trip was unlike what you expected from the still authoritarian, stern, colorless, and doctrinaire Red China of the time, Shanghai airport, where we arrived at dusk brought us back to earth. Unsmiling soldiers with tommy guns stood here and there in the terminal. The terminal was all but deserted except for our group of about thirty, accompanied by one permanent tour guide who had met us in Japan. No Chinese official smiled or displayed any outward courtesies as we went through the entry procedure. From the terminal we were escorted to a bus where we found a friendly and smiling young man who introduced himself as our tour guide while we were in China. Although it was dark you could sense the drabness of the countryside as we traveled into the city. Our hotel in Shanghai (Jing Jang Hotel) was slightly worn but still showed many signs of its former elegance. The commodious room we had and the friendly staff pleasantly surprised us. We were not expecting this, so it was indeed a surprise. Each floor of the hotel had a lady who served as an aide for any of the guests' needs. Her small desk was next to the elevator. She smiled and greeted us as we came and went.

We had heard of the "before dawn ritual" of Tai Chi that the population engaged in. Betty and I made it a point to be out on the streets well before dawn. We didn't participate, but only observed as we strolled along, pretending not to stare. The people in large numbers went about their exercise seemingly each lost in their own concentration—which is after all part of the Tai Chi ritual.

I was in awe of being in this great land. During World War II China was our great friend, and after the war our mortal enemy. Even more so than other Communist countries at the time, with the exception of Albania, China had isolated herself from the world for many years since 1948, and was only now opening her doors a bit, to include welcoming tourists. If we were surprised at our relatively luxurious hotel accommodations, we were more surprised to find the tour buses as modern as they made them in 1982. They definitely put the United States fleet of Grayline sightseeing buses to shame. All this was evidence of China's newfound interest in not only opening her doors from a political standpoint, but bringing in tourist dollars as well.

This was still the China of look alike unisex Mao suits with next to no color. Shanghai literally thronged with people and bicycles. We usually just inched along amongst the traffic in our big bus. People smiled and manifested a friendly demeanor if we had one-on-one contact with them. As a group though they were unsmiling but exhibited an industrious air. We observed no laggards, everyone had a mission, or seemed to. Each block had one or two older men who speared any piece of debris that somehow made its way to the street. A well disciplined, and to the casual observer, a somber but contented society.

On one occasion we visited a Shanghai department store. This was a four-story affair and the Chinese were obviously proud of it—which was why the store was on our itinerary. Betty was wearing a bright multi-colored sweater and it drew the Chinese women to her like a moth to a flame. Their friendly banter, which Betty could not understand, no doubt proved there was something primeval coming out in the women that was being suppressed in the then Red China.

From Shanghai we flew to Beijing,* the capital of China. Once again we enjoyed a more than we could eat box lunch and friendly smiling flight attendants. Our hotel was brand new, and probably rated at least four stars as we in our country rate hotels. This was yet more evidence of the Chinese now catering to tourists. Naturally we saw all the tourist

---

*Also known as Peking.

sights; the once Forbidden City, temples, Tiananmen Square, any number of small factories, and the Great Wall of China. Our bus trip to the Great Wall covered approximately forty miles of open countryside. Since all other travel in China was by air this was our only chance to see the countryside at eye level. What we saw was a throwback from a by-gone era. Here a gaggle of geese being herded along the road by a human; here farmers threshing with what looked like one of those familiar one-stroke Johnson and Johnson engines driving a flail bar as the farmer fed sheaves of grain into a feed trough.

I am a Wisconsin farm boy, a meat and potatoes type, and not too well attuned to foreign foods. But I resolved not to pass up any food on the menu, or drinks made available on this trip. The drinks were relatively easy to handle. There was the ever-present beer, and the one hundred proof high-octane drinks that came with many evening meals. Our evening meals were usually laced with many courses, many of which were epicurean adventures. I did my duty by them all.

Betty celebrated her fifty-first birthday in Beijing. The restaurant for that evening's meal was a typical colorless place dedicated to what it was in business for, serving food, so forget the frills. We were ushered past tables of diners who appeared to be a bit more boisterous than usual. As we walked upstairs our attention was attracted to a particularly rambunctious table of eight or ten men, all in typical drab dress, and all appeared to be angrily arguing. Plates of food and bottles of liquor seemed to weigh down the table. Initially a pang of concern hit me until I realized their anger was directed at each other, and was in all likelihood merely good-natured bantering Chinese style that occurred after a few drinks. I didn't see any playing cards, but I had to wonder if what was at issue here might not be a contested pot of money as occurred from time to time in those "buck euchre" card games on winter days in the bars of my home town of Norwalk.

Our tour group was ushered into a private dining room where we enjoyed a typical multi-course meal laced with delicacies I do not plan to ever eat again. At the end of the meal the Chef and two assistants wheeled out a birthday cake adorned with fifty-one candles. The Chef summoned Betty up front and in broken English, complimented by a big smile, asked her if she minded if "a bunch of Communists sang happy birthday to her?" She certainly did not! I suspect Betty rates that birthday celebration as her best to date, something like my most meaningful Christmas being the one which followed the Chosin Reservoir campaign in December of 1950.

One evening while in Beijing our tour group attended a light opera. We had been active all day on various tours. Our average age was around fifty-five. Most of our tour group fell fast asleep early in the performance. If I did not, I definitely did some serious nodding. The Chinese audience around us seemed to know the reason for our sleepiness, as evidenced by their good-natured smiles.

Our last stop in China was Canton. From there the trip took us to the Philippines. For me the highlight of the trip to the Philippines was visiting Corregidor. While all the ladies shopped in Manila, several of the men in our group made the forty-five mile round trip from Manila to Corregidor. This rocky fortified island was once known as the "Gibraltar of the Pacific." It guarded the entrance to Manila Bay on the island of Luzon. During the early days of World War II, United States and Filipino troops made a determined stand on Corregidor against overwhelming Japanese forces. Their surrender on 6 May 1942 marked the end of organized resistance in the Philippines.

Of the many historic battlefield sites on the Island, it was the Malinta tunnel that interested me most. Carved out a hill mass the tunnel was started in 1922 and completed in 1932. The main East-West corridor was 835 feet long, 24 feet wide, and at the top of its arch 18 feet wide. Branching from this main corridor were 21 laterals. Each lateral averaged 160 feet in length and 15 feet in height and width. In addition to General MacArthur's headquarters and associated military facilities, a 1000 bed hospital was located in the tunnel.

From the Philippines we visited Singapore, Malaysia, Thailand, Hong Kong,* Tokyo, and then home.

Kiwanis and Trip to Europe

Early during my job with Palomar College I accepted an invitation from a Vista Kiwanian, Bill Greenway, to look in on joining their Kiwanis Club. Joining Kiwanis ranks up there as one of those significant events adding spice to my life. After three years with the Vista club I transferred to the Escondido Kiwanis Club in conjunction with the Palomar College job site moving to Escondido. In the summer of 1983 my Kiwanis club underwrote the cost of sending Betty and me to the Kiwanis International convention in Vienna, Austria. This trip came our way by virtue of my being the incoming president of the Escondido Club. Our twelve-day trip took us to Rome, Vienna, Paris, and London in that order.

A must see for tour groups when in Rome is the Vatican. We did the customary group tour one morning, then went back on a free afternoon for a closer look. We found the grounds and church refreshingly clear of crowds and were able to wander around St. Peters Basilica at leisure. St. Peters is the largest Christian church in the world, capable of holding over 50,000 worshipers.

Earlier mention was made of the Japanese saying that there are two kinds of fools in Japan: those who climb Mount Fuji, and those who don't. I believe the same could be said as relates to climbing to the top of the dome of St. Peter's Basilica. The bronzed dome, designed by Michelangelo, covers the "high altar" in the center of the church where only the pope or a cardinal representing him is permitted to celebrate Mass. The dome rises 400 feet from the floor of the church, and is 138 feet in diameter.

The trip to the top of the dome started with an initial ride in an elevator. Then an additional 320 narrow steps took us to the top of the ro-

---

*The "Boat People" and the squalid area of the harbor I had observed when I visited in 1967 had disappeared. We were told most of these poor Chinese had been settled in government controlled low cost housing.

tunda. These were not ordinary steps. We passed through a combination of steep spiral stairwells, slanted hallways that learned inward, and narrow stuffy corridors. No place for one with claustrophobia!

It took some strenuous effort to reach the top of the dome, but the view from a narrow circular observation deck was superb. The 360-degree view over Rome made the physical effort worthwhile. We were also able to view the Vatican gardens, an area off limits to tourists.

While in Paris, along with another couple, we attended the "Lido Follies Bergeres." We arrived relatively early and while sitting at our table we were approached by one of the performers. He was a magician and asked if we (men) were willing to participate in the show. Why not? After all, I had experience on stage at the Palladium in Hollywood in September of 1949 so why not add the Lido Follies Bergeres to my resume. My friend and I, along with another volunteer, followed the magician to the back stage area. His part of the show was sort of a warm up before the main show began. I was the last of the three to appear. He arranged suspenders on me so as to make removal appear as magic. "Is this all that's involved?" I thought. Heck, my short dance with the showgirl at the Palladium in Hollywood was better than this. But it got better.

The magician dallied too long with his part of the show and now it was no longer possible for me to reach my seat in the audience by the route used by the other two volunteers. I was taken by a circuitous route to rejoin my companions. This circuitous route took us through a dressing room filled with a large number of gorgeous nudes waiting to go on stage for the opening number. I did what Father Mechler, my mother, and my wife expected me to do under the circumstances; I stared straight ahead—but oh thank God for great peripheral vision! Later my wife asked me to further describe the dressing room. Was it decorated in any way? What color were the walls? I did not note any decorations other than the ladies, and as for color; everything I saw was flesh tone.

In December of 1983 I went through, for the first time, that sweet-sad experience fathers have of giving away a daughter in marriage. This was our oldest, Diane, who we had welcomed into the world at the Naval Hospital at Camp Lejeune, North Carolina.

During my year as President of my Kiwanis club I kept my nose to the grindstone by presiding at all of the year's weekly meetings. At the end of my term (in October 1984) I rewarded myself with an AMTRAK trip. Train travel was not Betty's idea of a vacation. She chose to stay home with our youngest, seventeen year old David. I made it a comfortable trip by paying the extra cost for a sleeping compartment. This level of travel also came with three meals each day. During daylight hours I was usually in the observation car where I could watch and enjoy the ever-changing geographic scenes. The first leg of the trip took me from Los Angeles to Wisconsin via Portland, Oregon and the northern tier of states. After a few days in Wisconsin I traveled to Chicago, then New Orleans and on to Los Angeles and home via the southern tier of states.

To round out my association with Kiwanis, I remain active in the Escondido, California club and have now been a Kiwanian for over thirty years.

In early June of 1986 my three daughters hosted me to a rim-to-rim hike of the Grand Canyon. (I was close to age fifty-nine at the time.) This is a twenty-six mile hike, which for us started with a camp-out on the North Rim of the Canyon. All the next day we spent walking downhill on a narrow trail that dropped at a sharp angle as it clung to the side of cliffs. I thought this portion of the hike would be a "walk in the park." But the constant jarring on my thigh muscles was punishing. I was not at all ashamed to have some help from my daughters on this leg of the trip. Our first night was spent at a totally rustic campground called Cottonwood Camp. How refreshing to place my aching feet in the ice-cold water of the small creek that ran through the campground. The next day we had a much more comfortable hike to Phantom Ranch at the foot of the South Rim. That night we enjoyed a steak dinner and slept in a co-ed bunkhouse at the Phantom Ranch campground. The next day we hiked up to the South Rim on the Bright Angel Trail. Altogether an easier trek than down the Kaibub Trail from the North Rim. The martini my daughter Diane treated me to in the lounge at the South Rim was the best one I ever had.

Second Retirement and Law School

As previously mentioned, but worthy of repeating, is that I enjoyed the job with Palomar College and the vocational training program I was involved with. I considered it a near perfect second career. But as I approached age sixty the idea of going to law school became a temptation I couldn't resist. Besides, age sixty was an altogether ideal age to retire. My contract ended on 30 June of 1987, a little over three months shy of my sixtieth birthday. With my unused leave I actually left the job sometime in April of 1987. Much like leaving the Marine Corps, retiring from Palomar College carried with it a feeling of sadness. Now though I had a clear objective ahead of me and I was looking forward to being a full time student after all those night school and correspondence courses over the years. First though, yet another AMTRAK trip. This time the emphasis was on visiting Civil War battlefields. Once again Betty chose to remain at home while I retraced that familiar route back to Wisconsin where I spent a few days. From there I journeyed, again by rail, to Washington, D.C. Before picking up my rental car I spent a day as a tourist in the city, with a particular mission to visit for the first time the Vietnam memorial. As I left the memorial I chose to amble down one of three paths that led away from the memorial, and in the crowd on this particular path who should I meet but our daughter Joyce and her girlfriend. I knew Joyce was visiting this friend in Boston, but her trip to Washington was a surprise to me.

I spent the next week touring to my heart's content the Civil War battlefields in Virginia, Maryland, and Pennsylvania. I rented tape recorders from the Park Service and then followed directions for a guided automobile or pedestrian tour. What a luxury to have all the time I needed to visit a given battlefield for as long as I wanted, and to tour a given battlefield more than once, as I often did. The rolling acres covering the site of the Battle of Chancellorsville was of particular interest to me. This is where General Stonewall Jackson won his most stunning victory. Here I twice retraced the route Stonewall Jackson marched to hit the open right flank of Union forces late on the afternoon of 2 May 1863. His own men mortally wounded him that same day. This accidental wounding occurred after dark while he was reconnoitering in front of his own friendly lines to determine how best to continue the attack. The Park Service has marked the exact spot where this occurred. Other battlefields visited were those at Gettysburg, the First and Second Battle of Bull Run, Fredericksburg, the Wilderness, the Iron Triangle, and Cold Harbor. How relaxing knowing I wasn't subjecting Betty or anyone else to boredom while I toured to my hearts content. I returned to California by rail, this time via the central route through Denver

I arrived back in California for our daughter Cathy's wedding in May of 1987. Then a comfortable summer before law school classes started at National University. My interest in law school was initially perked when I read an article about how tough law school was, especially the first year. That was something of a challenge in itself. Then too, I was thinking of what I might want to do for the rest of my life and thought doing volunteer law work at Camp Pendleton might be something I would enjoy.

Law school started in September of 1987. In August Betty and I journeyed back to Asia. The South Korean government and people have shown deep appreciation over the years since the war to those who helped them liberate their country. Somewhere along the way their government started what was called a "Korea Revisit Program." This was a Korean government subsidized program for those who participated in the Korean War. Betty and I flew to Seoul in August of 1987 and visited some of the sites where we had military engagements in 1950. It had been close to thirty-seven years to the day since I had landed at Inchon. Inchon did not look at all like I remembered it, nor did I expect it to. We also visited the truce line at Panmunjon that still divides Korea today. This is something of a must see for tourist who travel to Korea. It remains as a grim reminder of the still icy-cold relations between North and South Korea. Then there was shopping—and then more shopping! On those days when the men were on military related tours, our wives often chose to shop, and who could blame them? On one occasion we men flew to Pusan on the Southeastern tip of Korea to tour some of the battle sites in what was in June of 1950 the Pusan Perimeter. At the end of the Korean tour, others in our party flew off to China, but we had been there and done that. From Korea we flew directly to Hawaii. After a few days in Hawaii we were on our way home.

Law school was at National University in San Diego, a thirty-two mile one way commute. I was one of twenty students in my class, and clearly the oldest. This was yet again in many ways another Boot Camp. Hard work, but I enjoyed the experience. It was great to once again devote full time to my studies. There was no job or family responsibility to speak of. At this time Betty was employed part time as an administrative assistant. Her part-time work permitted her to meet the home's domestic needs while I concentrated on my studies. There was no high school "muddling" now, I really put forth my best effort. My law school days were pleasantly interrupted by our youngest daughter Joyce's wedding in April of 1990. My Doctor of Jurisprudence was awarded in June of 1991. Next came the California bar exam. Each state approaches allowing lawyers to practice law in different ways. Some, like Wisconsin do not administer an exam if one graduates from a Wisconsin law school. Others require only a passing score on a multi-state (multiple-choice) exam. Others, like California, administer both a multi-state and an essay exam. I took the test one time, and along with eighteen in our twenty-person class, I did not pass. Should my entire class, save two, be presented here as dumb bells, the state bar did weave into the exam a new type of essay test involving a new essay test technique not yet familiar to law school teachers or the test preparers. I did okay on the multi-state exam. The passing score was 79, my score 103. Obviously, I did not do well enough on the essay tests to pass. If that was bad news for the class, the good news was that seventeen of my classmates passed the exam next time around. I am not sure whether I might have taken the exam again or not. I really didn't want to practice law for a paying job. But a series of surgical procedures for glaucoma ruled out any attempt for the next year (two test periods). It annoys me though that I didn't pass the bar exam as a matter of pride. Under a certain set of circumstances, I might venture into the bar exam jungle again.

Retirement for Real

Now it's late summer of 1991 and I am fully retired with no plans or desire to rejoin the work force, or go to school. I am constantly amazed how much time you can spend on projects around the home. Naturally you go about these chores in a relaxed manner and that takes time. Then too, gardens and foliage grow year round in the San Diego area so chores associated with gardening and landscape work are never ending. This former Wisconsin farm boy doesn't object to that at all.

On 10 August 1992 our daughter Cathy presented us with our first grandchild. A brother Aaron would join Johnathan eighteen months later. Daughter Joyce made her own contribution with Travis (1993) and Ryan (1995) to round out the grandchildren crew.

Retirees in the military are no different from their civilian counterparts in bonding together in fraternal organizations. In my case, eight military related organizations I belong to have either yearly or biennial gatherings around the country. Four have local chapters meeting monthly. Our area has no shortage of military retirees, especially from the Navy and Marine Corps. For most of us this was our last duty station, or we were once stationed here and were captivated by the pleasant climate. Another draw is having access to a number of large military bases. Betty and I find our way to Camp Pendleton at least once each week, and on a monthly or quarterly basis will visit one or the other three large bases in the San Diego area for what we call "recreational shopping."

Earlier mention was made of a unit of the British Royal Marines* participating in the Chosin Reservoir Campaign along with our 1st Ma-

---

*Designated 41 Commando

rine Division. In May of 1999 they held a reunion in London to which members of the organization (Chosin Few) were invited. A tour group of us veterans and our wives was put together and we set off for a twenty-four day tour of Europe before ending up in London for the reunion. Our tour guide was a reserve Major in the Austrian Army. Initially we toured by bus Southern Germany, Austria, Liechtenstein, Belgium, Holland, and Luxenborough in Europe proper.

The tour operators had set aside free days, primarily for shopping. With our wives concurrence (I think), we used these free days to tour battle sites not on the itinerary. One was the Bridge at Remagen. American forces captured this bridge, spanning the Rhine in March of 1945 when the Germans failed to demolish the bridge in time. The Remagen area had added interest to me for another reason. A fellow member of the Escondido Kiwanis Club, Jim Felix, won a Silver Star while leading a combat patrol in this area at the time our forces seized the bridge. Another visit was to the American Cemetery at Lorraine in France. This is the largest American cemetery in France and contains the graves of more than 10,000 America servicemen who died in World War II campaigns along the German frontier for possession of the River Rhine. Later we also viewed remnants of the French Maginot Line forts.* The final battle site visited was Waterloo where Wellington defeated Napoleon in June of 1815. We then traveled by ship (ferry) to England.

The Royal Marines treated us to several colorful events, each of historic significance where the British flair for pageantry was displayed. On one day a few of us took a one-day round trip to Paris via the "Chunnel"

---

*Our bus driver for the entire land tour of Europe proper was a Frenchman, who like our Austrian guide became a "member of the family." On this particular diversion from the planned itinerary we ended up a few miles from his home. He asked, through our Austrian guide, if we would like to visit his home and family? The answer was a resounding "yes." What a treat this promised to be! Imagine the surprise for his wife and four children when an entire busload of tourists showed up! Wine and French bread was served to all. Clearly one of the highlights of the trip!

on the bullet train where we traveled at an average speed of 157 miles per hour. After the reunion in London we flew to Frankfort, Germany to catch our flight back to the U.S.A.

Another trip of significance to us was a cruise to the Mediterranean Sea in April of 1999. We flew to Lisbon (Portugal) to catch our ship. From there we had stops in Majorca and Barcelona (Spain); Monte Carlo, Nice (France), Santorini (a Greek Island), Katakolon (Greece), Kusadasi (Turkey), Rome, Istanbul (Turkey), and then flew home after visiting Athens (Greece). On the bus tour at Nice (France), the tour guide (a lady) asked, "How many of you want to see the latest in women's fashions while on this tour?" While us men groaned audibly our wives thought this a great idea. But we men brightened up considerably when the fashions the tour guide referred to were those "three piece" women's bathing suits worn on the sun-kissed beaches of Nice, i.e. **sunglasses, sunscreen, and sandals.**

On 29 July 2003 we celebrated our fiftieth wedding anniversary. Our four children and four grandchildren could not have come up with a better place to mark the occasion than at Disneyland, and co-located California Adventureland. After that we went off on our own for an Alaska cruise, to include a trip to the North Slope oil fields at Prudhoe Bay (Deadhorse), Alaska. Our trip to Wisconsin in September of 2003 coincided with St. John the Baptist Catholic Church celebrating its 125th anniversary. As part of the celebration the church honored those couples who had been wed in the church, and were married for fifty years or longer. An altogether pleasant "anniversary year."

Every three years the Hedrick clan holds a reunion back on the farm in Wisconsin. In July of 2004, the family of my parents, George and Frances Hedrick, had blossomed to 188 attendees. Of that number sixteen were brand new to the family, all born after the last reunion in July of 2001.

Now here I am looking back from the vantage point of being seventy-eight years of age. All four of our children are established in the

Hedrick reunion (2004). Picture taken from a silo on home farm.

working world. As noted, four grandchildren, all boys have joined the family. There is a saying that the basis for judging a man should be his children. I am quite content to let that serve as the basis for the world's judgment of me.

Betty and I are now marching through our fifty-third year of marriage. Life has been good, and I suspect I feel all too smug about the cards life has dealt me. Might I do anything different if I had my life to live over? Well, I might try dancing with those El Paso USO ladies; and I certainly wouldn't have bought Lucent stock in January of 1999 at $72.875 per share (value in early December 2005 was $2.79 per share).

On a more serious note, I will forever wonder what would have happened if I had resisted that seductive and irrestable siren call from the Gods of War and remained at Camp Lejeune in 1950. The transfer to that aviation squadron very likely would have occurred. Given the rapid expansion of Marine Corps aviation over the three-year course of the Korean War, there is a distinct possibility that I would have had the opportunity to be trained as a military pilot.

Betty and I find it comforting to know our final resting-place will be "back home" in that little rural cemetery adjacent to St. John the Baptist

Catholic Church. Since I will join my dad there, I am pleased in knowing that the gravestones in our area of the cemetery are lined up like good soldiers, with not a **one out of line!**

Author's family (2004). From row left to right: Cathryn, Diane, Joyce. Back row from left: David, Betty, and Author.

Epilogue

Epilogue

Summit Ridge Today (2005)

Today, fifty-eight years after I left my farm home, Summit Ridge remains one hundred percent rural. However, in contrast to my day when fifty-five farmers worked the land, approximately twenty farmers currently till the soil on Summit Ridge. Of those twenty, less than fifteen operate dairy farms. Despite the reduction in the number of farmers involved, every acre continues in production. With modern farm machinery it's possible to double or triple the land that a single farmer can manage. He needs to cultivate all those acres. Today herds of milk cows have grown to sixty or more, and daily milk production is measured by the ton (2000 pounds). Giant tanker trucks arrive daily to haul the milk to market. My nephew Mike Hedrick, who operates the Hedrick farms today, and maternal first cousin Steve Berendes on my grandfather John Berendes' farm are two who have much expanded their herds and land under cultivation.* In my day, during the optimum spring and summer pasture time, our herd of about twenty cows produced approximately 400-500 pounds of milk per day. Now a herd of sixty produces from 5000 to 6000 pounds per day. Today it's not unusual for one 1500-pound dairy cow to produce 25,000 to 30,000 pounds of milk in one year compared to 10,000 pounds per

---

*As noted earlier, Mike Hedrick is the great-great-grandson of the original grantee of the Hedrick farm. Steve Berendes is the great-grandson of the original grantee of the Berendes farm

year in my day. This increase is due to a combination of breeding and the scientific ultimate in nutritious feed. Spring and summer pastures are irrelevant to milk production today.

To accommodate the increased size of milking herds, the old barns have been modernized and stretched out, in many cases with one story shed-like additions. But as you travel the ridge the old barns still stand out (along with the old two story houses).

As implied, it's one thing to build or expand a barn to accommodate doubling or tripling the cattle herd, but quite another to grow enough feed for those larger herds given a farm's existing cropland. You can go into debt quickly buying feed from outside sources. The answer is to buy out neighboring farmers or rent their tillable land. All of the farmers of my generation have retired, but a few continue living on their farms. The barns and other farm related buildings are empty, and all too often are deteriorating in appearance and structural integrity. These retirees pick up extra dollars by renting their tillable land for approximately fifty dollars per acre. They also rent out land that can only be used for pasture. Most dairy farmers have more young stock than they have pasture for. No one wants to buy or use up his supply of grain or hay to feed young stock when they do fine with only water and the grass growing in the forests and pastures. So a farmer pays a retired or gentleman farmer eight to ten dollars a month for each heifer pastured on the owner's land. Some of these gentlemen farmers live in the farmhouses and work in neighboring cities. In addition, they may maintain a small herd of beef cattle.

Something relatively new to the farm scene on Summit Ridge is the growing of soybeans. This is both a cash crop and a source of protein for livestock. It is harvested by a piece of machinery already in the farmer's inventory—a grain combine.

Something else new that may be coming to Summit Ridge is an electricity-generating windmill farm. Two Chicago, Illinois based firms are exploring the possibility of building a windmill farm on approximately

6000 acres atop the ridges of four townships in Monroe County. Ridgeville, one of the townships involved, embraces Summit Ridge. Depending on the size of the turbine installed, yearly income to landowners could range from $5475 to $7300 per turbine.

The appearance of the farm land when under cultivation has changed over the years. When I was growing up crops were grown on a patchwork of box-like fields. I can recall as many as twelve of these fields on the home farm alone. Many ran at right angles to each other. Here was a five-acre field of corn, there ten acres of grain, and over here a seven acre field of hay, etc. In the process a given crop, say of corn, could be spread out over three to four fields, each isolated from the other. Pretty in appearance, but inefficient to work and prone to soil erosion. Today, with the assistance of the state of Wisconsin farm agents, the fields are laid out in long graceful curves (contours) following the lay of the land. It's not unusual to see a given field, serpentine like, spanning the entire length of a farm. In addition to being much more efficient to work, contouring does wonders in preventing soil erosion as well.*

Farmer's sons today are no longer required to spend long hours harvesting wood in the wintertime. Part of the reason is that there is no longer any suitable firewood timber to harvest. The combination of cutting off hardwood timber for railroad ties and other heavy logging over the years has all but denuded the stands of hardwood trees on Summit Ridge. In their place fast growing softwood trees, not suitable for firewood, have sprung up. Besides furnace oil and liquefied propane (LP), two other fuel sources have come along for heating homes. One is wood pellets (made from sawdust); the other shelled corn. Nephew Mike Hedrick uses his plentiful supply of kernel corn to heat his 4-bedroom, 2800 square foot home. Shelled corn is hauled via a front loader from a storage bin to a 110-gallon hopper in the garage. A separate furnace in the shape of a large saucer shaped pan is

---

*My father-in-law, Fred Goetz, was the first farmer on Summit Ridge to have all his tillable fields contoured. He was proud of being in the vanguard of this progressive management of the land.

tied into the heating ducts. A thermostat controls an auger that carries corn to the furnace as needed. Based on the current price of corn, it costs about two dollars per day to heat his house. The LP furnace remains available as backup. Significantly, not a drop of liquefied propane was used during the winter of 2004-2005.

In keeping with the times, many of Summit Ridge's farm wives work off the farms. One major employer is the last truly functional Army base in the upper mid-west, Fort McCoy. Additionally, a Veteran's Administration hospital and a couple of Wal-Mart Super stores and related retail stores offer employment. These are all an easy commute away, as are manufacturing and clerical jobs.

The Chicago and Northwestern Railroad Roadbed Today (2005)

In conjunction with the abandonment of the line in 1966, the state of Wisconsin purchased the roadbed for the bargain basement price of $12,000 (see map page 508). The bike/hiking trail that evolved has turned out to be one of Wisconsin's major tourist attractions, with the long tunnel near the Hedrick farms being the highlight of the trail. In the wintertime the trail is used by snowmobiles, with the vehicles going up and around the tunnels.

Stand anywhere alongside the old roadbed during tourist season (between 1 May and 31 October) and you will see a steady stream of people going by. They will be traveling in both directions on the thirty-two mile trail running from Elroy to Sparta. The majority are bikers, with many pulling two-wheel kiddy-carts with one or two babies along for the ride. Others enjoy the pastoral scene by jogging, hiking, or casually strolling.

This is the granddaddy of bike trails, being the oldest existing rails-to-trails conversion in the United States. The railroad tracks were torn up and the roadbed surfaced with fine limestone or similar materials. The trail winds its way through the five picturesque communities of Elroy,

East end of tunnel today (2004)

Kendall, Wilton, Norwalk and Sparta. Services are available along the trail, ranging from food and overnight accommodations to bicycle rental and shuttle service. In 2005 the trail was used by visitors from forty-three states, plus Canada, England, and the Netherlands. An estimated 70,000 bicyclist use the trail each year. Approximately one-half are from Illinois and Minnesota. Bikers pay four dollars for a day pass, or fifteen dollars for an annual pass. There is no charge for children under age sixteen, or for hikers and joggers of all ages.

The thirty-two miles of trail includes three tunnels. Two are 1680 feet (under one-third mile) in length. If this is the granddaddy of bike trails, the three-quarter mile tunnel between Norwalk and Sparta is the granddaddy of the tunnels. This tunnel is clearly the main attraction on the trail. For safety's sake, riding bicycles while in the tunnel is not allowed. Bikers are required to dismount and walk their bikes through. The two-way traffic requires travelers in each direction to confine themselves to two narrow paths as they move through the tunnel. Since the tunnel

Thirty-two Mile Elroy-Sparta Bike Trail (Route of the Chicago and Northwestern Railroad, 1873-1965)

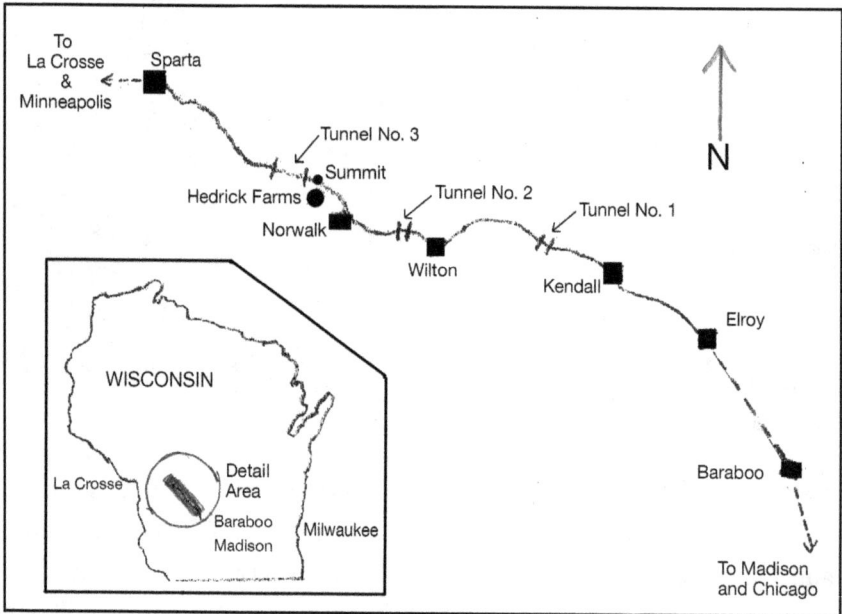

is usually pitch dark and/or foggy, carrying a bright flashlight is advised. The noisy waterfall at the mid-point, where the airshaft was drilled, has been diverted and muffled to the extent that the tunnel is now reasonably quiet. But water still drips from the ceiling along most of the route so wearing a rain hat is recommended. The temperature in the tunnel is a steady forty-five to forty-six degrees year round, which results in the tunnel feeling cool in summer and warm in winter. A jacket with a hood takes care of both the coolness and the dripping water.

The trip through the tunnel is both a bit scary (at first) and a delight for children. (Usually there is no "light to be seen at the end of the tunnel.") Something like one of the thrill rides at an amusement park. Small children will grasp an older person's hand extra tight as they move through most of the tunnel. When the end is clearly in sight they will drop that hand like a rock and run off ahead, all the while boisterously cheering themselves on as conquering heroes.

The same tunnel watchman's shack where Clarence Dittman spent his twelve-hour watches, and where I joined him on one occasion, stands as a small museum at the old location of the village of Summit. This is now a rest stop with bathrooms and the best drink in the world; cool spring water from a pump. Another delight for children is pumping water by hand. If children are in the area the chances are adults will not have to pump their own drink.

This area is something like a secular shrine to me. As I stand at the water pump and look directly across the trail I see a hill mass rising up within a few yards. At the foot of the hill mass are the cellar remains of my paternal grandmother's first home when she came from Germany in 1893. To my immediate left are the rotted remains of the old bridge I crossed many times when walking to or from St. John's Catholic Church. Another few yards west, and on the right is a relatively new bridge spanning the old water diversion flume. This is approximately where the old depot and post office once stood. The road on the other side of the bridge is now serviceable for vehicles. A few make the half-mile motor trip from the church to the bridge. From this point you are a quarter-mile from the tunnel. After a round trip through the tunnel you can return to the car to motor on out.* Those who want to remain close to nature will enjoy diverting from the trail to hike the one-mile round trip to and from the church. They will be treated to a pleasant stroll on a rustic tree-lined rural road gently weaving its way through the undulating hills.

As I face west down the trail and then turn slightly to the left I'm looking at the place where my paternal grandfather, as a boy, tended the oxen and mules used to build the tunnel. Turning further to the left, with my back to the trail, I can still make out the remains of the last three

---

*It would be wise to check with authorities before attempting the trip by motor vehicle. A heavy rain can create gullies in this dirt road hampering vehicle movement.

houses standing during my growing up years. A quarter-mile beyond and on top of the hill mass are the home farm buildings. All traces of the old road once running past those three homes and on up to the home farm have been all but obliterated by plant and tree growth. When I face down the trail (east) towards Norwalk, there on the right, next to the rest stop grounds is the northwest corner of the Bucholz farm. This was my old vantage point to watch the trains go by. That same vantage point also marks the location of the dreaded pickle patch where I and others in the family labored under the hot sun to make enough money to buy a washing machine. The very thought of that labor still makes me shudder a bit when I view the field.

St. John's Catholic Church Today (2005)

The church, social hall, and cemetery continue (as of 2005) to serve the community. Gone are the house (once the rectory) and outbuildings that once supported Pete Kroeger's family and their horses. Real or imagined fears persist that the bishop will in time close St. Johns. With the modern roads available it's but minutes to churches in Norwalk, St. Mary's Ridge, Wilton, Cashton, or Sparta. St. Johns is now one of four parishes served by a single priest. At one time five priests served the four parishes in Norwalk, Summit Ridge, St. Mary's Ridge, and Cashton. Gone also is that solid block of fifty plus Catholic family farms that existed during my growing up years. Today farmers who are members of St. Johns operate about ten dairy farms scattered around the ridge. (All are the sons or grandsons of the men who farmed in my day.) Although a small core of loyal parishioners remains, most attend whichever parish has the most convenient Mass for a given family's weekend plans. I suspect when my generation, with their sentimental attachment to the church are gone, the parish will be closed. In the meantime, Sunday Mass on Summit Ridge is a must for my wife and I when we are in Wisconsin. We can count on seeing many we knew while growing up.

Main Street in Norwalk looking south (2004)

Norwalk Today (2005)

The 2000 census gives Norwalk a population of 653—a significant increase from the 335 figure I recall seeing on a sign outside of town in the mid-1930s. The majority of the increase to the latest census count can be attributed to the approximately 200 employees and their families associated with a meat processing plant. Once the site of the Hollywood nightclub, the meat processing plant is one-mile south of the town limits. These additional residents are largely Hispanics, which required Norwalk to come to grips with weaving in a new culture. Naturally problems occurred along the way, but in general all went well. Since the year 2000 operations at the meat plant are much reduced with the labor force now (2005) numbering around 100.

But Norwalk has changed beyond its population, primarily in the area of businesses. Where once the creamery was the economic engine driving the town, now retirees and the meat processing plant carry the load. The old general store (Mercantile) still functions as a grocery store and bakery. Other convenience items are sold as well, e.g. health care products, light household supplies, etc. One small Mexican grocery store serves the Hispanic segment of the population with specialty food items. Two of the three taverns are still in business. The one run by Pete Schreier in my day is now called "The Place." The tavern is owned and operated by my paternal first cousin, Robert Cunitz and his son. The one full-service restaurant is adjacent to Cousin Robert's tavern, and is operated as an adjunct to the tavern. The restaurant is in the same room where Pete Schreier and his daughter Helen once served up hot buttered popcorn. The second tavern (Lil's Korner Bar) also serves food, but on a more limited scale.

Norwalk is still served by a bank and post office. A funeral home remains along with four churches. A small dispensary graces the west entrance to town where a doctor or physician's assistant is available Monday through Friday. The dispensary is in a new building adjoining what was once the old combined elementary and high school that served Norwalk and surrounding community for many years. Now school age children are bused to a consolidated school six miles away in Ontario. The old school gym has been converted into a community center. To round out medical support there is Doctor Michael Eastvold's chiropractic practice.

New to the downtown scene from my days are a combined real estate and insurance office and a tire store. On the southern end of town a convenience store has been established. As is typical of convenience stores, you can gas up here as well. This is the only place in Norwalk where you can buy gas today. Paul Flock operated one of the three gas stations in town for many years. He still does minor auto repair/maintenance work a few days each week at his former place of business—but only for his old long-term customers. For others, Bill and Bob Roy do vehicle repairs under the banner of "B & B Automotive." Finally, on the south end of town the Degenhardt brothers operate a farm machinery dealership

In the way of public service, the town has the typical municipal services as well as a small public library. A volunteer fire department serves both Norwalk and surrounding communities, and a part-time police officer meets public safety needs. Back-up police protection is provided by the Monroe County Sheriff's Department

In summary, a much-reduced business base. This is understandable since Sparta is but thirteen easy road miles away with its Super Wal-Mart and related business and entertainment attractions.

Norwalk remains a pleasant and picturesque little town. Stand on any of the hills surrounding Norwalk and you will be treated to one of those picture perfect post card views of small town America. Its church steeples and tree-lined streets remind one of a small town New England community or a picturesque Swiss village.

My wife and I are frequent visitors to Norwalk during our yearly trips back to Wisconsin. We especially enjoy visiting our cousin Robert at his place of business, conveniently called "The Place." Robert's restaurant is also where the current crop of local "good ol' boys," to include those from Summit Ridge, gather for coffee around 8 a.m. Monday through Saturday.

The Place (Norwalk)

Siblings (2004 photo) Front row left to right: Ronald, Author, Noel, Paul; Back row left: Elaine, Carolyn, Mary, Helen, Dorothy, Joan.

My Siblings

Today (2005) the ten of us are still living. We range in age from sixty-one to seventy-nine. Collectively we raised forty-six children. I am not even going to try and count the grandnieces and nephews. We hold a family reunion every three years at the old home (the Bucholz farm) where we all grew up. As noted earlier, at our last event in July 2004 the count was 188 attendees. Two of my brothers served in the military; Ronald for three years in the Marines and Paul was called up with his National Guard unit during the Berlin crisis in 1961.

High School

In September of 2005 my high school class met for our sixtieth year reunion. I attended, and logically expected to see my former classmates—but all that I saw were grandmothers and grandfathers.

Appendices

Appendix A
Non-Agricultural Land Use
on Hedrick Farms

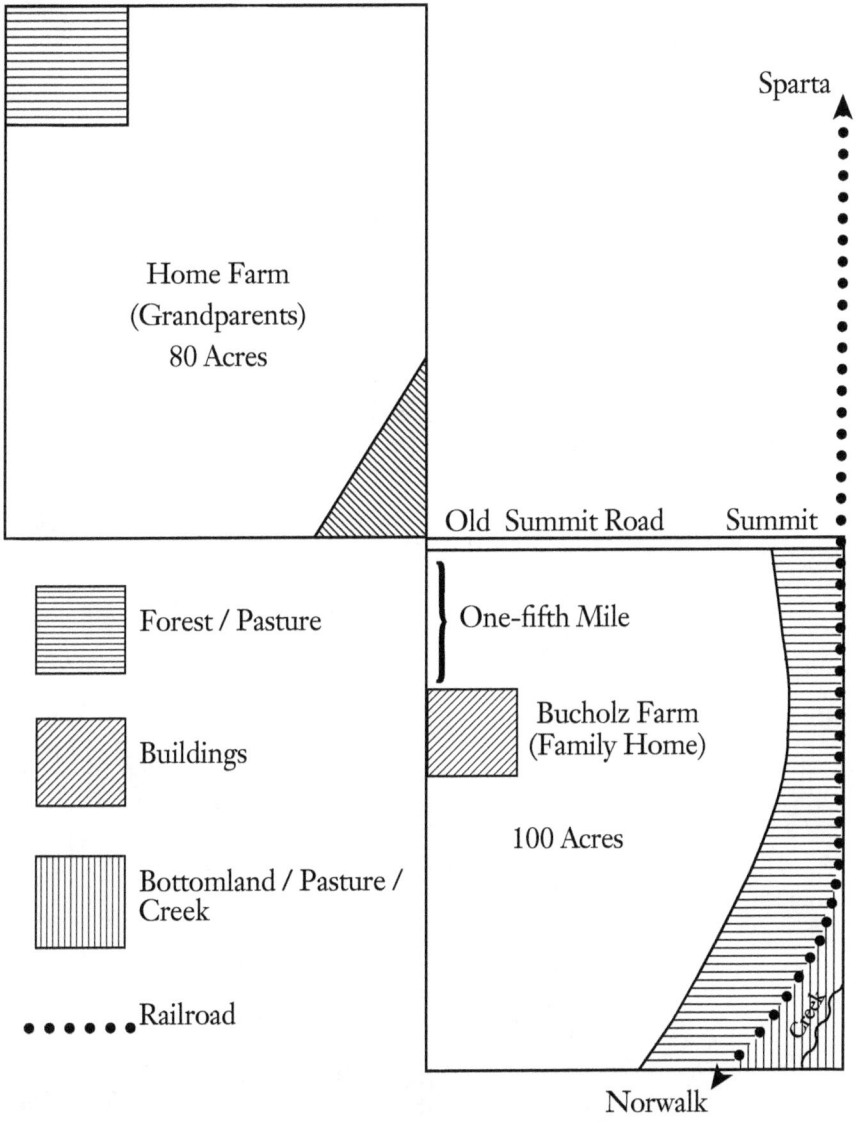

Sparta

Home Farm
(Grandparents)
80 Acres

Old Summit Road   Summit

Forest / Pasture

Buildings

Bottomland / Pasture /
Creek

Railroad

} One-fifth Mile

Bucholz Farm
(Family Home)

100 Acres

Creek

Norwalk

Appendix B
Building Layout on Farms

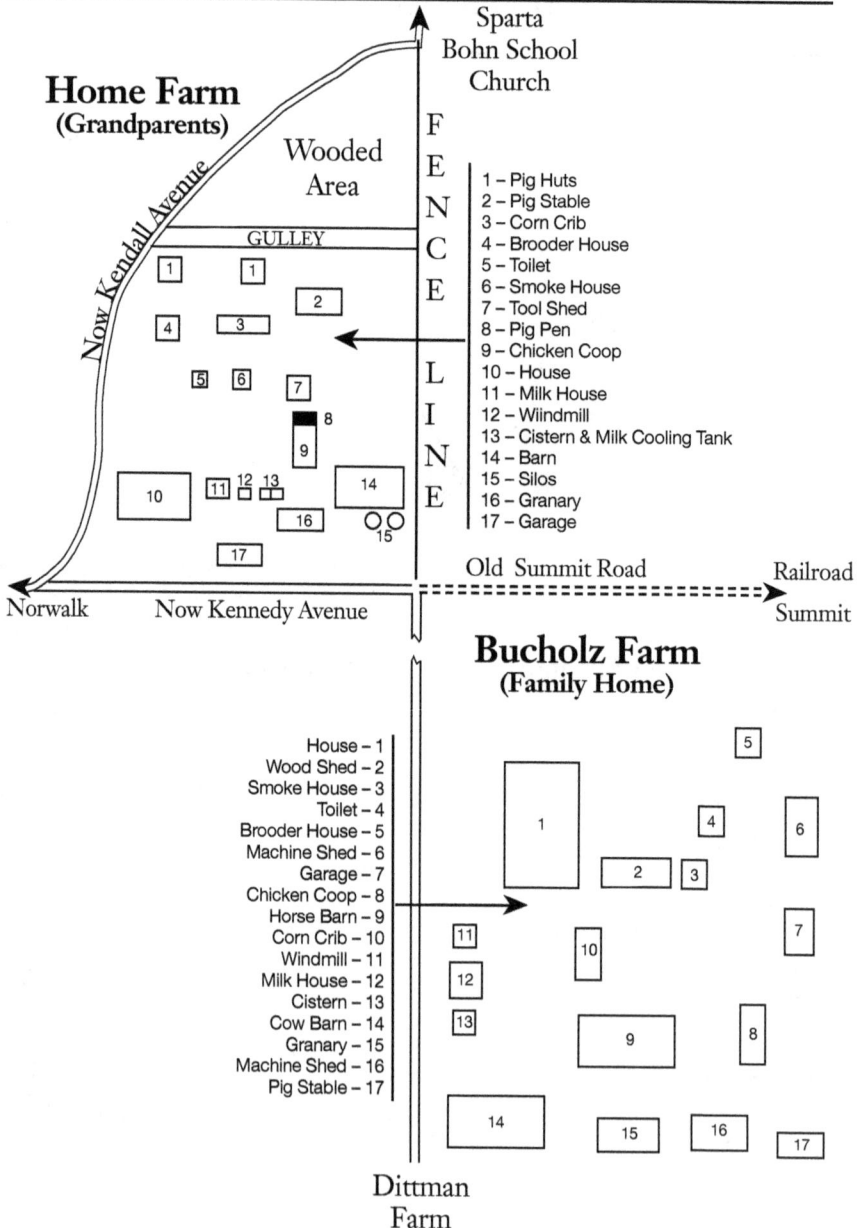

Home Farm
(Grandparents)

Wooded Area

Sparta
Bohn School
Church

F E N C E   L I N E

GULLEY

Now Kendall Avenue

1 – Pig Huts
2 – Pig Stable
3 – Corn Crib
4 – Brooder House
5 – Toilet
6 – Smoke House
7 – Tool Shed
8 – Pig Pen
9 – Chicken Coop
10 – House
11 – Milk House
12 – Wiindmill
13 – Cistern & Milk Cooling Tank
14 – Barn
15 – Silos
16 – Granary
17 – Garage

Old Summit Road   Railroad

Norwalk   Now Kennedy Avenue   Summit

Bucholz Farm
(Family Home)

House – 1
Wood Shed – 2
Smoke House – 3
Toilet – 4
Brooder House – 5
Machine Shed – 6
Garage – 7
Chicken Coop – 8
Horse Barn – 9
Corn Crib – 10
Windmill – 11
Milk House – 12
Cistern – 13
Cow Barn – 14
Granary – 15
Machine Shed – 16
Pig Stable – 17

Dittman
Farm

Appendix C
Sources and Recommended Reading on Korean War and Chosin Reservoir Campaign

Goulden, Joseph C., *Korea, The Untold Story of the War.* New York: The New York Times Book Co., Inc. 1982

Hammel, Eric, *Chosin.* New York: Vanguard Press, Inc. 1981

Owen, Joseph R., *Colder than Hell. A Marine Rifle Company at the Chosin Reservoir.* Annapolis: Naval Institute Press. 1996

Russ, Martin, *Breakout.* New York: Fromm International Publishing Corporation, 1999

Wilson, Jim, *Retreat Hell.* New York: William Morrow and Company, Inc., 1988

Appendix D
Block Diagram of a Marine Division

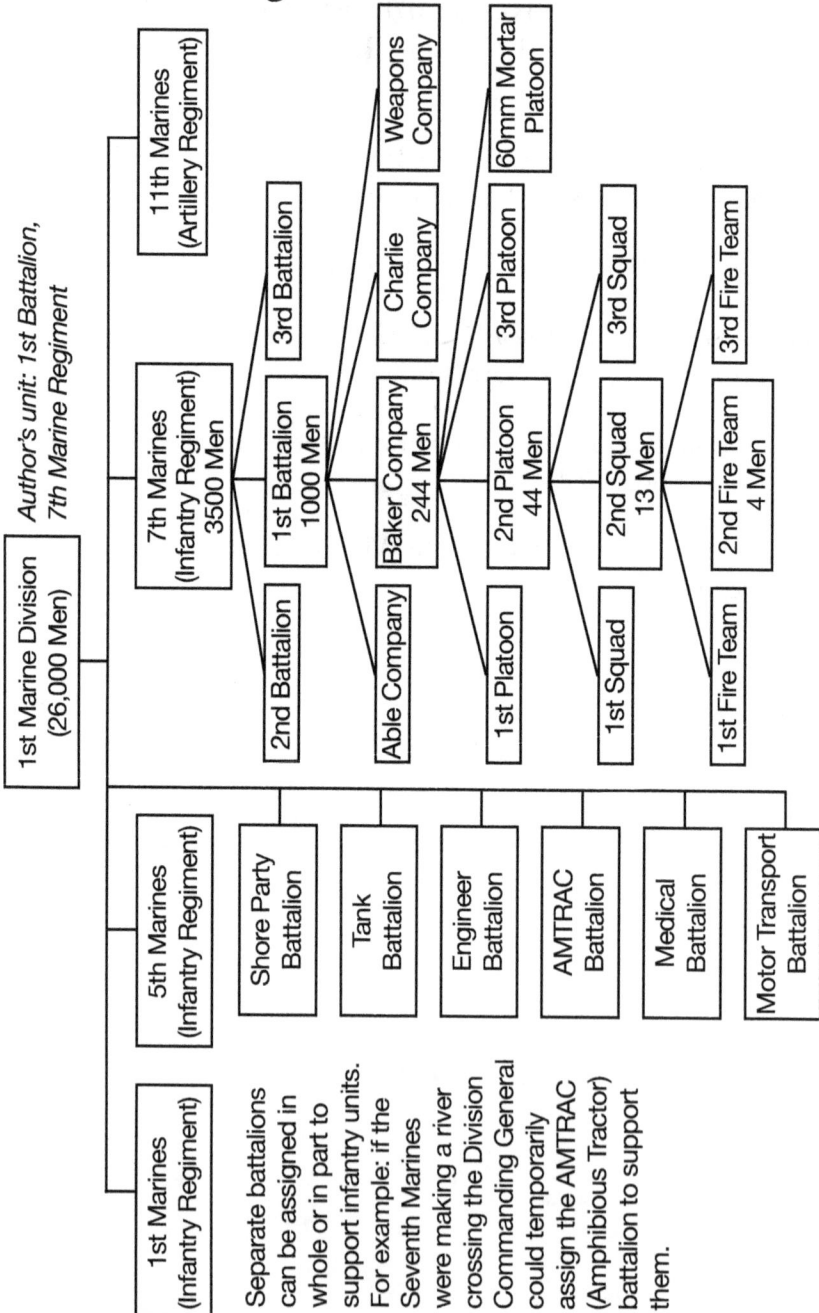

1st Marine Division (26,000 Men)

Author's unit: 1st Battalion, 7th Marine Regiment

1st Marines (Infantry Regiment)

5th Marines (Infantry Regiment)

7th Marines (Infantry Regiment) 3500 Men

11th Marines (Artillery Regiment)

Shore Party Battalion
Tank Battalion
Engineer Battalion
AMTRAC Battalion
Medical Battalion
Motor Transport Battalion

2nd Battalion
1st Battalion 1000 Men
3rd Battalion

Able Company
Baker Company 244 Men
Charlie Company
Weapons Company

1st Platoon
2nd Platoon 44 Men
3rd Platoon
60mm Mortar Platoon

1st Squad
2nd Squad 13 Men
3rd Squad

1st Fire Team
2nd Fire Team 4 Men
3rd Fire Team

Separate battalions can be assigned in whole or in part to support infantry units. For example: if the Seventh Marines were making a river crossing the Division Commanding General could temporarily assign the AMTRAC (Amphibious Tractor) battalion to support them.